RULING MINDS

RULING MINDS

Psychology in the British Empire

ERIK LINSTRUM

Harvard University Press

Cambridge, Massachusetts
London, England
2016

Library of Congress Cataloging-in-Publication Data

Linstrum, Erik, 1983– author.
Ruling minds : psychology in the British empire / Erik Linstrum.
pages cm
Includes bibliographical references and index.
ISBN 978-0-674-08866-5
1. Psychology—Great Britain—History. 2. British—Psychological testing. 3. British—
Psychology. 4. Great Britain—Colonies—Administration—History. I. Title.
BF108.G7L56 2016
150.9171'241—dc23
2015015035

For Sheela

CONTENTS

RULING MINDS

Introduction

A WOMAN DESCRIBES HER DREAMS in the Solomon Islands. A soldier takes an aptitude test in Calcutta. An insurgent talks about his childhood in Singapore. A baby plays in front of a film crew in Kampala. These are conspicuously disparate moments, imprinted by personal experience and separated in time and space. What binds them together, despite the differences, is the subject of this book: the history of psychology in the twentieth-century British Empire.

This is a story about the reach and the limits of human science on a global scale. It describes how new techniques in psychology around the turn of the twentieth century came to be accepted as reliable and useful sources of knowledge about the inner lives of people living in what was then the world's biggest and most diverse political system. These innovations marked a departure from late Victorian ideas about the supposedly inscrutable and alien "native mind," and they captured the imaginations of critics and rulers of empire alike. Laboratory experiments, psychoanalysis, and mental testing offered ways to challenge racial hierarchies and expose pathologies at the root of the relationship between colonizer and colonized. But they also furnished methods for governing populations: making factories and armies run more smoothly; recruiting the most talented subjects for government jobs and scarce school places; combating anticolonial rebellions; and remolding families, economies, and societies. From anthropologists and missionaries to bureaucrats, schoolteachers, and industrialists, the science of mind had wide appeal in the imperial context because it promised technical solutions to political

I

problems. The history of psychology and empire is thus the history of a paradox: how a field of expertise that generated critical and even subversive questions about British imperialism also captured the imaginations of the empire's rulers.

Superficially, at least, the techniques at the heart of this story traveled across geographic and cultural space with remarkable speed. Quantitative studies of perception, conducted for the first time among university students in Wilhelm Wundt's Leipzig laboratory in 1879, were replicated off the coast of Australia by the end of the 1890s. A little more than two decades after publication of Sigmund Freud's *The Interpretation of Dreams* (1900), a British researcher was collecting and analyzing dreams from Africa, India, and the Pacific. The Stanford-Binet intelligence test, released by Lewis Terman in California in 1916, was determining admission to mission schools in India as early as 1922. But the impressively rapid movement of these techniques across the world was always shadowed by disappointments and frustrations. Intellectuals who drew on psychology to advance egalitarian and liberatory aims repeatedly saw their ambitions thwarted. So, too, did the imperial rulers who hoped that psychology could strengthen British control by improving efficiency and governing emotions. The gap that opened up between far-reaching aspirations and disillusioned realities is a central theme of this book.

For a long time, historians have stressed the power rather than the frailty of expertise. Experts in psychology have figured as white-coated villains, establishing insidious standards of normality and sorting populations into rigid hierarchies.[1] In the colonies, psychology has appeared as another building block in the edifice of domination that branded whole populations as irrational and inferior.[2] This book takes a different perspective. Like other recent histories, it shows that human scientists sometimes challenged authoritarian and hierarchical ideologies.[3] It also stresses that the relationship between science and empire—a "logical alliance," according to Edward Said—was a tenuous collaboration marked by tensions and misunderstandings instead.[4] For researchers, local knowledge accumulated in the field fostered respect for indigenous practices, skepticism about plans for total control, and anxiety about the disruptive impact of imperial rule.[5] For the state, lack of resources, lack of ambition, and fear of triggering indigenous resistance all placed constraints on technocratic schemes.[6] When officials did embrace the goal of modernization after the Second World War, vastly increasing the numbers and influence of experts on the ground, the consequences spiraled beyond British control. Anti-colonial nationalists, postcolonial leaders, and international planners all laid claim to the idea of development that imperial rulers vainly tried to yoke to their own purposes.[7]

The political valence of imperial psychology was, in short, unstable. At their most subversive, mental testers used measurements of ability to refute racial generalizations. They made divergent test scores across the world a starting point for environmental, relativist, and functionalist explanations of difference. They also argued that quantifying innate ability could liberate imperial subjects from the burdens of discrimination and deprivation. The most radical psychoanalytic thinkers, meanwhile, questioned the mythology of a civilized and benevolent empire by arguing that aggressive drives and neurotic desires fueled the British quest for overseas rule. The evidence of dream narratives and free associations collected in distant places not only strengthened the case for universal models of the unconscious mind but also documented the psychic trauma of political dispossession. All these critiques had roots before 1914 but came to prominence in the years between the wars—a time when researchers across the sciences were increasingly questioning the significance of race.[8] In those years, too, many British intellectuals were growing disillusioned with empire itself. As George Orwell observed, joking about Colonel Blimps and the White Man's Burden—if not denouncing them outright—was a prerequisite of *bien-pensant* respectability.[9]

Why did psychology in particular seem to offer a useful vehicle for unsettling imperialist assumptions? If the human sciences always worked by dividing colonized populations "into manageable parts," as Said once observed, psychology accomplished this in a very different way than the familiar classifications of race, caste, and tribe.[10] Whether by revealing variation within groups through mental testing or universal forces of desire and conflict through psychoanalysis, the science of mind unsettled the "categorical knowledge" of difference which always played a central role in British rule.[11] In some cases, psychology produced new classifications that cut across established boundaries; in other cases, the knowledge it generated could not easily be contained within classificatory schemes of any kind. The spaces where psychology happened—the laboratory, the consulting room, the testing room—removed its subjects from the physical and cultural surroundings that helped to distinguish the "primitive" from the "modern."[12] Close, sometimes intimate, encounters between researcher and subject made generalizations about colonized populations even more difficult to sustain.[13]

But these radical currents never went unchallenged. Imperial researchers could not help identifying at some level with the power that guaranteed an umbrella of security and easy access to cooperative human subjects as well as information, hospitality, and funding. Even as some thinkers embraced the oppositional possibilities of psychological research, others always found ways to reconcile their findings with racial hierarchies and imperial rule.[14] Despite the popular image of an aristo-anachronistic British elite, after all, the twentieth-century state drew heavily on scientific expertise at home and overseas.[15] The belief that technical innovation could conquer distance and impose order on diversity shaped imperial ambitions from the age of the telegraph to the age of aviation and beyond.[16] In the same way, the uniformities that emerged from psychology—the standardized forms of knowledge produced by experiments and tests—could make difference appear malleable and manageable, opening up new possibilities for imperial power.[17]

These divergent political agendas emerged from an intellectual problem: how to make the science of mind a global science. The remaking of psychology with laboratory methods at the end of the nineteenth century held out the promise of "portable" rather than "place-based" expertise, applicable anywhere in the world with tantalizing ease and speed.[18] In practice, though, researchers had to strike a precarious balance between the universal models of the laboratory and the particularities of place and culture. They were forced, in other words, to reconcile the scientist's drive for replicable results with the fieldworker's sensitivity to difference. The familiar narrative of a shift from biological evolutionism to cultural relativism around the time of the First World War foreshortens what was in fact a persistent tension between universalist and relativist modes in the human sciences.[19] The equally familiar counternarrative of instrumental, one-size-fits-all rationality running roughshod over diverse forms of local knowledge likewise overlooks a more complex reality of compromise and coexistence.[20]

Navigating between the local and the global, migratory experts in psychology cast a skeptical eye on the most common explanations of the relationship between them. When confronted with sweeping narratives that located every human group in a hierarchical order, they often responded with relativism, stressing that apparent mental differences arose from social environments and cultural contexts to be understood on their own terms. When confronted with claims about "primitive" and "civilized" patterns of thought, by contrast, they stressed that all human beings inherited a common set of psychological capacities—a commitment to universalism never fully superseded by theories of adaptive difference.[21] Psychology in the British Empire explored the space between these poles. How did differences between groups emerge from the shared foundations of human nature? And how much did those differences really matter? Were they fixed and fundamental or plastic and superficial—"substance" or "surface," in the words of Clifford Geertz?[22] Merely asking these questions could raise questions about imperial hierarchies. But the answers also had the potential to produce useful knowledge for imperial rulers: how to adapt just enough to the realities of difference to impose British aims overseas.

The Second World War marked a turning point in the instrumentalization of psychology. Officials who had previously shown only fitful interest in the field mobilized it as a tool of empire after 1945, drawing selectively on its concepts, methods, and vocabulary to advance their own agendas. Taking inspiration from the wartime mental testing of colonial soldiers, bureaucrats worked to heighten the efficiency of British rule by measuring the aptitudes of students and workers. Taking aim at the psychological origins of anticolonial movements, they attempted to transform American-style "behavioral science" into a bulwark of authority. In peacetime, this meant designing education programs to discipline emotions and reshape attitudes; in the context of counterinsurgency, it meant crafting tactics for propaganda campaigns and justifying brutal practices of interrogation and detention with the language of mind science.

Experts in psychology did not always welcome these initiatives. Even as they sought opportunities for patronage, they remained uneasy about the racism and violence of imperial rule—reservations that made the enterprise of psychological warfare seem particularly problematic. They protested, too, that the bureaucrats and soldiers who made use of specialized knowledge often failed to appreciate its complexity. But the interests of officials and researchers were aligning in other ways after 1945. Where imperial psychology earlier took inspiration from anthropology, with its attention to cultures as complex systems, the field now increasingly followed the lead of psychiatry, with its diagnostic standards of normality and pathology. Reflecting the influence of modernization theory across the postwar human sciences, the balance in the science of mind shifted away from tolerance of diversity and toward global norms. The belief that nationalist movements arose from volatile unconscious forces—a lesson learned, rightly or wrongly, from the experience of the Second World War—endowed imperial plans for cultivating emotional stability with a benevolent aura. Whether in the empire-turned-Commonwealth or the expanding universe of international organizations, meanwhile, a new conception of world poverty cast development projects as altruistic and progressive opportunities for exercising authority in other societies. Although Americans were much better positioned after the war to realize their vision of a "New Deal for the world," the prospect of a welfare state for the world was equally appealing to many British intellectuals.[23]

The impersonal aesthetic of "high modernism" is often seen as the default mode of state planning in this period.[24] But postwar blueprints for development assumed that the inner sources of human behavior mattered at least as much as the material world.[25] Whether they considered changing agricultural techniques to boost productivity or changing hygienic practices to combat disease, political leaders repeatedly concluded that "the main problem was not technical but psychological," as one member of Parliament put it in 1955.[26] From the villages of Jamaica to the factories of East Africa to the rubber plantations of Southeast Asia, researchers commissioned by the imperial state ran experiments with mental tests, attitude surveys, and observational studies for nearly two decades after the war. Working for the World Health Organization, UNESCO, and other global institutions at the same time, British experts championed intervention in homes and workplaces around the world, seeking to uproot the patterns of emotional dependency they saw as impediments to modernization.

This history is not only the history of a discipline or a profession. At a time when clear-cut divisions between fields had yet to emerge in the human sciences, the boundary between psychology and other fields was porous.[27] Particularly before the Second World War, many of the researchers who brought mental tests and psychoanalytic theories to the empire held positions as anthropologists rather than psychologists.[28] Academic communities overlapped in part because they were small: as late as 1939, just six university chairs in Britain were devoted to the science of mind.[29] But psychology in Britain always found its greatest influence beyond disciplinary boundaries and even beyond the academy—in the schools, factories, barracks, and offices where professionals of many kinds diagnosed, classified, and managed minds.[30] The postwar welfare state drew on the same expertise to meet the challenges posed by imperial subjects—foster children, exchange students, migrants, and others—who came to Britain in the age of decolonization.[31] How psychology worked in the empire itself remains an open question by comparison.

Any attempt to tell a global history like this one must confront the problem of scale. Seeking to avoid an old-fashioned diffusionist model in which the European center imposes its knowledge on a passive periphery, historians of science have emphasized the particularities of place and the contributions of indigenous cultures in their accounts of how knowledge moves around the world. From this perspective, all knowledge is local, emerging in the imperial context from the interaction of Western concepts with peoples and environments overseas.[32] But these local influences always had to contend with movements of standardization and regularization that occurred on a global level. Although ideas traveled in multiple directions rather than diffusing from a single center, expert forms of knowledge did increasingly converge around the world from the late nineteenth century.[33] A purely local or spatially bound approach risks overlooking these larger attempts to impose uniformity—which are significant even if they often failed to realize their vision in practice. To understand the limits of globalization, it is necessary first to understand the specific, often specialized, fields through which it was imagined and why so many believed that the imposition of uniformity was an attainable goal to begin with.

This book therefore focuses on episodes of movement and circulation between places (which may be the best way of describing what global history is about).[34] Networks of empire—bureaucracies, military bases, commercial links, transportation channels, linguistic and cultural connections—enabled and accelerated the flow of people, goods, and ideas around the world.[35] In the case of psychology, the figures who mattered most—researchers, officials, missionaries, soldiers—ordinarily cycled through different territories rather than stay in one place. Convocations like the Universal Races Congress in 1911, the International Anthropological Conference in 1934, and the Indian Science Congress in 1937 attracted participants from far-flung imperial arenas. A malleable idea of "Britishness" gave distant and disparate researchers a sense of common enterprise.[36] At the end of the Second World War, the historically decentralized imperial bureaucracy even set up a funding apparatus based in London: the Colonial Social Science Research Council, which sponsored research in psychology along with anthropology, sociology, and linguistics.

But globe-trotting research did not grow exclusively from imperial roots. Institutions based outside the British world—philanthropic foundations, international organizations, multinational corporations—rivaled and in some ways eclipsed sources of patronage in Britain itself. The role of money and expertise from the United States illustrates the importance of Anglo-American exchanges in particular. Between the 1920s, when American missionaries pioneered intelligence testing in India, and the 1950s, when the Colonial Office fretted that American researchers were outnumbering their British counterparts in the field, psychology in the empire evolved into something like a transatlantic project. Fueled by diverse influences—missionary zeal, New Deal liberalism, academic theory—philanthropies based in the United States pursued global ambitions that brought them into contact with imperial experts and administrators.[37] In the Cold War era, the intertwined threats of anticolonialism and communism drew the British and American states closer together, cementing an older network of private and voluntary links. Psychology in the British Empire, in short, was not always very British, laying foundations for the internationalization of expertise in the postcolonial world.[38]

In some ways, this is a story about a paradox of globalization: how the achievement of uniformity at one level masked the diverse agendas and endless adaptations that marked the passage of psychology around the world. Any history that ranges across the far-flung territories under British rule risks exaggerating the cohesion of the imperial enterprise, which was far more fragile and varied than those splotches of pink on the map might seem to suggest.[39] For the same reason, the currently fashionable metaphor of the network can distort as well as illuminate. By conjuring a frictionless, almost immaterial process of transmission, it obscures the conflicts, the failures, and above all the unevenness that defined the circulation of knowledge about colonized populations.[40] The question is why the science of mind, like other human sciences, continued to fascinate despite many moments of disillusionment. Its resilience is testament to its allure—not only as a tool of observation and explanation but as a force for changing the world.

I

MINDS

CHAPTER ONE

The Laboratory in the Field

Inventing Imperial Psychology

HE WEATHER was calm and bright when the *Duke of West-minster* launched into the Thames at midday. It was March 10, 1898, and the Royal Albert Dock was crowded with well-wishers waving handkerchiefs in the air as the steamship moved toward the sea. A group of men on board watched their families recede into the distance, then settled in for a long journey, gazing at the stars and watching phosphorescent fish dart through the water as night fell.[1] The six of them were bound for the islands that studded the Torres Strait between Australia and New Guinea. Alfred Cort Haddon, the leader of the expedition, was a naturalist, ethnographer, and Cambridge University lecturer who had first traveled to the region a decade earlier. Sidney Ray was a London schoolteacher with an unlikely expertise in indigenous languages, and Anthony Wilkin was a recent Cambridge graduate commissioned to take photographs. The other three—W. H. R. Rivers, Charles Myers, and William McDougall—were medical men with an unprecedented mission. Along with a fourth British doctor, Charles Seligman, who joined the expedition from Australia, they set out to investigate the psychology of Britain's overseas subjects with newly invented experimental methods. It would be "the first time," Haddon later observed, "that a well-equipped psychological laboratory had been established among a people scarcely a generation removed from perfect savagery."[2]

For these pioneers of psychology in the British Empire, the juxtaposition of archaic and modern would become almost routine. Nearly two decades later, Rivers returned from the remote Pacific island chain of the

New Hebrides to treat British soldiers stricken with shell shock, famously drawing on Freud to help the war poet Siegfried Sassoon regain his senses during the First World War. Myers went on to amass a collection of traditional music from around the world while also serving as a shell shock specialist and later as the director of the National Institute of Industrial Psychology. Although McDougall drew on ethnographic accounts of "primitive" warfare to construct his theory of human psychology governed by instinct, he too made use of Freud and even entered psychoanalysis with Jung himself.[3] These contrasts all had their origin in the Torres Strait. Living in the region for at least six months, the Cambridge researchers helped to establish the ethnographic ideal of fieldwork, with its insistence on absorbing the particularities of an alien world "from the inside."[4] But in the hilltop house on Murray Island—where they performed experiments on the perception of indigenous people with a wide array of instruments—they also laid the foundation of an alternative tradition. By reconstructing the ostensibly universal space of the laboratory in an unfamiliar and distant environment, they were not simply observing difference but attempting to make it comprehensible and manageable.[5] The house on Murray Island, then, was not so much a "laboratory of modernity"—where the imperial context provided freedom to innovate away from constraints at home—as a testing ground for the portability of techniques conceived in European laboratories.[6] As they recorded measurements of vision, hearing, and reaction time, the Cambridge men were also testing whether the tools of Western psychology could be usefully applied so far from their place of origin.

The experiments conducted in the Torres Strait in 1898–1899 marked the opening act in a long series of attempts to map the mental life of Britain's imperial subjects. Unlike the evolutionary thinkers of the late Victorian era, the Cambridge men did not rely on data collected by others; they made observations of their own, bringing the laboratory methods pioneered by physiologists into the field for the first time. They also focused their efforts on a single community, testing around four hundred fifty individuals and getting to know them in the course of repeated encounters. In the Torres Strait, the laboratory and the field—mechanical instruments and personal experience—were not opposed but complementary, blending objectivity and immediacy to create a new kind of research in the human sciences.[7]

But the expedition's novelty was not only a matter of method. Belying the assumption that technology served as a reliable "tool of empire," laboratory experiments in the Torres Strait undermined the psychological assumptions of imperial ideology at the turn of the century.[8] Even instruments governed by strict procedures and freighted with theoretical assumptions—devices "dense with meaning"—could produce unexpected results and unsettling conclusions.[9] While armchair theorists portrayed colonized minds as inferior in ability, resistant to change, and lacking in individuality, the Cambridge researchers found evidence of intelligence, adaptability, and diversity instead. Criticizing the idea of a "primitive mentality" and—in one case—launching a parliamentary campaign on an anticolonial platform, they came to question whether the distinctions and hierarchies underlying imperial rule were so clear-cut after all.

¶ BEFORE THE ADVENT of the laboratory in the late nineteenth century, British thinkers privileged observation and experience over instruments and experiments as sources of knowledge about mental life. The physiognomic outlook of Victorian psychology held that surface appearances mirrored inner states—whether indelible traits of character or momentary bursts of passion—in a predictable way.[10] This tradition of "ocularcentrism" was, if anything, stronger in the imperial context. Although the epistemological value of fieldwork remained uncertain until the second half of the century, descriptions recorded by educated European travelers were long seen as reliable data about indigenous people and landscapes.[11] Throughout the nineteenth century, British officials in colonies around the world believed that they could gather useful information by observing their subjects face-to-face. Mistrusting written reports and indigenous subordinates as sources of knowledge about public opinion, they insisted on touring their territories and monitoring the crowds assembled at big public meetings.[12] Whether termed "sympathy" or "tact," the ability to grasp the collective mood in an instant was considered an essential but also an attainable skill for administrators in the field.[13]

Although scientific claims about the intelligence and emotions of imperial subjects sometimes drew on quantitative data—including, notoriously, skull measurements—quantification proved superfluous for many researchers.[14] This was true in part because physical features readily perceived by the trained eye—smooth-haired versus woolly-haired, "long-headed" versus "broad-headed"—served as the basis for defining racial groups. Even an inveterate quantifier like the mental-testing pioneer Francis Galton collected almost no measurements during his African travels in the 1850s, relying instead on skin color and facial features to guide his classifications.[15] But universal models of psychology also contributed to faith in visual knowledge. In an especially famous case, Charles Darwin in 1867 circulated a questionnaire to overseas missionaries for his study on the expression of emotion, asking them to observe whether astonishment raised eyebrows, anger curled lips, and embarrassment flushed cheeks in India and Africa as in Europe. He concluded that "the same state of mind is expressed throughout the world with remarkable uniformity," demonstrating "the close similarity in bodily structure and mental disposition of all the races of mankind."[16]

In the late Victorian years, however, this belief in the transparency of mental life everywhere was shadowed by growing doubts. After rebellions in India in 1857 and Jamaica in 1865, anxieties about the inscrutability of the so-called "native mind" proliferated.[17] As Raj administrator George Trevelyan wrote almost a decade after the uprising on the subcontinent, "their inner life still remains a sealed book to us." Contemporaries described African minds as even more opaque: the inhospitable climate of the "White Man's Grave" and the unfamiliarity of indigenous languages contributed to the sense that "the native mind [there] works on a different plane from that of the European," as a handbook for imperial officials put it around the turn of the century.[18] The distinctions drawn between diverse cultures and far-flung continents amounted to variations on the same theme: an epistemic crisis in imperial psychology. Armchair anthropologist Sir John Lubbock identified the crux of the problem in 1870. "The whole mental condition of a savage is so different from ours," he wrote, "that it is often very difficult to understand the motives by which he is influenced." At a time when the transformational promise of liberal imperialism was giving way to sharper-edged distinctions of political and racial authority, the possibility of understanding colonized minds looked increasingly problematic from the British perspective.[19]

Attempting to reconcile the universal biological responses chronicled by Darwin with this deepening sense of difference, late Victorian thinkers recast the science of mind as a set of evolutionary hierarchies. Since John Locke's *Essay Concerning Human Understanding* (1690), British psychology had been dominated by sensationalist and associationist theories of knowledge, tracing the most complex ideas back to perceptions of the world. As John Stuart Mill put it in 1873, the connections forged in the mind followed "the real connexions between Things, not dependent on our will and feelings," so that "things which are always joined together in Nature . . . cohere more and more closely in our thoughts."[20] For evolutionary theorists, the mind's tendency to learn from experience ensured that animal impulses in human nature would not inevitably thwart rationality. Instead, they argued, each generation adapted mentally to the environment and transmitted its improvements to the next. Evolutionists continued to debate whether the means of transmission among *Homo sapiens* was biological or social: Herbert Spencer held that instincts or reflexes developed into the subtler operations of memory and reason through a Lamarckian process of inheritance; others, like C. Lloyd Morgan, insisted that advantageous ideas were embedded in culture rather than the nervous system. But all agreed that the power of the environment to mold minds explained how conscious thought came to dominate unreflective impulses over the course of evolutionary time. When late Victorian neurologists referred to "higher" and "lower" mental functions, they confirmed a narrative of human development in which intellect gradually triumphed over instinct.[21]

From the British perspective, this narrative had the virtue of explaining, and perhaps justifying, the vast disparities in wealth and technology of societies among human societies. Defining prosperity as the byproduct of psychology validated a Victorian truism: that success in life represented the reward for hard work, foresight, and abstinence from sensual pleasures. According to this logic, Britain had leapfrogged past other societies—India inspired analogies to Saxon villages, while Africa drew comparisons to the more distant past of primeval hunter-gatherers—because the subordination of instinct to reason had proceeded so much further there. Spencer, perhaps the most influential proponent of this view, catalogued the defects that defined "primitive man" with an emphasis on failures of psychological efficiency: "impulsiveness," "improvidence," incapacity for complex thought, and preoccupation with "meaningless details." Even those who insisted that biological evolution was no longer an active force in differentiating human populations agreed that heightened powers of rationality and restraint distinguished "civilized" from "primitive" groups. The assumption that all knowledge was derived from the steady accumulation of sensory experience encouraged a finely graded view of human diversity in which mental, moral, and material differences corresponded neatly.[22]

In this way, evolutionary theory furnished an explicitly hierarchical schema for structuring the observation of colonized minds. It also offered a rationale for considering those minds legible. Where traditional communities like the caste, tribe, or village reigned, Victorian thinkers argued that the imperatives of group cohesion—embodied in elaborate ceremonies, rigid hierarchies, and strict sanctions for violating rules—created an environment that allowed for minimal variation in intelligence and temperament. Among the individuals in any one "primitive" society, in other words, homogeneity ruled—a corollary of the evolutionary principle that human groups inevitably progressed from simplicity to complexity. As the dean of British anthropology, Edward Tylor, put it, "there is to be found such regularity in the composition of societies of men, that we can drop individual differences out of sight, and thus can generalize on the arts and opinions of whole nations." Invoking the "amazing sameness" of "savage nations," Walter Bagehot stated this more succinctly: "when you have seen one Fuegian, you have seen all Fuegians."[23] Even Spencer, who did so much to define the "primitive" as a generic bundle of instinct, assumed that psychology varied strictly as a function of ethnic identity. Compiled from ethnographies and travel narratives, his encyclopedic *Descriptive Sociology* (1873–1881) presented "a comprehensive account" of groups around the world—including "emotional" and "intellectual" characteristics—in elaborate charts covering the pages of eight oversized volumes. While words like *impulsive* and *incapable* appear frequently, Spencer also noted aptitudes and dispositions that diverged from the norm. The so-called "Kaffirs" of southern Africa had a "quick power of comprehension and capacity of patient attention"; Bushmen were "lively, frank, and generous"; Fijians were "quick to receive ideas, both simple and complex." In Spencer's portrayal, the world contained an endless diversity of character types, but the psychological uniformity of "primitive" groups made generalizations possible.[24]

When applied to colonized populations, the language of group psychology often served as a language of rule. The recruiting policy of the Indian Army after 1857, which favored Punjabis, Sikhs, and other groups prized for their courage and toughness, is the best-known example of this.[25] But linking mental qualities with ethnic identities was a common technique of British rule across the empire. Stereotypes about martial races, lazy tribes, and other groups both favored and disfavored helped officials to make sense of the unfamiliar; they also legitimized the ethnic division of labor that structured the military, civil service, and private industry. Rudyard Kipling thought that a well-trained British agent in India could recognize "how such and such a caste talked, or walked, or coughed, or spat, or sneezed." In Nigeria, officials replicated the Indian template almost exactly, venerating the Fulani of the north for their manly, martial virtues and maligning the Yoruba in the south. In East Africa, they saw the Masai as markedly intelligent, unusually frank, and pleasingly free of servility, while other tribes had lesser virtues: the Luo, simple and stolid; the Kamba, loyal and cheerful; the Kikuyu, industrious but potentially untrustworthy. In Northern Rhodesia, the British reserved most of their opprobrium for the Lamba, who were seen as timid, lazy, and backward. In Southeast Asia, they contrasted the supposedly indolent Malays with shifty but industrious Chinese immigrants.[26] Since the time of Captain Cook, the British perceived the Melanesians who inhabited the Torres Strait as dark-skinned, barbaric, and hostile—near the bottom of the evolutionary ladder—especially in comparison with the cheerful and attractive Polynesian peoples to the east.[27] Although evolutionary theorists were not necessarily imperialist ideologues—Spencer, for instance, denounced the "mob-jingoism" and "filibustering atrocities" of overseas rule—their categories and hierarchies proved useful for British officials.[28]

At the outset of the expedition in 1898, the Cambridge group appeared unlikely to challenge those visions. Although Spencer's influence was waning in some ways, he still loomed large in the intellectual lives of the researchers. Myers had chosen Spencer's works as an undergraduate college prize and remembered him later as "that distinguished" and "courageous" philosopher; Rivers studied under the Spencerian physiologist Michael Foster at Cambridge and subsequently spent his spare time reading the Spencerian *oeuvre* while working as a ship's doctor. In fact, the expedition itself represented an attempt to enact Spencer's prescription for a "comparative psychology of man." Referring casually to the "lower races" of the Torres Strait, Haddon initially understood the value of psychological research there in terms of its potential to show how mental states changed over evolutionary time.[29]

This sense of hierarchy translated into the racial attitudes expressed by the researchers when they first arrived in the region. Shortly after landing,

Myers took umbrage at the egalitarian rhetoric of a Samoan missionary on Murray Island: "a troublesome fellow" who "comes among the people telling them how Samoans are all the same as white men." Myers's initial response to the physical appearance of the islanders was not favorable either: even "the most favorably impressed European," he thought, "could not term [them] handsome." Two of his colleagues expressed a more virulent sense of superiority. Wilkin complained in a letter home that "black-amores" and "savage minds" were incapable of yielding useful data; McDougall took the "inferiority of the black races" as a given and hoped that measurements of blood pressure would show whether "cessation of the growth of the brain at an earlier age than in the white races" was responsible. Although the group encompassed a variety of views on the causes and significance of racial differences, a sense of superiority united the researchers at the outset.[30]

So did the belief that British experts and imperial rulers were engaged in a mutually beneficial enterprise. Most of the funding for the trip came from an array of institutions at home: Cambridge University, the Royal Society, the Royal Geographical Society, and the British Association for the Advancement of Science. The resident magistrate on Thursday Island, John Douglas, added a subsidy of £100 to defray costs—making him one of roughly a dozen British officials who offered the expedition some form of material support. Another was Charles Hose, an administrator in the service of "white rajah" Charles Brooke in Sarawak; Myers and McDougall joined him on a diplomatic mission in the jungle after leaving Murray Island. Both men were among a growing number of officials across the empire who advocated ethnographic research in the service of imperial government at the end of the nineteenth century.[31] For the assistance provided by Douglas, Hose, and their colleagues—indigenous guides, letters of transit, overnight stays in comfortable residences—Haddon repaid the favor in *Head Hunters,* his popular memoir of the expedition, by praising the "generosity and erudition" of those "loyally respected" administrators. Haddon, too, had for years advocated a closer relationship between anthropologists and the state, seeking government patronage in Britain, South Africa, and Australasia while also dispensing advice to officials who asked for it.[32]

And yet, despite their ties to evolutionary theory and imperial power, the Cambridge researchers ended up raising questions about both. In some ways, their expedition revealed the difficulty of trying to navigate an enduring tension of empire—the need to see overseas subjects as different enough to justify their subjection but also similar enough to sustain the promise of progress through imperial rule.[33] Even at the end of the nineteenth century, the hardening of racial boundaries was not absolute. The notion of the British as a supremely accomplished "Anglo-Saxon race" enjoyed only a brief efflorescence in the mid-Victorian years, eclipsed soon afterward by disillusionment with mass democracy and the reassertion of class divisions against national unities.[34] The scholarly tradition of "Aryanism" parlayed ancient linguistic affinities into the romantic vision of an imperial family tree stretching from India to New Zealand—a deceptively benevolent image but one rooted in the assertion of similarity rather than difference.[35] The fascination with indigenous tribal and princely figureheads who could be idealized as colorful analogues to the aristocracy at home likewise cut across racial lines.[36] Perhaps the most powerful force working against rigid racial distinctions was the missionary community, which despite its own unmistakable sense of superiority remained committed to the biblical narrative of a common descent for humankind and the universal promise of Christian salvation.[37]

Of course, voicing vaguely egalitarian or colorblind opinions was made easier by the context of seemingly secure British dominance. The rhetorical minimization of racial differences was almost always pressed into the service of arguments for enlightened paternalism rather than self-government, which remained unimaginable for territories beyond the predominantly white settler communities of Canada and Australasia. Even those who drew attention to the resemblances and connections linking the British with their non-white subjects continued to assume that other identities mattered in powerful ways. But a note of ambivalence was nonetheless present in the imperial rhetoric of "race," an unstable compound of cultural, linguistic, and biological explanations.[38] Indeed, evolutionary theory itself pointed in two directions: toward ethnocentric hierarchy and also toward "psychic unity," the idea that every human being was endowed with the same mental functions and thus the capacity to progress through universal stages.[39] These tensions extended to the officials who hosted the Cambridge men in the Torres Strait.

John Douglas, the resident magistrate, embodied the optimism as well as the contradictions of an older liberal generation. Born in London in

1828, he had earlier served as a Liberal in the legislative assemblies of New South Wales and Queensland; anxious about the incursions of Japanese imperialism, he was a fervent backer of White Australia. But he also supported Mechanics Institutes and other initiatives aimed at working-class improvement, and as an official in the Torres Strait, he applied a similar logic of assimilation and uplift to the colonized population. The islanders, Douglas insisted, were "civilized" and "intelligent" British subjects "entitled to the same privileges that we enjoy"; the children even on rugged Murray Island were a "a very bright and orderly lot, quite equal in intelligence, according to my estimate, to the ordinary run of white children." The official in Sarawak, Charles Hose, was a younger man and a Cambridge-educated anthropologist. Like many other administrators, he played favorites among the ethnic groups in his territory, praising the morality and intelligence of the Kayans in an implicit rebuke to the rest. In the years after the expedition, however, Hose also followed the lead of the Cambridge researchers as they questioned the idea of an inferior and irrational "native mind." "The more intimately one becomes acquainted with these pagan tribes," he reflected in 1912, "the more fully one realizes the close similarity of their mental processes to one's own." If the inhabitants of Borneo sometimes acted impulsively and illogically, Hose pointed out to his fellow Europeans, "so do we also."[40]

Psychology mattered to debates on race and empire because claims to rule depended on generalizations about intelligence and character. What few people expected in 1898 was that the science of mind might unsettle those claims rather than strengthen them. As it turned out, the data that emerged from experiments in the laboratory and experiences in the field dramatized the tensions of imperial ideology.

¶ THE SIGHT that greeted the Cambridge men after almost six weeks at sea was far from paradise. Haddon described the main settlement at Thursday Island, Port Kennedy, as an "assemblage of corrugated iron and wooden buildings which garishly broil under a tropical sun, unrelieved by that vegetation which renders beautiful so many tropical towns." Kerosene tins and gin bottles floated in the sea; hastily erected hotels, some two or three stories, crowded the shore. It was a Conradian crossroads, with Britons, Frenchmen, Germans, Scandinavians, Greeks, and Pacific islanders all jostling for an edge in the pearl-fishing trade.[41] Looking out at the Pacific horizon months later, Charles Myers asked whether these signs of encroaching modernity portended catastrophe for the native people. As Spencer and most other Victorian thinkers saw it, the collision of cultures set the stage for a Darwinian drama in which only the fittest would survive, and Myers could easily imagine the grim final act.[42] "Will the plain be crowded with white men," he wondered, "the natives cowed & sweated in order to produce profits for the owner or to better the dividends of a company, until, sodden with drink & eaten away with diseases which today they know not, they sink into oblivion, as so many other races have done in the past before the approach of the European?"[43]

It was a vivid image of exploitation and extinction as evolutionary destiny. But Myers rejected it. "I believe in a better future," he wrote. As he saw it, the improving influence of English laws and English schools had the potential to transform the local population into a society capable of reckoning with the modern world. Its leaders "could be convinced of the utter lack of foundation for many of their own superstitious practices"; this newly enlightened elite could then mobilize against the deadening weight of tradition. "Under their own tuition and by the will and effort of the native," Myers declared, British rule might yet raise the islanders to "a high degree of civilization."[44] This marked a conspicuous departure from the racial fatalism common among British intellectuals in the late Victorian years. But the expedition that was drawing to a close as Myers wrote had cast doubt on many long-held assumptions.

In contrast to Thursday Island, the European influence on Murray Island—where most of the research in psychology took place—took some effort to discern when the researchers first arrived in 1898. The islanders' first sustained contact with Europeans had begun twenty-seven years earlier, with the coming of Protestant missionaries.[45] Although Haddon's friend John Bruce, the government schoolteacher and magistrate, was now the only white man living on the island, most of the inhabitants spoke the pidgin English they had picked up from the flourishing pearl trade. Many of them remembered Haddon from his zoological expedition a decade earlier. When he first came ashore in a dinghy on the return visit, he "was most affectionately greeted" by an islander named Pasi.[46] After lunching and bathing at Bruce's house that first afternoon—May 6, 1898—Haddon noticed an old mission building in the distance. "Although it is high up the hill & in bad repair," he recorded in his diary, "it will suit

The laboratory in the field, 1898. W. H. R. Rivers (seated) and Tom, an islander working as an assistant, demonstrate the use of color wheels in the mission house on Murray Island. (Copyright © 2014 Museum of Archaeology and Anthropology, University of Cambridge Museums. Licensed under a Creative Commons Attribution—Noncommercial 2.0 UK: England & Wales License.)

our purpose very well." He returned in a canoe a few hours later with Rivers, Ray, and a "lot of baggage," perhaps including the collection of psychological instruments they had brought around the world. The inventory was extensive: color wheels and wools (for testing vision), ohrmesser (for measuring power of hearing), Galton's whistle (for distinguishing frequencies), scents in test tubes (fourteen varieties for testing smell), and many others.[47] The more elaborate devices, including tachistoscopes to measure reaction time, were installed in an interior room, but the researchers also tested islanders on the verandah. They drew them to the house by offering to take photographs; providing medical care in a bare-bones dispensary; and giving away tobacco, sweets, and pocket knives.[48]

As their choice of apparatus suggests, the Cambridge men saw the study of perception by laboratory methods as an especially promising avenue.[49] The expedition came to the Torres Strait at a time when simple observation was losing credibility as a source of psychological knowledge. Scientists increasingly saw visual knowledge unmediated by instruments as tainted by the individuality of the observer and therefore unsuited to generalizations across place and time. Even—or especially—when it came to studying inner life, researchers preferred the "mechanical objectivity" of laboratory methods to the imaginative meeting of minds.[50] At a time when many British travelers went abroad in search of subjective, even mystical, transformations of the self, keeping the stigma of spiritualism at arm's length was indispensable to doing respectable science. For years after the expedition, Myers worried that the legitimacy of British psychology was threatened by groups like the Society of Psychical Research pursuing their own brands of "experiments" on hypnosis, telepathy, and spirit communication.[51] To mark out the boundaries of the science of mind, research at the turn of the century could only approach inner life by measuring bodily responses: ways of seeing, hearing, and feeling.

Curiosity about perception in other cultures had a long history. It was 1858 when then-future Prime Minister and polymath William Gladstone inspired speculation about variations in color vision by observing that Homeric poetry had no distinct word for blue.[52] More influential for the expedition, though, was Wilhelm Wundt, whose experiments in Leipzig from the late 1870s defined a new approach to the eternal question of psychology: how to develop an objective study of subjectivity? Wundt rejected the introspective method of his predecessors, identifying the senses as a rare domain of mental experience accessible to the new materialist methods of physiology. Hence the chronoscope (a device for measuring small time intervals) figured among his essential instruments because it produced the repeated trials and quantitative measurements that alone qualified as reliable experimental data in his view.[53] Although Wundt's philosophical idealism also led him to emphasize the importance of volition—which he argued could be investigated only through linguistics, ethnography, and other indirect methods—his legacy was appropriated by apostles of the new "scientific psychology," who championed Wundt as a strictly empiricist master of the laboratory. As a consequence, the reaction-time experiments he pioneered came to be seen as a source of knowledge about personality types, racial differences, and even the speed of thought.[54]

The measurement of the senses mattered, too, in the context of evolutionary theory. Because there were few obvious methods for verifying its claims empirically, researchers borrowed tools from disparate fields like physiology and optics to generate data.[55] The key evolutionary assumption in psychology was the "Spencer hypothesis," an explanation for the travelers' cliché that "primitives" possessed extraordinary sensory acuity, perceiving sights and sounds across great distances.[56] Herbert Spencer argued that less advanced races had sharper senses because their higher mental functions consumed little energy—that the simplest operations of the mind worked most efficiently among the simplest people.[57] When the researchers put the this hypothesis to the experimental test, however, they found it wanting.

The forty tables of data scattered throughout the second volume of the expedition's report told the story. In their ability to see, smell, and react to stimuli, the Torres Strait islanders performed comparably to Europeans, and in their power of hearing, they actually did worse. After returning from the Pacific, the researchers repeated their tests on control groups across Britain: villagers in Girton outside Cambridge, villagers near Aberdeen in Scotland, and patients in a convalescent home near Manchester. This process of replication confirmed the lack of meaningful differences in the perception of "primitive" and "civilized" people. Rivers concluded that the apparently impressive ability of the islanders to spot birds in trees or ships on the horizon was a habit honed in response to the demands of the environment rather than an evolutionary inheritance. By removing the islanders from their usual tropical surroundings the artificial space of the laboratory had unearthed universal capacities. Myers agreed that environmental influences had the greatest impact on the results, speculating that racial differences reported in earlier studies of reaction time might have reflected the fact that some groups simply practiced the test more than others.[58]

The comparison of two surprisingly convergent sets of numbers—one collected in the Torres Strait, one collected in Europe—made these conclusions possible. Setting out from the assumption that quantification transcended physical distance and cultural particularity, the Cambridge men allowed numbers to erode a sense of difference.[59] At the same time, however, this data only reinforced their subjective impressions. At every turn, the members of the expedition were confronted with reminders that they had traveled far from Cambridge; they struggled to carry out sensory experiments while the sun was shining brightly, wind was rustling in the palm trees, and surf was crashing on shore.[60] Yet they repeatedly counterbalanced the exotic with the analogic, constructing parallels between the

Pacific and everyday life back home. Myers commented that the inhabitants of the Torres Strait resembled the villagers he knew in Aberdeenshire; "the shrewdness and capability" projected by Tama Bulau, a formidable chief in Borneo, even reminded him of the former prime minister Lord Rosebery. Haddon, who was reminded of Ireland as he watched a funeral on Murray Island, once observed that even the most confounding markers of difference could coexist with depths of kinship. "An intimate and friendly acquaintance with savages," he wrote, "breaks down many prejudices, and while it often reveals modes of thought and traits of character which are all but incomprehensible to us . . . yet human nature is displayed at every turn, and common impulses and sympathies link the extremes of human kind."[61]

From a scientific standpoint, what the researchers saw in their subjects mattered. If even the most rigorous-seeming empirical data never spoke for itself, this was especially true in the case of experiments with "primitive" subjects. There was a long tradition in Western science of questioning experimental results generated by servants, women, and other subaltern groups; trained scientists with experience of observation were long considered the most trustworthy subjects.[62] Before leaving Britain, in fact, Myers found it "improbable that the reaction-times of a primitive people like the Murray Islanders could be profitably investigated." The experiments required elaborate procedures and industrial-style discipline: subjects had stare at a screen thirty-five meters away and lift their finger from a button when they saw a colored card slide into view. Only the testimony of the Cambridge men could confirm that the islanders understood this process well enough to generate meaningful data, sustaining the claim of comparability between Britain and the Torres Strait.[63]

As a result, the published report of the expedition stressed the diligence and intelligence of the islanders. Haddon lauded their "conscientiousness"; Myers reported that he "found no difficulty in explaining" the rationale of the experiment and collected reliable results from fifty-one of fifty-three subjects; Rivers reported a similar rate of success. Although earlier experiments with perception seemed to confirm racial differences in intelligence—and although the first ready-to-use mental test, the Binet-Simon, would not be published until 1905—the Cambridge researchers argued that the complexity of their experiments served as evidence of intellectual ability.[64] "Some of our investigations were distinctly laborious and made a considerable demand on the attention," Rivers remarked, "but in most cases [the islanders] exhibited a degree of application which was surprising in face of the widespread belief in the difficulty of keeping the attention of the savage concentrated on any one thing for any length of time." In a notebook used to record test results, he formalized this judgment by crossing out the word "General" at the head of a column for miscellaneous observations and writing "Intelligence" instead. Four of the six subjects evaluated in this way (Jimmy Rice, Liu, Charlie, and Tom) were classified as "good."[65] Perhaps Rivers and his colleagues recognized that their research would never have succeeded without the skill of their indigenous assistants—Jimmy Rice, Ned Waria, Tom, and Debe Wali—who helped to operate the equipment, translated the test instructions, and explicated their culture.[66]

To be sure, these abilities impressed some members of the expedition more than others. McDougall remained committed to scientific racism: in the years after returning home, he threw his support behind the nascent eugenics movement, using mental test results and crudely juxtaposed photographs to bolster the claim that "Anglo-American stock" was superior to any other. He worried that the least responsible and reflective groups were also the most prone to reproduce, subscribing to Spencer's belief that the balance of biological instinct and cultural achievement varied with race through the mechanism of Lamarckian inheritance.[67] While all of his colleagues acknowledged the existence of psychological differences between groups, however, several of them also stressed relativistic and cultural interpretations of those differences. Challenging researchers who claimed that reaction time translated directly into a measure of intellectual ability, Myers stressed the significance of "racial differences in temperament"—qualitative rather than quantitative traits akin to the "modal personalities" later described by relativist anthropologists in the United States. Comparing the "relatively unemotional" Malays of Sarawak with the "highly strung" Melanesians of Murray Island, Myers speculated that the Malays might have demonstrated more impressive reaction times because the high-pressure conditions of the experiment favored a phlegmatic "disposition" or "attitude." The ability measured by the test, in other words, was situational rather than absolute. Although Myers did not speculate on the origin of these temperamental differences, Rivers argued in later years that social structure rather than biological inheritance accounted for the varying frequency of personality types across groups.[68]

Several of the Cambridge researchers were struck by the diversity of abilities and personalities they encountered in the field. This too was reflected in the quantitative data—not in the comparisons *between* groups but in the variations *within* them. When each subject underwent many iterations of the same test, the pattern of results was anything but random. In the reaction time experiments, some improved their performance with practice, while others flagged as fatigue set in: Myers noted that Wanu and Baton got better over time, while Berò and Jimmy Dei got worse. In measuring reaction time, too, Myers had to closely observe his subjects to ensure that they responded only to the stimulus. Some focused intently on watching for the prompt; others concentrated on controlling their own movements; still others allowed their attention to relax completely. Myers ended up identifying individuals as the "dull steady-going" type, the "excitable" type, and "every gradation" in between. In explaining the outliers whose results had to be excluded altogether, he carefully distinguished between capacity and motivation, concluding that one of the underperforming subjects was simply "not doing his best." This approach to variation in psychological data—constructing complex profiles of situational responses rather than absolute rankings of ability—would shape Myers's career for a long time to come. As the director of the London-based National Institute of Industrial Psychology, which he founded in 1921, Myers advocated assigning British workers to factory jobs on the basis of a conviction forged in the Torres Strait: that the unique bundle of dispositions possessed by every individual might have a useful function to serve in the right context.[69]

Numbers told the story they did, once again, because personal encounters with the islanders shaped the outlook of the researchers. Psychological diversity proved difficult to ignore because the laboratory in the Torres Strait was less a pristine clinical space than a chaotic theater of humanity. It contained "a noisy crowd which made serious work impossible," hypochondriacs demanding medical exams, and so many photograph-seekers thronging the verandah that Myers once "trembled for its safety."[70] In the laboratory, at least, the researchers could attempt to order this chaos into a kind of "standardized individuality," plotting details on a diagnostic grid like a medical case history.[71] Just as the varieties of human nature contained in the crowd appeared infinite and unclassifiable, however, the standard variables of sex and age failed to explain all of the variation in

Charles Myers (kneeling) records a song on Murray Island, 1898. One of his favorite informants, Ulai, sits in front of the phonograph. (Copyright © 2014 Museum of Archaeology and Anthropology, University of Cambridge Museums. Licensed under a Creative Commons Attribution—Noncommercial 2.0 UK: England & Wales License.)

the data. As Myers put it, "the character of the natives appears as diverse as it would be in any English town."[72]

Turning aside the moralistic and evolutionary connotations of that Victorian word, Myers's understanding of "character" closely resembled the later concept of personality.[73] He described an islander named Pasi, who grew excited when telling stories, as "the high-strung 'nervous' type"; Tui, known as Dick, struck him as a "slow plodding reliable man"; Ulai appeared to be the "personification of cunning."[74] Other researchers noted that a robust sense of self differentiated the islanders from one another. Disproving the "widely spread" belief that "backward peoples" are "especially susceptible to suggestion," as Haddon put it, they deferred neither to the Cambridge men nor to each other. When confronted with a leading question, several made the pidgin retort: "that fashion belong another fellow, that no fashion belong we fellow." In the reaction-time experiments—which they were encouraged to treat as a kind of marksmanship competition—the islanders seemed eager to surpass those who tested before them, even checking the traces left on graph paper to assess their performance afterward. Far from conforming to social pressures, Haddon found, the islanders were "aware and proud of their own individuality."[75]

Like Myers, Haddon resisted moralistic judgments in the Torres Strait, taking pains to point out that the autonomy he observed did not translate into impulsivity, selfishness, or promiscuity. Initiation rites for young men embodied "a definite system of morals": a period of isolation put "self-restraint" to the test while elders extolled virtues including truthfulness, diligence, generosity, kindness to relatives, discretion in dealing with women, and a quiet temper. And yet Haddon also failed to detect what theorists of the "primitive mentality" would later describe as a slavish obedience to traditional rules. When custom dictated an overly harsh outcome, exceptions were tolerated, and the "strong personality" could flout regulations with impunity. Even more striking was that the islanders enthusiastically adopted customs from other cultures, suggesting that their attitudes "were not so conservative as is usually assumed." Departing from the conclusions he reached after his solitary journey in 1888–1889, Haddon after the turn of the century saw indigenous culture as flexible and dynamic rather than oppressive and static.[76]

After American researchers corresponding with Rivers confirmed his findings about visual perception at the St. Louis Exposition of 1904, human scientists on both sides of the Atlantic abandoned the Spencer hypothesis. Its refutation soon emerged as a key piece of evidence in the case for cultural relativism. In 1911, Franz Boas—whose skepticism about cross-cultural judgments may have originated with his own laboratory experiments on visual perception—cited the Cambridge experiments to bolster his claim that environment rather than heredity determined group differences.[77] As historians have noted with some puzzlement, however, the Cambridge researchers themselves did not immediately draw attention to the most dramatic implications of their research. In the years following the expedition, they seemed "reluctant to become involved in contemporary controversies," projecting "ambivalence" rather than certainty about the status of race in science.[78] Why did they not embrace the relativist cause as enthusiastically as Boas?

Spencer may have remained a daunting influence for the Cambridge group. So, perhaps, did Edward Tylor, another evolutionary thinker who reigned as the *eminence grise* of British anthropology.[79] Then, too, the authority of the human sciences—and the professional security that came with it—remained fragile around the turn of the century. Borrowing money from friends and relatives to pay bills from the expedition, Haddon did not receive a permanent appointment at Cambridge until 1905. When McDougall was hired at Oxford that same year, his position carried the title "reader in mental philosophy" because the science of mind was still tainted with the suspicion of godless materialism—a threat to the ideal of the morally autonomous subject. It was a similar story with Myers, who had to divide his time between Cambridge and King's College, London, until 1909, when he used his family's fortune to underwrite the construction of the first psychology laboratory in Cambridge. Seligman subsisted on work in clinical medicine and a series of anthropological expeditions to New Guinea, Ceylon, and Sudan before the London School of Economics (LSE) finally hired him in 1910. Only Rivers enjoyed a stable perch in the years after the expedition—and that may have owed something to the fact that his original appointment in Cambridge was in the field of physiology rather than psychology or anthropology.[80]

If a tenuous hold on gentlemanly status slowed the professional advancement of all these men, however, it may also have sharpened their skepticism of inherited ideas when they finally arrived in positions of influence.[81] As time passed, they cast an ever more critical eye on the reliability of the methods that researchers commonly used to produce racial classifications. Drawing on his experience of fieldwork in the Pacific and North Africa, Seligman observed that individuals who shared the same ancestry might look nothing alike, and, conversely, that people who appeared identical were often unrelated. He stressed that probing beneath the surface of appearances—gathering information, for instance, about kinship practices and artistic traditions—was sometimes more useful than the observation of faces and bodies in determining whether populations shared a common origin.[82] Reflecting on a trip to Egypt in 1901–1902, Myers agreed that basing racial classifications on "the outline of a face" risked an "utter lack of reliability." He went on to argue that quantitative data generated by instruments could likewise impose a false sense of coherence on group differences. Criticizing the common anthropometric practice of comparing races based on average skull sizes, he pointed out that such summary figures flattened the diversity within groups into misleading generalizations—both because individual measurements were subject to a large margin of error and because physical traits "vary enormously within a given community." By 1911, Myers extended this skepticism to racial comparisons based on intelligence testing, noting their susceptibility to the variables of temperament and fatigue that mattered so much in the Torres Strait.[83]

The decline of evolutionary hierarchies in the human sciences had many corollaries: distrust of visual knowledge, insistence on personal interaction with research subjects, attention to intragroup variation rather than intergroup differences. Each of these developments paralleled the incursion of laboratory psychology into territory once dominated by armchair anthropologists—a shift neatly illustrated by the fact that the British Psychological Society, founded in 1901 by a group including Rivers and McDougall, held its first meetings in the rooms of the Royal Anthropological Institute. As literary critic Samuel Hynes suggested long ago, this growing interest in "mental events" helped to displace the "purely mechanistic materialism" of Darwinism.[84] In a 1903 speech to the Anthropological Institute in London, Haddon acknowledged the change by placing physical anthropology on the "lowermost plane" of the profession—a striking concession in light of his training as a zoologist. The study of social institutions and customs came next; and then, at the summit of human self-knowledge, was the study of "sensations and mental operations . . . in which the limitations of classification in the animal plane are largely transcended." Psychology, Haddon argued, "takes us into the inner sanctuary of man." Seligman likewise applauded James Frazer for referring to social anthropology as "mental anthropology," heralding the rise of experimental psychology as a watershed for the human sciences. When anthropologists in 1905 proposed the establishment of the state-funded Imperial Bureau of Ethnology, they characteristically cited the need to understand the "mental attitudes" of indigenous people. Objective knowledge of the subjective—perceptions, thoughts, and feelings—now ranked as an important aim of imperial research.[85]

In 1911, Myers and Haddon decided to attend the Universal Races Congress held in London, signaling a new readiness to debate the politics of racial science beyond the academy. A remarkable congregation of imperial reformers, anticolonial leftists, and imperial subjects from Africa, Asia, and the West Indies, the Congress fell short of an interracial consensus on the evils of empire. Many European participants stressed their commitment to educating officials about cultural difference rather than ending imperial rule altogether.[86] But even speakers who resisted sweeping egalitarian pronouncements sounded a cautionary note about the significance of racial distinctions. "It was repeatedly emphasized," as one newspaper put it, "that the differences that separate race from race are almost always more apparent than real."[87]

In his address to the Congress, Myers explained why the refutation of the Spencer hypothesis mattered: what experts once saw as a fundamental biological difference turned out to be nothing more than a learned response. He also pointed out that the range of results captured by experiments in the Torres Strait exploded the myth of the monolithic "native mind": "In temperament we meet with the same variations in primitive as in civilized communities. . . . The average differences between different primitive peoples are as striking as those, say, between the average German and the average Italian." In intellectual ability, too, individual traits mattered more than group identities. Myers reported that the Scottish schoolteacher on Murray Island found the children there "superior in mathematical ability to those of an average British school." "Who knows what mental powers may be dormant even in primitive communities," Myers asked, "ready to burst into full flower as soon as the environment becomes appropriate?" This flourish came with a significant caveat: his time horizon for raising the least sophisticated societies to a "civilized" level stretched to "hundreds of thousands of years." But Myers took sides with those who believed in the value of education and development against those who insisted that racial difference was insurmountable.[88]

The appearance of Sorbonne professor Lucien Lévy-Bruhl's *Les fonctions mentales dans les sociétés inférieures* (1910) provoked the Torres Strait group to even stronger attacks on racial distinctions in psychology. Challenging a foundational tenet of British anthropology—"a 'human mind' completely the same as our own, in terms of logic, in all times and places"—Lévy-Bruhl insisted that it was not possible to transpose Western categories of thought to other cultures.[89] But he was no relativist. Rather than describing a multiplicity of mentalities, each rational in its own way, Lévy-Bruhl identified only two types: the "rational" and the "primitive." The animism that seemed to characterize many non-Western cultures did not arise from a universal reasoning process applied imperfectly—the classic explanation of Tylor and Frazer—but rather from a "mystical," "prelogical" psychology that obeyed its own rules. For the "primitive," Lévy-Bruhl argued, "objects, beings, and phenomena can be, in a way incomprehensible to us, both themselves and other than themselves."[90]

Although Lévy-Bruhl later conceded that examples of mystical thought could be found in contemporary Europe, his British critics pounced on the suggestion that the abstract categories of supernatural obscurantism and logical rationality could be mapped onto the boundaries between cultures. Myers argued that European peasants were as wedded to superstitious and supernatural beliefs as people anywhere and that "there is not a savage who cannot talk logically about matters of everyday life." Rivers warned of the danger that "prelogical mentality" might become "a convenient title wherewith to label any manifestation of the human mind we do not understand." Reflecting on his experience interviewing informants for hours at a time on frequently arcane points of genealogy and ritual, he concluded that "in intellectual concentration, as in many other psychological processes, I have been able to detect no essential difference between Melanesian or Toda and those with whom I have been accustomed to mix in the life our own society." Seligman stressed that mysticism was not confined to the exotic edges of empire; religious ideas, he pointed out, "call up complex worlds of emotion" for everyone. Even McDougall faulted Lévy-Bruhl for "the great error of assuming that the mental life of civilised man is conducted by each individual in a purely rational and logical manner."[91]

As a younger generation of intellectuals rose to prominence, they followed in the path of the Cambridge group, criticizing Lévy-Bruhl with an ever more emphatic blurring of the distinction between "primitive" and "civilized" minds. For British anthropologists in particular, attacking Lévy-Bruhl served a useful function, allowing them to salvage universalist principles from the hierarchies of evolutionary theory. Almost immediately after arriving in the Trobriand Islands, in 1915, Seligman's most famous student, Bronislaw Malinowski, became convinced of the "complete futility" of Lévy-Bruhl's theory because "the native mind works according to the same rules as ours." Any "apparent differences" in mental life, he later told his students at the LSE, are "due to differences in . . . cultural patterns, not to differences in methods of [mental] functioning." Jack Driberg, an Oxford anthropologist who was fired from the colonial service in Sudan and later converted to Islam, published popular books arguing that "primitive man" is "a being as human as ourselves, affected by the same emotions as ourselves, with thoughts, responses, and actions differing in no essential way from our own." In the psychology laboratory at Cambridge, Myers's student and successor Frederic Bartlett argued that Lévy-Bruhl had set up an asymmetric contrast between the scientific expert at home and the "primitive" overseas. In navigating the demands of everyday life, he argued, every human being "most clearly perceives, remembers, constructs and reasons as we do, displaying all the care, all the patience, all the skill and insight, and much of the logic of the highly trained investigator."[92] In the interwar period, social scientists and natural scientists, armchair scholars and university professors, researchers and bureaucrats all invoked a universal model of psychology against Lévy-Bruhl's theory of difference.[93]

This response was not unanimous. Some British thinkers renewed old clichés about the weakness of individuality in non-Western societies by insisting that feelings of group solidarity dominated inner life. This view—supported by readings of Durkheim as well as Lévy-Bruhl—had a high-profile proponent in R. R. Marett, the armchair anthropologist who succeeded Tylor at Oxford in 1910.[94] Many imperial officials, meanwhile, saw Lévy-Bruhl's emphasis on collective and ritualistic sources of meaning as a welcome justification of indirect rule—the practice of channeling British authority through supposedly traditional institutions. As late as 1935, a district officer in Northern Rhodesia asserted that "the idea of the western mind, that can conceive of an individual personality having an independent existence . . . is still beyond the scope of savage mentality." In Africa, especially, officials assumed that inner life and tribal identities were so profoundly intertwined that modernization or "deculturation" might cause mental breakdowns.[95]

Even among those who worked and lived in the colonies, however, arguments for the uniqueness of the "primitive mentality" did not go unchallenged. The most skeptical response may have from Christian missionaries, who often voiced doubt about hard-edged racial classifications.[96] "Underlying all differences of race," missionary administrator Joseph Oldham declared in 1924, "there exists a common humanity . . . the same dominant instincts, the same primary emotions, the same capacity of judgment and reason."[97] Among secular intellectuals, too, criticism of the "primitive mentality" thesis was widespread. This was true even in the set-tler societies of southern Africa.[98] Ecologist John William Bews, a Scottish-born segregationist and protégé of Jan Smuts who served as president of the University of Natal, emerged as perhaps the most surprising opponent of what he called Lévy-Bruhl's "extreme views." Bews in 1935 described the idea "that primitive man never thinks of himself as an individual but only as a member of the tribe or group" as "definitely disproved."[99]

Whether these echoes of the Torres Strait group reveal a direct line of influence is, for the most part, unknowable. But the veterans of that journey irrevocably altered the terms of the debate. By training a new gen-eration of scholars led by Bartlett, Malinowski, and Edward Evans-Pritchard, the Cambridge men helped to shape the future of research on inner life across the world. In their own distinctive ways, they also demon-strated the relevance of the human sciences to imperial rule. As the director of the National Institute of Industrial Psychology, Myers pro-moted the use of efficiency-boosting aptitude tests in factories and offices from Malaya to India to South Africa. As an adviser to imperial officials, instructor of recruits to the imperial service, and occasional commentator on the BBC, Seligman blended anthropology and psychology to illustrate the complexities of cross-cultural interaction. W. H. R. Rivers, meanwhile, followed the path from the Torres Strait to a more radical destination. Fusing expertise and activism, his brief career as a Labour Party candi-date for Parliament showed that the science of mind could even cast the legitimacy of empire into question.

¶ WHEN RIVERS AGREED in the spring of 1922 to stand for election to London University's seat in the Commons, the prospect of a don ven-turing into electoral politics was not unprecedented. Rivers's mentors Michael Foster and Victor Horsley, for instance, had earlier represented the same constituency as Liberal MPs. But neither had done so under the banner of socialism. The policies Rivers pledged to support were radical: the Labour Party platform in 1922 called for the nationalization of mines and railways and a progressive tax on large fortunes. It also conspicuously aligned itself with the cause of anticolonial nationalism around the world, advocating "real independence" for Egypt, "self-government" for India, recognition of the Irish Free State, and an "all-inclusive League of Nations" to hold the imperial powers in check. In private, Rivers observed that he had "furiously annoyed" some academic colleagues by making these new commitments. One of them was Charles Myers, who "remained the closest of friends" but "found it impossible to agree with some of the views which [Rivers] published so freely."[100]

What drove Rivers to risk his reputation for the uncertain rewards of a campaign? He expressed a feeling of obligation to bring scientific expertise into politics, describing the British future in apocalyptic tones. "The times are so ominous, the outlook for our own country and the world so black, that if others think I can be of service in political life, I cannot refuse." At home, he worried about the threat of unconscious forces disrupting the political system; joking that he wanted to get into Parliament to psychoanalyze Lloyd George only concealed a profound anxiety about democratic decision-making. In one campaign speech, Rivers railed against "the credulity with which the nation swallows the arguments and nostrums of a Yellow Press, allows itself to be swindled by the unscrupulous company promoters, and remains incompetent to engage in logical argument or consistent thought"—a striking echo of the language Lévy-Bruhl applied to "primitives." In the empire, Rivers deplored the cultural insensitivity of administrators who banned indigenous practices they did not understand, arguing that this "indiscriminate and undiscriminating interference" led to catastrophic depopulation in the British Pacific by producing a fatal "lack of interest in life."[101]

In some ways, Rivers's indictment of irrationality and ignorance in British life stemmed from the experience of the First World War. As one of the celebrated doctors who treated "shell-shocked" soldiers with psychotherapy, Rivers led the way in introducing Freud to British science. Like other wartime discoverers of the unconscious, he merged psychoanalytic theory with social criticism, suggesting that the upper classes overlooked their proximity to poverty through a process of "repression." His most famous shell shock patient, the poet Siegfried Sassoon, brought him into contact with pacifist and radical politics for the first time.[102] But Rivers's postwar platform also marked the continuation of a prewar tradition on the British left. His *entrée* into politics came through a London-based intelligentsia that advocated taming popular sentiment through expert knowledge and owed at least as much to fin-de-siècle crowd psychology as to Freud. Troubled in part by popular outbursts of Boer War–era "jingoism" at home, economist J. A. Hobson, political scientist Graham

Wallas, and psychologist Wilfred Trotter were among the Edwardian thinkers who voiced concern about eruptions of irrationality.[103] Rivers shared these anxieties in a qualified way: rather than fatalistically accepting the need for a permanent dictatorship of the rational elite, he argued that educating the masses about psychological principles could reduce the influence of unreason. As Rivers declared in the aftermath of war, the age of physical science was yielding to the age of human science, and political leaders could draw on therapeutic knowledge to lead the nation "back to health and sanity."[104]

Rivers found his first political home in a hybrid of social radicalism and technocratic elitism: the Fabian Society. One of his earliest political outings after the war was a salon at a Sussex country house attended by Harold Laski, Bertrand Russell, and Sidney and Beatrice Webb; his nomination as parliamentary candidate came with endorsements from card-carrying Fabians like epidemiologist Arthur Newsholme, suffragist Marion Phillips, and Sidney Webb himself. Accepting the nomination in 1922, he sang from the Fabian hymn book: "I cannot believe that political problems differ from those of every other aspect of social life in being incapable of solution by scientific methods, and the Labour party is far more likely than any other to recognize the value and utilize the results of such methods."[105] Rivers also echoed those Fabian thinkers who saw imperialism as a source of political instability. Hobson thought the "mass psychology" shaped by music-hall propaganda demonstrated how easily vested interests could manipulate public opinion; Wallas worried that conquering alien cultures without extending the promise of assimilation guaranteed a future of perpetual conflict.[106] The dysfunctionality of politics at home, Rivers agreed, was both cause and consequence of an unjust empire overseas.

Putting his ethnographic experience in the service of a topsy-turvy relativist gaze, Rivers used the example of other cultures as a foil for social criticism. The very qualities he and his colleagues had taken pains to decouple from the "native mind" in the Torres Strait—susceptibility to group pressures, emotionalism, and selfishness—Rivers now identified as threats to progress in metropolitan Britain. Speaking at University College, London, in the spring of 1922, Rivers took issue with conservatives who described socialism as an attempt to legislate against human nature. Using R. H. Tawney's recent study of *The Acquisitive Society* as a point of departure, he conceded the existence of an individualistic, competitive instinct

ρ.

W. H. R. Rivers in Vanuatu, 1914. (Copyright © 2014 Museum of Archaeology and Anthropology, University of Cambridge Museums. Licensed under a Creative Commons Attribution—Noncommercial 2.0 UK: England & Wales License.)

that motivated the drive for material possessions. Summoning the authority of his fieldwork in the Pacific, however, Rivers contended that alternative forms of social organization were possible. He described Melanesia as a communistic idyll where "co-operation in the interest of the community" reigned supreme and every individual was "allowed the use of the produce of the cultivated land of the group regardless whether they have taken any part in the cultivation." The Melanesians, it seemed, had "modified" the acquisitive instinct. While Rivers professed uncertainty about the mechanism that accomplished this, he speculated that a benevolent "herd-instinct" of the kind described by Trotter had been called into play. According to Rivers, then, the contrast between colony and metropole was not instinct versus reason but rather two different kinds of instinct: self-seeking greed versus communitarian benevolence. He was lauding the Melanesian model as one for Britain to emulate.[107]

But Rivers's attempt to construct a radical platform on the foundation of the human sciences was cut unexpectedly short. In the midst of planning a lecture series for workers in Manchester and trips to Europe and India, he died of a twisted intestine in June 1922. His students were devastated. On hearing the news, Frederic Bartlett remembered, "Everything seemed suddenly silly . . . for Rivers who was my friend and counselor had gone, and I should see him no more." In the general election that fall, the science-fiction writer and leftist activist H. G. Wells took his friend's place on the Labour ticket. Wells faithfully echoed many of Rivers's views: while he spent more time talking about Europe than about empire, he still found time to condemn "the dangerous British 'ascendancy' dreams of Lord Curzon" and "the reckless adventurousness" of then-colonial secretary Winston Churchill. Wells railed, too, against the coarsening effects of "swollen private fortunes" and newspapers filled with "plutocratic propaganda." But he fell far short of victory in a white-collar constituency Labour had rarely contested before, finishing in third place and trailing the winning Conservative candidate by around twenty-six hundred votes out of more than eight thousand cast.[108]

Rivers left a more lasting legacy than those election results might suggest. British intellectuals between the wars increasingly argued that the familiar equation of rationality and civilization could not be sustained because European minds were far from rational. Superstitious beliefs about knocking on wood and avoiding the number thirteen—or faith in the supernatural tenets of Christianity—offered proof enough of that. So did the persistent threat of regression into barbarism. In a 1922 lecture crafted with help from Rivers and Myers, Bartlett warned that "sudden outbursts" of impulses which had been "driven into secret may occur at any level of cultural development." University of Manchester professor John Murphy arrived at a similar conclusion: as he put it in 1927, atavistic passions threatened to "break volcanically to the surface" even in the most sophisticated societies. While the war provided one subtext for these arguments, the perception of an eroding boundary between "primitive" and "civilized" revolved around the disillusionments of everyday life as well as the extremities of the battlefield. Leading a seminar at the LSE in 1936, Malinowski mused that the "constant repetition of slogans" in advertisements for beer and Bovril operated on the same psychological principle as "primitive magic" in Africa. As British intellectuals took a more skeptical view of democracy, capitalism, and other institutions at home, psychology furnished a novel language for questioning differences between colonizer and colonized.[109]

One consequence of this novelty was that the methodological toolkit researchers had at their disposal was constantly evolving. Corresponding with Seligman in the early 1920s, Myers felt compelled to remind his old colleague that the science of mind had changed dramatically since 1898—and that one kind of knowledge, in particular, was not available to the Cambridge group in the Torres Strait. "Are you aware that Freud's [*The Interpretation of Dreams*] did not appear until 1900? How could the Expedition have utilized all the psycho-analytic developments . . . which have occurred since the Expedition left England?!"[110] Myers's frustration was understandable. British human scientists had gradually reached at the same conclusion as Wundt himself: studying perception with laboratory instruments failed to provide access to the richest depths of inner life. The advent of psychoanalysis heralded new ways of thinking about colonized minds.

CHAPTER TWO

A Dream Dictionary for the World

The Globalization of the Unconscious

WHEN CHARLES GABRIEL SELIGMAN sat down behind a microphone at the studios of the BBC shortly before eight o'clock in the evening on March 24, 1931, he had reached the twilight of a long and accomplished career. Since participating in the Cambridge expedition to the Torres Strait, he had carried out fieldwork in New Guinea, Ceylon, and the Sudan; trained a generation of British anthropologists; and instructed hundreds of imperial officials about the cultures they ostensibly ruled. Along the way, he had accumulated a long list of honorifics, become a serious collector of East Asian art, and put his medical training to work for the British Army. Seligman's talk on this occasion marked yet another role for the influential if unconventional scholar: psychoanalyst for a mass audience. He began by asking his listeners, "What do you dream about?"[1]

The question might have seemed impertinent, but it would not have been unfamiliar. Dream books touting prophetic interpretations had been a fixture of British popular culture for centuries; more recently, Freudian and Jungian theories had begun to circulate from the intellectual circles of London and Cambridge to the middlebrow print world of newspapers and self-help texts.[2] As one of the medical men who treated shell-shocked soldiers with elements of the talking cure during the First World War, Seligman himself belonged to the psychoanalytic *avant-garde*.[3] But the significance of his radio broadcast had less to do with the choice of subject than with the journey that led to it. Seligman's invitation to a national conversation about dreams was the culmination of a project he had pursued, sporadically, for nearly a decade. Inspired by his wartime foray into psychotherapy, Seligman assembled a network of anthropologists and administrators to collect dreams from indigenous peoples across the British Empire—from Nigeria to Sudan to India to the Solomon Islands. His appeal to the public at home represented another step in the service of a curious ambition: to construct a global dictionary of the symbols in dreams.

The "psychoanalytic moment" in British anthropology has been described as an intellectual cul-de-sac—a passing fashion that faded away by the 1930s.[4] But Seligman was confronting a problem that lasted far longer: how to reconcile a universal model of the mind with human diversity. Was psychoanalysis only an updated version of evolutionary psychology, with the id and the superego replacing the Victorian language of impulsivity and restraint? Freud and Jung may have thought so.[5] But the interpretation of dreams in Seligman's project blurred the boundaries of the "primitive" and the "civilized" in ways he did not anticipate—revealing the same condensed meanings, inner conflicts, and irrational drives in Britain and its colonies.[6] These universalizing possibilities made psychoanalysis a useful form of knowledge for anticolonial leftists between the wars. For them, unraveling the complex inner lives of imperial subjects meant exposing the trauma of political oppression and the pathological irrationality of empire itself. They anticipated, in some ways, the psychoanalytic radicalism made famous by Frantz Fanon and others in the postwar French empire.[7]

But the currents of protest and liberation in British psychoanalysis encountered limits.[8] At a time when rebellions around the world were challenging imperial authority, researchers also probed the unconscious origins of political behavior, seeking to explain why the deference and apathy of loyal subjects sometimes turned to aggression.[9] The conclusion they drew—that colonized minds were damaged minds—had a fatal ambiguity.[10] While studies of the unconscious revealed the wounds inflicted by imperial violence, they also focused attention on the supposedly disordered personalities and dysfunctional families of indigenous cultures. Even the radical insights of psychoanalysis, in other words, could serve imperial designs for managing intimate relationships and inner life. Seligman showed how this, too, could be done: by listening closely to the language of unconscious minds.

¶ ALTHOUGH HIS FASCINATION with the unconscious mind bore the hallmarks of modernism, Charles Seligman was a product of Victorian science. He never fully abandoned the taxonomic sensibility of his child-hood hero T. H. Huxley, whose "Science of Man" was explicitly modeled on zoology and aimed at locating human groups in a Linnaean scheme of classification.[11] Like several of his colleagues in the Torres Strait, Seligman trained as a physician and always retained the habits of the medical man. When he first went to the tropics in 1898 and again in 1904, he gathered information on disorders as varied as eczema, albinism, and cancer. Treating soldiers during the war, he could still use a stethoscope to pin-point the respiratory difficulties of a patient.[12] Seligman's affinity for the physical foundations of anthropology underpinned his most notorious work, *The Races of Africa,* first published in 1930 and reissued by Oxford University Press as late as 1979. "The chief criteria of race considered in this book," he declared at the outset, "include skin colour, hair form, stature, head shape, and certain characters of the face, e.g. prognathism, and of the nose." Although fieldwork around the world led him to recog-nize the fallibility of visual knowledge and racial classification, Seligman remained far more reliant on both than, say, Myers or Rivers.[13] His habit of discerning "Caucasian blood" in Africans with supposedly noble fea-tures led to his dubious affirmation of the nineteenth-century Hamitic myth, which held that all civilization in Africa—from the glories of ancient Egypt to the spread of pastoral farming—could be traced to the European-looking Hamites.[14]

But Seligman's involvement with race in anthropology was complicated by the disruption of hierarchies in another field: the science of mind. Even before Freud reached British shores, two foundational assumptions of evo-lutionary psychology—the origin of all knowledge in sensory experience and the subordination of instinct to rationality—were showing signs of strain. A surge of enthusiasm for idealist philosophy at the end of the nine-teenth century shifted attention from the environment's power to shape consciousness to the meaning imposed on it by consciousness itself. By arguing that volitional qualities such as desire and aversion were insepa-rable from perception, aesthetic judgment, and moral belief, some British psychologists increasingly blurred the boundary between emotion and intellect.[15] Others interpreted the Darwinian language of instincts to mean that mental life was neither purely conscious nor purely logical. A decade after the Torres Strait expedition, Charles Myers described "instinct-intelligence" as "one indivisible mental function," an amalgam of innate drives and learned behavior. Although many British intellectuals—including Myers—still insisted that minds were ultimately rational, this no longer seemed a foregone conclusion.[16]

If psychoanalysis could build on new directions in British psychology, however, the first appearance of Freud's books in English translation after 1909 did not inspire universal enthusiasm. Skepticism of a supposedly sex-obsessed theory with continental and Jewish roots dampened his theory's appeal in Britain for a long time to come. Even in the intellectual-friendly pages of the *Manchester Guardian,* references to Freud, repression, and the Oedipus complex were conspicuously sparse before 1945 and much less common than in American newspapers.[17] British popularizers of psychoanalysis tended to filter the language of the unconscious through Victorian traditions of self-improvement and dream interpretation. They played down the idea of sexual liberation while offering practical advice for introspection and enlightenment; they also drew on an eclectic range of sources, including Carl Jung and Alfred Adler, as well as Freud.[18] A more orthodox form of psychoanalysis did, however, become fashionable among the urban intelligentsia. The bohemian Bloomsbury circle left its imprint here: Freud's *Collected Papers* were first published in English by the Hogarth Press, Lytton Strachey's brother James did the translation, and Virginia Woolf's brother Adrian set up one of the first psychoanalytic practices in the country. The handful of innovative psychotherapy clinics that opened after the First World War likewise clustered in the cosmopolitan atmosphere of the capital.[19] This was a congenial milieu for Seligman—not only because of his own continental and Jewish origins but because medical specialists like himself were perhaps the earliest British students of Freud's work. Brenda Seligman began seeing a psychoanalyst sometime in the 1920s, and although it is unclear whether her husband did so too, he shared her practice of writing down dreams and attempting auto-interpretations.[20]

For Charles Seligman, the first opportunity to put psychoanalysis to professional use came with his involvement in the treatment of shell-shocked soldiers during the war—a celebrated early experiment in Freudian therapy that also served as an impromptu reunion for the Torres Strait researchers. Myers, on the front lines in France, and Rivers and McDougall, at the Maghull military hospital outside Liverpool, were among the first to argue that bizarre symptoms in soldiers sent down from the trenches did not result from the concussive force of artillery fire but rather from the emotional dislocations of war.[21] The concept of trauma, which British doctors had defined in psychological as well as somatic terms for decades, figured prominently in this diagnosis.[22] With far more freedom to experiment than Myers enjoyed in the combat zone, the group of experts assembled at Maghull interspersed their clinical work with lectures on Freud, Jung, and Janet; Rivers organized long afternoon walks in the "Cambridge fashion" to talk over theories of the unconscious. It was, in the words of one participant, "a society in which the interpretation of dreams and the discussion of mental conflicts formed the staple subjects of conversation."[23]

When Seligman ventured into this hothouse in 1918, his interactions with patients came to reflect the heterodox and eclectic spirit of the place. Like Rivers and company, he blended psychoanalysis with old-fashioned self-help; he prodded patients to read the war news and "face up to facts." But he took inspiration from Freud as well, probing childhood memories and eliciting detailed accounts of sexual encounters. With one patient, he launched into a mini-lecture on the concepts of dissociation and reintegration, explaining how painful experiences driven into the unconscious could generate physical symptoms.[24] The dreams that provided the richest information about his patients' inner lives also dramatized the obsolescence of the hierarchical progressions—from instinct to reason, from experience to knowledge, from simplicity to complexity—on which Victorian psychology had rested. Belying the associationist idea that all thought arose from repetitions and juxtapositions of sensory data, the strange mental journeys recounted by Seligman's patients could not have reflected any objective reality. Rather, they reflected a scrambling of it, a willful rearranging of events in which the observation of the world merely provided raw material for the machinations of the psyche.

The dream of a private from Birmingham, the manager of a livestock firm in civilian life, offered an especially striking case. He dreamed of standing outside a grocer's shop and gazing at a window display of vegetable marrows. A moment later, they have turned into artillery shells; when he remarks "those are funny marrows, aren't they?" the shopkeeper responds by putting her finger to her lips. The scene then abruptly shifts to a field where marrows, potatoes, and cabbage are growing in a row. The private is now a farmer, laying his plow across the furrows and walking behind two horses at the end of a day's work. A "motor-car" passing on the road suddenly kicks up a cloud of dust that frightens the horses and sends them tumbling into a ditch. At the next instant, the dreamer is holding a marrow in his hand and trying in vain to slice it open: "It seems hard, can't get knife in, seems as though it's frozen." The marrows look strange, like "little cut-glass bottles." Then, in another abrupt change of setting, he finds himself on a train bound for Manchester and finally in a car *en route* to the hospital.[25]

Seligman prompted his patient to free-associate with the images of the dream. The oval-shaped bottles glimpsed in his hand led back to a feverish recollection of pulling grenade pins and bracing for an explosion: "Can hear one terrible crash, that's when shells was dropping all round. Remember feeling as if my insides trying to change places." When Seligman asked about the significance of the price of the marrows in the grocer's window, the private realized that the card read "1/8," the number painted on the side of the ambulance that carried him away after his mental breakdown. The unconscious afterlife of trauma had fashioned an unlikely sequence from grocer's shop to farmer's field to military hospital. Yet it was not only the reordering of experience, but the multiplicity of meanings attached to ordinary objects, that demanded a new kind of psychology. The old paradigm of discrete sensations neatly interlinked had given way to a universe in which marrows were not only marrows but also artillery shells, glass bottles, and grenades.

The association of stable meanings with material objects was a hallmark of rationality in Victorian psychology. That is why the "object lesson," which prompted schoolchildren to list the qualities and uses of everyday commodities, figured so prominently in British schools at home and overseas.[26] It is also why Lévy-Bruhl identified the lack of stable associations as a defining characteristic of the "primitive mentality," in which, he argued, objects appear as "both themselves and other than themselves." After Maghull, Seligman always insisted that this multiplicity of meanings was not unique to "primitive" minds. When a correspondent in the early 1930s suggested that "savage" people "see the real world [as] suffused with subjective emotional values" so that "rivers are gods, trees are shrines," Seligman recoiled. "Getting back to Lévy-Bruhl," he scrawled in the margin. "No more than any religious person." If British churchgoers—like British soldiers—defied logical distinctions by projecting emotional meanings onto the world, Lévy-Bruhl's theory looked less like an account of the lower evolutionary ranks than of universal human dispositions.[27]

Although early psychoanalysts drew frequent analogies between the "primitive" and the neurotic—a legacy, perhaps, of Freud's example in *Totem and Taboo*—Seligman and his colleagues at Maghull did not see irrationality as a fixed marker of backwardness or madness. The doctors there diverged from convention by looking past the spectacle of bizarre symptoms and treating their patients as normal men whose experiences in the trenches exacerbated domestic and professional stresses.[28] When they conducted word-association experiments of the kind pioneered by Carl Gustav Jung, some of the responses given by patients rested on purely logical connections: phonetic similarity ("sigh–cycle"), description ("horse–swift"), or "causal dependence" ("cloud–rain"). But many answers were determined instead by individual happenstance ("lunch–bicycle" "because subject goes to lunch on his bicycle") and "emotional" associations ("sister–darling"). Along with Freud's *Psychopathology of Everyday Life,* one of the books he read in 1918, working at Maghull helped to convince Seligman that mental associations were intrinsically unstable and idiosyncratic.[29] In the years that followed, he repeatedly stressed that "modern psychology has given a place of importance to the unconscious—which is essentially emotional and non-intellectual—in the motivation of both civilized and savage behavior, normal as well as abnormal." He encouraged Malinowski to incorporate dream analysis into his fieldwork in the Trobriands, praised Freud as "a very great man," and in 1922 even wrote up a dream of his own and mailed it to 19 Berggasse in Vienna.[30]

The moment Seligman chose to share his dream with Freud was revealing in more ways than one. It showed the Englishman's newfound enthusiasm for psychoanalysis, of course, but also the limits of that enthusiasm. "No kind of Freudian psychology," he told Malinowski, "is ever going to make up, as far as anthropology goes, for common sense, the knack of making friends with natives, and a historical knowledge of what has already been done in the science." Those are the words of the old-fashioned empirical researcher, tempered but not overcome by the modernist frisson of the war years. Like Rivers, perhaps, Seligman was unconvinced by Freud's commitment to the sexual etiology of neurosis; his scholarship maintained a dignified silence on the subject of sex, even as Malinowski delved into the minutiae of coital positions.[31] It was the interpretation of symbols in dreams, however, that most clearly revealed Seligman's distance from psychoanalytic orthodoxy. Freud's chilly response to the request for a long-distance analysis hinted at the divide:

> Permit me to classify your question as a pre-analytic one relating as it does to the manifest content of a non-analyzed dream. The associations you give are so very few and do not even bring out a connection between your state of mind on the dream-day and the remembered dream. A birth-situation appears in the latter part of the dream which when submitted to analysis might have proved very interesting.[32]

Although Seligman and Freud were both concerned with the associations attached to images in the unconscious mind, they had very different ideas of how to make sense of them. From the opening pages of *The Interpretation of Dreams,* Freud took pains to distance himself from the dream dictionaries that had been a staple of popular culture for centuries. Stressing that "the curious plasticity of psychic material" made fixed, universal, and impersonal definitions far from certain, he remarked that "these [symbols] often possess many and varied meanings, so that, as in Chinese script, only the context can furnish the correct meaning." In particular, Freud argued, the interpretive work of the analytic session alone could elicit the meaning imparted to images by each individual. Even the tantalizing suggestion of a "birth-situation" in Seligman's dream—"we came to a longer narrower tunnel which we traversed with considerable difficulty and came out into a sort of natural amphitheatre with trees, water, etc., and knew that all pursuit and danger was over"—meant little in the absence of more information about the dreamer's inner life.[33]

For Seligman, by contrast, acknowledging the unpredictability and irrationality of mental associations did not mean that symbols had purely individual meanings. This conviction may have had something to do with the fact that the anthropology profession in which he built his career was consumed by debates about a particular kind of *socially* constructed symbol: the totem.[34] Freud intervened in that tradition by tracing customary prohibitions on marrying within the clan or eating the totem animal to feelings of incestuous desire and Oedipal rage. But Seligman always interpreted totemism primarily as an instrument of collective identity, a mechanism for marking out the boundaries of the group. To belong to a clan was by definition to invest a shared symbol with social meaning, the view famously expressed by Émile Durkheim.[35] Seligman never fully accepted the idea that every culture represented a closed system of meaning; like other anthropologists of his time, he was fascinated when identical tools, weapons, or artistic motifs turned up in far-flung places. But while Seligman conceded that contact between cultures played a role in diffusing symbols like the lightning bolt and the swastika across the ancient world, he kept his distance from the radical version of diffusionism—espoused by W. H. R. Rivers—which held that an immense collection of cultural forms originated in ancient Egypt and migrated outward from there. The old idea of psychic unity, Seligman maintained, also had relevance for the new frontier of the unconscious. The same symbol could have arisen independently in different places, he argued, because *"human needs & human psychology are the same"* everywhere in the world.[36]

For Seligman, then, the meaning of symbols offered a point of entry into debates about universality of psychoanalysis. If Freud went too far in individualizing symbols, stressing personal experience and unconscious fantasy to the exclusion of shared cultural forms, Rivers went too far in making them social artifacts, marginalizing the inventive force of the mind by focusing on practices of transmission instead. But there was another possibility: Jung's idea of the collective unconscious, a stratum of myths, memories, and images accumulated over generations and inherited by every human being. Rivers expressed withering skepticism: "we need far more evidence before there can be established even a probable case." Seligman was less dismissive. While confessing a predisposition for Freud's "materialistic" psychology over Jung's "semi-mystical" alternative, he took up Rivers's challenge, putting the collective unconscious to an empirical test by charting the symbolic vocabulary of dreams around the world. Questioning people in many places about the images in their dreams could establish whether the symbolic language of dreams took shape from personal history, cultural tradition, or the mind itself. The British Empire would serve as Seligman's laboratory.[37]

At a time when global applications of psychoanalytic theory provoked intense controversy, the decision to analyze unconscious minds in Africa, India, and elsewhere was a radical one. It was Seligman's protégé, Malinowski, who touched off a contretemps in 1924 by suggesting that the Oedipus complex necessarily took different forms in matriarchal and patriarchal societies. Although Malinowski initially described his work as a "confirmation of the main tenet of Freudian psychology," the ensuing criticism from Freudian loyalists drove him to a forceful rejection of psychoanalysis. By 1927, Malinowski was dismissing the anthropological significance of dreams altogether.[38] Then too—and despite his interest in the expansion of the psychoanalytic movement around the world—Freud himself demonstrated little enthusiasm for the cross-cultural study of the unconscious. The leading analyst in India, Girindrasekhar Bose, helped to establish a lively Freudian community in Calcutta but also proposed significant changes to the Freudian model of the mind. Drawing on the Upanishads and other Sanskrit texts, Bose rejected the tripartite division of id, ego, and superego; on the basis of clinical observation, he suggested that castration anxiety and Oedipal father-hatred were less prevalent in Indians than in Europeans. Freud responded by dismissing Bose and other Indian intellectuals with thinly veiled condescension, reportedly joking that they were obsessed with the idea of a mother complex.[39] Seligman diverged from both Malinowski and Freud by framing his tentative commitment to the universality of psychoanalysis as a methodological precept. He argued that the mysteries of the unconscious could not be unraveled in Europe alone.

Seligman's experiment challenged convention in another way as well. To the extent that psychotherapy had gained a foothold in the imperial context, it focused on the colonizer rather than the colonized, policing the identity of the European ruling class by marking out boundaries and upholding prestige. In India, the administration of state asylums was motivated less by fear of disorder in the indigenous population than by the desire to keep alcoholics, vagabonds, and other embarrassing elements of the European population out of sight. In East Africa as late as the 1930s, experts warned the white settler community about "tropical neurasthenia," a vague diagnosis of nervous exhaustion caused by the intensity of equatorial sunlight as well as the stresses of living among an alien population far from home.[40] Fictions like Joseph Conrad's *Heart of Darkness* (1898) and Somerset Maugham's Malaya stories (1926), followed later by Graham Greene's *The Heart of the Matter* (1948) and Doris Lessing's *The Grass Is Singing* (1950), attested to anxieties about the fragility of the European psyche amid climatic extremity, racial isolation, and casual violence. Dramatizing the fragility, and perhaps the futility, of British rule, these dark narratives hinted at the anticolonial edge of psychoanalytic politics. But they also exemplified the Eurocentric perspective that shaped the usual treatment of mental disorder in the colonies. Psychoanalysis in particular operated as a signifier of status, a luxury item requiring leisure as well as a rich inner world worthy of sustained exploration, wherever it traveled in the world.[41] This charmed circle often excluded colonized populations; the myth of the "happy-go-lucky" native, too simple-minded to experience depression or neurosis, was pervasive.[42] In this context, Seligman's decision to investigate the inner life of subjects rather than rulers was unconventional and even subversive.

Beginning in 1922, Seligman mobilized a network of agents to collect dreams from across the empire. Most were anthropologists, including a number of colonial officials and missionaries who studied indigenous cultures in their spare time and often acquired a reputation for eccentricity along the way. In the Sudan, there was Jack Driberg, a popularizer of the case against Lévy-Bruhl, who then served as a district commissioner and went around the desert with a spear in hand, wearing a kilt and a pair of sandals. ("He really looks a fine figure," Brenda Seligman once noted in her diary.) In West Africa, there was Northcote W. Thomas, a former habitué of the Society for Psychical Research and telepathy enthusiast who secured an appointment as the first government anthropologist in the British Empire. According to one of many officials irritated by Thomas's idiosyncrasies, he was "a recognized maniac in many ways. He wore sandals, even in this country, lived on vegetables, and was generally a rum person." Also collecting dreams in West Africa was Richard Rattray, another anthropologist employed by the imperial government but more respectable than Thomas. In Uganda, there was T. T. S. Hayley, a Driberg protégé who later served as an administrator in colonial Assam, became one of the few expatriates to retain an official post in post-independence India, and edited the *International Journal of Psycho-Analysis* after retiring to Britain. From the Naga Hills, a corner of northeastern India whose inhabitants—neither Hindu, nor Muslim, nor caste-observing— had long attracted British interest, a trio of colonial officers moonlighting as ethnographers also sent dispatches. In total, roughly twenty researchers canvassed for dreams on Seligman's behalf, including correspondents from Nigeria, Nyasaland, Malaya, China, and the Solomon Islands, as well as the Sudan, the Gold Coast, Uganda, and India.[43]

For some of these investigators, the world of dreams was already familiar terrain. Anthropologists had long studied magic and observed that dreaming provided raw material for prophecy and divination. Seligman's associates did not always agree on the significance their informants attached to dreams: Thomas concluded that "they are seldom cited as matters of importance" in Sierra Leone, while Rattray reported that the Ashanti would fine a man for adultery if he dreamed of sleeping with another man's wife. They did agree, however, that dreams were widely believed to predict the future in accordance with an unwritten symbolic dictionary. In other words, certain images or situations had the same prophetic import no matter who dreamed them.[44]

But Seligman wanted to know how those fixed social meanings could be reconciled with the dynamics of the psyche. Stung, perhaps, by his exchange with Freud, he drew up a dream-collection protocol aimed at pushing beyond the collective dictionary. He asked his agents to record a verbatim narrative of the dream and then probe the associations that arose along the way. "The dreamer should be asked of what each incident or figure makes him think," Seligman instructed. As he told one of his agents in the Naga Hills: "Try to get your associations as far back as you can, that is to say find out if something lies behind the association given." He also suggested eliciting multiple recitations of the same dream to yield new details.[45] Like more orthodox Freudians who went on to search for empirical confirmation of psychoanalysis in other imperial arenas between the wars—Hungarian anthropologist Geza Roheim in Australia and Russian-born analyst Wulf Sachs in South Africa—Seligman believed that therapeutic methods could be refashioned as research tools.

It soon became clear, however, that this was no easy task. As Roheim later pointed out, field-workers hoping to act as psychoanalysts could not expect their subjects to come calling like patients in search of a cure. The researchers were the supplicants, reduced to offering bribes of tobacco and rice and ultimately powerless to induce their informants to associate freely. Several of Seligman's agents reported difficulties in getting them to open up. "They seem to forget [dreams] later, or do not like to tell them," according to an American missionary in the Sudan. In the Naga Hills, an informant named Lengjang reluctantly agreed to share some dreams with John Henry Hutton but dwelled on the reasons for resisting: "It is not good to remember dreams and to think about them. For the one that does . . . there is no peace at all."[46] Religion contributed to this reticence in some cases: Muslims in northern Nigeria protested that taking dreams

Charles Seligman at work in Hula, Papua New Guinea, 1898. (Copyright
© 2014 Museum of Archaeology and Anthropology, University of Cambridge
Museums. Licensed under a Creative Commons Attribution—Noncommercial
2.0 UK: England & Wales License.)

seriously was a form of idolatry, making recent converts especially
"ashamed to acknowledge the superstitions which they formerly harbored." Another complication was posed by the fact that administrators,
missionaries, and other authority figures did not make the most natural
confidants for imperial subjects. Seligman's man in Nigeria reported that
if he did not phrase his questions carefully, the people there told him
whatever they thought he wanted to hear "without regard to truth."[47]

Even more daunting than the practical difficulties were the theoretical
complications. Qualms about the universality of psychoanalysis began to
percolate among Seligman's agents. "So far as the people concerned here
go," M. C. Blair wrote from Nigeria, "Freud is the worst of guides."
Echoing Malinowski, Blair held that sexual desire did not exert the same
overwhelming power in shaping the dreams of non-Western people
because their waking lives were virtually free of repression. But evidence

on this point varied from place to place and observer to observer. In the Naga Hills, Seligman's contact agreed that the liberality of sexual behavior relegated eros to a less prominent position in the unconscious. In the Solomon Islands, by contrast, anthropologist Beatrice Blackwood rejected the trope of carnal bliss in paradise, observing that "conjugal disharmony occurred about as frequently as among ourselves."[48]

Faced with conflicting evidence about the reach and the limits of psychoanalysis, Seligman distributed another questionnaire to his contacts around the world. In his eagerness to learn whether the phases of erotic development outlined by Freud held true for other cultures, he requested details on anal, oral, and genital behavior that dismayed even the most ardent field-workers. As Roheim remarked, "It is dreary beyond words and unappetizing to apply anything like statistical methods to the excretory habits of the young, but I will do my best next visit [to Australia]!" The results vindicated Freud's critics. From Australia to New Guinea to Tanganyika to South Africa, Seligman's correspondents could report almost no instances of typically anal behavior (playing with dirt and hoarding objects), few instances of oral behavior (thumb-sucking), and no evidence of a latency period before adolescence. These findings entrenched Seligman's conviction that the significance of libido as a mental force varied widely across cultures. If the developmental sequence Freud imagined as a biological imperative—from polymorphous perversity to repression, sublimation, and finally maturity—was not universal after all, then Freud's other claims about the unconscious mind suddenly looked doubtful.[49]

In fact, Seligman kept a flexible and pragmatic attitude toward Freudian concepts rather than discarding them altogether. When a woman in the Solomon Islands dreamed of refusing to have sex with her husband, enduring a beating, and then seeing her brother, Seligman suspected that she was struggling to repress an incestuous desire. Interpreting a dream from Nagaland, he mused that an ethereal figure with a long white beard might represent a death wish. Another dream from the Naga Hills, related by a Sema man named Lhuzekhu, inspired an especially elaborate interpretation in the Freudian mode. The narrative ended this way:

We all sat round the fire, there was a sudden gale of wind, I held the post fearing my house would be blown over. The gale stopped. I looked at all my posts especially at the carved one in front of the door and said if it

had not been for this post my house would have fallen and I should have
had a lot of trouble.

When asked for his own interpretation of the scene, Lhuzekhu replied:
"The gale of wind in my house means I shall have very bad crops this year.
No post fell so no important member of my clan will die. The excellence
and strength of my carved post means that I shall have fine sons and
daughters." This auto-interpretation neatly exemplified the prophetic tradition. But Seligman went further, eliciting a subtext of individual, emotional meaning from the final line: "His manhood (phallus) upholds his
home & ensures him fine sons and daughters." Where previous anthropologists had been content to catalogue conventional or proverbial interpretations, Seligman still wanted to pin down the affective forces that
lurked behind them.[50]

Seligman's desire to transcend Freud emerged more clearly in his insistence on reading these narratives in more ways than one. Moving between
case histories and cultural contexts, he noted the recurrence of one theme
in particular: the tensions generated by imperial authority. Lhuzekhu's
dream, for instance, began with a loose elephant stomping from the
bazaar to the courthouse where he worked as an interpreter with two
other Sema. "I felt it was yours," he told his boss, the district officer James
Philip Mills. "I was frightened it might hurt me and threw a stone at it."
Lhuzekhu interpreted this in characteristically prophetic terms, saying, "I
think I may quarrel with one of your staff." But Seligman was not convinced. Lhuzekhu's dream, he thought, suggested a classic case of transference: his encounter with the elephant revealed hostility to the paternal
figure of Mills and his flight into a nearby house represented an "escape
to the mother." The gale of wind threatening to topple his home dramatized the conflict between the comforts of tradition and an alien, imperial
power. Finally, his boast about "fine sons and daughters" offered a kind
of resolution—a desire to imitate Mills's authority by establishing himself
at the head of a family. As Seligman put it, "he lives his father hostility &
becomes the father himself."[51]

In this interpretation, whatever disagreements might actually have
existed between Lhuzekhu and Mills receded behind the inner drama of
Sturm und Drang. The essential truth of the dream was, as Seligman saw
it, the divided loyalties of the subaltern—just as the dreams of converts to

Christianity, collected by his missionary friends, foregrounded ambivalence and resistance in the journey to revelation.[52] The primacy of inner conflict also accorded with the model of dream interpretation proposed by Rivers at Maghull. But Seligman's agents also collected dreams in which imperial authority was less a metonym for social change than the focus of very real relationships of aggression and control. This came across most clearly in the dreams of Philipo Oruro, a chief or *Jago* appointed by the British in Uganda. He was an educated man and a Christian, but these advantages afforded little relief from the pressures of office. As Seligman's man on the spot observed, his dreams showed "how heavily the affairs of administration and fear of the D.C. [district commissioner] hang upon the mind of a native chief."[53] In fact, it was not only the D.C. who tormented Oruro in his sleep, but other representatives of British power, including schoolteachers and missionaries. The Swahili honorific *Bwana,* meaning "Sir" or "Lord," recurred frequently in his dream narratives, and it almost always preceded a reproach, an act of violence, or both.

On the night of February 15, 1936, Philipo Oruro had the following dream:

> Bwana D.C. beat the behind of *Won pacho* Asanasio Pule [a village chief] hard. Then he gave him to *Won amagoro* Etum [a more powerful chief] to beat. When the stick broke in pieces Etum went to fetch another and continued to beat him for a long time. Then I said, "Well, when are you going to leave off?" Bwana said, "Not yet sufficient."[54]

The attention to chiefly titles was itself a function of British rule, which imposed an alien Ganda hierarchy on Lango territory and brought in outsiders to occupy many of the new offices.[55] The district commissioner's use of force—unexplained, unavoidable, and humiliating—embodied this political violence in the most literal way. Four nights later, Oruro dreamed that another Bwana threatened to give him ten strokes with a cane for breaking through the fence behind the school. Three weeks after that, he dreamed that yet another Bwana, apparently a missionary, scolded him sharply: "not in the slightest do you help me in my work." Oruro humbled himself to the point of prostration—"Bwana, I am still fresh, I have only just started, come teach me"—but to no avail. After showering praise on another chief, the man called Bwana Cox drove Oruro from the house and threatened to beat him into submission.[56]

Seligman was fascinated by the "very large part played by white offi-cials" in these dreams of domination.[57] But another observation fascinated him more: images dreamed in different parts of the world were linked to the same emotional meanings. Motifs familiar from the treatment of shell-shocked soldiers in Britain—falling dreams and dreams of dead relatives—turned up repeatedly in the accounts collected by Seligman's agents overseas.[58] Other parallels emerged with European folk traditions cata-logued in the dream dictionary which Seligman kept close at hand.[59] In Ashanti, Malaya, Nagaland, Nigeria, Palestine, Sierra Leone, and the Sudan, to dream of losing a tooth had the same prophetic meaning as it did in England, Scotland, Ireland, Germany, and Hungary: the imminent death of a close friend or family member. This was "the most universal of type dreams," Seligman thought, but it was not the only one. The equally vivid image of raw meat was interpreted as a portent of looming mortality, or at least bad luck, in an impressive range of cultures, while dreams of flying were interpreted as good omens from Java to the Tyrol.[60] Impressed by the consistency of the links between manifest imagery and latent meaning in so many disparate places, Seligman now subscribed to something that sounded a lot like Jung's collective unconscious: a "common store on which fantasy may draw" in "the unconscious of the most diverse races."[61]

Even for some orthodox Freudians, Seligman's vindication of psycho-analysis as a universally applicable method outweighed the Jungian idiom in which it was couched. Roheim heralded his dream collection as evi-dence of "the fundamental unity of the human psyche," harkening back to German anthropologist Adolf Bastian's concept of "elemental thoughts" (*Elementargedanken*).[62] But Seligman, keen as always for empirical evi-dence, kept searching for corroboration. Although he presented versions of his argument to the British Psychological Society and the Royal Anthropological Institute in 1924, it was not until seven years later that he turned to a ready-made population of experimental subjects—the British radio audience—to bolster his case for the existence of a collective unconscious.

Doubling as a promotional stunt and a research tool, the *Radio Times* distributed in advance of Seligman's BBC broadcast on March 24, 1931, carried an appeal for readers to mail their dreams to the professor at his house outside Oxford. It came with a form asking respondents to describe their dreams of flying, climbing, and losing a tooth; their "frame of mind" or "affect" on waking; and any associations arising from the dream. Seligman received more than two hundred fifty responses, and although most of them did not deal with the particular types of dreams he requested, many did. By revealing familiar links between manifest content and emotional subtext, these provided additional support for the cross-cultural reach of the collective unconscious. Thirty-five respondents reported tooth-losing dreams, each one tinged with a feeling of dread, while more than one hundred respondents shared flying dreams, all of them pleasant. The crop of dreams harvested by the BBC also revealed an unexpected link between Britain and its colonies: many British dreamers, like their counterparts overseas, believed that dreams foretold the future. For Seligman himself, this supposed power of prediction could always be explained by Freudian and Jungian means: flying dreams figured as auspicious omens because the sensation of sexual arousal lurked beneath the surface, while dreams retrospectively interpreted as omens of misfortune in fact represented unconscious responses to real-world signs of trouble. Even in metropolitan Britain, though, many people resisted these disenchanting arguments.

In some cases, the interpretation of dreams as prophecies seemed to arise from the folkloric traditions of the countryside. In Norfolk, an old woman confirmed that raw meat in dreams presaged the death of a friend or relative; a correspondent from Ireland added that dreams of meat were also sometimes seen as harbingers of a birth there, possibly because new mothers customarily received roast beef as a gift.[63] But other responses were shaped less by the quaint anachronisms of rural life than by the occultist and spiritualist movements that had been thriving among educated urbanites since the late nineteenth century.[64] These correspondents either did not know about psychoanalysis or rejected its claim to the interpretation of dreams; several mistakenly assumed that Seligman was an ally of their not-quite-respectable quest for an anti-materialist understanding of mind. One London man told Seligman that he had "been developing a little psychic faculty" with the help of "an entranced medium" and added: "I am so glad a scientist is brave enough to take up this study, for I firmly believe there is something not of ourselves in it all." Not everyone was so amiable—especially once they realized that Seligman saw himself as a hard-headed enemy of mysticism. One man accused him of neglecting "the Science of Life called by the nick-name of 'Spiritualism,'" while a woman who initially identified Seligman as an "astrologer" angrily wondered why anyone would bother sending their dreams if not to receive a prophecy in return.[65]

Seligman tried to persuade these correspondents of a rational explanation for the seemingly prophetic power of their dreams. In the case of foreboding omens, he stressed, it was anxiety that operated at an unconscious level and organized dreams around real-life problems not yet perceived by the waking mind—a classically Jungian take. But his interlocutors refused to accept this, insisting that they had no possible access to the information that their dreams revealed. An old man dreamed that his son in India was ill with fever just before a letter arrived to confirm it. A man recovering from an operation in England dreamed that his fiancée, visiting family in Kenya, had fallen in love with another man, on the eve of a telegram announcing that she had indeed married someone else. A young girl dreamed that her older brother died in a corral filled with black water years before he actually died of black water fever in South Africa. These respondents were describing yet another empire of dreams: not a laboratory of the collective unconscious, nor a chronicle of trauma in the colonized mind, but an almost mystical network of kinship that allowed emotional bonds to triumph over distance. If Seligman ever had any sympathy for Lévy-Bruhl's dichotomy of colonizing reason and colonized irrationality, the results of the BBC survey dispelled it. "From the sociological standpoint," he commented, "the experiment is interesting as showing the very large proportion of people [in Britain] who consider dreams as prophetic." In the symbolism of dreams and the interpretation of dreams alike, the colonizer and the colonized were not so different after all.[66]

Following this experiment, Seligman issued his most expansive pronouncements yet on the universality of the unconscious. Speaking to the Royal Anthropological Institute in 1932, he recounted the dreams of a woman in the Solomon Islands, rich with the pathos of an unhappy marriage and incestuous longing, to illustrate that "psychological conflicts" in other races "are largely the same as our own." It was not only the "worldwide presence of certain symbols" in dreams, but the dynamics of repression and wish fulfillment, which supported the conclusion he announced on the BBC a year earlier: that "the unconscious of all these races is qualitatively much the same." Seligman went on to speculate that the higher functions of the conscious mind were no different. Because the mind is an "organic whole," he reasoned, "we may well be prepared to accept . . . that the savage mind and the mind of Western civilized man are essentially alike."[67]

Even couched in conditional terms, this was a striking conclusion. But Seligman's heterodoxy had clear limits. Unlike Rivers, he never saw himself as a critic of empire; he worked closely with the officials who ran it and promoted government funding for anthropology as a boost to the "well-being and security of our Colonial possessions." Arguing that "practical problems of administrations" were "inextricably interwoven" with indigenous "ways of thought," he believed that expert knowledge could train officials to avoid making faulty assumptions about the people they ruled. He also never doubted that some groups were *meant* to rule, sometimes invoking the logic of scientific racism without confronting the questions raised by his own research. Even as he led an intellectual campaign to discredit Nazi race theory in the 1930s, for instance, Seligman speculated that variations in brain structure might explain "why certain races have lagged behind in civilization" and endorsed the accuracy of intelligence tests that showed racial differences in mental ability. At other times, Seligman identified subsistence practices—hunting, pastoralism, agriculture—rather than biological traits as the key variable in the advancement of human societies. But even then, he assumed, the dynamic force of European expansion would leave some cultures "doomed to extinction" in an inevitable process of evolutionary change.[68]

Seligman, then, clung to some hierarchies while questioning others— an ambivalence that reflected tensions between the universal and the particular, the biological and the environmental, the physical and the psychological. Most of all, perhaps, it reflected the instability of meaning in the archive he created. Cataloguing dozens of dreams from around the world, and even decoding them in accordance with psychoanalytic theory, turned out to be possible. But the diversity and depth of individual dream lives proved difficult to contain in any one mode of explanation. Had his experiment documented the existence of a collective unconscious, the psychological tensions generated by imperial rule, or the cross-cultural portability of Western models of the mind? As Seligman himself recognized at different times, all three answers were possible.

This ambiguity may have blunted the impact of psychoanalysis in politics. But it also guaranteed its wide appeal. Amid the tumult of the interwar empire, anticolonial critics described aggression and dependency as the hallmarks of a pathological encounter between ruler and ruled. Defenders of the *status quo,* by contrast, claimed that probing the emotional origins of behavior could beat back challenges to British authority. By discrediting the mythology of the untroubled and uncomplicated "native mind," Seligman helped to ensure that debates about empire would increasingly turn on theories of the unconscious.

¶ LOOKING BACK across the decades, Francis Hislop could still vividly recall the day when, as the assistant district commissioner in a remote corner of Kenya, he came upon a safari car stopped on the side of the road. It was 1925. Three white men clambered out of the car, asked for directions to Mount Elgon, and introduced themselves. One of them was "a burly man, middle-aged, with a reddish-brown country face," but it was only after Hislop invited them into his bungalow for tea that he realized the identity of his guest. "Did you say Dr. Jung . . . of Zurich?" As they sat and talked, Hislop learned that the Swiss psychologist and his companions had embarked on a self-described "psychological expedition"; they planned on collecting dreams in the shadow of Elgon "as a change from studying them among the highly civilised people of Europe." Hislop felt obliged to inform them that the Karamojong and Sabei people did not speak Swahili, which Jung had studied in advance of the trip, and that they would probably need a special permit to cross the border into Uganda. The visitors seemed dismayed but not discouraged as they thanked Hislop for his hospitality and drove off toward Eldoret.[69]

As Hislop surmised, the expedition yielded a meager crop of information. After arriving in the Elgon foothills, Jung followed the same routine every morning: sitting under a clump of acacias and gathering about a dozen Africans (mostly porters hired by his traveling companions) for an hour-long palaver. Flanked by *askaris* and interpreters dispatched by the British government, he must have looked like a colonial official himself, which perhaps explains why only one African was ever willing to share a dream with him. For all its methodological shortcomings, however, the trip deepened Jung's own commitment to the idea of a collective unconscious—a consequence that had less to do with African dreams than with his own response to the landscape and people. Taking the train from Mombasa to Nairobi, Jung glimpsed a silhouetted figure leaning on a spear and experienced "a most intense *sentiment du déjà vu.*" It was, he recounted later, "as if I were this moment returning to the land of my youth, and as if I knew that dark-skinned man who had been waiting for me for five thousand years."[70]

It proved an influential image. The so-called "Dark Continent" offered a path to self-actualization for the likes of Graham Greene, who underwent analysis with a Jungian before traveling to Liberia in 1935, and Laurens van der Post, the Afrikaner writer and a friend of Jung who portrayed the Kalahari bushmen as the "lost soul" of modern man.[71] Jung's vision of a "dark child" lurking beneath the surface of Western rationality was the essence of the primitivist aesthetic: a romantic but evolutionary sensibility that cast Africa as an alluringly backward antidote to the alienated materialism of Europe. It also lent itself to the racial paranoia of "going native," a phrase used by the Kenyan settler press in reports on the expedition.[72] But Jung's primitivism did not stop him from protesting what he saw as the destructive impact of British rule and drawing attention to the traces it left in the unconscious mind. By transferring authority from tribal rulers to district commissioners, Jung argued, the British in East Africa inflicted a kind of cultural death that caused the visionary dreams of traditional healers to wither away. As an Elgonyi medicine man had told him, only the British still experienced vivid dreams because only the British exercised real power.[73]

Jung always claimed that the British Empire exhibition at Wembley Stadium in London in 1924–1925, with its colorful displays of hunters, herdsmen, and warriors, inspired his dream expedition to Africa.[74] As early as 1919, however, Seligman sent Jung a copy of Malinowski's article on dreams in the Trobriands and mentioned that he hoped to collect dreams in Sudan during his upcoming fieldwork. Jung responded with enthusiasm, describing himself "most anxious to know of the negro dreams," regretting that he had never encountered the dreams of "normal primitives," and asking for a full report from the field. Just before going to Wembley in 1924, Jung lavishly praised Seligman for his early work on dreams in Africa and India. "Such attempts as yours," he wrote, "bridging over the gulf between [anthropology and psychology], are quite particularly needed in our days."[75]

Whatever Jung owed to Seligman's example, he assumed a far more critical attitude toward empire. While Jung's lament for the passing of a mystical Elgonyi tradition drew on a well-worn ideology of empire—the "salvage colonialism" which aspired to preserve exotic practices otherwise doomed by the march of progress—his indictment of European rule in the early 1930s went beyond the disruption of indigenous traditions to condemn exploitation, violence, and hypocrisy.[76] He faulted the imperial powers for "setting the whole East in turmoil with our science and technology, and exacting tribute from it." Missionary work was sheer "megalomania," a veneer of benevolence for the prostitution and opium trafficking that proliferated in its wake. The only way to dispel the "moral incense" that rationalized this rapacity was for the colonizer to attempt to see himself through the eyes of the colonized. "What feelings do we arouse in the black man?" Jung asked. "And what is the opinion of all those whom we deprive of their lands and exterminate with rum and venereal disease?"[77]

In the years between the wars, explorations of the unconscious mind increasingly gave rise to protest, critique, and dissent. For many leftist intellectuals in Europe, psychoanalysis exposed the atavistic impulses that lurked behind bourgeois propriety and fueled the savagery of war, misogyny, and class conflict.[78] Distressed by the fate of socialist revolutions after the war, some thinkers speculated that unresolved complexes arising from sexual denial or patriarchal authority might help to explain the continuing deference of the working classes to conservative rulers. The politics of psychoanalysis were not intrinsically or necessarily radical; by stressing universal biological drives, Freudian theory in particular might also imply that economic inequality, family dysfunction, political oppression, and other social ills had no relevance to the treatment of neurosis. In practice, however, psychoanalysis fueled criticism of established institutions.[79] This held true in Britain, too, and perhaps especially there, since the eclecticism that defined British theories of the unconscious made it easier to mobilize them politically.[80] Jung and German psychologist Alfred Adler—who broke with the psychoanalytic movement by emphasizing the urge to dominate other people, rather than libido, as the motive force of behavior—loomed larger for anticolonial activists in Britain than Freud did.

Like the "oppositional fraction of the ruling class" known as Bloomsbury, to which many of them were linked, the first generation of British psychoanalysts tended to mistrust both the irrationality of mass democracy and the ineptitude of a traditional elite in government.[81] From this perspective, the empire represented another aristocratic preserve in need of expert management; critics now cast doubt on its legitimacy, in part, by questioning the unconscious forces motivating overseas rule. Bloomsbury luminary Lytton Strachey set the tone in *Eminent Victorians* (1918) by portraying the imperial heroes of the past as "strange characters, moved by mysterious impulses"—transforming the martyred General Gordon, for instance, into a violent alcoholic with a penchant for mysticism. Psychoanalyst Edward Glover later pursued this theme in a lecture on the BBC; the distinguished appearance of a Cabinet official, he warned, might mask the "attitude of the Jingoistic schoolboy," entranced by "red splotches" on the map and possessed by "phantasies of war and annexation." Glover puckishly suggested that, unless political leaders were routinely subjected to examination for symptoms of neurosis, Britain had no better claim to acting rationally in world affairs than an aboriginal tribe. The "Principal Secretary of State for Foreign Affairs" might as well be "an Australian black-fellow," "armed with spear and bull-roarer," roaming the corridors of Whitehall. Glover's friend and fellow analyst David Eder likewise questioned the rationality of the empire's rulers. Joseph Chamberlain's famous campaign for an imperial trading bloc in 1902–1906 had less to do with economics or geopolitics, Eder claimed, than with the desire of an insecure political dynast to carve out an identity of his own. Once Chamberlain "found a father—the Empire—which gave him a political fatherhood," he advocated surrounding the colonies with a tariff wall because he felt that "the father's children must be looked after and helped." This suspicion of unconscious motives reflected the sensibility of the modernist-socialist journal *New Age,* an occasional venue for Eder's writings which drew heavily on Adler's theory of a will to power in attacking the excesses of industrial capitalism.[82]

The radical impulse to put imperialists on the couch was not confined to metropolitan Britain. A retired administrator of the Indian Civil Service in Burma, Bernard Houghton, handed the nationalist movement a propaganda coup in the 1920s by publishing psychoanalytic critiques of British rule in collaboration with Krishna Menon's India League. Although Houghton hailed Freud as a discoverer on par with Christopher Columbus and Charles Darwin, his diagnosis of imperialism as "displaced aggression," "paranoid hysteria," and a "Narcissus complex" owed at least as much to Adler as to Freud. While the infantile "desire to dominate, to appear important," might be repressed within one's own social group, he argued, it ran riot against other groups. The military victories of European aggression produced a "feeling of arrogance . . . egoism and selfishness" as well as a garrison mentality which anxiously projected the "wish to rob" onto rival states. Like others on the interwar left, Houghton located capitalist self-interest in the unconscious mind, explaining the hypocrisy of the civilizing mission as a triumph of repression and endorsing Woodrow Wilson's call for national self-determination. "Will any man," he asked, "openly admit that he acts from selfish motives"?[83] His former colleagues at the India Office considered Houghton's pamphleteering so inflammatory that they weighed prosecuting him for sedition and searched in vain for a way to stop his pension.[84]

Even if they had succeeded in silencing Houghton, another disillusioned veteran of Anglo-India was soon making similar claims. When John Hoyland, a Quaker missionary, lay ill in Hoshangabad on New Year's Day, 1918, after five years in the country, he had a humbling epiphany: "I was profoundly ignorant of Indian character and psychology." One way that Hoyland attempted to improve his knowledge was to test more than one thousand Indian schoolchildren with a personality questionnaire designed by an American psychologist.[85] But he also turned a more critical eye on the imperialist mind. Like Jung and Houghton, Hoyland urged unsparing introspection; he warned against the "hypocrisy" of "pretend[ing] that our lives and actions are ruled by true altruism." Concluding from his research that Western children were more materialistic and less ethical than their Indian counterparts, he lionized Gandhi as a Christ-like figure opposed to the rampant individualism that governed a "world-order of selfish profit-hunting, of hatred, of oppression, and of warfare."[86]

Following Jung and many others, Hoyland was far from unique in contrasting Western materialism with Eastern enlightenment.[87] But he went further than most in tracing the defects of the colonizer back to defects in British culture. Rejecting Freud's emphasis on sexuality, which he faulted for reinforcing an unhealthy Western preoccupation with male authority, Hoyland turned instead to Adler, who replaced the Oedipus complex with the inferiority complex. Childhood feelings of weakness and dependence gave rise to the spirit of "acquisitiveness and possessiveness" lurking behind many social ills: not only "the profit-motive in industry" but also the "grab for Africa" and "the attitude of the average Britisher towards the Indian and the negro." This chauvinism had its origin in "snobbish middle-class" customs that segregated domestic life from the wider world, producing spoiled but insecure princelings whose striving for maternal affection laid the foundation for a lifetime of selfish competition. As long as the transference of emotional involvement from family to society broke down in this way, he warned, "national inferiority feelings" would continue to fuel war and conquest. Returning to Britain from India at the height of the Depression, Hoyland pursued a brand of Quaker activism aimed at stamping out "anti-social" sentiment and replacing it with "community-fellowship," organizing work camps for the unemployed and even advocating a global federation to supersede national states.[88]

If psychoanalytic critiques of empire often focused on the pathological mind of the colonizer, however, the inner life of the colonized received even more attention. In the 1920s, British anthropologists working in the Pacific pioneered the idea that administrative and missionary meddling with indigenous customs could inflict life-threatening psychic wounds. According to Rivers, Malinowski, and others, practices like polygamy and head-hunting might offend Western sensibilities but nonetheless represented vital sources of emotional satisfaction. Malinowski concluded that British officials in the Trobriands had heightened the islanders' susceptibility to disease by disturbing their "cherished diversions, ways of enjoying life, and social pleasures." Summoning the authority of "new developments in psychotherapy," he attributed "the rapid dying out of the natives" to this "exceedingly parochial and narrow-minded application of our own sense of morality." Anthropologist George Henry Lane-Fox Pitt-Rivers could not have been more different from Malinowski or Rivers in political terms—his fascist sympathies landed him in a British internment camp during the Second World War—but he too registered unease about the impact of overseas rule on unconscious minds. Invoking Jung's theory of personality types, he claimed that introverted people like the Aua Islanders placed a special value on cultural integrity more than others and so grew hopelessly despondent at the mere prospect of conquest "by an irresistible alien power." Australian researcher Stephen Roberts agreed that preventing the expression of "instincts" through strict regulations made Pacific populations fatally "apathetic." By causing depression, in other words, empires killed.[89]

These accounts owed little to the Freudian concept of trauma, which depended on the reactivation of repressed memories by much later events and derived its force from internal forces of fantasy and conflict rather than the events themselves.[90] As other human scientists pursued fieldwork in the psychoanalytic grain, however, free associations, dream narratives, and other data of the unconscious mind revealed the damage done by imperial power and the twisted emotional entanglements of rulers and subjects. One of Seligman's closest collaborators in the dream project, Geza Roheim, discovered this during his celebrated expedition to collect dreams from Australian aborigines in 1928–1930. When Doketa, chief of the Loboda, dreamed that he was rescued from a torrential rainstorm by a missionary, Roheim traced the image back to an episode of filial trauma: the jailing of his father and uncle for practicing sorcery. Because Doketa then "had to find new fathers," as Roheim put it, he converted to Christianity. But the transference of emotional loyalties to missionary and government remained dangerously insecure. In some of the associations arising from Doketa's dream, Roheim detected "a deeper trend of rebellion . . . a tendency to rely on his own strength and not that of the white man and his god." Quarrelsome behavior with friends and relatives risked erupting against Mr. Walker, the missionary glimpsed in another dream "trying to exterminate" indigenous customs, or Mr. Smith, the shopkeeper who was "very unpopular among the natives."[91]

A precarious balance between submission and rebellion likewise struck anthropologist Meyer Fortes in the Northern Territories of the Gold Coast in the 1930s. Before training under Seligman and Malinowski at the LSE, Fortes had studied psychology, and he experimented with psychoanalysis along with intelligence tests and personality tests in the field. He listened patiently as a chief named Tezin, "lying on his back chewing kola" and "as if speaking aloud his day dreams," complained of the anxiety he felt in a position which depended on competing with other chiefs to win favors from the British. Tezin exemplified what Fortes saw as a "conflict state of mind" in which "recrimination of [the] white man" mingled with the need for deference to the new ruling class. Like Roheim in Australia, Fortes interpreted this kind of ambivalence in West Africa as an uneasy truce rather than a stable equilibrium. Noting the invective that filled nationalist newspapers in Accra, Fortes suggested that British officials had been cast in the role of "common enemy," serving a unifying function like "the Jew in Hitler's Germany." Yet even the proudest traditionalists among the chiefs, fearing the consequences of resistance, would do almost anything "for the sake of the white man's approval." How to explain the discrepancy? Fortes saw aggression and deference in the Gold Coast as two sides of the same coin. What might be understood simply as obedience or loyalty was in fact hostility constrained by "elements of fear": the memory of military action "less than a generation ago" (still a "constant topic of conversation" in the Northern Territories) and the district commissioner's authority to levy punishments in the present. Acquiescence in British rule, Fortes suggested, had less to do with "some mysterious awe of the white man" than with the brute facts of power.[92]

These glimpses of discontented and reluctantly submissive subjects—a strikingly deromanticized vision of empire—may help to explain why many imperial officials remained wary of psychoanalysis between the wars. Of course, there were other, less political, reasons for this lack of enthusiasm among British authorities: above all, perhaps, the convention-defying frankness that also fueled discomfort with Freud at home. When Raj administrators asked a psychoanalyst to examine the erratic heir to the throne of a princely state in 1935, for instance, his talk of onanism and bisexuality soon caused them to regret it.[93] So why did other officials end up taking the claims of psychoanalysis more seriously? Many of them already perceived challenges to imperial authority as irrational outbursts rather than serious political grievances. Some seized on diagnostic expertise as a rhetorical tactic, attempting to delegitimize indigenous movements by portraying them as symptoms of madness.[94] But all of these appropriations had to navigate an unstable boundary between useful knowledge and radical protest. Combating the unconscious origins of rebellion forced researchers to confront the traumas, anxieties, and resentments of empire. As a result, some of the most damning observations of British rule—the lasting effects of violence and the unforeseen consequences of cultural insensitivity—ironically came from psychoanalytic thinkers who wanted to strengthen the imperial state against its enemies.

Sylvia Leith-Ross arguably pioneered the psychoanalysis of anticolonial insurgency by linking revolt to frustrated desires and traumatic memories. The widow of a British administrator in Nigeria, she later worked as an education officer in the colony and, for five years, as secretary of the Tavistock Clinic in London. It was during her time at the Tavistock that Leith-Ross knew Seligman, attending his lectures at the LSE and welcoming his encouragement to pursue a career in anthropology.[95] In 1934, she returned to Nigeria on a Leverhulme grant to investigate the roots of the Women's War that had shaken the colony five years earlier. Likening the Igbo towns she visited to the "unreal, super-sensitive, ego-centric atmosphere of neurasthenics," Leith-Ross argued that the boom and bust of the 1920s in commodities like palm oil had awakened materialistic urges and then abruptly removed the means of satisfying them, triggering a collective mental breakdown. Suspicion that the British had retaliated for the revolt by somehow provoking an economic depression was reflected in "the tense faces, the thin bodies and slightly glaring eyes" that met her questions, inviting comparisons to "the patients I knew at a certain clinic for psychological cases where I used to work." According to Leith-Ross, fear that officials might still punish them further—along with a secret satisfaction in having rocked the British back on their heels in 1929—kept Igbo women fixated on the past. Extravagant demands for water, education, jobs, and even cinemas supplied by the state were symptoms of an unsteady grip on the reality of the present—and a sign that the threat of rebellion had not yet receded. "Their voices were shrill with anxiety," she warned, "their bodies ready to dive off the deep end."[96]

In private, Leith-Ross delivered an equally dire diagnosis to William Hunt, the British lieutenant-governor of the Southern Provinces. But she now made a crucial distinction: it was not only paranoia but the long history of imperial violence that inspired so much hostility. Leith-Ross described the Women's War as just one in a series of "profound, and in different ways, terrifying experiences" that affected the "psychological life" of Nigerians. In particular, the Anglo-Aro War of 1902 had introduced a "new and surprising vision of organized force," while military reprisals following the murder of a British medical officer in 1905 still inspired "guilty and fearful" recollections. "The coming of the white man" represented a traumatic landmine, buried but not defused; distant memories of brutality remained vivid and emotionally charged, sowing distrust between Africans and the state.[97] In her emphasis on the deferred action of long-ago events, Leith-Ross echoed Freudian trauma theory more closely than other British researchers. Hunt predictably found this troubling: "It only shows how little we can judge of the effects of our actions. . . . I am very concerned at your picture." Faulting British heavy-handedness as well as African irrationality, Leith-Ross recommended a series of policies—expanding education and mission work to provide "new interest and a new outlet," keeping tax rates unchanged and opening craft workshops to instill "a greater sense of economic security"—aimed at achieving pacification without the use of force. She argued then, and for decades afterward, that officials did not know "as much of the background of their people as they should."[98]

Margaret Field, who served as government anthropologist in the Gold Coast from 1938 to 1944, likewise argued that British misrule contributed to an oubreak of neurosis in West Africa. Like Leith-Ross, Field worked at a psychiatric clinic in London, the Maudsley rather than the Tavistock, and then fell under Seligman's influence, touring mental hospitals and studying Freud with him in the early 1930s.[99] Field too blamed modernization—the price swings in the cocoa trade, the incursions of the mining industry, the pressures of competitive education—for the rise of schizophrenia, obsessive-compulsive disorder, and other pathologies in West Africa.[100] This echoed the ubiquitous rhetoric of "deculturation," which suggested that tradition-bound Africans responded to social change by going mad.[101] But Field also insisted that "the harsh persecution of socially valuable medicine-men" by British administrators exacerbated the problem. Religious cults classified as "barbaric" thanks to "official ignorance" were in fact vital safety valves for managing discontent; they "comforted the anxious" and "soothed the neurotic." What would become of those people now? Field's pseudonymous novel *The Stormy Dawn* (1946) suggested an ominous answer. The protagonist, a mentally unstable African student, ends up turning to nationalist politics, denouncing British oppression in front of left-wing crowds before finally committing suicide. Lacking diagnostic knowledge, Field implied, the imperial state risked undermining its own foundations.[102]

In comparison with Leith-Ross, Field criticized imperial policy as an outsider. Fired from her position after questioning an ordinance that undermined the already limited autonomy of the native authorities, she gave free rein to frustration with her former Gold Coast colleagues in *The Stormy Dawn*. In a characteristic jab, she described the character of the district commissioner as suffering from a "tropical neurosis which made his quinine-embittered life a burden bearable only with the help of whisky and the thought of his approaching pension."[103] But Field's equation of anticolonial nationalism with mental disorder showed that her deepest sympathies did not lie with African aspirations, either. She expressed the frustrations of the expert who craved a more enlightened state. Her sharpest ire was directed at British administrators not because she questioned the legitimacy of the system but because they challenged her influence within it.

When psychoanalytic thinkers did question the legitimacy of empire, they often did so in politically ambiguous ways. Paralleling the preoccupations of European psychoanalysis after 1919, they juxtaposed the logic of rebellion against unjust regimes with the mysterious inner compulsions that prevented most oppressed peoples from rising up. Submission to imperial authority, rather than resistance to it, represented the irrational phenomenon from this perspective. In seeking to explain how empires exacted obedience, however, these radicals turned a critical eye not only on the violent dominance of the state but also on the pathologies of indigenous culture. Dysfunctional families, they argued, produced dependent personalities and thus the foundations of political dependency. This strand in psychoanalytic radicalism mirrored the ambivalence of anticolonial sentiment between the wars: even activists who deplored the abuses of empire remained deeply paternalistic, exchanging the overt authoritarianism of the proconsul for the condescending support of the sympathizer or the benevolent guardianship of the "trustee."[104]

Wulf Sachs, a Russian-born Jewish analyst who settled in South Africa in 1922, made the most ambitious attempt to blend Freudian and Marxist thought with anticolonial politics.[105] While working in Pretoria Mental Hospital in the early 1930s, Sachs observed that the symptoms of insanity "are identical in both natives and Europeans" and speculated that "the working principles of the mind in its normal state must also be identical." Although he considered mental testing as a way to confirm his hypothesis, Sachs felt that a "mere collecting of answers to questions" would be hopelessly "superficial" in comparison with the study of "desires, conflicts, strivings." A devotee of orthodox Freudianism—he underwent analysis with Theodor Reik and corresponded with Freud himself—Sachs persuaded an African man named John Chavafambira to lie down on his couch in Johannesburg for sporadic analytic sessions over the course of two and a half years. It soon became clear that Chavafambira's complexes were not so different from those Sachs saw in white patients; he dreamed longingly of his mother and fantasized about replacing his stepfather as the head of the family, confirming the universality of the Oedipus complex. The meanings

Chavafambira attached to symbols in his dreams—for instance, the knife as a sign of sexual desire—likewise accorded with Freud.[106]

Sachs was more interested in chronicling the psychic damage inflicted by racial hierarchies than in reopening debates about the portability of psychoanalysis. Publishing the narrative of Chavafambira's analysis first under the title of *Black Hamlet* (1937) and then in revised form as *Black Anger* (1947), Sachs shifted his emphasis from the inner world to the state-sanctioned discrimination that continually intruded on it. The petty insults of white passersby, the segregation of public space, and the unending harassment of the pass laws bred a desire to "get away from white people" and be "free of their rigid-time tables" to the point that Chavafambira envied a man who committed suicide.[107] Taking the helm of a radical Johannesburg newspaper, *The Democrat,* Sachs criticized racism as a "social disease of the mind." Like others on the psychoanalytic left, he described stereotyping and scapegoating as irrational forms of aggression displaced from class conflict, and he predicted that only socialism would lead to the elimination of group hatreds. In Sachs's view, racism and anti-Semitism stemmed from the same pathological impulses. Some critics have even suggested that his Zionist sympathies caused him to over-identify with Chavafambira in a kind of counter-transference.[108]

Yet Sachs complicated his critique by finding pathology on both sides of the imperial divide. Submission to an oppressive system, he argued, was as much a symptom of neurotic disorder as the racist mentality that built it in the first place. That is why, in both versions of the book, the therapeutic process of psychoanalysis and Chavafambira's journey to political consciousness run on parallel tracks. If he had not encouraged him to "talk out his feelings with regard to the white people," Sachs suggested, Chavafambira would never have made a courageous public protest against police mistreatment of an African boy; nor would he have taken part in a tax revolt in his home village in Southern Rhodesia. It took the analyst's lessons about "the essence of the aggressive instinct, of the unavoidability and necessity of hating people whom we believed to be hostile to us," to make Chavafambira recognize the structural causes of discrimination. When Chavafambira finally exploded against Sachs's condescension by complaining about Europeans who treated Africans like children, Sachs blithely concluded that he had succeeded in curing his patient's apathy: "John was ready for revolt."[109]

How, then, did Sachs explain Chavafambira's earlier reluctance to act—the reason for comparing him to "Hamlet"? Although his answer involved the unconscious mind, Sachs crucially insisted that the pathology in question was not individual but cultural—a disorder of Africa itself. He argued that the practice of breastfeeding until age four, with mothers constantly holding their babies and feeding them on demand, fostered feelings of dependence that persisted into adulthood. Those early years of unregulated indulgence formed unrealistic expectations of abundance without effort; the "great, godlike" father, who kept his distance after birth and then abruptly usurped the child's privileged position when infancy ended, laid the foundation for an "irrational fear" of "every man, black or white, in authority." As Sachs saw it, the abrupt transition from maternal affection to maternal neglect had the effect of weakening the ego at the expense of the id and the superego, molding personalities that oscillated between selfish hedonism and slavish obedience for the rest of life. "This dramatic childhood experience had a retarding effect on John," Sachs argued, "and on every African child in his fight for independence."[110]

Although variations on this theory of traumatic weaning would remain a fixture of imperial expertise for decades, its origins lay in home-grown anxieties about child-rearing. Moving beyond the biopolitical preoccupations of the infant welfare movement at the turn of the century—a legacy of concerns about population decline and physical degeneration after the Boer War—experts between the wars stressed the psychological and behavioral dimensions of mothering. In advice manuals, clinics, and home visits, they praised regimented feeding times and strict toilet training as means of self-discipline. Responding to cries, showing too much affection, or otherwise indulging the baby's whims were castigated for instilling selfishness and aggression in future generations—an especially worrisome prospect in the aftermath of the First World War.[111] Although psychoanalysts advocated a more permissive approach than this, they too linked the mother–child relationship with the aims of social engineering, shifting attention from the fixity of innate drives to the plasticity of personality.[112] Psychoanalytic texts in this period represented the act of feeding as a crucial mechanism for conveying affection from mothers to children—an entwinement of physical and emotional sustenance. When caregivers withheld food and love, one writer warned, "the echoes come back in the terrors of war and revolution."[113] All these influences underwrote the expansive reach of infant welfare policies between the wars—not only in Britain but also, increasingly, in the empire.[114]

The tension between liberation and regulation shadowed the theory of traumatic weaning across British Africa. One of its most ardent exponents was in fact an imperial official: J. F. Ritchie, a longtime teacher and headmaster of the Barotse National School in Northern Rhodesia, who psychoanalyzed his students despite lacking formal training. His study of *The African as Suckling and as Adult* (1943) arrived at the same political diagnosis as leftist activist Wulf Sachs: Africans suffered from "psychic dependence," which meant that "individual personality, with all its latent powers, is never liberated." Because the state represented "the parent-surrogate *par excellence*," Ritchie worried that childhood experience caused Africans to "either turn away from politics altogether" or "ardently and blindly support every pronouncement of authority."[115] Writing confidentially to a fellow official, William Vernon Brelsford, who shared his interest in Freudian thought, Ritchie confessed that he was publicly downplaying the radical implications of his research "until I have retired and am (comparatively) economically free." A self-described "depth-psychologist who is also a socialist," Ritchie decried the educational system that employed him as one "designed to keep the privileged few of the ruling class still in power, with the assistance of the handful of Africans we educate highly." He also sided with those who insisted on the global validity of psychoanalytic theory: "the deeper I am able to penetrate into the African unconscious the more sameness I see in his mentality and ours."[116]

This dialogue between Freudian amateurs demonstrated once again that psychoanalysis could disrupt longstanding assumptions about difference. Brelsford voiced skepticism at the outset, claiming that "the Africans' sexual and family life is so vastly different from ours that I wonder if we are right in transposing a lot of Freudian ideas" and speculating that totem objects might complicate the interpretation of symbols in dreams. Ritchie replied that he too expected to find "innate differences" in the African unconscious but arrived "empirically" at the opposite conclusion. Even their dreams "have just the same basic elements and complexes" as those of Europeans, Ritchie wrote.[117] Perhaps because of his government job, he expressed more conventional opinions in public, declaring that African minds diverged from the "Anglo-Saxon" model with extreme emotions, illogical thinking, and sexual promiscuity. Like Sachs, however, Ritchie balanced his diagnosis of African pathology—itself rooted in "environments, experiences and activities" more than heredity—with an attack on the psychic oppression of British rule.[118] He confessed to ending several analyses prematurely because "the young men concerned showed unmistakable signs that they were on the point of plunging into subversive activities against tribal authorities." In contrast to the European analysand, who felt liberated by the discovery that his anxiety was rooted in an imaginary projection of the father figure, Ritchie argued that "the African living under our system, if he is induced to face and overcome that phantasy dread . . . only finds himself up against a real situation which is pretty well as bad as the imaginary one." This portrait of imperial authority as patriarchal tyranny came as a shock to Brelsford, who marveled that Africans—seemingly "so calm and placid"—might in fact be "subconsciously seething with political discontent."[119]

Ritchie's ambiguous position between radical criticism and imperial power played out in his work as a headmaster in Northern Rhodesia. Translating theory into practice, Ritchie treated the school both as a microcosm of the fears and resentments that afflicted Britain's African subjects and as a laboratory for techniques that might resolve them. Justifying his experiment to the education department in Lusaka, Ritchie portrayed a student body plagued by "excessive dependence on leaders" and "deeply-laid distrust of authority." The key, he argued, was to strengthen the fragile African ego—to encourage a sense of self that recognized the demands of the wider world without being dominated by them. Dismantling the house system that governed dormitories and sports teams, Ritchie ordered a constant reshuffling of groups to avoid "emotional dependence on 'the herd'" and a handful of prominent personalities. Rather than apply "hard and fast rules" in disciplinary matters, teachers now applied moral suasion instead, guiding "pupils to see their individual responsibility as members of society." Like the theory of traumatic weaning itself, this blueprint blended subversive and authoritarian elements to the point of contradiction. The cultivation of individual autonomy subtly challenged the collective structures of indirect rule; the encouragement of self-discipline strengthened imperial control by decentralizing and internalizing compulsion.[120]

In light of these tensions, it comes as no surprise that thinkers with very different ideological commitments sometimes co-opted the arguments of

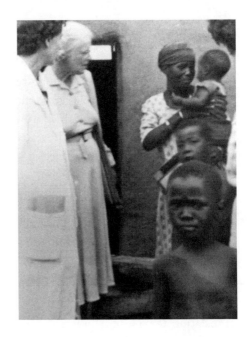

Cicely Williams in South Africa, 1954. (Photograph by Sam Wayburne. Image reproduced courtesy of Wellcome Library.)

the Freudian leftists. By suggesting that colonized populations could achieve political independence only after transforming their minds and cultures—and at a time when British activists around the world were protesting indigenous traditions in the name of child welfare—the weaning theorists found themselves aligned with full-throated defenders of the civilizing mission.[121] Jamaican-born physician Cicely Williams, an Oxford graduate posted to the Colonial Medical Service in the Gold Coast from 1929 to 1937, described the upbringing of African babies just as Sachs and Ritchie did: a wrenching passage from indulgence to deprivation provoked by the withdrawal of the mother's breast. The African infant "leads a thoroughly spoiled life," she wrote, "but this existence is rudely broken." Rather than bemoan the frailty of anticolonial resistance, however, Williams saw even the faintest stirrings of nationalism as expressions of emotional disorder. "Some of the peevish, ill-considered articles in the local press," she found, "are clearly a result of trauma at this [early] age." The "intellectual qualities" that resulted from defective mothering, including "lack of initiative" and "servile acceptance of superstitions and customs," lay at the root of African stagnation. Only continuing action by British experts—including education campaigns, the training of health workers, and the construction of maternity clinics—would "enable the African to take any high place in the economy of nations."[122]

Psychoanalysis, then, recast the politics of empire in unpredictable ways. By affirming a universal model of the unconscious, Seligman and the diverse group of thinkers who followed him raised uncomfortable questions about racial hierarchies and British rule. And yet, by making the inner world of people in other cultures accessible and legible with seemingly portable methods, psychoanalysis also gave rise to new possibilities of surveillance and control. The Rhodes-Livingstone Institute in Northern Rhodesia, which sponsored Ritchie's research, funded studies on juvenile delinquency, public opinion, and mental testing into the 1960s. So did the research arm of the Colonial Office, founded just after the Second World War, and more distant outposts of the imperial bureaucracy. Cicely Williams herself would assume a senior position in the World Health Organization at its inception in the late 1940s; from this influential perch, she continued to criticize indigenous child-rearing practices in India, Africa, and the Middle East. Long after the novelty of cross-cultural psychoanalysis faded away, the urge to remake unconscious minds endured.

Shortly before his death, Seligman grew curious about the possibility of another approach to imperial psychology. Corresponding with friends in the administrative service of Sudan in the late 1930s, he learned that at least two officials there were developing tests to measure the intelligence of the indigenous people. Seligman was fascinated. "I have no personal experiences of intelligence tests," he wrote, "& have only general ideas as to the intelligence of such black races as I have been among in the Anglo-Egyptian Sudan." Working from a list suggested by the British doyen of mental measurement, Cyril Burt, he proceeded to read everything he could find on the subject of intelligence testing across cultures.[123] Like psychoanalysis, psychometrics reflected the universalistic sensibility of mind science. With its promise of objectively quantifying inner qualities, however, the mental test appeared to be an exceptionally portable tool—even better-suited to migration across cultures, many believed, than the hermeneutic and interpersonal methods of the talking cure.

TESTS

CHAPTER THREE

Meritocracy or Master Race?

The Origins of Mental Testing in the British Empire

I N THE WANING DAYS of 1922, two Indian men sought admission to the United Theological College in Bangalore. It was a splendid facility, built with money raised by the faithful of several Protestant denominations in Britain and America, and equipped with a library, a harmonium, and a cook. The amenity both men had their eye on, however, was something else: a recently established scholarship. On paper, the competition was not a close contest. Paul Raj, the son of a minister, was a university graduate; his rival, Arumai Samuel, had been studying for only two years and had failed his last round of examinations. Yet the missionary in charge of making a decision hesitated to rule out Samuel. Too often, he observed, mission schools overlooked the most talented individuals because teachers had to rely on "guess work" or the recommendations of village elders swayed by caste or personal connections. Although David Scudder Herrick was sure that Raj deserved a place in Bangalore, he wanted to give Samuel a chance to prove his worth as well, in which case he might find the money to send both of them. So he asked Samuel to take an intelligence test: the Stanford revision of the Binet test, released by American psychologist Lewis Terman in California in 1916.[1]

Unfortunately for Samuel, the results were not promising: an intelligence quotient of seventy-seven and a "mental age" (in Binet's phrase) of roughly twelve years. "This settled his case as far as I was concerned," Herrick reflected, "and I could not recommend him." He feared that Samuel would never be able pass his exams, much less master the "abstruse and difficult subjects" required of a theology student, and so regretfully informed the other missionaries that he was "of lower caliber intellectually than is desirable for a pastor." But if this experiment in mental testing proved disappointing for Samuel, Herrick thought that Binet and Terman had emerged triumphant. "Mental tests score a point," he concluded, "in that the use of one saved the mission the useless expense that would have been incurred if he had been sent to us [at the theological college] and later proved unable to take the course." Rather incidentally, he noted, the test also spared Samuel "the disappointment that he would have suffered in such a case."[2]

When the Raj launched a nationwide experiment with mental testing in 1921, the British education commissioner praised David Herrick as a pioneering figure. Born in India to the son of an American missionary, he spent most of his life on the subcontinent. Like the British expatriates of the Raj, however, Herrick and his missionary colleagues lived migratory lives, cycling between home and colony for reasons of health, education, and status.[3] In Herrick's case, that meant studying at Williams College in Massachusetts around the turn of the century and spending most of the First World War in the United States, where his wife sought treatment for a nervous breakdown. He accompanied her to the Battle Creek Sanitarium in Michigan, consulted with a prominent psychotherapist in Connecticut, and spent a year teaching at the Hartford Seminary, alongside a psychologist who occasionally administered mental tests to missionary candidates.[4] Somewhere along the way, Herrick learned of the famous U.S. Army experiments with intelligence testing, which attracted enormous publicity at the time, and which he heralded a few years later as a breakthrough in the testing of large groups.[5]

When mental testing first came to the British Empire, proselytizers like David Herrick played a leading role. Contrary to their image as starchy traditionalists, missionaries brought medical, ecological, and other scientific knowledge to the work of saving souls, often working hand-in-glove with secular forces of change.[6] Thanks to the outsize importance of missionaries in Indian education, the experiments undertaken by Herrick and his colleagues profoundly shaped the psychometric initiative sponsored by the Raj in the 1920s. That initiative, in turn, established the template for mental testing in colonies around the world. Reaffirming a Victorian ideal of merit while promising new heights of objectivity and accuracy, mental measurement encouraged the belief that identifying talented individuals in colonized populations was both possible and necessary. When a different rationale for mental testing—the comparison of races rather than individuals—began to gain traction in the settler colonies of Australia and Africa, a coalition of missionaries, their official contacts, and their intellectual allies succeeded in pushing it to the margins of British policy.[7]

The arrival of the Stanford-Binet test in India marked an early moment in the entanglement of American and British expertise overseas—an encounter with uncertain consequences. Would the nativist ideology of "Anglo-Saxonism" that shaped mental testing in the United States reinforce the racial hierarchies of empire?[8] Or would the elaborate social hierarchies that dominated British psychometrics—the belief that every occupation, from the professional elite to the laboring underclass, required a certain level of intelligence—legitimize new kinds of distinctions?[9] In fact, British authorities between the wars showed far more interest in using intelligence tests to select applicants for schools and jobs—and trumpeting the rhetoric of opportunity, mobility, and merit—than in branding whole populations as inferior. Given the pervasive segregation of education and employment, British expatriates and overseas subjects did not often compete with each other in practice—a glaring exception to the meritocratic ideal. But even a nominal commitment to this ideal opened the way to criticisms of imperial rule: its fealty to racial and ethnic categories, its failure to mitigate inequality, its resistance to social change. The process of adapting Western tests itself demanded a relativistic awareness of the ways that language, upbringing, and education varied across cultures and within them.

Testing ability with written tests represented a longstanding imperial tradition. The fact that old-fashioned examinations of scholarly achievement persisted alongside novel measures of mental capacity showed that the idea of merit was malleable, blurring the distinction between character or temperament on the one hand and intelligence on the other. The British always had a flexible sense of what, exactly, their tests were measuring.[10] But this ambiguity did little to dampen enthusiasm for psychometrics as an instrument of efficiency and fairness. Long before British critic Michael Young coined the term *meritocracy* to describe a nightmare of self-serving elitism, the idea of a society where innate talent eclipsed inherited privilege captured the imaginations of the empire's rulers.[11]

¶ AT THE END of a quiet street in the West End of Hartford, Connecticut, past a procession of oak trees and brightly colored Victorian houses, you can still see a cluster of sturdy Gothic buildings. Home to a law school and some government offices today, their construction in the 1920s marked a triumph of church rather than state: a grand new setting for the pride of the city's Protestant establishment, the Hartford Seminary. In the closing decades of the nineteenth century, an influx of scholars trained in Germany transformed what was once a sleepy institution for the education of Congregationalist ministers into a "Theological university" where the pursuit of scholarly research took equal precedence with the defense of doctrine. The man who presided over the seminary's expansion in the first half of the twentieth century, William Douglas Mackenzie, was born in South Africa and educated in Edinburgh. His father was a pioneering missionary and critic of settler abuses in Natal; his son remembered him as one of those imperial heroes "who by sympathy, knowledge, and, above all, matchless nerve, could enter into the native mind, get a grip on it, and so drive it where they would." At the World Missionary Conference in Edinburgh in 1910, the younger Mackenzie stressed the necessity of training missionaries in secular subjects that might help to impart psychological insight: indigenous languages, world religions, and the human sciences. It proved an influential model, and by midcentury, more missionaries were being trained at Hartford than anywhere else in the United States.[12]

At least three of the missionaries who brought mental testing to India passed through Hartford Seminary on their way. Before David Herrick taught there, British Quaker John Hoyland graduated from the School of Missions, and Earl Leslie King, an American Baptist, followed shortly afterward.[13] The education they received there was suffused with a moralistic internationalism committed to the improvement and uplift of colonized peoples. It is fitting that a close friend of Mackenzie, Woodrow Wilson, who was serving as president of Princeton University, delivered a graduation address on the seventy-fifth anniversary of the seminary in 1909. A missionary seated next to Wilson on the dais commanded the graduates to remember "that we are not trying to save a few individuals here and there, but we are at work to remold and change empires." Mackenzie himself, later an enthusiastic supporter of the League of Nations, spoke of a "sense of world citizenship working through all barriers of race and of nationality." His deputy, Edward Capen, celebrated the spread of Protestantism in India and Africa for eroding institutions—"a guild, a caste, a clan, or a tribe"—which "stunted the growth of individuality."

Declaring that "the power of the old superstitions has been broken, the influence of the medicine-man and priestly class has been shattered," Capen argued that conversion and education in mission schools represented "first steps . . . towards preparing the people to desire and to be fitted for a larger share in the government."[14]

Like Wilson, the American missionaries considered self-determination for non-white populations a distant prospect even as they celebrated progress toward it. Herrick in 1918 proclaimed his "thorough loyalty to the British Government, which I believe is the best that India has ever had, or that any subject people have ever had."[15] Rather than overturn imperial rule, the missionaries sought new possibilities for reform within it, and few fields of expertise appeared to offer more powerful instruments than psychology. Even by the standards of early twentieth-century New England, which saw the emergence of an unlikely alliance between spiritual healing and Freudian psychotherapy, the seminary's leaders were unusually fervent believers in mind science.[16] They embraced the Child Study movement—then at the height of its influence—which held that empirical observation of how young minds developed would allow teachers to reach them more effectively. "There are aspects of our behavior which can be submitted to measurements," Mackenzie declared, "and we are learning from them to see how a character is gradually built up from the days of a baby's life." The curriculum in Hartford accordingly featured instruction in the "Psychical Development of the Child," including "Heredity and Variation" and "the dominating interests of each period," as well as more general courses in psychology.[17]

Although American psychologist G. Stanley Hall is credited as the movement's founding figure, Child Study rapidly evolved into a transatlantic enterprise, with Protestant ministers taking a prominent role in Britain as well as the United States. In both countries, anxieties about the quality of populations came to focus on variations in the innate abilities of children. Although school authorities in Britain introduced pencil-and-paper intelligence tests much more slowly than their counterparts in the United States, the drive to evaluate and classify young people according to observable criteria of "mental age" was widespread in both countries between the wars.[18] American missionaries could therefore draw on a transatlantic idiom of child development to justify the novelty of mental testing in the colonies. As a Hartford-trained missionary in Narsinghpur, Earl Leslie King, explained, it was necessary to classify Indian schoolchildren as "superior," "normal," or "retarded" because abilities varied so widely that "uniform treatment" in the classroom risked inflicting "harm."[19]

Among the half-dozen American tests King used in the mid-1920s, the best known was the Draw-a-Man test published by American psychologist Florence Goodenough in 1926, which assessed sketches of the human figure against age-specific standards of accuracy and detail. In Bangalore, David Herrick supplemented the Stanford-Binet test with the Goddard form board, which asked subjects to fit variously shaped blocks into matching slots as quickly as possible. "Not so easy as it looks," he commented, as the test "requires fair ability on the part of the subject in holding his attention to the task before him, in noticing similarities and differences, and in putting into execution rapidly the judgments formed."[20] John Hoyland, the British Quaker and Adlerian critic of empire who also trained at Hartford Seminary, constructed his own test in an effort to establish developmental benchmarks for Indian students in the Central Provinces. He surveyed one thousand schoolboys in 1916–1917 with questions like these:

What is a gentleman?
Describe the prettiest thing you have ever seen and say why you
    thought it pretty.
Of what are you most afraid?
What would you do if you saw a ghost? What is a ghost like?
Describe a punishment which you have received that you thought was
    just. Why was it just?

According to Hoyland, the results showed that self-interested and materialistic motives peaked around age eleven, while altruistic, ethical, and religious feelings came to the fore at age sixteen. He recommended redesigning the mission school curriculum to maximize conversions in each age group.[21]

One reason that so many different psychometric techniques flourished in British India was a persistent ambiguity about what, exactly, was being tested. How did intellectual ability, aesthetic sensibility, ethical commitment, and temperament relate to one another? In line with the emphasis on character building in Christian education, missionaries argued that mental and moral capacity were closely linked. After all, King warned his

Indian students, intelligence required self-discipline no less than virtue did: "if your mind is dead and stale NOW, you cannot expect it to suddenly become fresh and active, when you begin your life-work." He assessed students with the "trustworthiness" test devised by American Paul Voelker, which contrived situations in which students were tempted to cheat or lie. Herrick too believed that "moral qualities are closely linked with intelligence," citing Henry Goddard's now-infamous study that documented the prevalence of prostitution and criminality in one supposedly "feeble-minded" family.[22]

Although American eugenicists seized on this kind of evidence to argue that some groups were "fitter" than others, the missionaries who pioneered mental testing in India pointedly downplayed the significance of racial differences. Seeking to explain the divergent scores of low-caste Indians, high-caste Indians, and American children on the Goddard form board, Herrick stressed environmental causes—the "great difference in social and educational opportunities" between castes and "the thoroughness with which the kindergarten has been developed in America"— rather than heredity. Noting that other tests produced higher scores in India than in the United States, he affirmed that the "human mind the world over is essentially the same as regards the elements of intelligence." Hoyland likewise argued that if Indian schoolchildren seemed to lag behind their British and American counterparts in "critical faculty," the difference was "no doubt due to defective educational methods, and may in time be remedied." An American missionary in Raipur attributed low Indian test scores to a litany of environmental ills: malnourishment, chronic diseases like malaria and hookworm, illiteracy, limited exposure to printed material, and caste discrimination. "Poverty, disease, and under-privilege," he concluded, "are found to a greater degree in India than in any country in which standardization of intelligence tests has taken place."[23] Besides the durable doctrine of psychic unity, this critique reflected the growing willingness of missionaries between the wars to castigate the failures of British rule.[24]

The urgency of the need to identify candidates for education and conversion reinforced the minimization of racial differences. Unlike the comparison of Indians with Americans or Britons, comparing Indians with each other served a useful function in the everyday work of missions: selecting students for promotion through a stratified system. Astronomic growth in demand for secondary education in the first quarter of the twentieth century meant that only a fraction of those who sought entry to boarding schools could be admitted; those who failed to make the cut were left to attend lackluster village primary schools. "Upon the estimate formed of a child's capacities" between the ages of eight and twelve, one American missionary reflected, "depends his future, whether he is to remain a simple village worker or go on to higher study and become, perhaps, a future leader of his people." Confronting such momentous decisions about the fate of Indian children, missionaries turned to psychometrics for impersonal and apparently objective assessments of merit.[25]

Advocates of mental testing criticized the usual admission procedures in mission schools as arbitrary and irrational. The managers of the boarding hostels attached to the schools, rather than the teachers, often had the power to accept or reject applicants on the basis of character testimonials and even personal appearance. The result, as one missionary put it, was that "children were excluded who could profit by education, and those were admitted who were inherently stupid." Faced with five applicants for every place and little control over the intake, American Reformed missionaries who ran the Arcot boarding school west of Madras began to require mental testing as a condition of admission in 1922. The mix of tests varied over time; the Goddard form board, maze tests, picture completion tests, and adapted versions of the U.S. Army Alpha and Beta tests were all pressed into service in the next few years. Like other psychometric enthusiasts, the Arcot missionaries justified the novelty of their approach in part by stressing the fallibility of visual and intuitive knowledge. "Most people," one missionary argued, "have an unwarranted confidence in their ability to estimate a child's intelligence by some vague process of 'telling from their faces,' intuition, etc." Reliably assessing mental qualities, in their view, required instruments and expertise that lay observers lacked.[26]

The Indian children who were meant to benefit from this change did not always welcome it. Following the example of the wartime Army experiments, the missionaries' attempt to impose an atmosphere of military-style discipline in the testing room provoked considerable anxiety.[27] In one early session at Arcot, "two or three children were too badly frightened to go on with the tests," despite attempts to set them at ease with a round of games and songs. To make matters worse, concerned parents refused to leave their children's side, hovering anxiously and not always remaining silent. The missionaries' willingness to let them stay despite the disruption suggests that they saw the legitimacy of the tests as a fragile thing. "To surround the tests with an air of secrecy," one missionary worried, "may mean loss of confidence and the stirring up of needless antagonism." He rationalized that the unfamiliarity of the situation may have unsettled nerves but also made for a more accurate gauge of innate ability than tests that drew on past experience.[28]

The missionary mental testers did court controversy in one way: the rhetoric of selecting talented individuals, no matter what their social position, opened another front in the long-running missionary crusade against caste.[29] Confronting protests in the indigenous press that mission schools failed to respect caste distinctions, Christian proselytizers railed against the monopoly of knowledge by a Hindu "priestly class." Herrick pondered "how to eradicate the caste spirit"; Hoyland celebrated the Gandhian temple entry campaigns of the 1920s; the Arcot missionaries contrasted the "perpetual degradation" of the lower castes with the "opportunities afforded in Mission Schools" and the "ideals of equality inculcated" there. Mental testing figured prominently in this leveling project because it promised to disentangle innate capacities from the advantages of upbringing and education. "If we are to measure an ability," another missionary argued, "the only fair criterion must be one which gives an equal opportunity to the poor and the rich, the high caste and the non-caste, the literate and the illiterate." This rationale was not egalitarian but meritocratic; it sought to replace a hierarchy of birth with a hierarchy of talent rather than ensure a sound education for everyone. But drawing an opposition between mental testing and caste tradition was provocative nonetheless.[30]

The boldness of this vision raises a question. Why did habitually riskaverse Raj officials decide to collaborate with the American missionaries on a far-reaching program of psychometric research? In 1921, education commissioner J. A. Richey announced an initiative to replicate the U.S. Army experiments—an event that had "drawn the attention of the outside world" and "created a profound impression in England"—across British India. Researchers at state teachers' colleges in Madras, Bombay, Lahore, and Dacca were directed to adapt the Stanford-Binet test for use with Indian schoolchildren. Richey described the pioneering work of Herrick and King as a model while hiring another American missionary, Herbert Rice, as a consultant. Rice had studied with onetime Army psychologist Carl Campbell Brigham at Princeton before taking a teaching post at a mission school in Lahore.[31]

Although American missionaries supplied the operational knowledge for this initiative, British ambitions and British anxieties supplied the motive. Even before psychologist Charles Spearman proposed the existence of a "general factor" in intelligence in 1904, metropolitan reformers had argued that the essay-style exams which determined entry into elite schools and key professions were not always selecting the worthiest candidates. Evelyn Baring, the Earl of Cromer and former proconsul of Egypt, emerged as one of the leading advocates of a public inquiry into exam practices. Citing the glorious history of military officers promoted by merit rather than patronage, he declared that the future of British power was at stake: "What was it that enabled Lord Chatham to revive British spirit when it had sunk to a very low ebb, to march to victory on the banks of the St. Lawrence and the Ganges, and to found the British Empire? I say that it was the adoption of the principle of selection." One of Baring's closest allies in this campaign was Philip Hartog, a chemist and former University of London administrator who went on to serve as vice chancellor of Dacca University in East Bengal. Hartog adopted Baring's ambition for the creation of a new mandarin elite—"not the aristocracy of birth, but of intellect and of character"—as his own.[32]

It was Hartog who convinced Richey and other officials, at a meeting of the Central Advisory Board of Education in Simla in 1921, to study the use of mental tests in India.[33] An outsider to British society—his mother belonged to an Anglo-Jewish family in Portsmouth, while his father was a Jewish Frenchman—Hartog wedded the instincts of a reformer to a ferocious appetite for work. In his office at the University of London, he could be seen toiling "away screened off in a corner, correctly attired in morning coat but unaware of the specks which collected on it, calling out for his afternoon tea and then forgetting to drink it." His restlessness exemplified the "quest for national efficiency" prompted by anxieties about the Boer War defeat and the ascendance of Germany.[34] Like other professionals who wanted to replace the aristocratic habit of muddling through with rule by experts, Hartog warned that continued British dominance depended on a shrewder use of human as well as material resources. His inaugural foray into testing issues, a lecture to the Royal Society of Arts in 1911, was fittingly titled "Examinations and Their Relation to Culture and Efficiency."[35]

Following Baring's lead, Hartog initially stressed the importance of selecting a *British* elite by more sophisticated means. As he observed, "teachers, lawyers, doctors, dentists, engineers, architects, and the civil, naval, and military servants of the Crown, on whom the organisation and defence of the Empire rest, must pass examination tests." After visiting India in 1917, however, Hartog began to apply the logic of meritocracy to colonized populations as well. He observed that the mathematical genius Ramanujan once lost a scholarship in Madras because of a low exam mark in English composition—a dramatic instance of old-fashioned methods failing to recognize talent. As the chair of a commission on Indian education in the late 1920s, Hartog rooted an enduring concept in the imperial lexicon: the "wastage" of scarce resources caused by students failing out of programs to which they should never have been admitted in the first place. He quoted with approval the observation that "many of the pupils promoted to the higher standards have not the mental capacity for such studies and should properly have been weeded out of the secondary school at an early stage." An outspoken opponent of caste segregation in schools, Hartog was referring to intellectual ability rather than social status when he spoke of training "the best men."[36]

Hartog's psychometric campaign involved two ironies. First, the Victorian edifice of professional, matriculation, and graduation examinations he now deemed inefficient had in fact been designed by an earlier generation of reformers to serve meritocratic ends.[37] Second, this meritocratic tradition actually originated in India. Competitive examinations for the civil service were established there more than a decade before aspiring Whitehall functionaries had to sit for exams in Britain; former Raj officials Charles Trevelyan and Thomas Macaulay subsequently led the charge for reform at home. Although old-timers in the Indian Civil Service grumbled that the new breed of "competition wallahs" lacked finesse with everything from horses to cutlery, the principle of promotion through written tests was soon established as a routine practice.[38]

This was true for imperial subjects as well as British expatriates. By the end of the nineteenth century, Trinidad, South Africa, New Zealand, Malaya, Jamaica, Ceylon, and the Gold Coast were all using the Cambridge Local Examinations—still used today as a gateway for higher education and government employment in much of the world—as a school leaving exam. In many colonies, as in Britain, the names of those who passed and those who failed were treated as public knowledge—announced at assemblies, printed in newspapers, and commonly used to value the prestige of the schools that trained them. In India, the heroic status of high scorers on the Indian Civil Service exam—like Rabindranath Tagore's brother Satyendranath—provided a focal point for nationalist pride. Recurring controversies about exam rules, meanwhile, stirred outrage about the limited opportunities afforded to indigenous candidates. All these reactions revealed a high degree of what might be called test consciousness: a broad popular awareness that tests mattered because they determined entry into the narrow confines of an indigenous elite.[39]

From the vantage point of British officials, therefore, imagining psychometrics as a kind of autonomous technology had a great virtue: it depoliticized an increasingly contentious process for selecting students and workers. Quantifying intelligence with machine-like precision and a minimum of human intervention might allow administrators to escape the blame for unpopular decisions about selection procedures. And yet Hartog, like other psychometric enthusiasts, always offered more idealistic justifications for mental testing than bureaucratic self-interest. In selecting talented Indians for the ruling or "directing" classes, he recalled later, "we did not mean 'directing castes'; we meant those persons, of whatever origin, who by intelligence, character, and education were fitted to be leaders of their community."[40] This emphasis on the moral virtues of meritocracy echoed the American missionaries who helped to carry out the plan. But it also reflected the ethos of British mental testers—including, most famously, psychologist Cyril Burt—who believed in elevating lower-class schoolchildren with intellectual gifts above their social origins. Reconstituting the indigenous elite with every generation would serve the ends of efficiency and justice simultaneously.[41]

The first step in adapting the new tests to India was the translation of questions into indigenous languages. At Forman Christian College in Lahore, Herbert Rice produced Urdu versions of the Army Alpha and Stanford-Binet tests; in Dacca, an Englishman and two Indians translated the Stanford-Binet test into Bengali; in Madras, an instructor at the Saidapet Teachers' College translated Stanford-Binet into Tamil and Telugu.[42] The quest to create a fair assessment for children of every caste, ethnicity, religion, and class involved impressive attention to detail. The Urdu version of Stanford-Binet omitted *chair, fork, table, balloon,* and *battleship* from the vocabulary questions because it was thought that children living in towns would be much likelier to recognize them than their rural counterparts; the guidelines later published by the government of India suggested using *tiger, sepoy, mango,* and *tonga* instead. A series of questions on abstract concepts had to be omitted altogether because the performance of Muslims (and Hindus living in predominantly Muslim areas) varied dramatically, depending on whether the origin of the words was Arabic or Sanskrit. In Madras, where the Stanford-Binet test prompted four- and five-year olds to give their last name, the adapted version asked instead for the father's name. "Among Indians of the south," the instructions explained, "there is no family name as we understand it in the West," but if the child's "intelligence is normal, his interest in his father will ordinarily cause [that name] to be remembered." The same tester noted that the Sanskrit word *Bhakti,* meaning devotion to God, was familiar to Brahmins and Christians but alien to Muslims.[43]

Given the potential pitfalls of language, it is unsurprising that the use of images appealed so widely to the Raj mental testers. Yet pictorial questions, too, could be culture-bound—a limitation that psychometric enthusiasts often overlooked. The original Stanford-Binet test displayed images of everyday life; younger children were asked to name as many objects as possible, while older children had to describe the scene as a whole or tell a story about it. For Indian schoolchildren, though, these tableaux were hardly familiar. In Madras, an early version of the test included the "Post Office," set in an English village of thatched roofs and horse-drawn carts, and the "Dutch Home," complete with clogs, bonnets, and windmill. It also retained the aesthetic comparison question, which asked test-takers to look at pairs of European female faces and identify the more attractive. Echoing Terman, one researcher argued that "the development of aesthetic sense parallels general mental growth."[44] Even when the pictures were superficially adapted to show temples, markets, and Indian figures clad in saris and dhotis, their plainly representational style must have been alien to many children. The most widely circulated Western images in early twentieth-century India were perhaps the caricatures of *Punch* and its imitators, while the pictures in vernacular children's books tended to emphasize the playful, the fantastic, and the bizarre.[45]

Whatever its methodological shortcomings, the Stanford-Binet test did serve as an effective vehicle for advancing the missionary agenda. The "comprehension" questions, for instance, assumed that moral and mental development progressed in tandem. "What is the thing for you to do when

A Stanford Binet question in India, 1931. Schoolchildren were asked to identify the more attractive face as a measure of intelligence. (National Archives of India, New Delhi.)

you have broken something which belongs to someone else?" ("Satisfactory responses are those suggesting restitution or apology or both"; "mere confession" was scored as a failure.) The results, moreover, furnished at least some evidence of the potential for equality between castes. When Herbert Rice made a study of the depressed classes in the Punjab, he found that the untouchable Chuhras scored markedly lower than any other group. Yet Chuhras who converted to Christianity and attended mission schools performed about as well as Brahmins, Sikhs, and Muslims. While Rice conceded that these converts might not be representative of the caste as a whole, he contended that the results were enough to cast doubt on claims of a "necessarily inferior mentality." If even some boys of outcaste "stock and parentage" could thrive with the benefit of a "first-class education," he argued, then the missionary ideal of mobility might be possible.[46]

This conclusion is notable because it diverged so dramatically from the insistence of British and American psychologists that heredity, not environment, played the dominant role in shaping mental capacity. Over the course of his long career, Burt unwaveringly portrayed genetic inheritance as psychological destiny. Terman went even further by portraying it as social destiny; he refused to control for the effect of class status on test scores because he believed that success in life itself represented evidence of superior "native qualities of intellect and character."[47] When psychometrics

FIG. 4.—A STREET SCENE.

A Stanford-Binet question adapted for India. To receive a passing score, the youngest test-takers had to name at least three objects in pictures like this one, while their older peers had to integrate the elements of the scene into a brief story. (A. S. Woodburne, *Psychological Tests of Mental Abilities*, Madras: Printed by the Superintendant, Government Press, 1924.)

came to India, by contrast, hereditarian and environmental explanations coexisted in ways that undermined biological determinism. A government teacher in Madras, for instance, linked "the maximum capacity of the mind" to "the inheritance of an abundant supply of nerve-endings." But she also insisted that this innate capacity could be realized only through the "opportunity to learn from study and experience" in childhood. Another tester likewise stressed the interaction of "congenital" and "environmental" factors. Perhaps distaste for the caste system heightened their skepticism about the inheritance of abilities as well as their sensitivity to social causes of inequality.[48]

The Raj mental testers did absorb some attitudes from psychometric movements in Britain and the United States—above all, their distrust of inexpert conclusions about mental ability. "The trouble with the observational method," the teacher in Madras argued, "is its lack of a universal standard of judgment. . . . We are easily misled by appearances, the fluent talker is likely to be over-rated, the person of stumbling or monosyllabic speech likely to be under-rated." The missionary in Raipur bemoaned widespread ignorance of the concept of mental age, lamenting that some teachers feted fourteen-year-olds as star pupils for excelling at primary school assignments. When the Central Advisory Board of Education launched the testing project in 1921, officials described its objective as a kind of consciousness-raising about Child Study principles: "to stimulate teachers to take an interest in the individual characteristics and aptitudes of their pupils." Hartog and his allies hoped that demonstrating the effectiveness of Stanford-Binet—published by the state in a booklet of standardized tests in 1924 and again in 1930—would stimulate interest in measuring minds across the colony.[49]

In fact, mental testing diffused unevenly through government schools between the wars. Although teacher training colleges now imparted psychometric techniques and some local authorities—notably the Municipal Schools Committee in Bombay—appointed mental testers to classify students, traditional examinations remained a fixture of admissions procedures.[50] Even then, decisions often came down to factors other than intellect, such as athletic prowess, family connections, political horse-trading, and demographic balance.[51] For many Indian intellectuals, however, the experiments carried out in 1921–1923 inaugurated a sustained enthusiasm for psychometrics. From Calcutta to Lahore, at least half a dozen researchers attempted their own standardizations of the Stanford-Binet or U.S. Army tests between the wars. "The output," one observer remarked in 1938, "has been voluminous."[52] This movement was not confined to academic psychologists: an Indian social worker at a Delhi reform school asked an old missionary teacher for a copy of an intelligence test in 1928 because he wanted to approach his case work "in a systematic & scientific way." As one American missionary noted wistfully, Indian professionals were coming to play a leading role in a field once dominated by expatriates like himself.[53]

Although this pioneer generation of Indian psychologists would later draw criticism for slavishly imitating Western models, the reality was more complicated.[54] While echoing missionary criticisms of the caste system and other markers of cultural "backwardness," they also embraced an emerging tenet of the nationalist movement: that science could help to build a modern, independent state.[55] A schoolteacher in the princely state of Satara, H. A. Yeole, exemplified this subtle shift when developing an intelligence test of his own in the mid-1920s. Like American missionaries and British officials, Yeole invoked the dual logic of efficiency and fairness: measuring minds guided the allocation of resources that might otherwise be "wasted" and helped to identify talent regardless of caste. In condemning the "poverty" and "neglect" that degraded innate abilities, however, he sounded a sharper note of protest. Of "the so-called inferior races," Yeole asked, "are they not merely unfortunate in their lack of opportunity to learn?" Implicit in his account, too, was criticism of the favoritism and nepotism that allocated scarce spots to undeserving allies of the British. If "children of superior ability" were "properly and sumptuously aided," he argued, they would raise the name of the nation in the civilized world. . . . These God-gifted children are the hope of a rising nation."[56]

In British India, an education system dominated by missionaries and a tradition of competitive exams conspired to produce a psychometric movement in which meritocracy and mobility eclipsed theories of racial inferiority. But how well would this model travel across the imperial world? When a very different model emerged in the settler societies of Australia and Africa, it drew deep-pocketed sponsorship that forced officials and experts in Britain to take notice. As the Colonial Office took its first tentative steps to organize research in the science of mind, the debate provoked by settler psychologists moved to center stage.

¶ WHEN STANLEY PORTEUS traveled through central Australia on a train from Adelaide in 1929, a decade-long drought had left the desert landscape looking even more forbidding than usual. The edges of dusty basins were littered with dead cattle; dry riverbeds filled with stones and sand made it difficult for Porteus and his four companions to continue the journey from Alice Springs by car.[57] A professor of psychology at the University of Hawaii and an Australian by birth, Porteus was traveling between a series of remote mission stations, cattle towns, and aboriginal settlements for a research expedition focused on that most endangered of species: the Australian aborigine. Like most white Australians at the time, Porteus believed that the indigenous population was doomed to extinction in a matter of decades. The devastation of subsistence patterns in the drought had, in fact, brought many to the brink of starvation. This only heightened the urgency of Porteus's mission: using mental tests to quantify the intelligence of the aborigines. "Fifty years from now," he warned darkly, "it will be utterly impossible to establish the facts of Australian aboriginal psychology."[58]

Three decades earlier and a thousand miles away, Rivers, Seligman, and their colleagues had likewise brought a laboratory into the field. Like them, Porteus deployed the most sophisticated instruments available in a rugged antipodean locale; like them, he was consciously testing the limits of an ostensibly universal science; like them, he felt compelled to act before his subjects, or at least their cultural distinctiveness, disappeared. Yet one key difference remained: Porteus lived and worked at an immense distance from the academic centers of Cambridge and London, a source of tensions that would shape his career. Named for the explorer Henry Stanley, Porteus was born outside Melbourne in 1883 to a Methodist preacher who had emigrated from Northern Ireland. His hometown, Box Hill, was a modest frontier settlement thrown up during the Victorian gold rush where people conventionally referred to the British Isles as "home." From a one-room schoolhouse, Porteus won a scholarship to high school and graduated from the University of Melbourne before securing a job in the Victoria school system in 1913.[59] Like some other practitioners of what used to be called "colonial science," Porteus was acutely sensitive to traces of condescension in his encounters with researchers from British universities. But he would also prove adept at turning networks of empire—and the wider Anglophone world—to his advantage, winning allies from America to Africa when other paths to influence remained closed.[60]

Like Binet, Goddard, and others, Porteus first turned to intelligence testing as a means of identifying young "mental defectives" for special schooling or even institutionalization. But he faulted Binet's test for relying heavily on verbal knowledge and thus measuring education rather than ability. Noting that many of the "defective" or "feebleminded" pupils at the Bell Street School in Melbourne could hammer a nail or sew a line of stitches but not follow a pattern while doing so, Porteus concluded that "the most conspicuous lack in the mentally inferior person" was the "inability to hold [a] goal clearly in view." How might this capacity for "planfulness" be measured? A solution arrived in the form of an eight-year-old student named Claude, who scored poorly on the Binet test but managed to navigate the labyrinthine streets around the school with ease.

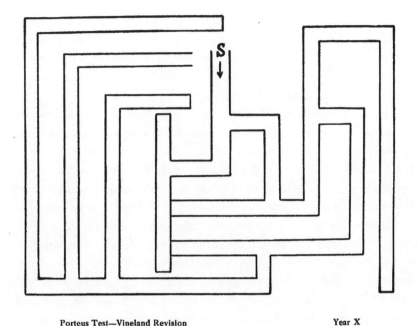

Porteus Test—Vineland Revision   **Year X**

The Porteus Maze Test. (S. D. Porteus, *Porteus Tests: The Vineland Revision*, Publications of the Training School at Vineland New Jersey Department of Research, no. 16, September 1919, p. 38.)

This display of practical intelligence captured Porteus's imagination: "A flash of insight hit me. . . . A printed maze of streets which could be graded in difficulty by multiplying the blind alleys and introducing false openings." This was the genesis of the Porteus maze test, which asked test subjects to trace paths through a series of printed mazes without lifting pencil from paper. The level of difficulty varied with age; points were deducted if pencil marks strayed onto the boundary lines or merely wobbled.[61]

The apparent portability of the maze test underwrote its striking success as a global export. Unlike other nonverbal performance tests, it required no apparatus beyond a pencil and paper; unlike Stanford-Binet, it required no verbal translation beyond a few simple words of instruction, which Porteus claimed could be put across "using pidgin English or dumb show." Embodying the promise of universality, the test circulated widely following its publication in 1914. The U.S. Army used it occasionally during the First World War; Cyril Burt featured it in the testing handbooks he compiled for London schoolteachers in the early 1920s; other researchers used it to evaluate garment workers in New York City, imprisoned convicts in Belgium, deaf-mute children in Holland, and schoolchildren in China.[62] The empire proved fertile ground for the test as well. By the early 1930s, researchers in India, South Africa, and Kenya were all testing its validity with indigenous populations.[63]

In some ways, Porteus fit neatly into an emerging imperial consensus about the uses of mental testing. Like the missionary psychologists in India, Porteus drew an imprecise line between intellectual ability and moral qualities such as self-discipline. Like the missionaries, too, Porteus rejected psychological judgments based on unmediated observation rather than impersonal instruments. Warning that "physical appearance may provide an unreliable index of mentality," he contrasted the awkward contortions of an intelligent but disabled person with the "profound mental vacancy" concealed by a pleasantly placid face.[64] But Porteus departed from the missionary mental testers in one crucial respect. He always believed that race—innate, hereditary, and fixed—shaped intelligence more profoundly than environment. As early as 1915, when he compared the test results of juvenile delinquents in Melbourne with those of aboriginal students at a mission station in South Australia, Porteus implicitly assumed that the psychology of other racial groups should be treated as pathological. When the aborigines complicated matters by outscoring the delinquents at an early age, Porteus stressed that the scores converged after the onset of puberty, suggesting the possibility of "arrested development" in the aboriginal group. This theory was a mainstay of scientific racism made famous by the South African writer Dudley Kidd, whose books Porteus read.[65]

In the years that followed, Porteus embraced a eugenicist view of racial struggle ever more enthusiastically. His belief in the inevitability of aboriginal extinction was now balanced by fears of "the white man's undoing" in an industrial economy: "the more time and effort he spends in turning out motor cars the less attention he may give to turning out children." Porteus branded psychologists who denied racial differences as "race levelers," complaining that their distaste for common prejudice led them to neglect the weight of empirical evidence. "The man in the street would no doubt wonder that there could be any question with regard to negro inferiority," he remarked, "and the scientist must not feel averse to siding with the popular view if the facts points that way."[66] These attitudes provided a ready foundation for collaboration with elements of the psychometric movement in America. In 1915, Porteus struck up a correspondence with Lewis Terman of Stanford University; a few years later, he was hired to direct the research department at the Vineland Training School in New Jersey, where Henry Goddard had recently achieved celebrity status for his warnings about the perils of mental deficiency.[67] Shortly after that, Porteus moved to the University of Hawaii, where he directed the Psychological Clinic, which had recently been established by the territorial legislature to diagnose the "feebleminded." Introducing the Binet test and the maze test to Honolulu's public schools, he measured the average mental ability of the Chinese, Japanese, Filipino, and native Hawaiian populations at various points below the Anglo-Saxon level.[68]

These studies, which Porteus described as "racial psychology," laid the foundation for a lucrative relationship with the Rockefeller Foundation of New York. In 1925, the philanthropic giant awarded him $215,000 (nearly $3 million today) for an ambitious ten-year project to measure brain size, "prudence, foresight, planning capacity," and other mental attributes in the various ethnic groups of the Hawaiian Islands.[69] Foundation officials between the wars—including one, Beardsley Ruml, who had participated in the intelligence testing of American G.I.s—believed that a scientific understanding of "human capacities and motives" held the key to social problems ranging from immigration to crime to education. Their interest in Porteus deepened over the course of the 1920s as thinkers across the Anglophone world argued that Australia's aborigines embodied the most primitive stage of evolutionary development still extant in the world.[70] Porteus agreed. He proposed expanding his research to the aboriginal population in his home country to establish "a kind of measuring or zero point" against which other groups could be compared. "The deficiencies of performance of this primitive race," he predicted, "might be so marked as to set at rest all doubt regarding the realities of racial inequality." In 1928, an Australian research fund endowed by Rockefeller sponsored a homecoming expedition so that Porteus could apply his methods to the aborigines on a much larger scale than ever before.[71]

This project ballooned into a massive undertaking. At different stages of the journey across the outback in 1929–1930, Porteus was accompanied by a doctor and a social worker from Hawaii; two cameramen equipped with film equipment; and a Melbourne nature writer named

Robert Croll. They traveled by train, truck, and ship to the farthest reaches of the continent—Perth in the west, Broome in the tropical northwest, Alice Springs in the center—with an impressive array of instruments. They had a steel stadiometer to measure height; at least four different dynanometers to measure muscular strength; a spirometer to gauge lung capacity; a xylophone to test auditory memory; and intelligence tests including, of course, the Porteus maze. In addition to hauling this inventory across rough country, Porteus had to hire local assistants who could recruit aboriginal subjects and speak their language. He also had to secure "quite a big item in the provision line (flour, tea, & sugar)" to feed those subjects as long as he wanted to keep them in one place. Setting up makeshift laboratories in the back rooms of mission stations, Porteus collected data from more than two hundred fifty aborigines, mostly adult men and children of both sexes, over the course of eight months in the field.[72]

Porteus's commitment to racial science imposed exacting standards for data collection. The record cards he brought into the field included entries for hair quality ("straight, waves, curly, frizzy"), the prominence of brow-ridges ("marked, medium, slight"), the axis of nostrils ("antero-posterior, oblique, tranverse"), and the thickness of lips. Concerned to ensure the comparability of results across races, moreover, Porteus set strict guidelines for the adaptation of Western tests. First, the task had to be self-evident enough that it could be administered with no verbal instructions beyond a few pidgin words. Porteus's ideal was the measurement of ability without any reference to language at all: he took it as a great validation when an aborigine named Garden Jimmy who spoke fluent English with "quite a superior air" received low scores. Second, the tests had to be relatively brief: recognizing that aborigines might be unconvinced of the value of such an unfamiliar activity, Porteus doubted his ability to hold their attention for long. Finally, he scrupulously excluded any images that might strike his subjects as unfamiliar, going so far as to create a test that involved matching photographs of footprints on muddy earth. The desire to rank races ironically led Porteus to modify his techniques with an eye toward functionalism, relativism, and cultural sensitivity.[73]

Of course, human scientists today would have no difficulty picking apart the flaws in Porteus's methodology. Without a deep or ethnographic knowledge of aboriginal culture, he had no way of knowing whether his subjects could understand the elements of intelligence testing that often seem strange to non-Western peoples: the redundancy of asking questions to which the asker already knows the answer; the apparent aimlessness of seeking information not immediately relevant or useful; the insistence that problems be solved individually rather than socially.[74] Indeed, Porteus himself acknowledged that this last condition posed a special difficulty for aboriginal test-takers. "Not only is every problem in tribal life debated and settled by the council of elders," he wrote, "but it is always discussed until a unanimous decision is reached." As a result, the test subject was often "extremely puzzled by the fact that I would render him no assistance. This was the cause of considerable delay as, again and again, the subject would pause for approval or assistance in the task." Some aborigines, Porteus added, seemed "very slow to get the idea."[75]

Despite these qualms, Porteus felt confident enough to draw some sweeping conclusions. "Australians as a race," he declared, "are unadaptable to our kind of civilization, although excellently adjusted, both socially and psychologically, to their own natural environment." Unlike the mental testers in India, Porteus made no effort to restandardize the scores for a new population; he simply reported the results for aboriginal subjects in terms of Western norms. On the basis of the maze test, he concluded that adult male aborigines had an average mental age of 10.47 years and an IQ of 75; tests of memory and speed yielded even lower scores. Although the mental testers in India also made unwarranted assumptions about the portability of their tests—which relied on language and representational imagery to a much greater degree—Porteus compounded the error by moving from the comparison of individuals within a single population to the comparison of populations with each other. The abstract, geometric simplicity of the maze, shorn of language and naturalistic imagery, may have encouraged the illusion of universality.[76]

Considering the relatively small samples Porteus tested, it is little wonder that even sympathetic critics voiced skepticism about some of his comparative judgments. As Australian anthropologist A. P. Elkin pointed out, white ranchers who employed aborigines as cattle hands usually assessed ability in a less dogmatic way: "sometimes good, sometimes not, according to the individual concerned, his training, and the way in which he is worked." Porteus himself understood that individual capacities varied widely within every population. As in the Torres Strait, verifying that test-takers understood their task and put forth their best effort made it necessary to observe them closely. Watching Tapinah, a Luritja native in central Australia, work through the maze test, Porteus noted his perspicacity with approval: "Excellent response, studies test in advance, good planning capacity." Another Luritja named Sambo likewise demonstrated a "very careful, prudent response; considered all possibilities before committing himself to any course." When the time came to formulate conclusions, however, Porteus showed little interest in the possibility of identifying talented individuals for education or work. The abiding separateness of aboriginal culture—its incompatibility with settler culture even when relegated to a subordinate position—remained an unshakeable assumption of his research.[77]

This conviction reflected a very different demographic reality than mental testers faced in India. In light of the aboriginal population's apparently inexorable decline, the dominance and even the self-sufficiency of Australia's white population seemed assured. Some observers, including Elkin, faulted the state for not doing more to integrate aborigines into settler society; arguing that racial differences could be overcome through education and conversion to Christianity, they saw the civilizing mission as an effort "worth making." Porteus disagreed. Racial groups at the bottom of the evolutionary ladder, he thought, risked extinction whenever they came into contact with a "greatly superior civilization." As a consequence, it was "folly for the Government to apply to the blacks the ordinary system of education evolved for our civilization."[78] Like his traveling companion Robert Croll, Porteus blamed depopulation on well-intentioned "protectionist" policies that removed aborigines from their supposedly natural environment while failing to acknowledge the effects of expropriation and violence. Tellingly preoccupied with racial purity, the two men also expressed the same distaste for Australia's "half-caste" problem, suggesting that the unhappy products of mixed-raced liaisons embodied the irreconcilability of the two groups.[79]

In denying the aborigines' capacity for assimilation, Porteus joined a debate taking places in settler colonies across the British Empire. From southern Africa to the antipodes, eugenicists between the wars claimed that indigenous races could never benefit from Western education because of their supposedly innate incapacity—their limited "educability" in contemporary parlance.[80] This rhetoric drew in part on the familiar refrain that modernization or "deculturation" led inevitably to social disintegration and mental breakdown. The fear that educated subjects would find themselves better equipped to challenge white dominance was usually left unsaid; the racialists preferred to rely on empirical data instead. Like Porteus, mental testers in South Africa pointed to the racial gap in scores as definitive proof of inequalities in intelligence.[81] Like Porteus and other Australian researchers—who used supplemented psychometrics with measurements of aboriginal skulls—researchers in East Africa measured, weighed, and dissected African brains in a series of postmortem studies. One of these researchers, Nairobi asylum director H. L. Gordon, disseminated his views on the irremediable inequality of the races in a highly publicized visit to London in 1933–1934.[82]

When a few years after returning from the outback Porteus decided to widen the geographic scope of his psychometric project once again, southern Africa made an appealing choice because the fabled Bushmen of the Kalahari offered a superficially apt parallel with the aborigines. Porteus was also a "good friend" of Charles Loram, a South African educator who affirmed African inferiority based on intelligence testing.[83] Although the Rockefeller Foundation in the 1930s was shifting away from the eugenicist associations of "racial psychology" and toward cultural anthropology instead, Porteus managed to find support from another American philanthropy: the Carnegie Corporation. His aspiration to unite Australia and southern Africa in a grand research scheme fit neatly with Carnegie's commitment to strengthening ties between British dominions. His familiar self-presentation—the hardheaded empiricist resisting the blandishments of "race levellers" and white supremacists alike—evidently still appealed to the technocratic sensibility of some foundation officers.[84]

Over the course of fourteen weeks in 1934, Porteus moved his laboratory through the desert in Bechuanaland Protectorate, to a series of mission stations in Southern Rhodesia and the Transvaal, and finally to a mining compound in Johannesburg.[85] As in Australia, the observations he made in the field did not always neatly align with his agenda. In a dispatch to the Carnegie staff in New York, Porteus noted "that there is considerable variability in intelligence among the individuals in each tribal group and that the upper 15 or 20% of Bantu should be capable of assimilating modern education." In his published account of the expedition, however, the emphasis shifted back to "the rank and file" who "possess certain mental and temperamental disabilities." Porteus stressed that groups, not just individuals, showed meaningful variations in intelligence. He dismissed environmental explanations by stressing that family life, education, and culture "are themselves the products of human invention and intelligence"; the African, like the aborigine, had little hope of adapting to a "white man's environment." The fact that aborigines—contrary to their reputation as a "psychological zero"—actually outperformed the Bushmen did not inspire a revision of his previous research.[86]

Porteus wanted the book that arose from the expedition, *Primitive Intelligence and Environment* (1937), to play a role in imperial debates about educability. He sent copies to officials in Uganda, Jamaica, the Transvaal, and Trinidad, as well as Colonial Office advisers in London, although he claimed to care about opinion in the settler colonies most of all. "I hope that [*Primitive Intelligence*] will have a good sale, both in South Africa and Australia," he told Croll, "as I feel that criticism from both those countries means more than reviews in America or even in England." While prominent representatives of the liberal intelligentsia—R. F. A. Hoernlé in South Africa, Alfred Radcliffe-Brown and A. P. Elkin in Australia—were critical, the book found a warmer reception in the Dominions than anywhere else.[87] Porteus's pronouncements always received respectful attention in newspapers across Australia.[88] South African researchers in ecology, linguistics, and medicine now added their own admiration for his attempt to apply psychometric methods to so-called "dying races."[89]

The response was different, however, in the wider Anglophone world. One sign of the changing political atmosphere was that race theorists in Nazi Germany were now favorably citing Porteus's work—an association that seemed to confirm the worst suspicions of his critics.[90] In the United States, Boasian anthropologist Ruth Benedict and progressive psychologist Otto Klineberg were among those who reproached Porteus for imprecision in his definition of race, for unwarranted faith in the results of mental testing, and for susceptibility to "popular prejudices," "bias," "suspicious enthusiasm," and "logical fallacies."[91] When applications for funding from Rockefeller and Carnegie went nowhere in the second half of the 1930s, Porteus recognized that the rise of Nazism had complicated his position but ventured into anti-Semitic innuendo anyway. "With Hitler leading the race theorists and all the Jewish scientists rushing to combat them," he wrote, "there seems to be an urgent need for some fundamental studies which are untouched by racial bias." Porteus complained that his research "in its unfinished state" had been used to support "various untenable theories of racial superiority" and even pitched a project that might have rehabilitated his image: a study of the cultural achievements of "primitive" races from cave painting to tribal government. But there were no takers among the foundations this time.[92]

The response to Porteus in Britain was even less forgiving. At a time when liberal intellectuals were already battling the case against African educability—trumpeted by Kenyan eugenicist H. L. Gordon from the corridors of Parliament to the pages of the *Times*—it was easy to see Porteus as part of the same retrograde provincial movement. Cambridge psychologist Frederic Bartlett declared that Porteus had fallen "far short of what should reasonably be expected in any scientific treatise," not least because he failed to justify his assumption that the maze test gauged adaptability to "white civilization." Anthropologists Meyer Fortes in Cambridge and R. R. Marett in Oxford were equally harsh. These critics and others voiced many of the same objections: subjects from non-Western cultures might be baffled by intelligence tests for reasons having nothing to do with intelligence; the ability to trace a pencil through a maze made a very imperfect measure of foresight, perseverance, adaptability, or whatever Porteus claimed to measure; actual mental differences, if they existed, probably reflected environment rather than inheritance. Across the British human sciences in the 1930s, Porteus became a byword for shoddy research—and a cautionary tale. "The prevailing assumption" that mental tests assess the same abilities in Europeans and others "must be proved," Fortes privately observed. "What it leads to can be seen from Porteus's work."[93]

The chilly reception demonstrates how far the climate in metropolitan Britain had hardened against racial comparisons of mental ability. Oxford anthropologist Beatrice Blackwood won Rockefeller funds for mental testing on Native American reservations in Arizona and New Mexico in the 1920s but returned home doubting whether mental tests could ever "bring within the same realm for comparison on an equitable basis the civilized man and the savage." As Philip Vernon, a psychologist who spent most of his career at the University of London, observed a few years later, "the medium of test material used in tests for civilized people may have entirely different meanings to the primitive mind." Even Cyril Burt, who saw the biological inheritance of mental ability as an ironclad law when it came to class distinctions at home, hesitated to extend the same principle to racial differences overseas. "I am afraid none of the work is very convincing," he confided to Charles Seligman. "Under existing conditions, it is almost hopeless to plan a really cogent inquiry into racial differences. At the end of it all, if not at the beginning, one is always tempted to ask what precisely is meant by a race and what is meant by being different."[94] These methodological obstacles did not foreclose the possibility of testing in other cultures altogether, but they did suggest restrictions on the uses to which testing should be put. In the words of education researcher William Bryant Mumford: "The main object in the further development of mental tests should be not comparisons destined to prove one race better than another, but rather for . . . selecting the most intelligent individuals from within a group of people . . . with a view to their being given promotion or better educational opportunities." Other thinkers agreed that the proper function of psychometrics in the empire was the measurement of ability for schools and jobs.[95]

Although couched in relativistic language, protests against interracial comparisons often arose from a universalistic belief that intelligence did not vary with race. If low test scores could not possibly reflect actual ability, critics argued, the instruments themselves must be less portable than their champions claimed. Siegfried Nadel of the LSE observed that "most tests" applied to other races "seem to contradict completely the knowledge which the anthropologist has gained of their cultural achievements and their intellectual capacity." He added that some cross-cultural experiments registered scores "so low as to seem absurd." A district officer in Tanganyika named Arthur Theodore Culwick arrived at a similar conclusion. After paying a visit to Bartlett's laboratory in the mid-1930s, Culwick returned to East Africa with an array of verbal and nonverbal tests; for almost every one of them, the failure rate was near-universal. And yet, as Culwick and Bartlett both recognized, the experiment demonstrated the limitations of boundary-crossing tests rather than the abilities of the people being studied. Subjects who traced intricate patterns in pottery or weaving or performed other complicated tasks in everyday life routinely failed to solve analogous problems when they appeared on pencil-and-paper tests—a conspicuous disjuncture between actual and measured performance. The psychological laboratory that traveled too far afield appeared to be in danger of breaking down.[96]

For researchers who remained enthusiastic about the possibilities of mental testing, drawing a *cordon sanitaire* around indefensible applications of the technique now took precedence. Bartlett took the lead by praising Culwick's research, which he said disproved the assumption that "similar methods & similar material will produce similar results independently of the social background." In fact, he argued, mental measurement could never be pried apart from culture; tests that isolated tasks from their functional context amounted to esoteric puzzles with scant empirical value. "Every cultural element is a part of a *working* pattern," Bartlett insisted. "Take it out of what works and the intelligence that manifests it is changed." Even if comparisons *between* groups would always lack reliability, however, he believed that comparing narrowly defined abilities *within* groups remained possible with the right kind of culturally adapted tests. Bartlett and his protégé, Cambridge psychologist Eric Farmer, soon emerged as vocal advocates of aptitude testing for industrial jobs in British Africa.[97]

Imperial officials in London—habitually skeptical of racial claims from the settler colonies and closer to missionary interests than their counterparts overseas—arrived at similar conclusions about the proper uses of mental testing.[98] Guidelines issued to colonial governments in 1929 threw the influence of the Colonial Office behind the Raj model of psychometrics rather than the alternative championed by Porteus. They were written by Arthur Mayhew, a close ally of the missionary lobby and a former administrator in India who had participated in the decision eight years earlier to sponsor psychometric research. A devout Anglican, Mayhew always affirmed "the oneness of human mentality," attributing "a rational behaviour, an unimpeachable logic, and a definite power of observation" to people everywhere.[99] Mayhew drew much of the language in his "Note on Psychological Tests of Educable Capacity and on the Possibility of Their Use in the Colonies" from a similar report issued to British schools by the Board of Education in 1924. Crafted by Cyril Burt and Charles Myers, among others, it suggested uses for mental testing that centered heavily on the classificatory aims of the Child Study movement: the selection of scholarship candidates, the identification of the "mentally defective," and the detection of vocational aptitudes.[100] Mayhew repeated these aims verbatim, recommending that colonial governments "classify children according to their 'educable capacity,' that is, according to the probability of their profiting from instruction." Although he also commented that tests could aid in the "detection of important points of difference between the European and non-European races in the various modes of intellectual reaction," this likely referred to pedagogical tactics—what Mayhew elsewhere described as the need to avoid "unfamiliar language or ideas" with students in the colonies—rather than variations in mental ability. The guidelines, after all, included a skeptical reference to the ways in which "the native mind ... is *alleged* to differ from the English mind."[101]

Many of the British officials who attended the International Anthropological Conference in London in 1934—which included administrators from India, Kenya, Uganda, Tanganyika, Nigeria, and elsewhere—reported that they had begun to experiment with mental testing on the populations in their colonies. Following the tone set by Mayhew, Bartlett, and others, however, enthusiasm for the novelty of psychometrics was accompanied by an anxious effort to define its legitimate uses. The director of education in Nyasaland, A. T. Lacey, told the delegates that Africans could unquestionably benefit from education, so mental tests suggesting otherwise were worthless. "As the difficulty of finding any common yard stick is almost insuperable," Lacey argued, "any comparison between the general intelligence of African and European peoples is bound to be of little value." Participants in the psychology section of the conference found this skepticism persuasive: they adopted a resolution calling for further research and declaring interracial comparisons "in our present state of knowledge both unscientific and unjust."[102]

The meritocratic model of mental testing gained strength across the interwar empire as eugenicist thinkers like Porteus and Gordon confronted growing criticism. One of their most influential opponents was James Dougall, a Church of Scotland missionary who directed the Jeanes School at Kabete, Kenya. "It is not difficult to show," he argued, "that individuals among the so-called primitive communities can attain to the most civilized standards and the most purely logical modes of thought." When Frederick Keppel, the president of the Carnegie Corporation, paid a visit to East Africa in 1927, Dougall suggested that a "scientifically trained psychologist" might help to translate "the pedagogical axioms of England and America" into the Kenyan context. The pitch worked. Keppel commissioned a British psychologist named Richard Oliver, who had studied at Edinburgh and then trained with Terman at Stanford, to relocate to Kenya for two years beginning in 1930.[103]

Following Dougall's advice, Oliver made his first task the construction of an intelligence test to select Africans for teaching training at the Jeanes School. In contrast to the usual method of choosing candidates for scarce jobs and school places—relying on "missionary recommendation" or "the good opinion of some native commissioner or other official"—Oliver wanted to measure innate "learning capacity." Although his initial battery of sixteen tests included the Porteus maze, he arrived at a very different conclusion from its namesake, observing that most subjects could solve even the most difficult mazes and consequently casting doubt on "the African's alleged impulsiveness."[104] Oliver celebrated the value of efficiency above all else: selecting the "innately brighter boy" for schooling, assigning students to appropriate courses, guiding them to the right career. When he found that the average African score on his own intelligence test reached only 85% of the European average, he downplayed the result as a "crude" "conjecture" "based on the scantiest of data." Even if the African mean were slightly lower, Oliver pointed out, the distribution of scores would overlap between races to a considerable degree. Most Africans would benefit from the same education as Europeans, and a few would thrive as university students.[105]

Oliver and his wife quickly learned to enjoy what he called "the largeness of this colonial life," the "open air feel" and the "splendid tennis." Intellectually, though, he did not find the settler world so appealing. Working closely with Dougall and conferring frequently with another well-connected Scottish missionary, Joseph Oldham, in London, Oliver shared their distaste for the eugenicist campaign waged by Gordon in the colony. Frustrated with the local press for trumpeting "conclusions definitely uncomplimentary to African intelligence on the ground that SCIENCE has proved this and that," as Dougall put it, all three men advocated an expert inquiry to resolve the racial dimensions of the educability debate. Oliver warned that such an undertaking could succeed only if metropolitan researchers took the lead because the white community in Kenya was hopelessly tainted by prejudice. "It is almost impossible for a local man to be unbiassed," he argued; after all, Gordon commanded "great local influence" despite obviously having "an axe to grind." To counteract that influence, Oldham convinced Prime Minister Ramsay MacDonald to refer the controversy to Colonial Office researchers then compiling a massive compendium of expert knowledge about Africa.[106]

When it was finally published in 1938, the *African Survey* leveled harsh criticism at proposals to compare the abilities of races. "Such inquiry," it announced, "tends to lose its value as soon as it ceases to be objective." The *Survey* even faulted Gordon by name and disclaimed any research in which "the abnormal condition of the Kenya native is taken for granted." It also pointed out that more than an eighth of the Africans tested by Oliver surpassed the European average "in spite of the group's undoubtedly lower level of environment and education." Given the fact that individual abilities varied so widely in every group, the *Survey* pronounced "any general investigation into the comparative mental capacity of the African" virtually useless. This judgment—translating the implied position of Mayhew's memorandum a decade earlier into explicit disapproval—demonstrated Whitehall's determination to resist the entanglement of imperial psychometrics with scientific racism.[107]

Although Oliver left Kenya in 1932, his legacy endured in the intelligence test he created. The colony's director of education—another champion of African educability and critic of eugenicist research—had ten thousand copies printed, encouraging teachers to use it with their students and send the results back to his department. Because the test relied heavily on images familiar to African children, such as goats and acacia trees, officials believed that it could transcend differences of tribe, language, and geography across Kenya. They even began to consider the scores on Oliver's test as a factor in admissions to secondary school—likely the first time that a colonial government in British Africa used mental testing for such a purpose.[108] Interest in the test soon spread beyond the borders of the colony. By the mid-1930s, a Church of Scotland missionary in Nyasaland sought Oliver's advice as he sought to adapt the test there, and an American missionary in the Central Province of India, Emil Menzel, considered it the most reliable test he had yet seen. Menzel's enthusiasm may have stemmed in part from the antipathy for racial comparisons that he and Oliver shared. "There is no Intelligence test in existence," he believed, "that can show Indian children on the whole to be either superior or inferior in mental ability to the Chinese, French, English, Negroes, or Americans." By the end of the decade, that was a commonplace sentiment in the British Empire.[109]

Looking back from London in 1939, Philip Hartog reflected on the success of the psychometric vision he had outlined in India years earlier. The principle of meritocracy, he thought, had guided the Raj since Macaulay insisted on the need to recognize and cultivate an aristocracy of talent in the colonized population. Although Hartog deplored the insistence on Anglophone education that went along with this, he argued that the innate capacities of the empire's Indian subjects allowed them to thrive anyway. "The Indian intellect must be singularly strong," he concluded. "In Bengal, which I know best, I believe that the average intelligence is certainly not inferior to the average intelligence in England." Rather than marking a radical departure, in Hartog's view, mental testing updated and solidified a long imperial tradition: absorbing indigenous talent into the institutions of British rule.[110]

If anything prevented officials in London from realizing this vision in a more systematic way between the wars, it was not ideological opposition but lack of resources. In Kenya, for instance, Oliver had no successor because even the backing of education and medical officers in the local bureaucracy could not overcome the Depression-era imperative to retrench.[111] With the coming of the Second World War, however, that picture changed drastically. The recruitment of hundreds of thousands of soldiers in India and Africa forced attention to the challenges of promoting officers, assigning specialized tasks, and organizing humanpower despite daunting differences of language and culture. Aptitude testing emerged as a solution, making psychology a tool of empire on a previously unimaginable scale and opening up new possibilities for managing minds in the military and beyond.

CHAPTER FOUR

Square Pegs and Round Holes

Aptitude Testing in the Barracks and Beyond

TAKING THE 5:10 TRAIN from Paddington Station on a February evening in 1943, assistant adjutant general Hubert Vinden disembarked at Swindon, where a Royal Air Force car whisked him to a nearby hotel. After a late meal, he took a midnight drive to an airfield, boarded a military plane "sketchily converted for passengers," and flew to Cairo for an overnight stay at Shepheard's Hotel. He then caught an Imperial Airways flight and disembarked at Gwalior for a rail journey to his final destination, Delhi. As the Indian capital drew near, Vinden confessed to feeling "apprehensive at the task which faced us in this unknown country with an entrenched hierarchy [which] we felt would be hostile to the new methods . . . we were to introduce." The imperial networks that brought him from London to Delhi had been mobilized in the service of an unusual mission: the use of psychological expertise to transform officer selection in the Indian Army. Avoiding the "square peg in the round hole"— the worker with abilities ill-suited to the job—was already a wartime cliché in Britain. Vinden would now test its viability as a global project.[1]

Aptitude testing among British troops in the Second World War represented an epochal feat of social engineering, sorting millions of men according to their fitness for service and their suitability for specialized tasks. But wartime psychometrics in the overseas empire—where language barriers, political tensions, and cultural differences presented a distinctive set of problems—has received little attention. When the imperial military used psychology to distinguish officers from infantrymen, radio operators from porters, and gunners from drivers, the consequences reverberated beyond the barracks, accelerating the movement of expertise across borders and drawing British officials into a deeper involvement with the science of mind than ever before. Guided by a newly influential vision of the "universal worker," imperial authorities in the postwar era made the aptitude test a fixture of factories, offices, and schools from India to Africa to the West Indies.[2]

But this apparent moment of triumph for the psychometric movement also revealed its frailty. Systematically testing aptitudes across the empire involved a process of scaling up that was ill-suited to ideological cohesion. The machinery of mental measurement encompassed many different groups: British expatriates and imperial subjects; critics and defenders of empire; metropolitan researchers and overseas administrators; experts, amateurs, and skeptics in the field of psychology. Not for the first time, imperial rulers saw their ambitions frustrated because imperial subjects proved adept at resisting, reorienting, and refashioning attempts at standardization from above.[3] Psychometric experts who criticized racial hierarchies as barriers to efficiency and opportunity saw their hopes disappointed, too, because the path to influence ran through government bureaucracies, industrial firms, and other established institutions. To make psychology a useful form of knowledge, they had to decouple the values of efficiency and fairness, elevating the promise of rationalization over the drive for social justice. As tests amassed ever greater quantities of data about human abilities around the world, measurement for its own sake emerged as the only justification everyone could agree on.

¶ IN THE YEARS between the wars, testing workers' abilities to perform specific jobs became a routine feature of industrial life in Britain and the United States. In the British Empire, though, private employers and government officials resisted proposals by psychometric experts to apply their methods to the indigenous labor force.

Charles Myers was one of those experts. He resigned his position at Cambridge University in 1922 to become the founding director of the National Institute of Industrial Psychology, a not-for-profit outfit that offered consulting services to private firms. Visiting the subcontinent in 1937 to drum up new commissions, Myers declared his conviction that Indian workers no less than British workers harbored complex attitudes requiring scientific study. While "the measures advised and applied . . . in one country . . . could not be unthinkingly applied to another," he told a crowd in Bombay, "the broad lines of the principles determining the improvement of the human factor throughout occupational life must be universally the same." Myers even wrote to the viceroy's office, suggesting that his institute could help to resolve "defective working conditions in India and the flocking of young Indians to 'black coated' occupations, with consequent unemployment."[4]

Despite a succession of high-profile speeches and meetings, however, Myers's Indian tour yielded few tangible accomplishments. In the quest for new business, the manager of a jute mill gave no firmer commitment than a promise to call on Myers during his next trip to London, while the chairman of the Tata Iron Works pronounced himself only "mildly interested" in the institute's services. The most disappointing response, however, came from the imperial state. While the viceroy, Lord Linlithgow, had the "highest opinion of Dr. Myers's capacity," he ignored his proposal for an institute devoted to industrial psychology in India, seeking advice on the treatment of "psychosis" in political prisoners instead. But Myers had nothing to suggest on that score. His ambition to revolutionize the Indian factory was treated as an intellectual curiosity rather than a realistic blueprint for business and government.[5]

Industrial psychology may have appeared suspect to the imperial elite because the field was fast evolving beyond time-and-motion studies to encompass the analysis of subjective forces—motivation, satisfaction, interpersonal relationships—in the workplace. Even before the First World War, Harvard professor Hugo Münsterberg had departed from the mechanistic model made famous by American Frederick W. Taylor by suggesting that differences in personality could affect productivity. By 1929, Elton Mayo's famous Hawthorne experiments were prompting workers to reflect on their "individual adjustments to industrial conditions" in psychoanalytic-style sessions.[6] In Britain, industrial psychology effectively began with the Quaker chocolate manufacturer Seebohm Rowntree, who oversaw wartime studies of worker fatigue as an official in the Ministry of Munitions and then hired psychologists to give aptitude tests in his massive Cocoa Works at York. Rowntree's paternalistic—if also self-interested—attention to worker satisfaction made Taylorism looked exploitative and dehumanizing by comparison. It also left a lasting mark on the British tradition of industrial psychology. Myers always took pains to profess the humanism of the profession against those who "time-study the worker as if he were a machine." He portrayed "the satisfaction of each worker's instincts and interests" as an important goal and the disturbance of the "mental atmosphere" by neurotic managers as a threat to efficiency.[7]

In the empire, though, even factory owners eager to boost productivity had little interest in investigating the job satisfaction of their workers. Industrialists in India long claimed that inefficiency had no more complicated explanation than idleness: "I say my workers are lazy, yes," one of them told a government panel in 1929. Factory owners implicitly denied the relevance of industrial psychology in the imperial context by arguing that Indian workers did not respond rationally to incentives. Lacking ambition, supposedly, they refused to work harder in exchange for higher wages; incapable of sustained effort, it was said, they would rather spend ten lackadaisical hours than eight strenuous hours on the factory floor each day.[8] It did not help that British and Indian researchers who tried to study industrial conditions on the subcontinent often did so from a leftist perspective. Turning the usual invidious comparisons of Indian and British efficiency on their head, they judged welfare provisions for Indian workers by metropolitan standards and found them wanting. "This circle must be broken," a typical expert declared in 1933, "by providing . . . primary and industrial education, by improving the working conditions, the environment and the health of the workers, by shortening the hours of work, and by raising the efficiency of management." Against the backdrop of labor researchers advocating massive outlays, trade unionism, and even political independence as remedies for inefficiency, it is easy to see why the expertise Myers promoted in India found few takers.[9]

Attempts to bring aptitude testing to Africa between the wars proved no more successful. On his way back from a trip to Cape Town in 1929, Cambridge psychologist Eric Farmer stopped in Kenya to lay the groundwork for a project he had been discussing with his colleagues at the Industrial Health Research Board back home. Farmer wanted to investigate the "mental and physical suitability" of East Africans for industrial labor in two ways: by studying the "incentives, hours of work, and methods" that governed their productivity and by inventing tests of mechanical aptitude based on the "social background and interests" of various tribes. Like his mentor, Frederic Bartlett, Farmer believed that aptitude tests which accounted for cultural difference could identify "the most suitable natives" for "technical training schemes."[10] But even this capitalist-friendly approach failed to convince the Colonial Office that industrial psychology had any relevance in Africa, where labor policy was traditionally concerned with recruiting the maximum number of workers from a severely limited pool rather than selecting the most able. Even Granville Orde Browne, the Colonial Office labor adviser who pushed employers to spend time training their workers rather than relying on an endless stream of migrants, argued that individual differences in ability and temperament did not have the same significance in Africa as they did in Europe. "Crowd psychology" so "dominated behaviour," he claimed in 1933, that "the African had little incentive to the evolution of person-ality." Failing to overcome those kinds of assumptions, Farmer's proposal foundered on the belief that matching workers with jobs suited to their talents could not proceed until anthropologists, pathologists, and other specialists had acquired "more fundamental knowledge" about the pecu-liarities of the African mind. In Africa as in India, experts in the interwar period failed to convince imperial authorities when they argued that apti-tude testing rested on universal principles.[11]

That skepticism remained difficult to dislodge until the British Army embraced mental measurement during the Second World War. In psycho-metrics, as in other fields, the war dramatically boosted the prestige of expert knowledge.[12] Military leaders in metropolitan Britain concluded as early as 1941 that the usual rules for managing people—assigning soldiers to regiments on the basis of geographic origin and occupational back-ground, promoting them to officer rank on the basis of interviews and rec-ommendations, and providing almost no role for technical specialists aside from routine medical exams—were breaking down amid a huge influx of recruits. One study found that four percent of British infantrymen lacked the mental ability to serve as soldiers at all, while a full twenty per-cent were wrongly excluded from more skilled units; among candidates selected for officer training, meanwhile, the failure rate hovered around thirty percent. A new section of the War Office, the Directorate for the Selection of Personnel (DSP), was formed in 1941 to devise methods of selecting and sorting soldiers that accounted for intellect, temperament, and other psychological determinants of job performance. Staffed by a combination of soldiers and psychologists, including several from Myers's National Institute of Industrial Psychology, the DSP worked closely with the Royal Army Medical Corps, which employed a number of psychiatrists from the Tavistock Clinic.[13]

The translation of psychometric principles into military practice was eased by some superficial continuities with tradition. Above all, the new testing regime assimilated meritocracy into the chain of command, distinguishing the basic competence required of workaday soldiers from the lofty leadership qualities expected of commanding officers. Charles Myers, who helped to design the testing program for the rank and file, sought only to weed out the "unstable," the "mentally dull," and the "untrainable." He approved the use of a nonverbal intelligence test known as the Progressive Matrices, developed before the war at an asylum in Colchester, which involved recognizing patterns in series of abstract geometric images. New recruits were also required to take tests in English and mathematics, a test designed to gauge facility with clerical work, and two different tests to measure mechanical skill. Based on their test scores and a brief interview, they could be assigned to one of seven occupational categories, from driver to signaler to clerk to storekeeper; placed in the general combatant pool; or recommended for discharge. Rather than strive for a textured portrait of the psyche, Myers and his colleagues evaluated ordinary soldiers in narrowly functional and purely quantitative terms.[14]

For officers, by contrast, promotion depended on a far more exacting evaluation. Working under the supervision of adjutant general Ronald Adam and his deputy, Hubert Vinden, at Edinburgh University in early 1942, the experts drew on an eclectic array of influences—Gestalt psychology, Lewinian field theory, even an intelligence report on officer selection in the German Army—in their search for the unconscious origins of officer material.[15] Under their system, candidates for promotion to officer rank had to endure three consecutive days of assessments, including a verbal intelligence test; a nonverbal intelligence test; a word association test of the kind developed by Carl Gustav Jung; the Thematic Apperception Test, developed by Harvard psychologist Henry Murray, which involved writing brief stories in response to ambiguous pictures projected on the wall; a private interview with a psychiatrist; a group discussion moderated by a testing officer who posed questions to stimulate debate; and a series of outdoor exercises, like carrying heavy loads across obstacle courses, meant to reveal leadership qualities in the spontaneous behavior of the group.[16] The rationale for probing so deeply into mental life,

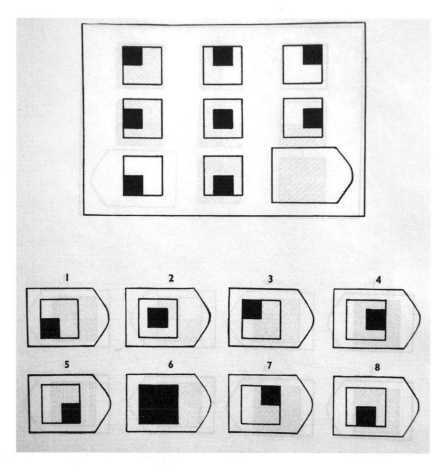

The Progressive Matrices test. Developed by British psychologist John C. Raven for use with mentally deficient children in 1938, the test was administered by the British to more than a million soldiers during the Second World War. It became one of the most widely used intelligence tests in the world. (J. C. Raven, *Progressive Matrices: Sets A, B, C, D, and E, 1938.* London: H. K. Lewis & Co. Ltd., 1940.)

examining inward compulsions as well as outward behavior, involved an old-fashioned ideal of command. In the words of John Rawlings Rees, the Tavistock medical director and a leading Army psychiatrist, "the capacity for leadership, the ability, character, and insight of the officer are of paramount importance for the happiness and welfare as well as for the efficiency of the men he commands." This was Victorian paternalism updated with technocratic authority: the fighting strength of the enlisted soldier, redefined as morale, depended heavily on his officer's mental state.[17]

Although very low scores on intelligence tests could be disqualifying for officer candidates, the selection boards paid far more attention to character or temperament. Rees defined this as the "capacity for a mature, independent social relationship." The evaluation form used by testing officers disaggregated the relevant traits in more detail: "appearance and liveliness," "relations with others and their attitudes to him," "self-reliance and attitude to difficulties," "powers of command and organisation." The projective tests (so called because they involved ambiguous situations aimed at prompting their subjects to project or reveal unconscious preoccupations) played an important part in systematizing impressions gathered from interviews and questionnaires. In the Thematic Apperception Test, experts interpreted stories with happy endings as evidence of a "well balanced and energetic" psyche; stories portraying the protagonists as passive victims of fate, by contrast, suggested "an ineffectual person with little drive." When the picture of a woman standing with her back to a young man inspired stories about a mother objecting to her son's decision to marry, this was deemed a troubling hint of "parental dependence." In the word association test, soldiers who seized on the military meaning of ambiguous prompts like *barrel, arm,* and *front* fared well, while emotive responses to *mother, afraid,* or *home* raised the prospect of an "anxious, spoiled, homesick youth." Even the intelligence tests indirectly served as another measure of temperament. The ability to answer timed questions, one expert argued, provided an index of "performance under pressure."[18]

Amid this barrage of tests, the outdoor activities known as leaderless group tests acquired outsized significance because they seemed to dramatize the virtues and flaws of the candidates in vivid fashion. Testing officers looked out for recurring types like the "thruster" ("trying to dominate" without "the real quality of leadership") and the "wallflower" ("always on the fringes of what was happening . . . a 'hand offerer' rather than a 'hand giver' "). The task itself assumed elaborate dimensions: one group was told to move "a bomb, unexploded, not to be tipped, tilted, rolled, etc., weighing quite a lot (it took six to lift it) . . . across the stream using two scaffolding poles that wouldn't reach across, and the stream too deep to stand in." In this kind of situation, intellectual ability and manual dexterity both mattered less than a combination of adaptability, determination, and pluck. The ideal candidate, one expert wrote, was "quick to size up the tactical possibilities" and make "rapid adjustment to the changing conditions" of the game. Another went so far as to suggest that

Which of These Men Shows The Greatest Dash?
One takes care to reach the stile first and climbs over. Another waits his turn to follow. A third scrambles through the wire at the side.

19

The "leaderless group" test in action, 1942. (Photo by Haywood Magee/*Picture Post*/Hulton Archive/Getty Images.)

"the word intelligence . . . would perhaps be better replaced by the term mother-wit . . . a measure of the ease with which a person gets into the picture in any normal situation."[19]

Despite their apparent fealty to an aristocratic ideal of character, then, the selection boards actually defined character in a deeply subversive way—as something situational and relational rather than as an unchanging essence of the self. As one military psychiatrist argued, "leadership is not a single quality possessed by some and not by others, but is a way of describing the effectiveness of an individual in a specific role within a specific group united for a particular purpose." This, of course, undermined the claims of a permanent elite distinguished by birth and tradition. The selection boards attached strikingly little importance to knowledge acquired through education—so that an understanding of military strategy, for instance, counted for nothing. Above all, the boards rewarded the ability to navigate highly structured situations, whether in solving the geometric puzzles of the Progressive Matrices or the concrete challenges of the obstacle course. Mirroring the background of those who ran them, this selection regime enacted the triumph of the self-made man: rational rather than imaginative, dutiful rather than effortless, clever rather than cultured.[20]

Reflecting the outlook of the field in Britain as a whole, psychologists in the military cast a suspicious eye on rigid social hierarchies. With their discipline still marginalized at the university level, many mental testers pursued unglamorous careers in schools and asylums, engendering a sense of distance from the traditional elite that carried into wartime. Only "scientific methods which penetrate surface appearances," as Rees put it, could counter the influence usually exerted by posh accents, public school pedigrees, and Oxbridge connections in decisions on promotion. An Army testing officer named Walter Greenhalgh pursued this argument further. "The only way in which you can find out the potential of a person," he insisted, "is to examine what that potential is, rather than what he has done, because what a man was capable of doing was quite different from what he has done in our present society." In other words, he admitted, the rationale for aptitude testing was essentially "Marxist." Although few mental testers could match Greenhalgh's ideological commitment—he was a lifelong Communist who fought with the International Brigades in Spain—many of his colleagues likewise viewed psychometrics in the Army as a force for social justice.[21]

The men who established mental testing in the Indian Army embodied the same trajectory of upward mobility as many of their counterparts at home. Hubert Vinden, the son of a pharmacist, described his family background as comfortable but "not rich."[22] One of his deputies, Donald Portway, rose from even humbler origins on the strength of technical know-how: the son of a foundry owner in Essex, he won an engineering scholarship to Cambridge and ended up as master of St. Catharine's College. For both men, crucially, mistrust of class privilege translated into suspicion of racial privilege. Portway made friends with Indian students in the dormitories and tennis courts at Cambridge, coming to share their indignation that British youth who failed to make it into the civil service at home had a fallback in the Indian equivalent. He would later irritate imperial service trainees at Cambridge by insisting that lower-ranking officials (including a growing number of non-white officials) should be treated as equals. For his part, Vinden used the occasion of a BBC talk in 1947 to criticize Anglo-Indians for their "color prejudice," for imposing a "yoke of paternalism" on their subjects, and for seeing India as a preserve of "backwardness, pigheadedness, idleness, and everything that was inferior."[23] Neither man, therefore, was likely to approve of the selection and promotion practices that reigned in the Indian Army when they arrived in the country in 1943. Although Queen Victoria had pledged almost a century before that colonial "subjects, of whatever race and creed, shall be freely and impartially admitted to offices in our service," that promise had long remained unfulfilled. A kind of second-class commission for indigenous officers, signed by the viceroy rather than the monarch, marked their subordination to British officers and confined them to advising rather than commanding. Although a handful of Indians were granted full commissions, they were restricted to units with no British soldiers.[24]

The difficulty confronting Vinden, Portway, and their expert collaborators was that the mission to India involved several kinds of radical innovation at once. Critics at home were already complaining that the selection board represented a uniquely intrusive means of selection—what a Tory M. P. later described as "a sort of glorified hotel with a 'snooper' behind every palm tree, and a man liable at any point to hop out and ask you: 'How round is a cricket ball?'" Prime Minister Churchill himself objected to the "charlatanry" of forcing soldiers to field impertinent questions about sex. Army officers, meanwhile, argued that regimental assignments based on test scores rather than the usual links of territory and family undermined *esprit de corps;* they also blanched at the prospect of psychologists and psychiatrists subverting the chain of command by overriding their own recommendations for promotion.[25] Perhaps the most fundamental objection, however, was their insistence on the value of subjective judgments of character. "What you really needed," one officer argued, were experienced men "who knew people and could say at a glance what they were good for."[26] In India, British officers held this assumption with special conviction when it came to indigenous soldiers. A sixty-year-old general named Ralph Bouverie Deedes, an accomplished cricketer who had commanded Indian troops in the trenches during the First World War, told Vinden that the new system simply "wouldn't do for Indians." He observed that the Indian Army had developed its own rough-and-ready selection methods, including a "test for courage" that a candidate passed if he managed not to flinch when an inflated paper bag was burst behind his back. Even though commissions during the war were issued on a temporary basis only, the prospect of Indian and British candidates competing side-by-side for the same officer rank in accord with methods devised by experts loomed as a dramatic break with tradition.[27]

This vision ultimately became a reality through a confluence of war-time circumstances. The massive expansion of the Indian Army—which grew almost tenfold over the course of the war—coupled with a shortage of British soldiers on the subcontinent made it necessary to recruit large numbers of untrained and untested Indian officers beyond the traditional "martial races." Although the advent of the selection boards in Britain had reduced training failure rates only slightly, even modest improvement would have been welcome in India, where as many as eighty percent of officer candidates were flunking out in the early years of the war.[28] Another important factor was the growing authority of psychiatry in the imperial military. As in Britain, specialists with the Royal Army Medical Corps overseas had drawn lessons from the First World War, insisting on the need to properly diagnose battlefield casualties with mental illness. Convinced that these cases often arose from preexisting neuroses or pre-dispositions to neurosis, psychiatrists advocated the expert selection of officers and enlisted men alike.[29] Some of them considered racial prejudice among British soldiers a neurotic symptom in itself: one psychiatrist con-cluded that ignorance of Indian customs contributed to "intense unneces-sary dislike" of the country that risked devolving into mental illness.[30]

The technocratic outlook of Archibald Wavell, the recently installed commander-in-chief of the Indian Army who would go on to become viceroy in 1943, ensured that the claims of mind science were taken seri-ously at the highest level. Wavell had stirred controversy in Britain a decade earlier by suggesting that the military could improve "man man-agement" in the rank and file by hiring experts to study the "psychology of our own citizens"—a proposal the conservative brass dismissed out of hand. As one of Wavell's opponents remarked then, "every regimental officer, if he is worth anything at all, has worked with men, and if he has not learnt after a year or two how to manage men he will never learn." Now Wavell finally had his chance to build an army on the basis of psy-chological expertise. Casting old-timers like Deedes as a foil, he remarked that "the officers of the Indian army had, in some cases, rather a limited outlook and also were convinced that only they knew how to deal with Indians." He authorized Vinden to install his first selection board at Dehra Dun, a garrison town in the foothills of the Himalayas.[31]

The belief that new selection methods could advance military efficiency and equality of opportunity at the same time pervaded the new bureaucracy. Following Wavell's advice to "employ as many Indians as possible," Vinden plucked seven Indian psychologists from university departments to work as testing experts and appointed another seven Indian soldiers to serve as deputy board presidents. When the first batch of thirty Indian candidates proceeded through the new course, Vinden recalled, "we were all apprehensive at the outcome, but everything went like clockwork. . . . It was a replica of the reactions in the Boards at home." He credited "the psychiatrists and psychologists" who had "showed that, basically, human beings were not so very different from each other whatever their ethnic groups." Portway went even further in linking the portability of psychometric techniques with the dismantling of racial hierarchies. Making an implicit claim about the benevolence of British imperialism in contrast to its fascist rival, he proclaimed that "leadership is a universal attribute and there never has been and never will be a master race."[32]

The apparent success of the selection board at Dehra Dun led to the establishment of others at Calcutta, Bangalore, Jabalpur, Meerut, Lonavala, Rawalpindi, and Karachi within a few months. Vinden and Portway legitimized the promotion of a new generation of indigenous soldiers, effectively overruling the conservative officials who believed that expanding the Indian Army beyond Punjabi Muslims, Sikhs, and other tried-and-true ethnic communities imperiled its fighting strength. Between 1943 and 1945, as the boards processed more than twenty thousand candidates, the proportion of Indians in the officer corps increased from thirteen percent to nearly twenty percent.[33] If this movement toward Indianization was largely inevitable given the staffing pressures of the war, the meritocratic pageant of the selection process represented the change as a matter of fairness rather than demographic necessity. British officer candidates now competed alongside Indians in exam halls, obstacle courses, and interview rooms, with Indians as well as Britons observing and evaluating them. In theory, at least, there were no fixed percentages to pass or fail. The outcome depended solely on whether the board discovered "some indefinable thing about a chap . . . any sort of qualities of leadership," as one officer put it.[34]

In an echo of the egalitarian logic expressed by mental testers at home, testing officers in India told the candidates that they would be judged on their future potential rather than the past performance reflected in their service records or employment history. Portway argued that work history provided an unreliable guide to battlefield mettle because limited opportunities concealed depths of character. Some Indians who had been languishing in dead-end jobs in peacetime, he observed, had "blossomed" "under the load of responsibility" in war.[35] A lighthearted parody of Kipling's "If" by one British testing officer made clear that while education might count for something, the balance of the assessment depended on qualities more innate than learned:

> If round the obstacles you idly hop
> If in the Group Task you are quite unnerved,
> If on the phone you're hesitant, perturbed.
> If you have no B.A. or LL.B.,
> If background's plunged in mediocrity,
> If pointers say you're anxious or upset
> Then here's the grading you are sure to get
> For you're a "U" [for unfit] my son.

In the world of the selection boards, quick wits and cool heads mattered more than conventional markers of status.[36]

The conviction that psychological qualities did not vary with race led Vinden and Portway to import the British model of officer selection almost unchanged. Aside from superficial changes to test questions about weights and measures, everything about the procedure—the Thematic Apperception Test images designed by Henry Murray, the verbal aptitude test given in English, the European-style food served to applicants—remained identical. Even the timing stayed the same: word association prompts were shown for fifteen seconds each, while images in the Thematic Apperception Test each lasted thirty seconds.[37] If this failure to account for cultural differences imposed a clear disadvantage on Indian candidates, however, it could also be presented as a selling point. A process that treated all candidates as generic Anglophone subjects, concealing religious affiliation, caste status, and even personal names from the testers, offered an escape from the classifications and categories that usually governed Indians under the Raj. As the *Madras Mail* enthused, "all war service candidates, whether Captains or Major or Lieutenants or Havildar clerks, were stripped of their uniforms and placed on an absolute footing of equality as mere candidates with numbers . . . to feel and behave like comrades irrespective of any distinction of birth, rank or social status." Portway likewise stressed that the "ladder" of the selection board was designed "for the best man to finish at the top without regard for community, caste, or creed."[38]

Not everyone found the world the psychologists made so appealing. British soldiers, in particular, often saw the experts themselves as figures of fun: the "queer bloke," the "trick cyclist," the eccentric snoop "always hovering about in the background" with a clipboard. According to the writer George MacDonald Fraser, who attended his own selection board in Calcutta, "the general view throughout the Army was that they weren't fit to select bus conductors, let alone officers." Then, too, the overwhelming majority of British officers in India—ninety-nine percent of them, according to one contemporary—wanted to dispense with a system that radically curbed their influence.[39] But many Indian soldiers welcomed the change. The application of expertise was not only fascinating in itself—"great training and experience for assessing people," in the words of future Pakistani president Mohammad Ayub Khan—it also represented a bulwark against the retrograde influence of the Anglo-Indian officer corps. As one newly minted Indian officer declared, "good man-management" proved that "courage, determination, and resourceful leadership are not the monopoly of any race." By defining an ideal of fairness against the discriminatory traditions of the past, the selection boards legitimized surprisingly explicit criticism of British rule. Under the old system, the *Times of India* concluded, "prejudice and favouritism" had long promoted "unworthy persons" on the basis of "parentage, class (martial or otherwise), social standing, and even wealth and influence." The advent of "a rational and scientific method" appeared to be changing that.[40]

As the war went on, the experts in charge of the selection boards increasingly gave voice to a utopian hope: that their showpieces of meritocracy would offer a model for transforming India beyond the military. Visiting the selection boards in 1945, War Office psychiatrist J. R. Rees believed that "something of value will be almost bound to survive after the war from this first effort to make honest and fearless election of the best Indian material for specific tasks." Portway, too, was looking ahead. Envisioning a postwar program of economic development anchored by irrigation networks, hydroelectric power, and other infrastructure projects, he saw the labor force assembled by the military as ideally suited to undertake the engineering feats required for modernization. The selection boards, he argued, had unearthed previously neglected reserves of "fine material" in the Indian population.[41] Already in 1944, Vinden scored a major victory in the campaign to extend psychometric authority beyond the military when he convinced British officials to establish a parallel selection board system for applicants to the Indian Civil Service (ICS). As in the military, open competition for government jobs marked a departure from tradition, which had long relied on racial quotas and geographically segregated exams to maintain British dominance of the bureaucracy. But traditions changed quickly in wartime. When a London official visited one of the new civil selection boards at Dehra Dun in 1945, he saw seven Indian soldiers and two English captains vying for positions in the ICS. Only one of the Englishmen, he noted, performed well enough to get the job.[42]

Thanks to Vinden's bureaucratic entrepreneurship, the military officers and civil servants who triumphed in wartime selection boards would go on to compose a significant portion of India's elite in the early years of independence. But how did the rhetoric of fairness and opportunity that legitimized this process square with reality? Although Vinden and Portway apparently never acknowledged it, some Indians at the time saw no difference between the putative meritocracy of the new system and the explicit racialism of the past. The failure rate for indigenous officer candidates was so high that nationalist voices in the Central Legislative Assembly in Delhi puckishly suggested that the selection boards should be rechristened "rejection boards." According to the most complete study conducted at the time, more than seventy-three percent of Indian candidates for commissions were rejected, while fewer than half of British candidates were.[43] As one British officer pointed out, this did not necessarily indicate intentional discrimination: newspaper ads touting generous pay for officer rank brought in a flood of Indian applicants with no military experience, while the much smaller pool of British candidates was drawn almost entirely from the Army. But others pointed out that the formal colorblindness of the process had perversely discriminatory consequences.[44]

Perhaps the most damning critique came from K. G. Rama Rao, a psychologist who worked for the selection board at Jabalpur and reviewed the case files of more than six thousand officer candidates who passed through the boards in 1943–1944. Rao pointed out that Vinden and his colleagues failed to verify that test scores in India followed the same distribution as in Britain by restandardizing them with an Indian sample.

This failure was compounded by the mandatory use of English in test questions, test answers, and the instructions given to candidates. Rao asserted that "the amount of mental confusion" resulting from this policy was "real and significantly large" for the vast majority of Indian candidates whose native language was not English—and at least one British officer agreed.[45] But Rao reserved his greatest ire for the British psychiatrists who conducted diagnostic interviews and scored many of the tests. "By race and nationality an utter stranger," he claimed, the expert who had recently arrived in India for the first time "cannot easily establish 'rapport' with a people foreign to him in every way." Quoting from psychiatric evaluations of candidates, he showed how easily they could "degenerate into pure and simple 'mind reading' stuff":

> [Candidate R3] Well balanced. Lacks confidence. Sense of inadequacy. Variety of interests. Poor education record. Lacks drive. Trainable.

> [Candidate C4] Alert keen little sikh. Well integrated and quite positive personality . . . Honest reliable type . . . Average intelligence. Has sufficient drive.

Both of these candidates received the same grade, D. Given British experts' unfamiliarity "with Indian conditions," as another Indian testing officer put it, the temptation to fall back on generalities and stereotypes inevitably contaminated the process.[46]

Neither expertise in psychology nor commitment to meritocracy was a prerequisite for service on the selection boards. As the system expanded rapidly, testing positions were filled by military officers and civil servants whose training was confined to a crash course in psychometrics. A typical example is G. M. Ray, an ICS official who bitterly resented his exile to selection boards in Dehra Dun and Madras in 1945–1946. Longing to be back "in the thick of it" and "in charge of a district," he had to settle for long days working alongside experts whose authority he questioned at every turn. "How these psychologists can pretend to interpret the Indian character, knowing nothing whatsoever about the country or the people, is something more than I can understand," Ray confided to his diary. "Of course they *can't*, but when tackled on the subject get very sore, and blandly maintain that 'human nature' is the same everywhere." He reserved special opprobrium for the psychiatrist at Dehra Dun, Colman

Kenton, "who struts about the place pretending that he knows all about the Indian character although he has been in the country barely a month." Ray was no nationalist; in fact, he held an even lower opinion of the indigenous applicants than he did of his colleagues. "How these people imagine they are qualified for the Imperial Services just staggers me," he complained. "The average Indian is completely lacking in imagination and originality." And yet Ray agreed with Indian critics like Rao on one point: British experts who had just parachuted into the country lacked the local knowledge they needed to make sound assessments of personality. Even as they agreed on little else, this degree of relativism united indigenous nationalists and expatriate colonialists with long experience in India.[47]

Absorbing local manpower as it expanded, the selection bureaucracy was hardly insulated from the culture of the Raj, making it difficult for Vinden or anyone else to maintain ideological consistency across the system. The tradition of favoring ethnic groups seen as innately martial and eternally loyal, for instance, proved resilient despite the nominal reign of colorblind meritocracy. Ray drew the usual contrast between "unattractive" Madrasis and "the tall, fair martial races of the north"; another testing officer, despite feebly warning that "we mustn't stereotype," concluded that "the Bengalis were much better at talking than doing." At least one psychiatrist insisted that assigning Indian soldiers to units with others who shared their caste, linguistic, and village background was essential to preventing mental breakdown.[48] Political pressures infiltrated the selection process as well. One promising candidate was rejected because his father edited a nationalist newspaper; conversely, a wealthy rajah's son judged mediocre by Ray made it into the civil service anyway because the board president was "tipped off" and scored him higher. Some British officers even argued that candidates whose ancestors "rendered meritorious service to the Raj during the Mutiny" should be promoted without question. "It was precisely to stop this kind of nepotism and favoritism that these independent Selection Boards were set up—or so I thought," Ray fumed.[49]

Arbitrariness prevailed even where discrimination and string-pulling did not. One of Ray's Indian counterparts wrote deliberately vague reports on all the candidates and copied down grades from a colleague just before the final meeting.[50] A British officer appointed to verify the effectiveness of the system across the country failed to find any correlation between assessments given by the selection boards and those given later by training units in the field. Because the wartime boards were inundated with inexperienced candidates, he found, even those who received relatively high scores from the testing officers underperformed later. In one ten-month period, more than half of the candidates recommended by selection boards either failed out of their training units or were asked to resign. "We didn't prove the case," the officer recalled. "The samples weren't good enough." He was sacked and replaced by another researcher who likewise could not establish a meaningful correlation.[51]

The men in charge of the Raj selection boards proved adept at projecting success despite evidence to the contrary. When Rees voiced concern that the high rejection rates for Indian candidates "led to a considerable amount of political trouble," a series of "very long discussions" with Vinden and his team helped to reassure him about the "first-class importance" of their work.[52] Stepping down as director of the Indian Army's Directorate of Personnel Selection on the eve of Partition in 1946, Vinden handed the reins to Brigadier Thakur Nathu Singh in a transition that seemed to validate the meritocratic ethos of the system. The *Times of India* proudly announced that the military would never return to the days of "prejudice and favouritism" that promoted many "unworthy persons" on the basis of "parentage, class (martial or otherwise), social standing, and even wealth and influence." As Singh's new deputy put it, "there are now going to be equal opportunities for all." Vinden himself moved to a new bureaucracy called the Employment Selection Bureau, where he supervised a team of former Army psychiatrists and psychologists screening job applicants for the ICS in the run-up to independence.[53]

The legacy of the Raj selection boards extended far beyond India. What British officials perceived as the success of the procedure fueled the replication of the same techniques wherever the imperial military needed to identify officer material, evaluate recruits for assignment to training programs, or diagnose breakdowns across racial lines. By the end of 1943, full-fledged selection boards were also operating in Cairo, Tripoli, and Rangoon.[54] From Malta to Lagos to Ceylon, meanwhile, Army psychiatrists and lay officers used the same intelligence tests and personality tests in less systematic ways. By the end of the war, British forces had administered the Progressive Matrices test to a million and a half people around the world, retiring it only for fear that it was becoming too widely known.[55]

In the wider imperial world, as in India, this sprawling system did not always stay true to the values of its founders. Even as they used the same tests, experts outside the Raj insisted on adaptations for different ethnic groups. Selection experts for the Middle East Force headquartered in Cairo restandardized the tests so that Indians, Palestinian Arabs, Jewish settlers, white South Africans, and Cypriots could be evaluated against their own norms; they also translated the test questions into Arabic, Hebrew, and Greek. A round of low scores from Maltese troops on the Progressive Matrices prompted one Army psychiatrist to stop using the test with non-British populations altogether because he believed that "language difficulties and temperamental factors" made cross-cultural measurements impossible. Although Vinden's universal models gave rise to stirring rhetoric, they did not travel very far.[56]

Wartime psychometrics diverged most dramatically from the Raj model in sub-Saharan Africa. With so many Africans disinclined to fight or weakened by disease and malnourishment, British military leaders were less interested in culling the applicant pool than in enlisting the maximum number of able-bodied men. Officer selection mattered not at all because the color bar remained virtually intact: imperial authorities never contemplated granting commissions to more than a handful of African soldiers.[57] South African premier Jan Smuts, a key British ally, refused to participate in a War Office conference on psychometric research because of the possibility that it could legitimize the promotion of African soldiers to officer rank.[58] These demographic and ideological pressures sharply circumscribed the use of mental testing across the continent. At the West Africa Command headquartered near Accra, the British Army tested only a fraction of the 200,000 soldiers recruited over the course of the war, confining the procedure to educated men who might serve as clerks, storemen, and teachers. The English proficiency test required for appointment as a senior noncommissioned officer (NCO) simply asked candidates to count up to one hundred, to "intelligently" answer questions about their tribe and birthplace, to give the correct names of objects commonly found in the barracks, and "to pass simple verbal messages on to a third person."[59] In accordance with local variants on the theory of martial races, many recruiters considered high intelligence a demerit rather than a virtue, clinging to a romantic vision of simple but sturdy warriors in which the ability to perform basic tasks mattered more than subtleties of personality.[60] Many, too, held fast to assumptions about the relationship between aptitude and ethnicity, like the commander in the King's African Rifles in East Africa, who believed that members of the Wakamba tribe had "a much greater aptitude for learning the Morse Code."[61]

Over time, however, the sheer variety of technical specialists required by the Army—drivers, repairmen, medical orderlies, signalers, censors, gunners, and engineers, among others—opened a wider path for psychometric expertise in British Africa. Some commanders in the field pointed out that assigning recruits to training programs based on tribe and educational background alone "resulted in a considerable waste of experience, special abilities, and exceptional intelligence." As a reform-minded officer in West Africa observed, soldiers who might have made excellent orderlies ended up as mediocre joint fitters because they never had to take a manual dexterity test. If illiterate recruits with no credentials or experience appeared unqualified at first, testing for "general intelligence or special aptitudes" might identify some who could benefit from particular kinds of training.[62]

Military leaders heeded this call in August 1944 by commissioning an experiment at the biggest British base on the African continent. In Cairo, an Army unit led by Lieutenant-Colonel Alan Macdonald—who worked in peacetime as an industrial psychologist at Rowntree's Cocoa Works—measured the aptitude of hundreds of East African Pioneer Corps soldiers with tests including the Progressive Matrices and the Goddard form board. Staking out a more relativistic position than his counterparts in India, Macdonald argued that British experts were ill-equipped to assess personalities through interviews because "the effect of social and cultural background on [the] character and behavior [of African soldiers] is so marked." By contrast, he argued, aptitude tests which minimized subjective judgments through rigid protocols could yield valuable data. Macdonald concluded that the test scores of his subjects matched later evaluations by commanding officers about as well as DSP testing predicted the success of British soldiers at home—a vindication for treating African soldiers less as an assemblage of ethnic monoliths and more as a heterogeneous population with "a wide range in performance."[63]

Like the selection boards in India, psychometric research in Africa fueled ambitions that transcended the war effort. According to Macdonald, "the existence of large organized groups of Africans" was an opportunity to be seized before the conflict was over—not so much for military aims as for "educational and industrial authorities interested in the economic use of African manpower." A War Office functionary noted approvingly that researchers had "not been unmindful of the civilian problems of educational and vocational selection." An official in the Colonial Office added that Macdonald's report had "been read with great interest" there.[64] The contrast with India came both in Macdonald's relativistic insistence on restandardization and in his quiet abandonment of the lofty ideals Vinden championed. Macdonald heralded the productive management of human resources without appealing to the values of mobility, fairness, and equality. It was a sign of things to come: at a time when Africa had already eclipsed India in planning for the postwar empire, bureaucrats in London were warming to the prospect of modernizing societies through psychological knowledge. If testing experts wanted to pursue egalitarian ideals in the future, they would find it useful to do so through the language of efficiency.

¶ MEASURED BY THE INFLUENCE flowing to its boosters, 1943 was an *annus mirabilis* for psychology in the British Empire. Moving forward with plans to distribute funds under the Colonial Development and Welfare Act passed by Parliament three years earlier, the Colonial Office now commissioned teams of scholars to outline research agendas for the natural and human sciences.[65] The psychology group was chaired by Frederic Charles Bartlett. It was an unsurprising choice not only because of his eminent position in the field—a legacy, in part, of the lineage he could claim from the Torres Strait generation—but also because he had long operated at the intersection of psychology and anthropology. Visiting Swaziland in the late 1920s, Bartlett conducted a version of his famous memory experiments among African cattle herders, showing them pictures for a few seconds at a time and then asking them to replicate the scene with pencil and paper. He concluded that "the results were much the same as they would have been for similar tests in a typical European group." During the war, Bartlett cemented his influence in Whitehall by studying fatigue among gunners and pilots in his Cambridge laboratory and advising the military on aptitude testing.[66]

Reflecting on his assignment for the Colonial Office, Bartlett mused that the time had come to replace the ancient idea of the philosopher king with the "psychological governor." "Every problem of government," he argued, "is at bottom a problem of the control of organized group behavior." Reflecting the magnitude of the policy shift from indirect rule to development, Bartlett now defined empire as a project of overt social engineering in which "one group tries to control and direct the behavior of another," with the aim of reproducing "the kind of behavior . . . already well established in the governing group." He stressed that achieving this objective would require a new commitment to the science of mind, proposing that recruits to the colonial service receive training in psychology besides the usual courses in law, language, and anthropology.[67]

It is striking that Bartlett's faith in this updated version of the civilizing mission did not diminish his calls for cultural sensitivity in imperial rule. Echoing his mentor, W. H. R. Rivers, Bartlett believed that the young district officer "imbued with the superiority of his own culture" went astray when he tried to "turn the little native into the nearest possible copy of the bright young European." Unlike Rivers, though, Bartlett saw relativism as a means to an end rather than as an end in itself. He argued that British officials needed to distinguish the "hard" elements of indigenous culture, the bedrock foundation of identity, from the "soft" beliefs and customs that might be changed through intervention. "If change is first sought at the former," Bartlett warned, "it will provoke resistance and very likely open discord, while the latter are yielding, and it is from them that reformation will spread."[68] He cited the example of Swaziland, where British policies aimed at combating overstocking and disease among livestock collided with entrenched traditions of pastoralism. Because cattle signified wealth and status, their African owners amassed as many as they could. Appeals to preserve the quality of the stock by limiting the quantity, meanwhile, went nowhere. According to Bartlett, the Swazi only began to cooperate when the British announced that they would shoot all the cattle that eluded inspection, communicating an alien concept of livestock management through a familiar idea of wealth in numbers. "What made the regulation effective was not the force," he concluded, "but a definite change of group attitude. . . . Slowly there is growing up within that native group a glimmer of an appreciation of quality as distinct from quantity of beasts." By acknowledging the "hard" symbolic power of large herds rather than attempting to impose scientific management from the outset, the British made the Swazi more receptive to their way of thinking in the end—or so Bartlett believed.[69]

How, then, could British administrators hope to disentangle the hard and the soft in the cultures under their authority? Bartlett thought that the usual ethnographic practices of fieldwork should be supplemented with new techniques for surveying attitudes: "tests, inventories, opinion scales and ratings, polls, questionnaires, 'mass observations,' organized interviews."[70] He argued that aptitude tests used during the war had a special part to play: mapping the "distribution of abilities" in each culture and so helping to identify which kinds of industrial production were likely to flourish there. Given the endless variety of skills required by "our mechanical kind of civilization," measuring aptitudes could guide the deployment of resources across the empire. Bartlett proposed testing for every conceivable kind of ability: "for heavy, medium and light muscular work involving simple but accurate co-ordinated response of related muscle groups; for skills involving a high order of accuracy of observation with long intermittent periods of monotony; for operations of code sending and receiving; and for a good many other psycho-physical skills up to the complexity of piloting a modern aircraft." The four psychologists assembled by the Colonial Office under Bartlett's direction agreed that a network of "experimental research teams" should be deployed throughout the empire to begin collecting this data in a systematic way. One proposed using intelligence, aptitude, and personality tests to guide schoolchildren into the careers that would best suit their talents, while another suggested dispatching industrial psychologists to boost productivity in plantations and mines.[71]

When a permanent organization charged with distributing government funds, the Colonial Social Science Research Council (CSSRC), came into being in 1944, social anthropologists led by E. E. Evans-Pritchard took a dominant role.[72] Yet the science of mind also received significant support: more than £25,000, or roughly £500,000 today, in the first five years of its existence. The only psychologist in the group, University of Edinburgh professor Godfrey Thomson, was well suited to advancing the psychometric agenda. A fervent believer in meritocracy, he had himself won scholarships to high school and university by competitive examination. His Moray House tests became a mainstay of the eleven-plus system (so called because the scores on mental tests taken at age eleven determined whether students would attend selective grammar schools or less prestigious "secondary moderns").[73] Thomson also trained a series of Indian psychologists at Edinburgh between the wars, suggesting after independence in 1947 that their expertise could help to steer young Indians into the positions "most needed by the nation." Thomson saw Macdonald's wartime research as "extremely promising" and imagined a global program growing out of it: classifying the occupational skills of demobilized soldiers in East Africa, measuring intelligence and aptitude in the West Indies, and studying labor efficiency from the Copperbelt of Northern Rhodesia to the cocoa plantations of the Gold Coast.[74]

The CSSRC played an important part in consolidating the gains of military psychometrics, helping to make mental tests an ever more ubiquitous technology across the postwar British world. But the agenda outlined by Bartlett and Thomson flourished in part because other networks of empire were operating along with those of the Colonial Office. The armed forces remained important, of course, although the methods used to select non-British soldiers varied widely from place to place after 1945. In East Africa, the most sophisticated test given to recruits in the King's African Rifles was still a conversation with a British officer. In West Africa, by contrast, the British Army commissioned mental tests from researchers at the University College of the Gold Coast in the early 1950s to select African technical specialists and NCOs. As the independence of the West African colonies approached a few years later, the psychometric apparatus of officer selection—including leaderless group tests—was applied to African soldiers for the first time.[75] Indigenous recruits to the British Army in Malaya were required to take a series of aptitude tests for the first time after the war. So were Papuans and New Guineans recruited to the Pacific Islands Regiment of the Australian Army. British Army researchers even traveled to the mountainous reaches of Nepal in the late 1950s to try out aptitude tests with the fabled Gurkha population—perhaps the final redoubt of the "martial races" theory.[76]

Industrial capitalism represented another powerful force for the diffusion of psychometric expertise. Experts at the National Institute for Personnel Research (NIPR), founded in Johannesburg in 1946, pioneered the use of aptitude testing on a wide scale in African industry. NIPR grew out of a psychometric program in the wartime South African Air Force but shifted subsequently to the selection and promotion of black miners, drawing funding from the giant mining companies of the Witwatersrand as well as the South African state. With a staff of roughly fifty people constructing, validating, and publishing tests, NIPR grew into the biggest organization of its kind on the continent.[77] Many of its initiatives— including the transformation of the British Army's officer selection boards into assessments of so-called "boss boys" or midlevel managers in the mines—were quickly replicated by employers beyond the Rand. Even the experts at the National Institute of Industrial Psychology in London turned to NIPR in the late 1950s when Royal Dutch Shell asked for help selecting engineers in West Africa.[78] By 1960, African candidates for supervisory positions in Kenyan oil fields, Northern Rhodesian copper mines, and Nigerian government offices all had to navigate the obstacle course of the leaderless group test (sometimes called an "initiative test" or a "social interaction test"). Firms such as Shell and British Petroleum also used the Progressive Matrices and the Thematic Apperception Test to evaluate managerial prospects.[79] At the same time, form boards, cube puzzles, and other mechanical aptitude tests proliferated as the mechanisms of selection for entry-level jobs and trade schools across the continent.[80]

This kind of mental measurement has often been seen as a means of degrading African workers into narrowly skilled proletarians, reinforcing the color bar that kept better-paying jobs in European hands.[81] The reality is more complicated. Despite its reliance on support from mining interests and the apartheid state, NIPR psychologists often challenged assumptions of African inferiority. The director, Simon Biesheuvel, made his reputation in the early 1940s by criticizing interracial comparisons of intelligence based on mental testing. "In apparently unique features of African behavior, at first seen as intrinsic to African cultures or races," he argued, "there may be detected parallels with the behavior of other groups . . . which constitute general human responses to environmental circumstances." Biesheuvel believed that Africans performed less well than whites in managerial jobs but held that differences in ability would diminish if the state provided "better feeding, housing, and education for the majority of Africans."[82] His staff, which included Africans as well as whites, challenged Rand tradition by stressing work experience rather than ethnic identity as the essential qualification for mining positions. When it came to turnover and absenteeism, one expert concluded, "the black industrial worker in the Republic does not differ very strikingly from . . . Australian, British, or American operatives." Most controversially of all, NIPR experts criticized apartheid as a drain on productivity, arguing that it installed mediocre whites in important positions and weighed heavily on the morale of black workers. Longstanding tensions finally broke into the open in the early 1960s, when Biesheuvel and most of his acolytes left NIPR to work in the private sector.[83]

The drive for efficiency, in other words, could open the way to arguments against racial ideology. This was true even in the most unexpected places—including Mau Mau-era Kenya, where the British government established an Aptitude Testing Unit (ATU) at the height of the counterinsurgency in 1954 to classify imprisoned suspects for industrial training. Only 509 detainees were tested before the British simply diverted them all into forced labor on construction projects: psychometrics was another aspect of "rehabilitation" policy that failed to materialize as punitive aims took precedence.[84] But ATU director J. H. Vant, a prison administrator who had no background in psychology or statistics besides a six-week training course with NIPR in Johannesburg, mounted an energetic effort to find a new *raison d'être* for his fiefdom. He signed up a clientele of private firms and government offices interested in aptitude testing of African workers: Shell, Unilever, the East African Tobacco Company, the Bata Shoe Company, the Kenya Bus Services Company, and the education, labor, medical, and police departments of the colonial government. By the early 1960s, ATU was testing more than six thousand job applicants—including seven hundred candidates for skilled or semi-skilled positions—and five thousand trade school applicants annually.[85] The prospect of aiding economic modernization through psychometrics attracted a grant from the Ford Foundation in New York, which provided $93,000 (approximately $700,000 today) to bolster ATU's budget from 1959 to 1963. "In Africa," a foundation officer argued, the "proper identification of talented individuals is a major requirement of development." Appealing to powerful interests on the continent and overseas alike, meritocracy seemed to be good for business in postwar Africa.[86]

Buoyed by client fees, philanthropic support, and continued government funding, the ATU operated on an impressive scale. At its height, the staff consisted of Vant, two other testing officers, three African testing assistants, two European clerks, a receptionist, an orderly, and a driver. Its offices on the grounds of Nairobi's Wilson Airport housed a testing hall that could accommodate fifty-six subjects at a time. A custom-designed "mobile testing centre"—a van equipped with desks, fluorescent lights, and

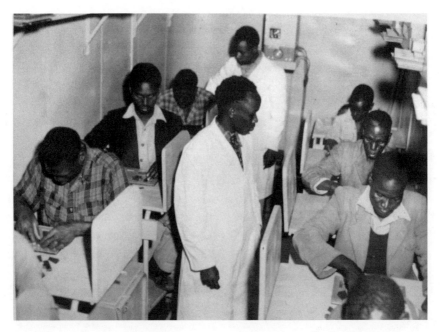

Aptitude Testing Unit, Nairobi, circa 1960. (Image reproduced courtesy of National Archives of Kenya, Nairobi.)

a film projector for demonstration purposes—traveled to locations outside the capital. For managerial candidates, an adapted version of the officer selection board promised to identify "energy, drive, staying power . . . mental alertness . . . leadership . . . personality make-up." For artisans and technicians, ATU used a combination of object-based and pencil-and-paper tests, and it measured the scores against a master chart of psychological attributes required for success in ten different trades. Based on a survey of industrial supervisors and trade school inspectors, the chart ranked thirty-eight different attributes—including hand–eye coordination, fatigue resistance, memory, and emotional stability—on a one hundred-point scale.[87]

The experts of the ATU, like their counterparts at NIPR, contrasted racial ideology with economic rationality. As they recommended Africans for employment as mechanics, drivers, clerks, telephone operators, air traffic controllers, prison wardens, engineers, and civil servants, they also challenged the settler orthodoxy that portrayed indigenous labor as hopelessly inefficient. In the words of an ATU pamphlet for prospective clients, "the Unit's experience, when working for commercial and industrial

Aptitude Testing Unit, Nairobi, circa 1960. African job-seekers participate in a leader-ship test of the kind used to select officers for promotion in the British Army and Indian Army. (Image reproduced courtesy of National Archives of Kenya, Nairobi.)

concerns in East Africa, shows that Africanization does not mean a low-ering of standards." Underlining the failures of imperial rule, ATU staffers claimed that their methods had special relevance in Africa because "a man's education, experience, and industrial advancement [here] have been determined more by limited opportunity than by basic ability." Scientific techniques were required to overcome injustice, they argued, because ordinary credentials were inevitably tainted by the racism of the society that produced them.[88]

If the bottom-line interests of productivity helped to make these argu-ments possible, however, it also constrained them by subordinating exper-tise to the needs of established institutions. Ultimately, patronage-dependent mental testers had to justify their usefulness to industries and govern-ments, and they could not force clients to follow their recommendations. One of the most vocal advocates for aptitude testing in African industry, industrial psychologist C. H. Northcott, collided with this reality when he led a CSSRC research team to study labor efficiency on the Kenya-Uganda

Railway in 1947–1949. A colleague of Alan Macdonald at Rowntree's factory in York, Northcott spent weeks interviewing workers on the ground with the self-proclaimed intent of replicating the Mass Observation Project in Britain. His conclusions were not flattering to the British settler class. Taking issue with the "residents of Kenya" who "generalized" about irresponsible and inefficient Africans, Northcott reported that most of the railway mechanics he saw "worked continuously and well, manifested initiative, did work of good quality, and took pride in it." Where African workers did appear less productive, Northcott placed blame squarely on the "European administrators, business executives, and foremen who control them." Citing the lack of psychometric selection in hiring, the weakness of supervision and training, and above all the meagerness of wages, Northcott argued that Africans could work as effectively as anyone else if only they had competent managers and decent pay.[89]

Far from spurring the railway to overhaul its practices, however, Northcott's field experiment in industrial psychology provoked a polarizing debate about African labor. The railway's general manager pressured him to tone down the criticism before publication while striking an old-fashioned note of managerial authoritarianism, warning that "African political agitators" might exploit the report to provoke "a good deal of unrest." He also rejected the validity of universal models of economic behavior as far as his employees were concerned. "I am afraid that none of us, even those with long experience, knows very much about the African mind," he remarked. Northcott disagreed. Denied opportunities for promotion, treated disrespectfully by supervisors, and compensated at a level inadequate "to meet the needs of the African and his family," black employees were demoralized, malnourished, and prone to turnover and dissension. These were all predictable consequences, he argued, of a labor policy that prized racial hierarchy over meritocracy.[90]

The CSSRC forced Northcott to remove the most inflammatory language from the published version of the report, although it remained critical enough to provoke a fierce exchange in the House of Commons. The rhetorical charge was led by Labour MP John Hynd, a former railway worker, who pressed the government to act on the problems Northcott exposed: "grave discontent among African workers as a result of continued colour discrimination, grievances concerning alienation of land, and lack of opportunities for advancement." Another Labourite took aim at the pernicious role of stereotypes in African industry, blasting "those few remaining apologists for colour discrimination and the colour bar who talk about the inherent 'laziness,' 'shiftlessness,' and 'irresponsibility' of the Negro."[91] On the other side of the aisle, however, the Northcott report left conservatives unmoved. One Tory MP castigated the railway's critics for "belittling the work done by private enterprise in developing the resources of the Colonial Empire." The *Economist* entered the fray with an affirmation of settler folk wisdom, insisting that higher wages failed to improve productivity because Africans simply worked fewer hours as a result. While the combination of moral outrage and expert knowledge commanded by Northcott and his allies could mobilize partisans, few minds were changed in the end.[92]

The limits of expertise in this debate reflected a larger truth: the psychometric movement fell short of its most ambitious goals in postwar Africa. Even within the walls of Government House in Nairobi—home to one of the most elaborate psychometric programs in the empire—the egalitarian rhetoric of ATU staffers failed to win many adherents. Most officials "considered that the tests applied demanded too high a performance in relation to local products," meaning African workers.[93] When employers did accept the validity of aptitude testing, this often rationalized the competition for jobs already open to Africans rather than widening the field of opportunity. At a time when political pressure to dismantle color bars in employment was increasing—albeit unevenly—across the continent, it is doubtful whether test scores alone ever persuaded a manager to hire an African instead of a European. The Ashanti Goldfields Corporation in newly independent Ghana embarked on a testing initiative in the late 1950s only after an Africanization drive yielded "a class of men" deemed "very low" in quality.[94] In some of the most heavily industrialized areas, like the Copperbelt of Northern Rhodesia, elaborate tests coexisted for years with a rigid color bar. When psychometric experts failed to convert their clients to a more enlightened perspective, they risked lending their legitimacy to discriminatory practices by adorning them with a meritocratic façade. It is no surprise that some British expatriates invoked the same language of meritocracy—hiring the "right man for the job" regardless of race—to oppose Africanization. Efficiency made a frail vehicle for idealistic aims precisely because it was so susceptible to co-option.[95]

For most British officials after the war, updating the machinery of selection was less a project of social reform than a bureaucratic imperative.

The number of indigenous applicants for coveted positions in the civil service and for places in secondary schools and universities far exceeded the number of openings after 1945; the newly established technical schools and vocational training programs likewise attracted many more applicants than they could accommodate.[96] British officials from Accra to Freetown to Dar es Salaam told the CSSRC that they wanted to use wartime research in psychometrics for government hiring and school admissions. They complained about the "very great amount of time and labor" required to sort through applications, the "low standard of efficiency" among those chosen on the basis of interviews and academic credentials, and the "heavy excess costs" imposed by "wasteful use" of human resources.[97] Perhaps, too, they recognized that casting social mobility as a function of individual aptitude rather than imperial policy had political advantages. Administrators feared that the demobilization of hundreds of thousands of African soldiers would fuel discontent about the persistent lack of opportunities under British rule.[98]

When the CSSRC sent a researcher named Geoffrey Tooth to West Africa in 1947 to study the causes of mental illness and juvenile delinquency, British officials on the ground urged him to shift his attention to aptitude testing instead. "Belief in the infallibility of tests," Tooth reported, "is widespread."[99] Like other psychometric experts, Tooth instinctively gravitated against racial hierarchies. A graduate of Rugby School and St. John's College, Cambridge, who trained as a psychiatrist before serving with the Royal Naval Volunteer Reserve during the war, he listened with disgust as British expatriates in Nigeria insisted on the intellectual inferiority of Africans. Those "neurotic attitudes," Tooth argued, were a symptom of self-imposed segregation. "The few Europeans I met, who had taken the trouble to get to know the Africans, spoke highly of them and clearly had no difficulty in working with them and for them." Racial isolation, on the other hand, encouraged a retreat into noxious stereotypes—"more a defensive rationalization for their failure to make a satisfactory contact with the African than a serious judgment of African character." Despite encouragement from administrators in West Africa and London, he worried that research in the human sciences risked offending local prejudices.[100]

In other ways, too, Tooth echoed the rhetoric of earlier imperial researchers. Like a good public school graduate, he saw mental ability and moral fiber as intertwined: "calmness, indistractibility, and persistence to the point of exhaustion are just as necessary in the examination hall as in the playing field." Anyone who endured "an exam covering a number of subjects and lasting several days," he argued, had passed "a fairly exacting test of character." Even as he placed faith in the value of tests, however, Tooth worried about their overuse by non-experts. "The assessment of one human being by another" was "a chancy business," he observed, and the results were "not always wisely used." While his research in the Gold Coast in 1950–1952 suggested that Moray House intelligence tests could "improve the quality of the Secondary School intake," he cautioned that this bottom-line conclusion obscured a significant number of failed predictions. Some students performed well on the intelligence test but failed the final certificate exam, while an even larger number who did poorly on the intelligence test managed to clear this hurdle. Fixing a rigid pass mark based on psychometric scores, Tooth suggested, would be like treating "Old Moore's Almanac" as an "infallible machine." He told the CSSRC that "there is probably no branch of science in which numerical symbols carry more weight with less justification."[101]

Few officials heeded Tooth's warnings about the fallibility of aptitude testing. Bureaucrats in the Gold Coast began using the Progressive Matrices to hire African workers in hospitals and asylums as soon as they could get their hands on the test booklets.[102] The Education Department official in charge of training new teachers in the colony, meanwhile, encouraged his pupils to master psychometric techniques for classroom use.[103] By the end of the 1950s, officials in Nigeria, Southern Rhodesia, and Tanganyika were using intelligence tests to determine entry to some secondary schools; their counterparts in Northern Rhodesia did so in a uniform way across the colony.[104] All of these experiments hewed closely to metropolitan models, taking the puzzle-like quality of the Moray House tests as a template. This question, for instance, appeared on the entrance exam in eastern Nigeria in the late 1950s:

> Tom, Dick and Harry are three men, one of whom is a doctor, one lawyer, and one an engineer. The doctor is the tallest. Tom is taller than Harry. Harry had a fight with the engineer. Dick is receiving treatment from the doctor. Give the names of (a) the lawyer, (b) the engineer, and (c) the doctor.

Since the vast majority of test-takers could answer that one, it served merely to "show up the ineffective candidates," as one official put it. More difficult questions, by contrast, helped to "sort out the top candidates from the rest":

> The series of letters in (a) and the series of figures in (b) are parts of a sequence. Add the next set of letters in (a) and figures in (b) to continue the sequence in each case.
>
> (a) PMH, QMG, RMF
> (b) 604, 703, 802

Nonverbal tests also found favor with many British administrators. These too involved find-the-pattern questions—but in the form of abstract images (shapes, arrows, squiggly lines) or everyday images "common to most countries with hot climates" (lions, umbrellas, hand saws).[105]

Some officials professed idealistic motives for the adoption of these new methods. Portraying psychometrics as a force for social justice, they wanted to neutralize the effects of "political pressure," "the ability to pay school fees," and other inequities of background and upbringing in determining which students advanced to the all-important secondary level. In contrast to the British system, a bureaucrat in Nigeria observed, talented students who underperformed on entrance exams in Africa were not merely placed in a less-than-ideal school but prevented from continuing their education altogether. The dire shortage of school places heightened the moral imperative to select the very best.[106]

More prosaic aims, however, usually fueled the pursuit of psychometrics. A 1964 study in Southern Rhodesia concluded that incorporating aptitude tests into the selection process for African secondary schools could reduce the failure rate among admitted students by five percent, saving the colony £40,000 (more than £500,000 today) annually.[107] Then too, psychometrics had the virtue of making decisions about school admissions appear technical and impersonal. Many officials welcomed parallels to the eleven-plus regime in Britain because it allowed them to justify the inadequate supply of school places by pointing to innate variations in mental ability. Mirroring the language, the numbers, and even the bell curves used by educators at home, administrators in West Africa and East Africa alike estimated that no more than a third of the African population had the capacity to benefit from literary and scientific studies. The majority, they argued, should receive "a less academic type of education" aimed at "the practical problems of living." Where the most idealistic advocates of the eleven-plus model envisioned a ladder extended to gifted children of humble background, most imperial bureaucrats preferred the image of the ceiling, suggesting that barriers to advancement were imposed by limits of intellect rather than resources.[108]

In Africa, as in Britain, the discretion granted to local officials on education policy resulted in a patchwork of selection regimes. In the settler-dominated society of Southern Rhodesia—where aptitude tests governed admissions to segregated schools for white and mixed-race students but not for Africans—racial ideology dictated the uneven application of psychometrics.[109] In the Eastern Province of Nigeria, a lack of technical training contributed to the halfhearted and inconsistent use of aptitude testing. As one administrator commented, "we were not sure what it did test—it was a sort of Christmas Day after-lunch quiz from [the humor magazine] *Lilliput!*" That experiment ended after just a few years; it was only after independence, in the mid-1960s, that aptitude questions reappeared on Common Entrance Examinations across Nigeria. In Ghana, too, Common Entrance Examinations did not include aptitude questions until 1964, and the results did not actually count toward the final score until 1970. Kenya only introduced aptitude testing for secondary school admissions in 1971.[110]

Many postcolonial states in Africa, then, only fully embraced psychometric selection when the British state was moving in the opposite direction, dismantling the eleven-plus regime to make way for "comprehensive schools" open to all.[111] An influx of American experts in the 1960s encouraged the use of aptitude tests to manage an ever-expanding population of students and deemphasize the Oxbridge-style essays that often remained the gateway to advancement.[112] But the postcolonial boom in psychometrics represented continuity as well as change from the imperial era. The British had long supported local research centers—the Institute of Education at the University College of the Gold Coast in Legon, the Rhodes-Livingstone Institute in Livingstone, Northern Rhodesia, the Institute of Education and the East African Institute of Social Research in Makerere, Uganda— which designated, validated, and standardized aptitude tests. Along with migratory experts like Geoffrey Tooth, these institutions generated a stockpile of proven techniques and ready-to-use norms for later adoption by independent states.[113] In some cases, too, British psychologists continued to advise African governments on aptitude testing after independence.[114] In

Ghana and Kenya alike, researchers in the 1970s found that aptitude tests favored the children of the same prosperous urban Anglophone families who enjoyed disproportionate access to the finest schools under British rule.[115]

Although Africa emerged as the central arena for postwar experiments with aptitude testing, the same pattern of frustrated idealism defined psychometric initiatives elsewhere in the empire. A pair of CSSRC experts in the West Indies in the late 1940s argued that poor performance on mental tests imported from Britain reflected a failure to adapt the instruments of measurement rather than low intelligence in the population being measured. Questioning the "so-called 'backwardness' of Colonial peoples," Deans Peggs of the Bahamas argued that low scores had environmental causes: "lack of education, environment, physical welfare." Echoing the interwar consensus against racial comparisons, Benjamin Bedell of Trinidad insisted that testing should reveal "what can best be done with a particular brain" and not "whether a particular race had a better or worse brain than the English." Both men agreed that only tests tailored to cultural contexts could provide a fair measure of minds.[116] In 1948, Peggs persuaded imperial officials in Jamaica to supplement entrance exams in English and math with an aptitude test he designed; it featured images like palm trees and baseballs while excluding unfamiliar Anglicisms as far as possible. The Jamaican state continued using the test until it became too widely known, then switched to Godfrey Thomson's Moray House tests in 1957.[117] When British psychologist Philip Vernon visited Jamaica as a government consultant in 1962, however, he concluded that the introduction of aptitude testing had done little to promote mobility or equality. "We must not expect to increase the proportion of well-educated people simply by finding tests which eliminate differences of background," Vernon argued. "There are no such tests." Because mental ability depended on "intellectual stimulation" and "emotional atmosphere" in "early childhood," the persistence of poverty and dysfunction in Jamaica made social progress through psychometrics an unlikely prospect.[118] Here, as elsewhere, aptitude tests forged in a spirit of meritocratic optimism ended up as tools of bureaucratic convenience—and as props, arguably, of the status quo.

Networks forged by empire—the War Office, oil and mining firms, the CSSRC—made the measurement of aptitude a global commonplace. The culture of meritocracy outgrew its Victorian roots by acquiring the armor of scientific authority and securing a place in blueprints for modernization.

Leaderless group tests, the Thematic Apperception Test, and the Progressive Matrices test, among others, ended up selecting workers and students around the world as a result. But the globalization of the psychometric movement came at a cost: the subordination of fairness and opportunity to productivity and efficiency as paramount values.

As imperial authorities after the war awakened to the science of mind as a useful form of knowledge, aptitude testing was only one of the techniques that promised technical solutions to political problems. How did British officials attempt to turn other kinds of psychological expertise against the growing threat posed by anticolonial movements? In fighting the battles of decolonization, they would draw not only on mental measurement but also on the language of psychoanalysis, behaviorism, and social psychology.

EXPERTS

CHAPTER FIVE

The Truth about Hearts and Minds

Development and Counterinsurgency in the Postwar Empire

W HEN COMMUNIST CHINESE rebels were captured by British forces during the postwar counterinsurgency in Malaya, they could expect sharp questions, grim conditions, and perhaps physical abuse. A few fighters captured in the early 1950s, however, also encountered something else: a questionnaire designed to probe the psychological roots of insurgency. On a scale of one to five, they registered their agreement with various statements: about their home lives ("I feel ashamed of the house I am living in"), their social habits ("I prefer to be alone, I do not wish to associate with others"), their attitudes toward self-help ("A person should depend on his own efforts to improve his livelihood"), and their sense of security ("I consider it is dangerous to talk about politics in public places"). Other questions covered job satisfaction, gambling habits, and emotional drives, including "fear" and "the need to belong to groups."[1]

The design of the study—carried out by British Army researchers with advice from American social scientists—was ambitious. For every individual in a sample of 100 "Surrendered Enemy Personnel," researchers would find a control subject in the civilian population who was born in the same place, belonged to the same ethnic group, worked on the same rubber estate, and had the same kind of job but did *not* join the Communist insurgency. The idea, of course, was to identify the subtle differences of outlook and temperament that drove some Chinese Malayans to take up arms and others to remain loyal. Although it proved difficult to meet those standards in practice—the total sample size in the end was only sixty-three—the results proved interesting. Among the insurgents, toleration of grim housing conditions and a propensity for gambling suggested that personalities able to bear material hardship and take risks were more likely to rebel. Although that finding had few obvious strategic implications, the results also indicated that a government crackdown on nonviolent Communist activism was one factor driving workers to insurgency. As one British Army psychologist concluded, branding Communists as illegitimate produced "feelings of guilt" and encouraged them to seek validation underground.[2]

Belying the familiar theme of postwar decline, the "British school" of counterinsurgency emerged as a robust global export. From America's war in Vietnam to its second war in Iraq, strategists on both sides of the Atlantic heralded British policy in the Malayan Emergency as a model to be emulated.[3] The promise of a "clean" counterinsurgency—what the British high commissioner in Malaya, General Gerald Templer, famously termed the battle for "the hearts and minds of the people"—hinged on the idea that rebellion could be defeated by persuasion as well as force. In Malaya, propaganda aimed at insurgents stressed the hopelessness of their cause and the imperative of surrender; for the rest of the colonized population, so-called information campaigns emphasized the rapacity of the rebels and the benevolence of British rule.[4] As Templer's lieutenants told journalists at the time, the "shooting war" amounted to a mere twenty-five percent of the counterinsurgency effort, while attempts to change "the attitude of people"—including material inducements, welfare services, and political reforms as well as propaganda—represented seventy-five percent.[5] Yet critics have since pointed out that even the most sophisticated methods of persuasion never displaced the violence of British counterinsurgency. Whether in Malaya or subsequent conflicts in Kenya, Cyprus, and elsewhere, search missions and collective punishments swept up innocent civilians; ordinary people were forcibly settled into armed villages and grim detention camps; draconian restrictions on food aimed at starving out the insurgents. Perhaps the rhetoric of "hearts and minds" was simply a convenient fiction—a "public relations device," as one historian has put it, that helped to legitimize indiscriminate brutality in the eyes of the world.[6]

The use of questionnaires with captured insurgents, and other experiments like it, hints at a more complicated reality. "Hearts and minds" was no empty slogan. Neither was "psychological warfare" (a neologism that could signify propaganda aimed at insurgents rather than non-combatants but which contemporaries often used interchangeably with "hearts and minds").[7] Both phrases suggest how far the promise of defeating anticolonial resistance through psychological knowledge captured imaginations across the postwar empire. When British officials set out to secure their African, Middle Eastern, and West Indian colonies after the Partition of India in 1947, the science of mind reinforced their belief that nationalism reflected emotional volatility rather than rational self-interest. In peacetime, development planners supplemented the material improvements of schools, clinics, and roads with attitude surveys and initiatives in emotional training. In counterinsurgency campaigns, military leaders put theories of mind to work in everything from propaganda posters to interrogation techniques. In war and peace alike, the imperial state worked to thwart rebellion in part by understanding motives, charting the unconscious origins of behavior, and ultimately changing minds. Like the French tactics known as *action psychologique* in Algeria and Indochina, British efforts to mobilize psychology did not simply coexist with coercion but rationalized and justified it.[8]

Is the use of psychology in the postwar empire, then, just another episode in the militarization of the human sciences—a case of experts taking their intellectual cues from the interests of the state? In some ways, British human scientists and government officials did grow closer together in this period. Fears about the volatility of nationalism, dramatized by the recent history of European fascism, made even left-leaning intellectuals uneasy about anticolonial movements overseas. Then, too, the refurbished image of the postwar state—redistributing resources through welfare programs at home and delivering technical aid through the British Commonwealth overseas—enlisted experts in seemingly benevolent projects of government authority.[9] But these shifts did not eliminate tensions from the relationship between researchers and rulers. Confronted with the realities of coercion, many psychologists raised ethical and practical objections to the instrumentalization of their expertise, even as administrators and soldiers continued to draw on the science of mind to advance their own aims. The postwar history of imperial psychology is less a morality play about the corruption of intellectuals than a cautionary tale about the state's selective use of expert knowledge.

¶ IN THE UNITED STATES, a massive infusion of government funding enlisted human scientists in a central front of the Cold War: combating the spread of Communism in the so-called Third World. They constructed models for the transmission of information in preliterate societies, the behavior of political elites, and the causes of insurgency; they compiled handbooks on the customs and mores that soldiers would have to navigate during an invasion. Empirical studies considered the relationship between child-rearing practices and personality, the reception of propaganda, and the motivations of enemy soldiers, while real-world experiments from Peru to Vietnam dramatized the process of controlled social change.[10] Although Cold War politics did not determine everything that happened in the postwar human sciences, the modernization theory that provided a framework for research in many different fields—by eliding cultural particularity into a universal vision of progress—was well matched to a moment when the potential field for American intervention encompassed almost every country in the world.[11]

A "military-intellectual complex" on this scale was not replicated in Britain.[12] Although anticolonial nationalism, like Communism, presented a diffuse global threat, funding levels for the CSSRC did not approach the resources commanded by, say, the U.S. Operations Research Office. Even as the influence and prestige of other kinds of technical knowledge grew, skepticism about the utility of the human sciences lingered in the British bureaucracy.[13] A Foreign Office mandarin in 1949 described wartime research on the German and Japanese "national characters" as a "luxury" of "doubtful value." The newfangled propaganda techniques known as psychological warfare drew special scorn in Whitehall. Even at the height of counterinsurgency conflicts in the 1950s, one official complained that "phoney people" were trying to "build themselves an empire" in the bureaucracy by laying claim to an "esoteric branch of the military art." Another sneered at "High Priests who claim to be the experts in a cult."[14]

But these kinds of protests also suggest that psychology was gaining influence in some quarters despite the skepticism. In contrast to the United States, where officials concentrated on supporting academic research through government contracts, the equivalent nexus in Britain—fellowships offered by the CSSRC—was only one measure of the relationship between the human sciences and empire. The rapid postwar expansion of the British university system created new career opportunities for psychologists, anthropologists, sociologists, and other researchers who studied the colonies or spent time there.[15] At the same time, a growing number of specialists trained in the human sciences found positions in the corridors of power. This happened in London: a principal administrator in the Colonial Office from 1949, Edith Mercer, was a protégé of Charles Myers at the National Institute of Industrial Psychology who worked on personnel selection in Britain, Egypt, and India during the war. It also happened overseas: the director of social welfare in postwar Malaya, Charles Rawson, studied psychology and wrote a dissertation on "the phenomenon of aggressiveness" at the LSE in the early 1930s. But the armed forces remained perhaps the leading imperial institution for the science of mind. The Army Operational Research Group in the 1950s had a staff of ten psychologists based at West Byfleet, Surrey, who periodically traveled to locations across the empire. In short, the entanglement of expertise and the state was not only reflected in funding for academic research, but also in the production and circulation of knowledge outside disciplinary spaces.[16]

If the postwar mobilization of the human sciences comes into sharper focus beyond the boundaries of the academy, so too does it emerge more clearly beyond the boundaries of the nation-state. The existence of a "British academic community" with outposts in Australasia, South Africa, and Canada extended to imperial research centers like the Rhodes-Livingstone Institute in Northern Rhodesia and the East African Institute of Social Research in Uganda, which supported at least five human scientists using attitude questionnaires and projective tests in the decade after 1945.[17] Then too, the psychological study of colonized populations developed as an Anglo-American dialogue. Itinerant experts like Geoffrey Gorer, who penned "national character" studies for various Defense Department agencies, and Kenneth Yarnold, a British Army psychologist who settled in America as a Pentagon consultant in 1949, were among those who found a receptive audience in Washington.[18] Belying the conventional wisdom that mind science in Britain lagged far behind the field in America, U.S. officials paid surprisingly close attention to British expertise. The Office of Naval Research in the 1950s and 1960s commissioned American researchers to visit psychology departments and psychiatric clinics in Britain with the aim of monitoring new directions in the field.[19] Pentagon consultants ransacked writings by British imperial veterans—Lord Cromer on Egypt, Lawrence Durrell and John Harding on Cyprus, Verrier Elwin and J. H. Hutton on India—when compiling handbooks for soldiers to carry with them during future interventions.[20] American researchers flooded into Britain's African colonies at such a rate, meanwhile, that they outnumbered their British counterparts in the field by the end of the 1950s.[21]

One factor leading at least some British officials to encourage these exchanges was the calculated self-interest of alliance-building. As a Foreign Office report noted in 1955, "the Americans are convinced of the value of psychological warfare. . . . If we did not . . . show ourselves willing to keep in step with [them], then they would go ahead on their own without consulting us further."[22] But a genuine intellectual convergence was taking shape, too. The promise of introducing and managing social change from above, co-opting nationalist and Communist forces in the process, had relevance for late imperial and Cold War agendas alike. Although modernization theory has sometimes been described as an attempt to universalize American history, one of its leading proponents, W. W. Rostow, famously pointed to Britain's Industrial Revolution as the model for the "take-off" into economic growth. British imperial policies aimed at transforming peasants into industrial workers, meanwhile, always rested on an "implicit theory" of modernization.[23] The idea that societies could be transformed by exploiting the interpersonal dynamics in groups grew out of institutions shaped by German-American psychologist Kurt Lewin on both sides of the Atlantic, including the Research Center for Group Dynamics at MIT and the Tavistock Institute of Human Relations in London.[24]

Shedding the fatalistic sensibility, exemplified by Freud's *Civilization and Its Discontents* (1930), that haunted psychology after the First World War, the science of mind after the Second World War had a utopian quality. Explanations of the aggression that caused conflicts played down the significance of innate instincts while emphasizing the ability of schools, governments, families, and other collectivities to reshape minds in predictable ways. The assumption that fascism could be treated like a mental illness pervaded the postwar era: that is why the Nazi leaders tried at Nuremberg were interviewed about their childhoods and tested with Rorschach inkblots, while the "denazification" bureaucracy in occupied Germany used interviews and questionnaires devised by psychoanalysts.[25] One of the most influential sources for molding attitudes through expert intervention—and for the paradox of forcing people to think and feel in autonomous ways—was Lewin's theory of group dynamics. Lewin and his followers tried to show that sensitivity training groups, or "T-groups," could correct racist and authoritarian attitudes by forcing individuals to examine their interactions with other people.[26] These experiments reflected the nascent field of cybernetics in their assumption that leaders and followers influenced each other in a continuous feedback loop rather than a hierarchical pattern of command.[27] Inspired in part by Lewin's work, American efforts to promote democracy overseas increasingly revolved around the idea of "community": social networks forged by egalitarian, face-to-face relationships rather than impersonal technologies of mass society or traditional hierarchies of caste, tribe, and village. The massive development effort launched by the U.S. government and the Ford Foundation in India in the late 1940s characteristically assumed that Western authorities should promote change by building consensus rather than imposing new practices by fiat. Identifying the sentiments, opinions, and "natural leaders" of the indigenous population, and then mobilizing them in the service of reform, was a hallmark of this approach.[28]

British officials were quick to adapt the principles of group dynamics to their own purposes. In 1941, a Colonial Office committee led by Labour activist Arthur Creech Jones had proposed a new education initiative aimed at subjects beyond the reach of formal schooling. The purpose of "mass education," later termed "community development," was to impart the practical skills—literacy, cooking, soil conservation, financial prudence—that enabled full participation in modern society. But its architects came to assume that transferring knowledge was less an end in itself than an instrument for reshaping thought and feeling. As Creech Jones declared after becoming colonial secretary in 1946, the postwar empire required a "revolution of habit and mental capacity," one guided by administrators who could take "the emotional fervour attached to nationalism" and "channel" it "towards constructive courses." This kind of development depended less on the "substance" of technical plans than on the "emotive power" elicited from the community. Because "people will move forward only so far as they have the inward compulsions," he told an audience of officials at Cambridge in 1948, the "fundamental problem" of governing colonized people was "breaking down their resistance and stimulating their desires."[29]

British administrators on the ground did not always welcome these attempts to reinvent their role with therapeutic language. But the postwar expansion of the imperial bureaucracy brought in a new generation of officials who stressed "the psychological aspect" as well as the "physical manifestations of progress."[30] The welfare and development administrators who proliferated after the war approached their work as an experiment in psychological change. Portraying the apathy of the tradition-bound villager as their greatest enemy, they assumed that transforming "an attitude of mind" mattered more than "the building of bridges, latrines, clinics, drains, water supplies."[31] Realizing this objective required an alternative to the traditional model of imperial authority, one that catalyzed emotional responses in the population without exercising power in an overt way. Rather than deliver lectures in the hierarchical setting of a palaver or baraza, development officers prided themselves on a "personal and human approach" that induced people to trust them as "valued friends." In Nigeria, a British administrator warned that sanitary inspectors who criticized too much while visiting villages awakened "deep-seated resentment"; treating people "as equals and not as children" made them more receptive to advice. In Kenya, a welfare officer contrasted the "fear" inspired by the "mighty voice" of provincial commissioners with his own desire for "recognition as [a] guide and friend." The ideal administrator invited people to discuss "their problems, their difficulties and differences, with a view to giving all his assistance to effect a change of heart and attitude." While a veteran of the agricultural service in Uganda found the manipulation of "shame and envy" especially useful—"Have you looked over the hedge and seen how Farmer X is doing?"—he also favored praise rather than blame and suggestion rather than argument. Peasants were much likelier to stick with innovations, he argued, if they could be led to see them as their own ideas.[32]

The training of imperial officials after the war introduced these methods through canonical texts of the American human sciences. At the University of London in the early 1950s, courses on community development assigned James Plant's *Personality and the Cultural Pattern* (1937), John Dollard's *Frustration and Aggression* (1939), Hadley Cantril's *Psychology of Social Movements* (1941), and Kurt Lewin's *Resolving Social Conflicts* (1948), among other works.[33] A key technique of Lewinian psychology in America—the T-groups designed to promote harmony between the races—was paralleled by the systematic self-criticism in which the trainees were instructed. While participating in discussions, they were told to consider not only the practical impact of their decisions but also the impulses that governed their behavior. Did they truly have the best interests of their subjects at heart or merely "seek personal gain, prestige, power"? This sort of enforced introspection—tracing "the ways in which the community interpreted his purpose, his behavior, and reacted to it," as one instructor said—aimed at forging sympathetic bonds between ruler and ruled.[34]

The shelves of the Colonial Office library in London provide another measure of the turn to psychology in postwar imperialism. By midcentury, the collection included Karen Horney's *The Neurotic Personality of Our Time* (1937), a key text of neo-Freudian psychoanalysis; Margaret Mead's *Coming of Age in Samoa* (1928), a classic of the culture and personality school; and Dollard's *Frustration and Aggression* (1939), a pioneering synthesis of psychoanalysis and behaviorism.[35] The Dollard volume, co-authored with his colleagues at Yale University's Institute of Human Relations, might seem especially alien to British sensibilities. By explaining all aggressive behavior as a response to the stimulus of frustration, it resorted to the kind of rigid behaviorist formula that psychologists in Britain traditionally resisted; by implicitly denying the existence of an innate drive for violence, it reflected a "perennial optimism" that some saw as deeply naive and, therefore, characteristically American.[36] Yet the predictability of the frustration-aggression hypothesis, with its implied promise of controlling behavior by manipulating the environment, appealed strongly to the architects of development policy. Leonard Barnes, a Colonial Office adviser who helped to draft a 1948 report on community development, judged that the "intensity of frustration" among educated Africans was to blame for "the passionate and often directionless lashing out of the young nationalist movement." The training instructor at the University of London, Thomas Reginald Batten, cited Dollard to support his claim that Nigerian protests, Ugandan riots, and Kenyan insurgency were all outbursts aimed at "agents of the outside world" who brought promises of material progress but not the means of achieving it. Arthur Lewis, the pioneering development economist and Colonial Office adviser, was among the United Nations's "Group of Experts" who in 1953 warned of "painful adjustments" and "frustrated" emotions in the shift from agriculture to industry.[37]

The influence of American social psychology merged with postwar currents in the British human sciences. An eroding distinction between mind science and social science encouraged the sense that behavior could be modified by intervening in the institutions of everyday life. British texts assigned in Colonial Office training courses, including James Halliday's *Psychosocial Medicine* (1948) and Alex Comfort's *Authority and Delinquency in the Modern State* (1950), touted therapeutic techniques as tools of governance and portrayed even the most intractable problems— crime, war, fascism—as objects of expert management. At a time when British officials worried that any imperial initiative risked triggering popular resistance, the model of group therapy pioneered by Tavistock Clinic psychiatrists during the war suggested that minds could most effectively be changed by building lateral relationships among community members rather than authoritarian relationships between rulers and subjects.[38] This new therapeutic language of minimizing transference and downplaying hierarchy was increasingly echoed by the empire's administrators. One Colonial Office adviser warned that officials overseas, perceived by nationalists as "a main source of their frustration," had to learn to subordinate their own plans to the will of the group. Another simply defined community development as "the psychology of disengagement . . . a gradual freeing of the people from the invisible ties which bind them to [their rulers]."[39]

The strategic renunciation of authority was a recurring theme in development policy after the war. A classic exposition came in the film *Daybreak in Udi,* released by the Colonial Film Unit in 1949, and winner of the Best Documentary Oscar the following year. It shows a British district officer, played by an actual official named E. R. Chadwick, overseeing the construction of a maternity hospital in a village in eastern Nigeria. Although Chadwick, with his khaki shorts, plummy accent, and retinue of subalterns, bears all the outward trappings of imperial rule, the film is careful to portray him as a figure who simply responds to popular demand. By encouraging a pair of African teachers to take the lead and insisting that they first seek the approval of the village elders, Chadwick ostensibly confines himself to a supporting role. But his attention to attitudes and relationships in fact makes him indispensable to the success of the project. Chadwick uses flattery to win the support of an influential woman, stokes a rivalry with the neighboring villages that already had hospitals of their own, and undermines a prominent skeptic with some lighthearted mockery at a public meeting. *Daybreak in Udi* shows how a savvy administrator could deflect opposition by posing as the instrument of collective self-help.

The district officer as non-authoritarian personality. (E. R. Chadwick in *Daybreak in Udi,* 1949, directed by Terry Bishop. A Crown Film Unit producton. British Film Institute.)

The most influential British theorist of community development was Batten, a longtime education officer in Nigeria who helped run the training course at the University of London after 1949. A prolific author of handbooks and manifestos, Batten served as a consultant to the colonial governments of Nigeria, British Guiana, Trinidad, and Jamaica in the 1950s and 1960s. His signature concept, the "non-directive" method, was adopted from the jargon of psychotherapy. As Batten conceded, it was often used with "problem children, problem families, delinquents, alcoholics, and mental health patients" as well as imperial subjects; it confined experts to asking questions, mediating disputes, and pointing out obstacles rather than advocating a point of view.[40] Criticizing the technocratic sensibility of many postwar development projects, he argued that individuals would never "conform to the same blue-print" because everyone had "his own small world of hopes and fears." By encouraging people to translate vague feelings of dissatisfaction into concrete plans for change, non-directive workers helped them to regain a "basic feeling of security." Batten argued that collective participation in development projects had therapeutic value because the motives behind individual behavior, the drive for "status and significance," were irreducibly social.[41]

This uneasy blend of authority and democracy in development planning reflected the fragility of British rule after 1945. Navigating between a rhetorical commitment to eventual self-government and a substantive commitment to retaining control, postwar officials placed conditions on the conferral of political independence. They did so, in part, by casting doubt on the psychological maturity of colonized populations. Nationalist sentiment could not be rewarded with sovereignty, they argued, because it was nothing *but* sentiment, a craving for recognition without a sense of responsibility. The use of psychology by the postwar imperial state drew strength from the belief that nationalism was an irrational, emotional, and potentially dangerous force.[42]

This mistrust of national feeling—a striking departure from the valorization of the nation-state that prevailed, at least in theory, after the First World War—had special resonance in Britain. Against the backdrop of a liberal imperial tradition that portrayed empire as a model of transnational solidarity and even world government, anticolonial movements could appear as atavistic eruptions reminiscent of European fascism. The threat of "some little African Hitler," as political theorist Martin Wight put it, invited Third World analogies to the Frankfurt School's identification of nationalism with psychopathology.[43] After all, even leftist intellectuals who criticized the violence and exploitation of empire in the 1950s and 1960s usually wanted Britain to maintain a dominant role overseas. They praised the British Commonwealth for strengthening cosmopolitan sentiments; Labour

THE TRUTH ABOUT HEARTS AND MINDS

Party thinker John Strachey in 1960 heralded it as "a psychological mechanism for making the British people care about the undeveloped world." Nationalism, by contrast, represented a barrier to material progress because it discouraged postcolonial states from accepting much-needed technical aid. Bertrand Russell mistrusted anticolonial nationalism for this reason; so did the left-leaning planners of the Fabian Colonial Bureau, who likewise worried that the "emotional upsurge" of anticolonial movements could divert energy from the more important business of building roads, schools, and clinics.[44] The assumption that nationalist movements pursued independence in opposition to tangible interests led many thinkers to perceive unconscious forces lurking behind them. Jurist Ivor Jennings labeled Indian nationalism as "not rational in its essence"; psychologist Robert Thouless described Colonel Nasser as a candidate for psychiatric treatment; political scientist William Gutteridge identified "anti-white emotion" as the motive force of West African nationalism; and psychoanalyst Alix Strachey saw "the child's desire to be equal to his elders" as the cause of aggressive behavior in anticolonial and postcolonial leaders.[45]

Other intellectuals, of course, took a more sympathetic view of nationalism against empire. But even sympathizers often filtered their observations through explanatory and diagnostic models that—inevitably if not intentionally—generated useful knowledge for officials who wanted to combat resistance movements. Hewing closely to Dollard's theory, British intelligence adviser Brian Crozier suggested that a chief cause of frustration and therefore aggression among anticolonial rebels was "the sense of inferiority" and the experience of being "humiliated by members of another race." He scrutinized the biographies of rebel leaders for clues about the insults and indignities that provoked them to violence.[46] In collaboration with Dollard's Yale colleague Leonard Doob, a pair of American psychologists working at the CSSRC-supported Institute of Social Research in Uganda found that Africans attending the most "acculturated" schools—those close to cities, staffed by European teachers, and using English as the language of instruction—expressed the greatest hostility toward white people and their indigenous collaborators in response to questionnaires. Those students also reported the most intense interest in politics. Proceeding from the assumption that Western education involved more "training for self-discipline, responsibility, etc.," the researchers concluded that the pressures of individualism were converting Africans to the nationalist cause. As Doob observed, social upheaval bred discontent, and "those bringing changes from the outside"—Western rulers, traders, and missionaries—often served as "targets for aggression."[47]

The imperial arena where British researchers pursued the frustration-aggression hypothesis most enthusiastically after the war was the West Indies. With limited self-rule on the basis of universal suffrage established in Jamaica by 1944, a loosely knit circle of human scientists argued that the island provided an ideal laboratory for studying nationalist politics. University of Liverpool social scientist Thomas Simey set the tone for this research. Sent to Jamaica by the Colonial Office to oversee welfare programs during the Second World War, he perceived everyday life as a cauldron of psychological tension. "There can be no doubt," he claimed, "that the amount of aggressiveness . . . is quite abnormal." Citing Dollard's classic *Caste and Class in a Southern Town* (1938), Simey identified one source of frustration above all: "the social relationships between coloured and white peoples." In a perverse legacy of the slavery years, Simey reasoned, status turned on minute gradations of skin color that made feelings of insecurity and self-consciousness endemic. This hypersensitivity translated into what Simey saw as the shrill, aggrieved tone of nationalist politics in the region. Responding to one Trinidadian politician who criticized the British Empire as a bastion of racism and exploitation, Simey declared that "his mind is a tortured one, caught in the toils of a powerful psychological mechanism which he has little power to control."[48]

After returning to Liverpool in 1945, Simey encouraged other researchers to investigate the pathologies he glimpsed in the West Indies. Another instructor of government social workers in the region (a former researcher in Bartlett's psychology laboratory) published an article tracing the supposedly quarrelsome personality of the middle-class Jamaican back to "feelings of insufficiency and inadequacy."[49] A Scottish missionary who worked with Simey to organize welfare programs through the Presbyterian Church, Lewis Davidson, applied for Colonial Office funding to support an ambitious scheme of mental testing and field research. Invoking Ruth Benedict's concept of the model personality, he argued that the ubiquity of matriarchal households in Jamaica created a unique "cultural pattern," which was marked by "ambivalent feeling," "high suggestibility," and "common hysterical neuroses." Davidson tailored his appeal to the modernizing ethos of the postwar moment: "in order to be developed," he argued, "Jamaica needs not merely the expenditure of considerable sums of money, but a social therapy which will transform family life, develop a culture capable of directing sexual energy, [and] create a new framework for society." But a research team led by Edith Clarke—a Jamaican planter's daughter and social worker who trained as an anthropologist under Malinowski at the LSE and also worked with Simey during the war—had already secured CSSRC funding for a similar project.[50]

Clarke envisioned an expansive social survey of Jamaica framed in the Malinowskian terms of "culture contact." By mapping the interaction of indigenous, African, and British influences, she hinted shrewdly, the study might shed light on the rise of nationalism in Africa. As Clarke assembled a small army of field assistants to collect life histories in four different locations across the island—in the village of Duckenfield alone, the records covered 444 individuals and ran to more than 2,000 pages—Godfrey Thomson suggested the addition of a psychologist to the research team. The appointment fell to Madeline Kerr, then a lecturer in psychology at Bedford College in London who had collaborated with Margaret Mead on a study of national stereotypes during the war.[51] Following Mead's methodological example, Kerr and her assistant, Vera Dantry, administered a battery of projective tests to several hundred Jamaican schoolchildren.[52] They used Rorschach inkblots; a custom-made version of the Thematic Apperception Test in which the students had to describe what was happening in pictures of everyday Jamaican life; and the Lowenfeld mosaic test, invented by British child psychologist Margaret Lowenfeld and championed by Mead for cross-cultural studies, in which students had twenty minutes to arrange a set of colored shapes "in any way you like."[53]

Cutting against the grain of an emerging consensus in the United States, where human scientists issued relativistic warnings against facile comparisons of projective test results, Kerr simply measured the Jamaican scores against European norms.[54] In the Lowenfeld test, she found that Jamaican children in all age groups replicated the patterns of British children who "lacked control of their emotional forces," scattering the tiles across the tray in groups of two and three rather than building symmetrical patterns from the center. Supplementing this observation with her own fieldwork in homes, schools, cinemas, and street corners, Kerr arrived at the neo-Freudian conclusion that a dysfunctional culture was causing mental dysfunction. Life in Jamaica, she argued, was pervaded by unreality: domineering mothers invoked absent fathers, textbooks valorized a distant British culture, and dark-skinned people clung to a myth of white superiority. The Rorschach results, which showed scores for introversion and repression increasing with age, seemed to confirm that the socialization of young Jamaicans into these perverse expectations was stunting their emotional development.[55]

Stressing the impact of high unemployment, Anglocentric schooling, and a pervasive racial hierarchy, Kerr saw Jamaicans as victims of a system they had little role in choosing. Limited opportunity rather than innate pathology figured as the key causal force—and in fact, she attributed the same forms of family dysfunction and mental disorder to the stevedores of Liverpool in a study a few years later.[56] But Kerr's account nonetheless implied a grim outlook for the advent of self-government. In Jamaica, she argued, ambivalent emotions centered on mothers were transferred to authority figures in general, so that "white people" appeared as "benefactors and oppressors" simultaneously: "Mother gives you everything, but she also disciplines you." This dependent personality was prey for "demagogues" like nationalist leader Alexander Bustamante, who made "meaningless speeches" which promised to "take on his shoulders all your troubles." Kerr wondered whether Jamaica's "odd choices of leaders is due to the fact that boys have not experienced male leadership" and warned, ominously, that "dangerous situations would result" if the aggressive impulses of the crowd ever settled on a target.[57]

This attempt to balance criticism of British rule and unease with nationalism exemplified a dilemma for human scientists. Was it possible to study anticolonial movements on psychological terms without delegitimizing them? Some researchers tried to avoid this by explicitly affirming the rationality of African nationalists. In his study of the Gold Coast on the eve of independence, psychologist Gustav Jahoda described the new generation of African leaders as "friendly and easy-going, balanced and tolerant" and criticized the "naïve psychologism that would single out reactions to frustrations and inferiority as *the* efficient cause of political action." Other psychologists labeled imperialism rather than nationalism as the true mental disorder, attributing racial prejudice among British colonialists to status anxieties, sexual conflicts, and feelings of insecurity.[58] But even sharp-edged critiques of this kind could aid imperial officials by shedding light on the origins of discontent. During his stint at the

Colonial Office in the late 1940s, historian Ronald Robinson cited Gunnar Myrdal's damning study of race relations in the United States, *An American Dilemma* (1944), as a model for research with "the greatest practical value to the Colonial Office and Colonial Governments." A CSSRC administrator underscored the bureaucracy's willingness to make use of radical voices: "we knowingly recruited persons with left-wing connections and convictions."[59] Although human scientists themselves remained unreliable allies of imperial authority, their ambivalence toward the nationalist mind opened up a space for British authorities to approach anticolonial movements as problems of the unconscious.

Drawing on the language of psychology to discredit nationalist aspirations was not new. After 1945, however, claiming emotional control as a prerequisite for sovereignty grew almost routine in official circles. Proconsuls and soldiers attributed independence movements to "egotism," "sadism," and "resentment of parental authority." Former Kenya governor Philip Mitchell compared African politicians to rebellious adolescents who chafed at chores and homework. Even those who acknowledged the legitimacy of nationalist grievances, like Colonial Office adviser Margery Perham, could still insist that these did not "sufficiently explain the deeper emotions of those who used them."[60] Perham, who helped to train the last generation of colonial administrators at Oxford in the 1940s and 1950s, taught that the "inferiority complex" among African leaders represented "a force of great, of dangerous, of still incalculable power—a mental atomic energy." Humiliated by the consciousness that their states, economies, and schools bore the imprint of European conquest, they resorted to the "projection of guilt," blaming Britain for all their problems and seeking independence before they could realistically hope to stand on their own. A veteran of the imperial service in Nigeria agreed that the "pathology of wounded self-esteem" was fueling nationalist demands. So did the governor of the Gold Coast, Alan Burns, who also perceived an "inferiority complex" and described educated Africans as suspicious, touchy, and aggressive. Besides questioning the viability of independent states on pragmatic grounds, in short, officials pointed to the aspiration for a national state as evidence in itself of a disqualifying immaturity.[61]

If invocations of the inferiority complex echoed Dollard's *Caste and Class* once again, British officials always tempered novel American influences with the moralistic and developmental language of an older psychology. The rhetorical strategy conditioning political self-rule on emotional self-mastery was nowhere more apparent than in the civic education curriculum that became a centerpiece of postwar initiatives.[62] As an internal Colonial Office report argued in 1946, calls for independence were "merely symptoms of a deeper semi-conscious feeling of frustration"; imperial subjects had to be taught to recognize the practical demands of government. The report explicitly invoked "the analogy of adolescence," suggesting that rebellious passions coexisted with "lack of self-confidence" and therefore dependence on demagogic leaders. A reference to the need for "straight thinking" in democracies echoed Cambridge psychologist Robert Thouless, whose *Straight and Crooked Thinking* (1932) deplored the dangers of emotionalism in politics. The guide to civic education in Africa published by the Colonial Office in 1948 likewise stressed "character training" and "emotional adjustment" "as a foundation for self-reliance and responsibility." For traditionalists like Philip Mitchell, the language of "personal character, honesty, and public spirit" made the otherwise objectionable prospect of training in self-government more palatable.[63]

The moralistic strain in psychological training for citizenship served British aims. Although the pioneer of community development in the Gold Coast in the late 1940s, Alec Dickson, blandly described his work as the "training of leaders," the apparently freewheeling village discussion groups he organized were carefully structured to discredit nationalist politics. Dickson's development officers used leading questions to demonstrate that "every social issue is a moral problem," displacing blame from systematic inequalities to individual actions. By asking whether African market women were "more to blame for high prices than the big European firms," for instance, they guided the conversation away "from denunciation of imperialistic, capitalist exploitation to frank and humorous admissions of African joint responsibility." The same logic dictated that officials should not ask whether the villagers wanted "Self-Government Now," as the popular slogan had it, but whether the entire British population should pack up and leave—language calculated to sow doubts about readiness for independence. As Dickson shrewdly observed, even an exercise in democratic debate could advance imperial interests as long as officials paid attention to the fine points of "phrasing."[64]

The most elaborate effort to define citizenship in psychological terms came in the Sudan. Heralded by Creech Jones "for building up character, a sense of responsibility and ability," the Institute of Education at Bakht er Ruda was heralded in the Colonial Office report of 1948 as a model for the rest of the empire. The British civil servant in charge, Vincent Llewellyn Griffiths, played an outsized role in the colony's education system as a trainer of teachers, inspector of schools, and prolific author of textbooks. During the war, he wrote a pamphlet on the character traits required of civil servants in a "rising nation," declaring that educated Sudanese in particular would have to change their habits "if Sudan is to become self-governing." Yet Griffiths still envisioned that outcome as "a far-distant future" in 1953, just three years before independence. His regime of character training was designed as much to justify the continuation of British rule as it was to prepare the indigenous elite for self-government.[65]

Griffiths argued that functioning effectively in modern institutions—following instructions, meeting deadlines, communicating clearly—required the cultivation of inner discipline. Some of the qualities he promoted, such as "self-reliance," "obedience," and "loyalty," had a Victorian flavor. But the unifying concept was the need to manage "fundamental flow of energy" in every individual, a process of "canalization" achieved through the "irrigation system" of self-control. Like others who regarded emotions as socially disruptive forces, Griffiths favored hydraulic metaphors.[66] He warned that an "inferiority complex" could breed excessive sensitivity to criticism, cautioned against "rationalizing" personal failures, and recommended "the habit of suspecting one's own motives" as an alternative to "hasty emotional action." Prescribing constant introspection as a brake on neurosis, he constructed a five-point scale for fifteen different character traits so that his readers could evaluate how they measured up. Did they work steadily or take frequent breaks? Did they think before speaking or make conversation for its own sake? In all things, Griffiths asked his Sudanese readers, "are you criticizing yourself severely enough?"[67]

This punishing program won official support far beyond the borders of Sudan. The longtime education adviser to the Colonial Office, Christopher Cox, helped to broker the publication of three of Griffiths's texts as a "Good Citizen" series: *Character Aims* (1949), *Character Training* (1949), and *Character: Its Psychology* (1953). Cox circulated the galleys to his missionary contacts and persuaded Griffiths to replace some Islamic quotations with biblical material to secure its adoption in mission schools across Africa.[68] Griffiths's implicit critique of nationalist movements may have had something to do with its popularity among the British: he warned against "crowd emotions" and stressed that "the improvement of society is more dependent on the improvement of the individual than on any better organization, however well devised, of that society."[69] Officials in Northern Rhodesia designed a curriculum inspired by *Character Aims,* while their counterparts in the Gold Coast and Uganda required teacher trainees to read *Character Training.* In Lagos, the principal of the King's College secondary school ran a civics course built around the opposition between "emotion and reason" and the dangers of "mob oratory."[70]

Other officials tried to illustrate the demands of political independence in more dramatic fashion. After taking up a new position in Nigeria in 1950, Alec Dickson launched a character training course at a rugged coastal spot called Man O' War Bay, across the border in the British Cameroons. Taking inspiration from the new Outward Bound courses back home—an amalgam of military discipline and Quaker moralism that stressed character-building through physical exertion—Dickson and his wife Mora transformed an old banana plantation into a government camp for young Nigerian men who worked in the public service and other essential jobs.[71] With encouragement from Chadwick, the guru of Udi, they recruited hundreds of clerks, teachers, police officers, sanitary inspectors, and district scribes to participate in month-long courses aimed at instilling "the qualities of hand, head, and heart that the New Independent Nigeria needs." Like Griffiths, the Dicksons blended a Victorian ideal of character with newer psychological theories, interspersing mountain hikes and construction projects with lectures on the perils of the "aggressive instinct." Like Griffiths, too, they offered homilies on personal responsibility with a subtle political message. Pointing to the selfishness and laziness that he saw as an epidemic among educated Africans, Alec Dickson reserved special opprobrium for the "young intelligentsia" which expended its energies "writing letters to the Press" and casting blame on colonial officials. If anticolonial nationalism was "more psychological than political, more individual than general," as an exam question in Margery Perham's Oxford course put it, then the acrimonious relationship between ruler and ruled could improve with a carefully designed program of emotional training.[72]

When anticolonial movements crossed the line from activism to revolt, however, a new set of questions arose. What motivated insurgents to take up arms? What kinds of emotional bonds secured their loyalties? What appeals and images might persuade them to give in? For many of the most influential voices in British counterinsurgency, defeating rebellions against empire meant waging psychological war.

¶ RANGING ACROSS SOUTHEAST ASIA, sub-Saharan Africa, and the Middle East, British counterinsurgency campaigns of the postwar period did not follow an identical path everywhere. But if observers on the other side of the Atlantic sometimes exaggerated the cohesion of a "British way" or "British tradition" in counterinsurgency, imperial officials none-theless followed a consistent script in responding to postwar uprisings.[73] At the outset, the declaration of a state of emergency effectively suspended civil liberties, enabling new forms of control over physical space and the movement of populations. Police and military authorities restricted some subjects with curfews and identity cards while transporting others to armed settlements. The indefinite detention of suspected insurgents was relegated to shadowy bureaucracies where torture became possible. Just as police officers and soldiers circulated from one hot spot to another, the same tools of repression—bombing runs in jungles, tear gas in city streets, even the black hoods that informants used to disguise their identities—united counterinsurgency campaigns across the empire. How did psychology fit into this program of violent repression?

Attempts to heighten military effectiveness by acting on opinions, atti-tudes, feelings, and motivations had a decades-old history in Britain. In the First World War, the propaganda outfit at Crewe House crafted pamphlets trumpeting Allied victories and exploiting old grievances to encourage desertions from the armies of the Central Powers. More elaborate efforts targeted European civilians as well as soldiers during the Second World War.[74] It was during the Second World War, too, that morale on the home front—monitored by the Ministry of Information through an extensive surveillance network in 1939–1941—emerged as a pressing concern of the state.[75] The Janus-faced ambition to build up support among British sol-diers and civilians while chipping away at the enemy's will to fight remained influential in the postwar era of counterinsurgency. At home, the state tightly managed press coverage to build support for campaigns in distant places and minimize outrage about cases of brutality.[76] Overseas, British strategists argued that tried-and-true propaganda themes—playing up military defeats, material hardships, and ethnic divisions—could succeed in demoralizing fighters everywhere. They stressed the universality of the emotions they targeted, arguing that the old label of "political warfare" should be replaced by "psychological warfare" because primal impulses and unconscious forces provided a vital opening for propaganda appeals. A Royal Air Force (RAF) report in 1956 identified an array of potential vulnerabilities in any audience: "curiosity, gregariousness, feelings of isolation, discomfort or frustration, humor, hunger, sex and family feelings, discipline and resentment of it, fear of the unknown, or the dark, and indeed all sorts of fear and terror." As a 1959 guidebook for military officers advised, "propaganda must arouse or play upon an existing need in the audience . . . and it must suggest a way of satisfying that need."[77]

Even as they insisted on the portability of these blueprints for psychological warfare, however, British strategists also recognized that counterinsurgency in the colonies presented unique challenges. The unfamiliarity of jungle and urban warfare, the superior motivation of ideologically driven rebels, and the pervasive yet unpredictable threat of guerilla attacks all weighed heavily on the morale of their own side. As early as 1949, a military researcher in Palestine tracked the psychological effects on British troops of "disturbing stories, gloomy prognostications, and well-meant cautions" about "sniping in orange groves and riots." Using an apparatus for measuring hand tremors as an index of fear, he observed that even Army clerks who had seen no combat experienced elevated levels of anxiety as a result of merely anticipating these dangers.[78] Then, too, the exotic and irrational psychology that officials invariably attributed to anticolonial rebels—"sentimental and excitable" in Palestine, "oriental" and inscrutable in Malaya, "demonic" and "bestial" in Kenya, vengeful and sadistic in Cyprus—raised questions about the limitations of universal models.[79] According to a Colonial Office report drafted in 1952, propaganda campaigns needed to account for "mental attitudes" particular to colonized populations: feelings of "dependence," "suspicion arising from ignorance," and "jealousies" provoked by the global disparity in living standards.[80] Cultural variation posed challenges as well. Military strategists perceived Greek Cypriots, the only Europeans among the postwar rebels, as "highly emotional" but also educated, media-savvy, and propaganda-resistant foes; they concluded that technological novelties like aircraft equipped with loudspeakers were unlikely to impress them. For the so-called

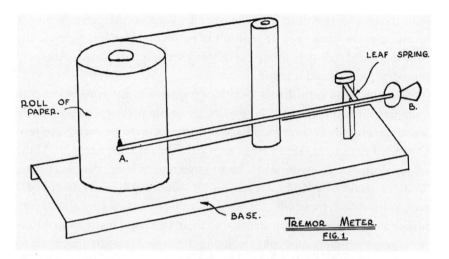

The apparatus used to measure fear among British soldiers fighting insurgents in Palestine. (Kenneth Yarnold, "Fear: A Field Survey in Palestine," 1949. Private Papers of Major General W. S. Cole CB CBE. Imperial War Museum, London.)

"tropical savage" in Malaya and Kenya, by contrast, the "awe-inspiring ju-ju" of technology would figure prominently in British efforts.[81]

If the practice of psychological warfare always required balancing universal principles with local adaptations, the campaign in Malaya served as a critical early test. British officials at the outset saw the psychology of ethnic Chinese Communists as insuperably alien: "I can't really believe," one of them remarked, "that we have the technique to win the hearts and minds of chaps like this."[82] The task of proving otherwise fell to one of the top psychologists in the British Army, Howard Lakin, who directed a nine-man research team charged with investigating the origins and vulnerabilities of the Malayan insurgency beginning in the fall of 1952. Working alongside MIT political scientist Lucian Pye and two other Americans from a military-sponsored research center at Johns Hopkins University, they interviewed more than four hundred captured insurgents about their family backgrounds, their personal relationships, their reasons for joining the Communist Party, and their reactions to propaganda from both sides of the conflict. These sessions, which took place in an interrogation center at Kuala Lumpur, lasted up to forty hours across several days.[83] Some insurgents also took a mental test, the results of which suggested that those who had already surrendered were less intelligent than those who remained in the jungle. To keep up the pressure on the insurgency, therefore, and appeal to the hard core of jungle fighters, the British decided that they needed to devise a more sophisticated message.[84] But what form should it take?

The interviews furnished a wealth of insight into the frustrations and longings of the insurgents. Complaints about the perks enjoyed by party leaders, especially access to food and women, recurred frequently, so propaganda began to highlight tensions within the insurgent group. "Many of you desire to give yourselves up to government," one pamphlet read, "but are afraid of your brutal leaders."[85] While most rebels described a happy childhood, those who reported an unhappy upbringing almost uniformly cited the absence or cruelty of their fathers. This reinforced the belief of government advisers—including Chinese Malayan official C. C. Too, who took the lead in designing propaganda appeals—that intergenerational tensions in the Confucian household had triggered a crisis of authority in the Chinese population. The result was a distinctive iconography of the family in British propaganda. Pamphlets contrasting the miserable life of the jungle insurgent with the "happy home" of the reformed civilian placed frail and aging patriarchs in the background, with an affectionate wife or mother dominating the foreground.[86] Finally, questions based on the hypothesis that isolation and loneliness drove Communist recruitment uncovered a very different reality. In fact, the interviews showed, it was not the need for comradeship but the promise of a more equitable society in material terms that motivated the insurgency. As a result, British propaganda edged toward a more substantive treatment of politics, looking to the future by suggesting that surrender would give the Communists a chance to "play a part in building the New Malaya."[87]

Psychology in Malaya bolstered the rationale for a massive propaganda machine by certifying the knowability and accessibility of an enemy once seen as inscrutable. Under Templer's command, tens of millions of pamphlets were dropped by air every year, ninety cinema vans traveled between remote villages, and a fleet of five aircraft equipped with loudspeakers targeted fighters in the jungle.[88] While Lakin and his colleagues shaped the subtext of this propaganda by probing emotional life, another researcher influenced its formal qualities by investigating visual perception. In 1953, a University of Reading psychology student named Peggy Thornton—whose husband worked as the manager on a Dunlop rubber plantation—applied

British propaganda pamphlet in Malaya, 1953. Note the frail patriarchs relegated to the background in the domestic scene on the right. (National Archives of the United Kingdom, Kew.)

for CSSRC support to study ways of seeing among Malays, Chinese, Indians, and Europeans. Buoyed by an endorsement from Meyer Fortes and a back-channel report that "General Templer was interested in the use of visual aids in propaganda," she received a grant of £300.[89] Following the model of Frederic Bartlett's seminal experiments in the 1930s, Thornton asked schoolchildren, rubber workers, and others to look at a series of picture cards and then reproduce the scenes from memory. Concluding that exposure to Western print culture affected perception more than anything else, Thornton argued that "the similarity between the ethnic groups is greater than the differences," suggesting that the British did not need to vary the visual style of their appeals to different subsets of the population.[90]

Touting the research-propaganda complex in Malaya as a model for counterinsurgencies elsewhere, Lakin estimated that psychological warfare "played an important part" in roughly half the cases of rebel surrender.[91] In light of the political concessions the British were forced to offer before finally granting independence in 1957, the claim that any kind of tactical sophistication defeated the insurgency was questionable. But the perceived success of Templer's strategy secured the status of psychological warfare in the British military for years to come. Throughout the 1950s, a coterie of Army officers argued that anticolonial unrest could be contained with more energetic efforts to mold opinion and manipulate morale.[92] One Malaya veteran, Major R. J. Isaac, crossed the Atlantic with several other British officers in the mid-1950s to receive training in psychological warfare from the U.S. Army; he then returned home to launch a similar course for senior officers at a military base in Wiltshire, where Peterson and other Malaya veterans took leading roles as instructors. A course for junior officers was established soon afterward at Episkopi, the British base on Cyprus. At least two hundred civil servants and two thousand military men participated in these programs over the next two decades.[93] In 1961, the Army heeded calls to set up psychological warfare units in Aden, Nairobi, and Singapore, each one prepared to deploy to trouble spots with planes, loudspeakers, tape recorders, film projectors, and printing presses.[94]

As the idea of psychological warfare secured an institutional home in the military—and as attention shifted from Malaya to Kenya and Cyprus—British strategists redefined the meaning of expertise in the field, stressing practical knowledge of operations and technologies over research on minds and cultures. This was, in part, a function of constrained supply: as Lakin observed in 1957, the quasi-psychoanalytic methods used in Malaya were unlikely to be replicated very often because they depended on capturing "cooperative" insurgents willing to lay bare their inner lives.[95] But military officers also interpreted Templer's campaign as a triumph of tactics rather than controlled experiments and empirical studies. Aside from Lakin's occasional lectures on "Social Psychology, Social Groups, Communication, Attitudes, and Opinions," the training course in Wiltshire rarely featured human scientists. The lecturer on the "Arab Mentality" in 1957 was Alec Kirkbride, a longtime Foreign Office hand who championed T. E. Lawrence's "warlike exploits" as a model for "what was needed to impress and to appeal to the Arab." Geoffrey Gorer spoke on the "Asiatic mentality," although his experience of fieldwork on the continent was confined to a few unhappy months in a Himalayan village. The guidebook issued to military officers, meanwhile, focused squarely on the mechanics of typography and loudspeakers while ignoring theories of culture and personality altogether.[96] "When one comes down to it," a skeptic in the Colonial Office observed, "psychological warfare

High-tech propaganda. Airplanes equipped with loudspeakers were considered especially useful for communicating with insurgents concealed in jungles and other remote environments. ("The Talking Aeroplane" leaflet cover, 1955. National Archives of the United Kingdom, Kew.)

seems to resolve into talk about pamphleteering and sky-shouting"—the instruments of mass communication that another official puckishly described as "bullshit machinery."[97]

In overseas operations, too, the balance of power in psychological warfare shifted from professionals to amateurs. Although Lakin paid a visit to Cyprus in 1957, the task of developing a "personality sketch" of EOKA guerilla leader George Grivas fell to MI5 officer William Magan. Drawing on a cache of Grivas's diaries discovered by British troops, he portrayed Grivas as a grimly determined fanatic who perpetrated violence with the stoicism of a Greek peasant: "the shepherd is unmoved at the slaughter of a lamb." Tracing Grivas's antipathy for the British to the lack of recognition he received as a partisan fighter during the Second World War, Magan concluded that this "soured and embittered man" who had burned with the "instinct of revenge" for more than a decade was unlikely ever to surrender. While Magan worried that novelistic flourishes like these might seem "a trifle colorful for an official paper," speculation about the psychology of Greek Cypriots was far from unusual among British officials. Claiming that the rebels lacked "reason, logic," and "all the processes which are usual in the Western mind," after all, helped to justify the disappointing results of the propaganda effort.[98]

Although veterans of the Malaya campaign pointed out that the effectiveness of propaganda there depended on harvesting insights from indigenous informants, their successors in later conflicts failed to heed this advice.[99] In Kenya, an intelligence agent who grew up in the colony was considered "the only man on the [Psychological Warfare] Staff who can forecast, *as far as it is possible for a European to do so,* the probable reactions of the Kikuyu." This was a telling qualification, but officials did not try to overcome it by recruiting indigenous informants. Instead, they praised the reports by asylum director J. C. Carothers and archaeologist Louis Leakey as "valuable contributions" for their sensationalistic portrayals of Mau Mau as collective psychosis.[100] They also proposed outlandish tactics, inspired by lurid visions of African sorcery, to encourage insurgents to surrender: a witch doctor to prophesy doom for recalcitrant fighters; the use of chemicals to dye forest rivers red as an apocalyptic omen; and a "mumbo-jumbo ritual" in which insurgents' family members lit bonfires, prayed for peace, and cast a curse on the forest where rebels were hiding. When a Colonial Office administrator visiting the colony "tried to obtain an assessment of the way in which the Kikuyu are thinking," he found that "no one could give it to him." As an Army officer observed years later, "little appears to have been known about the psychology of the Mau Mau."[101]

In Kenya, too, military officials cited the strangeness, irrationality, and "extremely suspicious nature" of the population to justify what they later acknowledged as a failed attempt to sway hearts and minds.[102] Even as the language of psychology remained pervasive in British counterinsurgency, however, it was drifting ever further away from the knowledge produced by human scientists. Far from reflecting an intellectual consensus, the equation of Mau Mau with mental illness triggered fierce opposition from British experts beyond the settler community. In one of the few scholarly reviews of Carothers's *The Psychology of Mau Mau* (1954), anthropologist Kathleen Gough dismissed the book as "nonsensical verbiage" resting on "confused, unsubstantiated assumptions." Mental-testing pioneer Arthur Culwick took a veiled shot at Carothers, insisting that "data from all over Kenya must be studied painstakingly before we can with any certainty diagnose the psychological ills of the Kikuyu" and faulting "unscientific speculation of a type which may postpone the day when peace and concord return." In the pages of the *Manchester Guardian,* anthropologist Max Gluckman argued that Mau Mau had less to do with "reversion to ancient rituals" than with labor exploitation, land alienation, and the proscription of African unions and political parties by the British. Psychologist Madeline Kerr likewise asserted that a "traumatic experience of deprivation or oppression" lay behind the rebellion.[103]

The increasingly strained relationship between human scientists and counterinsurgency was nowhere more apparent than in the treatment of captured rebels. Some recent histories have portrayed an unholy alliance of researchers and interrogators as the point of origin for torture by British authorities.[104] For most of the postwar era, however, experts doubted that cutting-edge psychological knowledge could transform the art of interrogation. Ministry of Defence scientist Henry Tizard asserted in 1951 that "there had been nothing new in the interrogation business since the days of the Inquisition." Psychologist Cyril Cunningham, who worked for the RAF in the 1950s, contrasted the reliable tradecraft of hidden microphones, background intelligence, and stool pigeons with the chimera of mind control. "Supposedly scientific behavioral principles" of interrogation, he believed, amounted to "laughable" and "ludicrous speculation." Other experts kept their distance on ethical grounds. Psychiatrists serving on an Army advisory committee in the early 1960s declined to participate in interrogation training as "a matter of individual conscience," citing their professional obligations under the Geneva Convention and the possibility of inflicting long-term damage to mental health.[105]

Howard Lakin, too, repeatedly passed on opportunities to apply his expertise in the interrogation room. When the head of the Army Intelligence Corps's Interrogation Branch suggested that psychological knowledge might help "in bringing a subject to a 'breaking point' and in recognizing that point during interrogation," the psychologist threw cold water on the idea. "The concept of a breaking point," Lakin argued, "was probably far too definite." He pointed to the uselessness of "generalizations" when British soldiers might encounter an endless variety of nationalities on the battlefield. Above all, he bridled at the suggestion that his expertise could be translated into a mechanical formula, declaring the subject "a matter for discussion between psychologists" and voicing doubt that "a superficial theory of personality structure would be of very much use" to the "lay interrogator." The use of sensory deprivation and other forms of psychological torture provoked Lakin to even stronger opposition. Despite the official pretext of simulating Communist methods, he worried that training exercises in which British soldiers were confined in steel lockers, subjected to stress positions, and exposed to high-pitched noises while physically restrained would "contaminate" the real-world practices of the interrogators involved. "All too easily," he observed, those soldiers began "acting out" "sadistic fantasies."[106]

Despite skepticism among the experts, British military and intelligence officials in the 1950s showed enthusiasm for the science of interrogation. In the United States, anxiety about "brainwashing"—touched off by public confessions in Eastern Bloc show trials and the indoctrination of military prisoners in Korea—launched a government-sponsored cottage industry of secret research.[107] Sir Alwyn Crow, a ballistics expert posted to the British Joint Services Mission in Washington, served as a transatlantic conduit for the results of these experiments, relaying correspondence between American psychiatrist Irving Janis and British psychiatrist William Sargant in 1949–1950. When Janis concluded that "conditioning techniques" and "drug treatments" played a role in Soviet interrogation, however, scientists consulted by the Ministry of Defence remained unconvinced.[108] Nobel Laureate E. D. Adrian, a physiologist, conceded the possibility of hypnosis but doubted that it was the most important factor. Medical researcher Harold Himsworth argued that the Communists were unlikely to have employed a sinister form of mind control because more prosaic methods would suffice: "under-feeding, inducing extreme fatigue by lack of sleep, the relentless maintenance of the 'sword of Nemesis' atmosphere, the adroit alternation of hope and fear."[109] It was not until CIA-funded experiments at McGill University in the mid-1950s documented the hypnotic symptoms produced by long confinement in sensory deprivation tanks that MI6 commissioned research in British hospitals "in continuation of the work of the Canadian observers." British intelligence at this time also briefly followed the lead of the CIA in studying the psychological effects of LSD: the drug was administered to soldiers in the chemical warfare facility at Porton Downs in 1953–1954.[110]

But even the science-fiction cachet of this new research did not transform British practices of interrogation. Some military advisers pointed out that the time needed for sensory deprivation to take effect made it an impractical tool in the heat of battle. Mind-altering drugs, meanwhile, were considered too unpredictable for use outside the laboratory.[111] In 1956 and again in 1964, expert panels concluded that "there was little in the way of scientific or technical aids which could improve the interrogation techniques already being taught." A huge public controversy ensued when newspapers reported in 1960 that training exercises for British soldiers involved stress positions, sensory deprivation, and other kinds of so-called brainwashing, circumscribing the military's ability to carry out similar experiments in the future. Soldiers and police officers working overseas, meanwhile, showed little interest in opening up their interrogation rooms to the scrutiny of researchers. As Lakin had observed in Cyprus, securing the cooperation of Special Branch interrogators in an observational study "would be very difficult if not impossible to obtain."[112]

The relationship between experts and interrogators was shaped by skepticism on both sides. As one Army consultant put it, mastery of "theoretical psychology" mattered less than an "instinctive understanding of [one's] fellow men." When military and police interrogators laid claim to the language of expertise—as they habitually did—they were touting powers of intuition rather than technical knowledge. As one interrogator in Palestine and Malaya put it, "you had to be a psychologist . . . to decide whether the person had told you everything or was holding something back." Almost like a human lie detector, another interrogator recalled, the skilled questioner could pick up on the nonverbal cues that indicated truth or falsehood: "the vital aids afforded by voice inflexion, tonal range, unusual hesitancy, the too-eager reply, and the monosyllabic answers habitually given . . . when he fears a trap or the questions are 'hitting near home.'" Of course, claiming these almost fantastic powers of psychological insight—the interrogator's capacity "to know his prisoner, understand his fears, desires and motives," as one of them put it—laid the foundations for a reassuring narrative about the possibility of extracting information from reluctant subjects without resorting to force. British interrogators interviewed in later years almost invariably claimed that they had no need to perpetrate violence because they could learn what they wanted by other means.[113]

Military officials' eagerness to appropriate the authority of mind science for their own purposes made them receptive to invocations of expertise from dubious sources. When a representative of the Church of Scientology turned up uninvited at the War Office in 1957, promising insight into what he called "the mental mechanics" of interrogation and brainwashing, some high-ranking officers actually took him seriously. Even as an Army psychologist protested that this man had "all the outward signs of being utterly bogus," his superiors ordered him to review a small library of Scientology literature for possible use in interrogation. Only after inquiries confirmed the checkered past of the organization did military officials give up on the project.[114] Although the CIA's infamous KUBARK interrogation manual (1963) contained more substantive information about sensory deprivation, the tactics most often cited by British officials in the years that followed—assuming the role of "the father figure" and using "the momentum provided initially by the shock of arrest" to weaken resistance—reflected pop psychology rather than laboratory research.[115]

During the Troubles in Northern Ireland, revelations that British forces interrogated some IRA insurgents with the "five techniques"—black hoods, stress positions, white noise, limited diet, and sleep deprivation— touched off an intense controversy about the link between psychology and torture.[116] British troops employed the "five techniques" with about two dozen suspects in a seven-year period, beginning with Aden in 1964 and continuing in Malaysia (1965–1966), Oman (1970–1971), and Northern Ireland (1971).[117] But the novelty of bringing all five methods to bear simultaneously operated on the surface of deeper continuities. As early as the 1850s, British police in India prevented suspects from sleeping through the night, and in the first half of the twentieth century, stress positions were used in India and Palestine. In Malaya in the late 1940s, one interrogator recalled, sleep deprivation served as a powerful tool: "You'd keep [them] awake, you'd make sure they suffered from fatigue, and by these means you'd break their resistance down." In Cyprus, Kenya, and Aden, suspects were kept awake with punches or noise and forced to stand for hours at a time.[118] These methods, which have sometimes been described as "psychological torture," might better be understood as attempts to inflict pain and injury without leaving visible marks—an explicit aim of training imparted by the British Army Intelligence Corps in this period.[119] The fantasies of mind control that recurred in cinematic thrillers like *The Mind Benders* (1963) and *The Ipcress File* (1965) were just that: bloodless projections with little relation to the reality of beatings, floggings, and other low-tech tortures in British interrogation rooms.[120]

At the most brutal extremes of British decolonization, then, what function did the language of psychology serve? The promise of "rehabilitation" that officials used to justify the existence of detention camps in Kenya, Cyprus, and Aden posed this juxtaposition in especially stark fashion. Amid grim living conditions, forced labor, and pervasive violence, the reality of the camps was far from therapeutic. But even here—in the "total institution" of the camp, where British officials ruled the world behind the barbed wire with virtually unfettered authority—they proved deeply reluctant to abandon the vocabulary of expertise. The commandant of the Pyroi camp in Cyprus, for instance, saw his mission as "prevent[ing] future delinquency." He encouraged his functionaries to forge "free and easy relationships" with the detainees and then enlist family members in the villages back home to ease their transition from "destructive habits" to "creative activities." Concerned to prevent the "problem characters, "the aggressive, unstable, unbalanced," from infecting the rest, he stressed the need to identify the vulnerable as well as the pathological in the detainee population. A "lay assessment" of three hundred twenty detainees concluded that seventy-one of them had below-average intelligence, and two were "mentally defective," while more than ten percent overall were neurotic.[121]

In Kenya, reports by J. C. Carothers and Louis Leakey describing Mau Mau as a kind of mental disorder underlay the idea of the "Pipeline": a series of gradually less oppressive camps through which suspects would be channeled as their rebellious impulses weakened. Coupled with the isolation of the camp environment, officials argued, education in literacy, crafts, and Christian morality would constitute a therapeutic process culminating in the confession and renunciation of Mau Mau loyalties. Continual references to the "anxiety," "imbalance," "insecurity," and "frustration" of the camp population reinforced a sense of therapeutic mission. After confessing and recanting their links to the insurgency, one officer claimed, prisoners' "health and physical appearance improves, their eyes become clear, their address direct and confident, their skin begins to shine and their hair blackens."[122] At least some officials believed that measuring mental ability could help in "the classification and the rehabilitation" of individual cases: more than five hundred detainees at the Athi River camp in 1953 were given an intelligence test originally designed for the selection of Gurkha Army recruits in South Asia.

Psychological language guided the treatment of even the most recalcitrant detainees. After arriving in a specially designated camp, this so-called "hard core" underwent a ritual of submission suggested by KUBARK, shaving their heads and removing their clothes and bracelets. According to Kenya Attorney General Eric Griffith-Jones, changing detainees into uniforms served "to condition them psychologically to shed the past and look to the future." As he put it, "psychology and symbolism play a decisive part" in breaking down resistance.[123]

What happened when detainees refused to cooperate in this process of conversion is revealing. "Any who showed any reluctance or hesitation" to change clothes, Griffith-Jones reported, "were hit with fists and/or slapped with the open hand." If the detainee continued to resist, "three or four of the European officers immediately converged on the man and rough-housed him, stripping his clothes off him, hitting him, on occasion kicking him, and, if necessary, putting him on the ground." Because the pseudo-therapeutic pathway imagined by the British could have only one outcome, the threat of force always lurked behind promises of psychological change. If the science of mind captivated officials with the illusory promise of a clean counterinsurgency, no veneer of technical language could alter the underlying rationale for resorting to force. The trouble with hearts and minds was that violence proved much easier to justify when coupled with subtler methods of coercion.[124]

CHAPTER SIX

Psychology beyond Empire

Global Expertise and
the Postcolonial Mind

F ROM ITS BEGINNINGS in postwar London, the World Federation for Mental Health (WFMH) carried the burden of utopian hopes. Moving beyond the comparatively modest goals of the mental hygiene movement before the war, the therapists, social scientists, and other professionals who founded the organization in 1948 sought an end to global conflict.[1] Citing the formative role of childhood training in shaping political behavior, they boldly proclaimed "the plasticity of human beings" and "the modifiability of man," seeking to build sturdy psychological foundations for democratic citizenship around the world.[2] According to one participant, British psychiatrist John Rawlings Rees, the science of mind offered valuable insights for "many different lands and cultures, for, fundamentally, all have the same problems."[3]

Even at the moment of the federation's founding, however, this lofty internationalism had to contend with a more provincial reality. When the inaugural meeting took place in the Ministry of Health building in Whitehall, a decisive bloc of delegates came from the British Empire and the Commonwealth. Representing Australia, British Guiana, Canada, Egypt, England, Hong Kong, India, Ireland, Malta, New Zealand, Pakistan, Scotland, and South Africa, they accounted for roughly one-third of all the territories there. Unilever, Imperial Chemical Industries, and Courtaulds were among the British firms that acted as sponsors; Rees, who had just finished serving as a psychiatric consultant for the War Office, was installed in the federation's London headquarters as its first president; Raj selection board veteran Kenneth Soddy and West Indies expert Thomas Simey also served as top administrators. With American psychologists and psychiatrists playing prominent roles as well, it is not difficult to see why anxieties about "Anglo-Saxon influence" haunted the organization for so long.[4]

The gap between cosmopolitanism in rhetoric and Anglocentrism in practice did not diminish the influence of the WFMH. The World Health Organization (WHO), the United Nations Educational, Scientific, and Cultural Organization (UNESCO), and other international agencies repeatedly turned to the federation for personnel and ideas in the postwar years. However insistently they proclaimed the values of global cooperation and national self-determination, all of these institutions sprang from imperial interests that shaped them in lasting ways.[5] British experts, meanwhile, discovered that experience of empire conferred intellectual authority even as imperial power was waning. They succeeded in translating imperial theories about trauma, the family, and the unconscious mind into a central assumption of technocratic planning: that modernization required the mastery of psychological forces. Independence from authority figures, tolerance for change, and an empirical outlook, they argued, decided the fate of development initiatives as much as material self-interest or engineering know-how. Even when postcolonial and American experts eclipsed the authority of their British counterparts—and the Anglocentrism of the postwar moment did not last forever—they shared the same faith in the transparency of emotions and the measurability of aptitudes. By giving currency to a scientific language of manageable minds, imperial psychologists-turned-international consultants helped to underwrite the expansive claims of expertise in the postwar world. No matter how they felt about formal imperialism, British mind scientists could always champion technical intervention in the name of development.[6]

¶ DESPITE ITS SHRINKING range of action in financial and military terms, postwar Britain remained influential in the global economy of ideas. Drawing on the knowledge accumulated and tested through imperial rule, expertise represented an enduring source of prestige.[7] Roughly a third of British imperial officials, mostly technical specialists rather than political administrators, kept working overseas after decolonization: for the states the emerged from empire, for the various foreign services of the British state, and for an expanding universe of international organizations. Many of these new global institutions were based in London and dominated by British personnel; observers saw some of them, like the International Planned Parenthood Federation, as a "virtual extension of the British Civil Service or Colonial Office."[8] At WHO, more officials came from Britain than from any other country in the first years after its founding. At WHO and UNESCO alike, Britain provided the second-highest amount of funding after the United States; the two Anglophone powers together underwrote more than half of those agencies' budgets into the 1950s.[9] It was a propitious time for veterans of imperial psychology to segue into international roles. Tavistock psychiatrist Ronald Hargreaves, the inaugural director of the mental health section at WHO, awarded jobs and consultancies to several old empire hands: child nutrition expert Cicely Williams, Kenya asylum administrator J. C. Carothers, West Africa testing expert Geoffrey Tooth, and Unilever personnel specialist A. T. M. Wilson. At UNESCO, selection board pioneer Hubert Vinden served as a personnel officer, while the "project on world tensions" included Meyer Fortes, Madeline Kerr, and Thomas Simey as advisers.

The Anglophone intellectuals who led these institutions in their formative years were ardent believers in the possibilities of psychological knowledge. The first director-general of UNESCO, British biologist Julian Huxley, hailed "the importance of psychology to every branch of social science" and envisioned a worldwide program of mental testing for government employment and job training. Canadian Brock Chisholm, the inaugural director of WHO, was a Freudian psychotherapist who had trained both at London's Maudsley Hospital and at Yale's Institute of Human Relations. He argued that feelings of guilt and fear arising from subjection to parental authority in childhood represented the leading cause of neurosis and therefore war.[10] While scholars from continental Europe protested that the dominance of psychology in postwar research overlooked the material causes of conflict, this focus aligned with Anglo-American interests in the context of the Cold War. Hard-edged social and economic analysis risked playing into Soviet hands by drawing attention to capitalist failures and global inequalities.[11]

To be sure, the diverse array of experts recruited by international organizations could not always be herded into conformity with geopolitical imperatives. An early group of consultants for the UNESCO tensions project—including British Quaker psychoanalyst John Rickman, Harvard psychologist Gordon Allport, and several others—warned that imperial rule inflicted trauma with potentially grave consequences. Citing the damaging psychological effects of "a continuing inferior status," they declared in 1948 that "neither colonial exploitation nor oppression of minorities within a nation is in the long run compatible with world peace"—a striking statement more than a decade before the United Nations (UN) General Assembly approved a similar resolution. In 1953, likewise, a technical assistance manual written for UNESCO by Margaret Mead and several American colleagues detailed the devastating effects of British rule on indigenous societies in Burma and Nigeria.[12]

The internationalist rhetoric of postwar research also opened up a path to influence for imperial and post-imperial subjects. Nigerian psychiatrist and WHO consultant Thomas Lambo suggested in 1959 that mental illness was rising in Africa because the culture of imperial Britain was itself pathological, a breeding ground for the "suburban neurosis" of "boredom, social isolation, and a false set of values."[13] When an American psychologist appointed by UNESCO to study social tensions in India proposed investigating the link between childhood discipline and adult aggression, Indian social scientists insisted on exploring the legacy of the Raj instead. What happened to emotional life, anthropologist K. P. Chattopadhyay asked, when a colonized population "resents" its "domination and control" by another nation? Other Indian researchers pointed to the institutional forms of British *divide et impera* as sources of postcolonial conflict: railway stations segregated by religion and caste, electoral districts organized on communal lines, patronage doled out to favored groups.[14]

If the contentious politics of imperialism and decolonization did infiltrate the corridors of Geneva and Paris, however, the technocratic sensibility that reigned there usually dampened conflicts. Mind scientists shared a widespread sense among development workers that the world beyond the West could not advance without expert guidance.[15] This faith in psychological knowledge was premised on a triumphalist vision of Western science. According to a 1949 WHO report by Ronald Hargreaves, "the socio-economic development of a community" and "the conception of mental health" progressed in tandem. Although people in the poorest societies might recognize "flamboyant psychoses and grave cases of mental defect" in individuals, Hargreaves argued, they overlooked the neuroses that affected entire populations in subtler ways. WHO's mission was therefore to raise awareness about the insidious chains of causality that led from defective child-rearing and educational methods to pervasive personality disorders. Hargreaves stressed the economic cost of these pathologies, identifying them as "sources of considerable productive loss . . . which obstruct the country's development."[16] While international organizations after the war are sometimes said to have neglected systemic problems in favor of narrow technical interventions, mind scientists were simultaneously intent on remaking societies and confident that their own specialized knowledge could be usefully employed to that end.[17]

Psychology mattered to international development planners not only as a means of identifying mental obstacles but also as a mechanism for overcoming them. Hargreaves observed in 1949 that the advent of group dynamics—what he called "operational techniques" to minimize "resistances"—made it newly possible to "modify behavior and environment." Although "deep psychological roots" were "not susceptible to modification by didactic means," he suggested that they could be reshaped through interpersonal influences and emotional identifications.[18] Experts at the World Federation for Mental Health agreed that development workers had to elicit desires and channel motivations rather than simply impart lessons. Echoing the architects of mass education at the Colonial Office, Kenneth Soddy insisted that experts were more likely to inspire an "impulse to change" if they positioned themselves—misleadingly—as vessels of the collective will. "In harnessing the system of values" unique to every society, he argued, "you get . . . an enormous source of power and then you can do what you want to do."[19]

This cadre of experts—like others after the war—placed cultural sensitivity in the service of universal standards for health and sickness, adjustment and maladjustment, normality and pathology.[20] If British imperial psychology had always involved an unstable tension between diagnostic and relativistic sensibilities, the postwar campaigns for "mental health" marked a tipping of the balance toward influences from psychiatry. Shifting away from the fatalism of orthodox Freudianism and toward a more interventionist neo-Freudian model, British mind scientists after 1945 evaluated child-rearing and other intimate practices for their ability to temper and train the dangerous instincts that had seemingly caused the war. Summarizing the report of a federation panel on "leadership and authority" in 1950, psychiatrist Leonard Browne drew a sharp distinction between "mature" and "immature" "culture patterns," warning that the absence of emotional control created an opening for authoritarian leaders. As London alderman W. J. Garnett argued at a federation meeting in 1949, "self-indulgence, frustration, self-deception"—and thus the potential for "an aggressive attitude leading to dictatorship"—were "common to every home."[21]

The drive to cultivate emotional control by regulating family life loomed large in the postwar construction of European welfare states. After mental disorders spiked among British children evacuated to the countryside during the Second World War, the bond between infants and mothers came to be seen as the single most important variable in personality formation—a belief reinforced in Britain by the postwar vogue of "Bowlbyism."[22] Although John Bowlby's attachment theory has long figured in debates about the domestic politics of the welfare state, it is less often noted that his influence extended beyond the metropole, fostering a global ideal for family life across cultures.[23] The frontispiece of Bowlby's magnum opus, *Attachment and Loss,* pointedly featured a photograph of a naked Amazonian woman cradling her infant son—the only image to appear in three volumes.[24] Although Bowlby used ethology, or the study of animal behavior, to ground his theory in biological science, its first empirical test came in British East Africa. His closest collaborator, American psychologist Mary Ainsworth, came to the Tavistock after studying the behavior of Ganda mothers and children during her time at the East African Institute of Social Research in 1953–1955.

Ainsworth managed to draw universal conclusions and simultaneously account for cultural particularity by reviving an old idea in imperial psychology: the theory of traumatic weaning. In the first year of life, Ainsworth argued, variations in mother–child interaction were no different in Africa than anywhere else. The baby who cried when his mother left the room and laughed when she returned was a universal type; this behavior occurred at almost exactly the same age in Uganda as in a study conducted later by Bowlby's Tavistock colleagues in Scotland. But how could Ainsworth reconcile the power of these innate human instincts with the peculiarities of the Ganda personality—what Ainsworth's friend, the British anthropologist Audrey Richards, described as an "obsessive, anal-erotic" type? Speculating that "the crucial bit occurs later than the period I studied," Ainsworth pointed to "the implicit rejection when the mother turns her attention from the weaned child to the new baby" around the second year. This "could be quite a traumatic happening," as she put it in 1962, especially since fathers tended to place a new emphasis on "control and decorum" around the same time.[25]

By distinguishing phases of development in this way, attachment theory served a dual function: legitimating an ideal for parenting everywhere and explaining divergences from it. WHO lent its prestige to both parts of this project. Hargreaves voiced support for the idea that children deprived of continuous maternal care in early life suffered "a degree of permanent damage of personality development—damage particularly to the capacity to form relationships with others and to the cognitive capacity we call abstraction." He commissioned Bowlby to write the report *Maternal Care and Mental Health,* which appeared under the WHO imprint in 1952 and later sold four hundred thousand copies as an abridged paperback edition.[26] Hargreaves also commissioned another round of observational studies from East Africa, approving a grant to the Infant Malnutrition Unit operated by Britain's Medical Research Council at a Kampala hospital. A pair of researchers—a British nutritionist and a French psychiatrist—ran experiments in 1954–1956 with the Gesell test, which evaluated manual dexterity as an index of mental maturity. They prompted African babies raised in two different environments—"traditional" and "Europeanized"—to handle balls, cubes, and other objects. The results supported Ainsworth's belief in the impact of traumatic weaning. Babies in traditional homes matured earlier than their Westernized counterparts, the researchers concluded, because constant proximity to their mothers provided stimulation and security. In the first two years of life, this closeness even compensated for the lack of mechanical toys, which forced children to play with sticks and banana peels instead. Around the second year, however, mothers in the "traditional" sample withdrew their attention, and the psychological development of their children slowed sharply, falling behind the "Europeanized" sample for the duration of the study. A parenting style that encouraged independent play with real toys, it seemed, was better-suited to producing healthy and productive minds than a regime of intense but impermanent affection.[27]

The continuity between imperial and international theories of arrested development was cemented by continuity among the experts themselves. Cicely Williams, the Colonial Medical Service veteran who warned about

Gesell testing with African infants at the Infant Malnutrition Unit, Kampala. An Anglo-French research team concluded that the combination of material scarcity and traumatic weaning in "traditional" Ugandan households imposed a burden on a mental development. (*Tests de Gesell et de Terman-Merrill: Application en Ouanda,* 1957. Image reproduced courtesy of Bibliothèque de l'Université de Genève.)

traumatic weaning in the Gold Coast in the late 1930s, became the inaugural director of WHO's Maternal and Child Health division in 1948. Although trained as a pediatrician and best known for her work on malnutrition, Williams always stressed "the effect of mental and emotional factors on bodily form and functions," as she told an audience in Beirut in 1949. Wherever she went in the world, Williams encouraged mothers to breastfeed—and learn how to do it properly—for psychological as well as physiological reasons. On a tour of Britain's African colonies in 1955, she warned about the trauma of weaning in almost exactly the same words as she had two decades earlier. She worried that the newborn African baby, favored with "constant attention" and "very attached" to the mother, was "rudely displaced" when the next child was about to be born. Rather than spending money in "under developed" countries on high-tech clinics, Williams advocated dispatching Western consultants to disseminate enlightened practices through teams of training nurses and welfare workers, stressing the necessity of "prolonged and intimate" intervention in home life.[28]

Even as Williams complained about rival agencies diverting resources from the Maternal and Child Health division, she scored some significant bureaucratic victories. In 1947–1948, WHO dispatched thirty-five experts in child health—the vast majority of them welfare workers rather than medical professionals—to advise national governments in Latin America and Eastern Europe. In New Delhi, where Williams ran a WHO outpost from 1949 to 1951, a training program for nurses stressed the importance of monitoring "maternal care, feeding, sleeping, training in toilet habits" in the home. The rationale for this kind of surveillance struck an uneasy balance between sensitivity to cultural difference and the ambition to create global standards. During her career at WHO, Williams always paid lip service to relativism: as she put it in 1949, "one cannot consider one society's methods as 'better' than another without regard for the kind of person they aim to shape." In the very same speech, however, she offered support for "universal principles" adopted at the inaugural meeting of the World Federation of Mental Health that year. She suggested that certain "positively harmful" practices should be avoided everywhere even if total uniformity were not possible. She also argued that every welfare worker in the world should understand the developmental theory of American psychologist Arnold Gesell so that they might recognize the danger of creating "distorted adult patterns of behavior and feeling" through misguided mothering. Relativism for Williams was less an absolute value than a means to the end of rooting out pathology in other cultures.[29]

One of Williams's most fervent admirers within WHO was Hargreaves. He cited her research as evidence of "the extreme indulgence of the Gold Coast woman toward her infant, and the complete withdrawal of that indulgence from it on the birth of another child." These emotional dislocations, he concluded, "must by their effect on adult personality structure play a large part in obstructing the development of individuals and communities in under-developed areas." But anti-relativistic superiority when it came to other cultures mingled in Hargreaves's account with antiracist opposition to racial determinism. What outsiders saw as innate "laziness and fecklessness" in much of the world could in fact be attributed to malnutrition and disease as well as "the local pattern of childhood upbringing." The plasticity of minds was crucial for Hargreaves because it created an opening for expert intervention. Like Bowlby and other contemporaries, he drew an analogy between psychological and physiological forms of deprivation, suggesting that doses of maternal affection could cure emotional disorder just as reliably as vitamin pills treated malnutrition.[30]

Hargreaves's conviction that child-rearing held the key to international development helps explain one of the strangest episodes in his tenure: the appointment of an obscure psychiatrist named Colin Carothers to a WHO consultancy in 1952. A South Africa native and longtime director of the government asylum in Nairobi, Carothers would achieve his greatest fame as the author of *The Psychology of Mau Mau* (1954), which portrayed the Kikuyu rebellion in Kenya as an atavistic eruption of barbarism. A physician with no formal training in psychology or psychiatry, Carothers is usually seen as a champion of settler views on racial inferiority.[31] Why did Hargreaves elevate him to a distinguished place in Geneva, publish his views with the imprimatur of the WHO, and then defend him against a wave of criticism from outside experts?

The report Carothers wrote during his Geneva sojourn, *The African Mind in Health and Disease* (1953), laid the foundation for *The Psychology of Mau Mau* by presenting stereotypes as scientific fact. It claimed that Africans lacked the capacity for rational thought, relied on supernatural explanations of natural phenomena, and failed to develop qualities of "personal uniqueness." Drawing on cranial measurements collected by Henry Gordon and his collaborator in Kenya as well as EEG data on brain activity from French Guinea and South Africa, Carothers pointed to "frontal lobe idleness" as a possible explanation for psychological differences between Africans and Europeans.[32] Those comments provided ample fodder for critics like the American anthropologists Melville Herskovits and Jules Henry, who bombarded Geneva with expressions of "shock and concern" about the WHO's involvement in the book. "Prejudice against African Negroes in this book is great, and the auspices under which it is published are exalted," Henry complained. "No evidence is produced by Carothers to prove the untenable generalization that child rearing is consistent in 'Europe' and inconsistent in 'Africa.'" Herskovits for his part faulted Carothers as "not a competent ethnographer," who obliterated distinctions between African cultures and employed "an outworn concept of 'primitive' life"—criticisms echoed by reviewers in other American journals.[33]

What allowed Carothers and his allies to cling to the veneer of scholarly respectability was a causal story that downplayed heredity in favor of environmental forces. Carothers stressed that infectious diseases such as malaria, trypanosomiasis, and syphilis caused many symptoms of mental disorder. So, in his view, did the dysfunction of the African home. Like Hargreaves, Williams, and others, Carothers identified the practice of breastfeeding babies at all times of the day as a precursor to traumatic weaning and lasting emotional damage. But he conceived the scope for expert intervention in even more expansive terms than the modification of feeding practices. Carothers urged that the "musical, dramatic" emphasis of traditional education—the cradle of illogical thinking—should be replaced with the "balls and building blocks and mechanical toys" of the European nursery to introduce ideas of causality. He argued, too, that the sprawling extended families of African culture—a source of confusion about the boundaries of the self—should give way to the disciplined affection of parents alone.[34]

Carothers's prescription for psychological transformation could, of course, serve imperial as well as international ends. His most detailed blueprint for an African welfare state—with expanded housing to accommodate two-parent families, training courses in child welfare for mothers, and toys in every home and school—came at the conclusion of *The Psychology of Mau Mau,* a handbook for suppressing the insurgency. But Carothers's account of *The African Mind* was also well calculated to appeal to like-minded experts at WHO and the World Federation for Mental Health. By rejecting the idea of inherited biological inferiority for a narrative of behavioral dysfunction, he opened up a vast space for development initiatives. According to Carothers, this conclusion came as the unanticipated result of his research. Although "I set forth in the expectation that differences of innate potential between Europeans and Africans would emerge," he wrote in 1955, "to my surprise I found no evidence of these." He added that "the environmental, and especially the cultural, influences, had been so overwhelming that innate differences, if such exist, are . . . quite negligible. . . . Human beings start off with 'minds' that are practically clean slates and on which each society writes its own peculiar message." Reengineering the world of early childhood, Carothers claimed, held almost unlimited potential for reshaping mental life.[35]

This radical environmentalism provided a rallying cry for Carothers's allies. With Hargreaves's encouragement, Margaret Mead heralded the

African Mind in the journal *Psychiatry* as an "urgent plea for better education and public health for Africans [based] firmly on the assumption that there are no known racial differences which would interfere with Africans learning and functioning as Europeans learn and function." While conceding Carothers's shaky grasp of the latest ethnographic details, she suggested that these shortcomings should not count too heavily against "a pioneer effort" with a practical bent. WHO officials likewise clung to the distinction between hereditarian and environmental explanations—even when the latter involved conspicuously tenuous generalizations. Hargreaves stressed Carothers's conclusion that differences were "not genetically determined" but echoed his claim that African culture "sets itself to stamp down any basic independence or development of personal responsibility in the African adolescent."[36]

International authorities put a benevolent face on the idea of transforming personality overseas, in part, by eliding the distinction between psychological and medical imperatives. According to Hargreaves, Carothers had demonstrated that "the provision of education and the solution of nutritional problems are absolutely essential if technological development is to take place in Africa." Hargreaves argued that even the most dazzling infrastructure projects were doomed to fail unless the workers running them possessed an aptitude for objective, empirical, mechanical thought. Pointing to the most ambitious development project of the day, he questioned whether progress "can be achieved by damming the Volta River [in the Gold Coast] and attaching an aluminum industry, without, at the same time, enabling Africans on a wide scale to learn the Western post-Reformation mental trick which made it possible to work out how to refine aluminum." The only way to establish the mental preconditions of economic growth, Hargreaves insisted, was to remake "cultural and nutritional influences during the period of child development." Feeding practices kept recurring in these debates because they brought together mental and physical forms of nourishment.[37]

Although child-rearing research sponsored by WHO focused on Africa, experts at the World Federation for Mental Health extended the link between psychology and economic development to other parts of the world. Kenneth Soddy, the longtime scientific director of the organization, was one of them. A psychiatrist who trained with Bowlby, Soddy spent the war as deputy director for personnel selection in the Indian Army. The experience of applying personality tests on a massive scale in India heightened his confidence in the possibility of managing emotions in other cultures. Invoking his wartime experience in federation meetings after the war, he cited the behavior of British officers in mess halls and Indian candidates at selection boards to illustrate universal principles of motivation and identity. But this universalism coexisted comfortably enough with a hierarchical sense of difference: Soddy described British imperial history as an ongoing narrative of cannibalism, slavery, polygamy, human sacrifice, and other barbaric customs crumbling under the "impact of certain new ideas." The challenge for development planners was to continue revolutionizing attitudes in the world beyond the West without triggering a conservative reaction. In many cultures, Soddy warned, traditionalist anxieties about rampant individualism and "moral deterioration" outweighed the desire for a higher standard of living.[38]

According to Soddy, the central question for the psychology of economic development was "how a climate of change may be created in the individual." Drawing an analogy between Britain's Industrial Revolution and Third World development at a 1958 conference in Manila, he noted that material progress often generated feelings of loss and insecurity. But some individuals were better equipped to handle the transition than others. Discontent was inevitable only "when, after a childhood spent in a rigid family environment where the way of life is accepted and unquestioned, the individual passes on . . . without having had 'built in' . . . a capacity to adapt harmoniously." Soddy, like Bowlby, portrayed the "standard nuclear family" as a prerequisite for emotional adaptability. The bond between mother and child determined an individual's tolerance for change throughout life: by establishing a "warm and secure relationship" through breastfeeding and then gradually training the child to feed independently, the ideal mother taught her offspring "to gain satisfaction from the very acceptance of new things." In the extended families Soddy claimed to observe in Asia, however, this critical shift never materialized. Because a profusion of siblings, grandparents, aunts, and uncles weakened the intensity of emotional connections, the experience of growth into adulthood lacked the sense of joy that only a mother's love could impart. As a consequence, Soddy argued, "change may be no more than a passive conformity that is likely to maintain the rigid form of relationships" outside the family. Growing up with a deficiency of affection, in other words, heightened resistance to nontraditional means of making one's way in the world.[39]

Another expert with the World Federation for Mental Health reached strikingly similar conclusions in the very different environment of India. Born to Church of Scotland missionaries in Mussoorie, Morris Carstairs spoke fluent Hindi from an early age, studied anthropology under Meyer Fortes at Cambridge, and served as an RAF medical officer during the war. The Colonial Office—where his brother Charles worked as a senior official—considered him "an exceptionally competent research worker," tried to commission him for a study of mental illness in Borneo, and consulted him on a planned survey of "African attitudes to Westernization" in the late 1940s. But Morris Carstairs went to New York instead and trained in the methods of culture-and-personality research with Margaret Mead. When he arrived in the Rajasthan village that would serve as the site of his Rockefeller-funded fieldwork in 1951–1952, Carstairs had an arsenal of mental tests with him: a nonverbal intelligence test, a word association test, and the Rorschach test (then a staple of Mead's toolkit in the field).[40] Interpreted alongside data from dozens of interviews, the test results suggested an epidemic of neurosis among high-caste Hindus. Although outwardly friendly, they formed superficial and transitory relationships; plagued by doubt and uncertainty, they suspected the worst of others and fell prone to outbursts of aggression. Like other theorists of traumatic weaning, Carstairs concluded that a generous, undisciplined style of mothering prevented young children from learning how to manage frustration. Thanks to the untrammeled affection they briefly enjoyed, Indian babies could entertain visions of omnipotence until the harsh experience of maternal deprivation shattered this idyll. As Carstairs saw it, "the underlying mistrust which seems to cloud so many of my informants' adult personal relationships may well be derived from the fantasy of a fickle mother who mysteriously withholds her caresses." This sense of insecurity had implications for economic development because, according to Carstairs, it encouraged conformity and passivity rather than ambition and risk-taking.[41]

The influence of the World Federation for Mental Health extended throughout the UN bureaucracy. Within a few years of its founding, the organization effectively functioned as the research arm for Hargreaves's mental health section in Geneva, carrying out contract studies of child guidance services, prison psychotherapy, and mental illness in student populations around the world. A key intermediary between WFMH experts and UN planners in New York was Charles Hogan, an American who held various high positions in the secretariat of the Economic and Social Council. Hogan, who counted Rees as "a close friend" and commended him to colleagues as "a very sensible person," arranged to hold WFMH meetings in the UN complex on the East River in 1955, 1957, and 1959. Before audiences of diplomats, bureaucrats, and representatives of other nongovernmental organizations (NGOs), Rees and his fellow experts rehearsed their arguments for the significance of psychological impediments to modernization.[42] Mental states would have to adapt, they argued, as urbanization and industrialization wreaked havoc with traditional cultures. According to Rees, "many people cannot take [change] and are not sufficiently adaptable, perhaps because of their upbringing."[43] UN officials took seriously his insistence that "stress due to industrialization and mechanization" was causing pervasive emotional disorder in the world beyond the West. Noting the "psychological and social strains" imposed by the new "habits and attitudes" of economic development, the UN technical assistance budget in 1949–1950 allocated $1.6 million (the equivalent of more than $15 million today) for the training of psychologists, psychiatrists, and "psychiatric social workers."[44]

Theories about the psychological afterlife of childhood cast a long shadow in the UN. Officials in the Bureau of Social Affairs, citing Bowlby, identified the family as "the basic unit within which preventive and protective social welfare measures should be centered." British economist Hans Singer noticed a widespread conviction among his UN colleagues in the 1950s that the "welfare of children was an economic necessity." The United Nations Children's Fund (UNICEF) was classified as a development program rather than a humanitarian enterprise, he recalled, because "children who had been malnourished in their early years and pre-birth would have a lower brain capacity." If this emphasis on psychological efficiency could bolster benevolent programs, however, it also sharpened invidious distinctions between cultures. Echoing Soddy almost word for word, a UN panel concluded in 1952 that the extended families of the developing world discouraged entrepreneurial initiative by dissolving individual initiative into diffuse webs of obligation.[45]

Another preoccupation of British experts—the non-coercive leadership style inspired by group dynamics—likewise found its way into the heart of international organizations. Perhaps the most influential development manual ever published, *Cultural Patterns and Technical Change* (1953), was the product of a UNESCO contract with the World Federation for Mental Health. The WFMH committee that proposed the study at a conference in Geneva in 1949 was chaired by Colonial Office adviser Thomas Simey.[46] Emerging four years later from a drafting committee led by Margaret Mead, the final version of the manual paid homage to relativist principles, imploring Western experts to recognize that their own preconceptions about everything from the expression of emotions to the nature of time and space were far from universal. But this restraint had clear limits: although respect for cultural difference altered the means of approach, it did not affect the ultimate goal of modernization. Mead and her colleagues recommended easing the frustrations of rapid change by turning to group therapy, encouraging the subjects of development to share their difficulties with each other. New practices would be accepted more readily if development workers could attach "some form of satisfaction to them . . . consistent praise, approval, privilege, improved social status, strengthened integration with one's group, or material reward." Conversely, if the inevitable consequence of emotional upheaval went untreated, individuals risked regression into apathy, escapism, or violence. These guidelines bore the imprint of Simey's belief that building up "mutual confidence between individuals" was a prerequisite to conquering the "backwardness" that persisted "in all forms of rural social life."[47]

If inducing social change depended on finite calibrations of feeling, then modernization required a certain kind of personality among Western development workers as well as the people they worked with overseas. In the late 1950s, bureaucrats at the UN and the U.S. State Department asked the WFMH to investigate the possibility of using psychological tests to evaluate candidates for international work. While these administrators were initially most concerned about the threat of emotional breakdown, human scientists saw a more profound danger in the temperamental disposition to issue commands instead of gauging emotions. A few even suggested using the F-scale designed by Frankfurt School researchers to identify the unconscious wellsprings of fascism: ethnic prejudice, intolerance of ambiguity, and lust for power. As Unilever psychologist A. T. M.

Wilson argued, "much may depend on the distinction" between "an authoritative personality" and an "ethnocentric authoritarian"—a difference that only formal personality tests could reliably assess. Other federation experts likewise concluded that overseas influence rested on a delicate balance of intervention and restraint, shifting attitudes gradually across the generations without appearing to dictate terms.[48]

The World Federation for Mental Health was not alone in warning that overt racism and authoritarianism could endanger Western influence overseas. Newspaper editor Henry Vincent Hodson founded the Institute of Race Relations (IRR) in 1951 to promote what he called an "attitude of mind which makes the commonwealth system work, the attitude of tolerance." Like the WFMH, this organization drew support from a combination of American foundations and British companies doing business abroad. The inaugural director, Philip Mason, was an ex-ICS administrator who issued a *mea culpa* in 1954 for what he retrospectively described as complicity in the racial hierarchy of the Raj. "I begin to perceive," he reflected, "the anaesthetizing effect such a situation had . . . in the case of almost everyone who took part in it from the privileged side." Defining the relationship between colonizer and colonized as a neurotic entanglement that ensnared Britons and Indians alike, Mason argued that working through the psychological legacy of that relationship offered the only path to easing "friction between the races of mankind."[49]

Like many other Anglophone thinkers, Mason found Octave Mannoni's theory of a "dependency complex" more congenial than Frantz Fanon's vision of therapeutic violence. Mason seized on the idea that paternalism endured in the minds of imperial subjects—sapping autonomy, turning to hostility at the first sign of abandonment, and otherwise throwing up mental roadblocks to modernization—after formal rule ended. In places with "a long history of exploitation," he argued, entrenched attitudes of passivity and fatalism stunted progress no less dramatically than the physical symptoms of malnutrition. Other IRR researchers agreed that "emotional resistance" to development—even a "Slave Mentality"—could be attributed to the lasting effects of British imperialism.[50] But the indictment of Western dominance implicit in this diagnosis went only so far. Reflecting the preoccupations of the postwar moment, the language of paternalism and dependency blurred boundaries between the public and the private; the trauma inflicted by imperial rule, in these accounts, could not easily be separated from the trauma inflicted by dysfunctional families. Like their counterparts at the World Federation for Mental Health, Institute of Race Relations experts dutifully chronicled variations in toilet training and other parenting practices around the world. Mason even cited traumatic weaning as an explanation for the supposed rarity of entrepreneurial initiative in Africa. As long as they learned to navigate around the pitfalls of imperial authority, in other words, experts still had a role to play in easing the disorders of decolonization.[51]

Identifying inner life as the key to economic development had many consequences. It sketched a "thin," or schematic, model of the ideal post-colonial subject, charting cultural variations as barriers to the realization of universal norms. Where Freudian radicals had once seen the mother–child relationship as the wellspring of liberation, the same emotional nexus now appeared as a target of regulation. Harnessing the family as an engine of social change was not, of course, a uniquely British ambition: experts in America and France likewise envisioned far-reaching benefits from the guidance of mothers and children.[52] But the global dimension of this movement was shaped by British experts and imperial institutions in ways that have not often been recognized. The same theories and methods that helped define anticolonial rebellion as pathological disorder now por-trayed child-rearing, personality, and social change as interconnected problems. Seizing on this research, British internationalists echoed their Colonial Office counterparts in warning that development projects were doomed to fail unless emotions could be stabilized and reformed.

In some ways, the prominence of British expertise on the world stage declined quickly from its postwar apogee. Julian Huxley served as UNESCO director-general for only two years, stepping down in 1948; Williams and Hargreaves left the WHO in 1951 and 1955, respectively. As the number of member states in these agencies climbed, the proportion of the budget covered by Britain dropped, and so did its claim on top jobs.[53] British think tanks likewise saw their influence wane as the war became a more distant memory. Sent into decline after the retirement of Jack Rees in 1961, the World Federation for Mental Health had to shutter its head-quarters for lack of financial support a few years later. A bitter dispute about migration to Britain, meanwhile, divided the Institute of Race Relations as a generation of radical scholars shifted their attention to the problems of home-grown racism.[54] But the declining prominence of British experts in the world did not always translate into a rejection of their ideas. When postcolonial and American thinkers stepped into the void created by decolonization, they continued to accept the assumptions of late imperial psychology: the inadequacy of purely material solutions to development problems; the link between psychometrics and social efficiency; and the need to reshape volatile attitudes toward authority and change. To modernize the postcolonial world, it was said, the postcolonial mind had to be analyzed, measured, and managed.

¶ ACROSS THE BRITISH WORLD, researchers discovered that colonies made less congenial laboratories after political independence. Doing fieldwork in Ghana in the late 1950s, Institute of Race Relations psychologist Gustav Jahoda noticed that schoolmasters no longer afforded him easy access to research subjects, as they had during the colonial period. "They would keep me waiting," he remembered, "perfectly pleasant and so forth, but there wouldn't be this great adoration of the white man." When British officials complained about the hostility and resentment encountered by visiting technicians overseas, their postcolonial counterparts pointed out that the history of imperialism was not so easily forgotten. At an Oxford conference in the early 1960s, African delegates led by Tom Mboya of Kenya stressed "the importance of a sense of dignity and equality" among nations; they said that imperialism was not merely a matter of foreign domination but also the "psychology of superiority which so often went along with it." In India, where Nehru initially expressed enthusiasm for the UNESCO study of social tensions, concern that researchers might feed stereotypes about Third World backwardness led him to change course. Advocating a shift of attention away from communal riots in India and toward the world leaders who "sit in Chancellories and prepare to break and smash millions and billions of heads," Nehru puckishly suggested that UNESCO human scientists should focus their energies on the UN's New York headquarters instead.[55]

British experts sometimes made matters worse by parachuting into former colonies with a long list of prescriptions and a minimum of local knowledge. Despite management consultant Lyndall Urwick's self-professed "ignorance" of India, the British Department of Technical Cooperation sent him to the subcontinent in 1956 to impart his knowledge

The imperial expert in a post-imperial world? Lyndall Urwick in India, 1956.
(Image reproduced courtesy of Henley Business School, Henley-on-Thames.)

of industrial psychology and personnel selection over the course of a two-
month tour. From the commercial hubs of Ahmedabad, Bangalore, and
Hyderabad to the metropolises of Bombay, Delhi, and Calcutta, Urwick
greeted audiences with a simple message: running efficient organizations
required knowledge of how to "motivate" and "integrate" groups. Insisting
that a well-administered business in the "mechanical" sense could not
hope to succeed unless their managers also won loyalty and respect,
Urwick suggested that psychology could help in two ways: by offering "a
more objective approach to problems involving individual personality,"
alerting the manager to "the dangers of his own emotions," and by

furnishing "valuable techniques for testing various physical, moral, and intellectual capacities" at every level of the workforce.[56]

Urwick, a former Rowntrees manager, and his official sponsors conceived the trip as an emergency infusion of expertise for a benighted indigenous elite. As he put it, "India is desperately in need of a very rapid development of an appreciation and knowledge of management." In fact, however, efforts to maximize the productivity of human resources were already flourishing across the country. Private firms, government agencies, and the armed forces all commonly used psychological tests to select and promote employees in the early years of independence. The massive Tata steel factory at Jamshedpur hired military selection officers as industrial psychologists and used the Progressive Matrices test to select job applicants.[57] Prime Minister Nehru's director of development planning, P. C. Mahalanobis, was a statistician and mental-testing pioneer whose blueprint for the Indian economy depended on the precise allocation of resources. This included human resources: a Mahalanobis put it, "appropriate tests and examinations . . . have to be developed" to ensure that young Indians were appropriately placed in training programs and jobs.[58] Bureaucracies devoted to mental measurement proliferated accordingly: the Bureau of Psychology, Allahabad (1947); the Psychological Research Wing of the Ministry of Defence, Delhi (1949); the Psychological Research Wing of the Central Institute of Education, also in Delhi (1950); the Vocational Guidance Bureau, Bombay (1950); and the Central Bureau of Educational and Vocational Guidance, Delhi (1954), which was the model for twelve similar offices at the state level. According to one estimate compiled at the time of Urwick's visit, at least one hundred researchers were working to standardize and adapt tests for the Indian population: intelligence tests like the Binet and the Progressive Matrices; personality tests like the Rorschach and the Thematic Apperception; and aptitude tests to select nurses, engineers, social workers, teachers, and medical students.[59]

While Urwick imagined himself launching a "mental revolution" in a land where "customs and practices" threatened progress, Indian leaders in business and government were innovating new techniques of psychological management that blended British, American, and local knowledge. A representative figure in this movement was Gautam Sarabhai, a scion of the leading textile family of Ahmedabad, who acquired his enthusiasm for psychoanalysis while studying at Cambridge and was later analyzed by

Anna Freud herself. Sarabhai drew in part on a rich Indian current of Freudian thought which assumed the unity of individuals and their surroundings in a way that European psychoanalysis did not; the pioneering figure of Indian psychoanalysis, Girindrasekhar Bose, helped establish the vocational selection unit at the University of Calcutta in the 1930s and designed pencil-and-paper tests like the "neurotic questionnaire" to assess the temperaments of job applicants.[60] When Sarabhai did seek advice from foreign experts, he did so on his own terms, taking cues from different traditions at different times and translating them into his own idiom. As the chairman of the Ahmedabad Calico Mills in the early 1950s, he hired a Tavistock Institute researcher to reorganize the factory floor on the model of "the close-knit family and village community which formerly provided traditional opportunities for the satisfaction of group needs." The resulting recommendation—that weavers work as members of small groups rather than "independent isolates"—bore the imprint of its Nehruvian moment, synthesizing modernizing efficiency with cultural traditionalism.[61] But Sarabhai took inspiration as well from the famous Hawthorne experiments in the interwar United States, proposing "interpretive group discussions" to uncover "unconscious attitudes" that weighed on productivity. Sarabhai hosted one of the Hawthorne researchers, Harvard professor Fritz Roethlisberger, in Ahmedabad in 1959. His mill managers drew on Roethlisberger's works as they met for weekly sessions to discuss the workplace dynamics of "dominance and dependence."[62]

The multinational expertise that new states had at their disposal was partly a function of the geopolitical moment. With psychology serving as a putatively nonideological meeting ground for human scientists around the world, the technical assistance offered by international organizations often took the form of expertise in constructing and validating mental tests. UNESCO, for instance, sent psychometricians to India, Malaya, and Nigeria in the 1950s. At the same time, the Cold War ensured a buyer's market for technical aid, allowing postcolonial leaders to play Americans and Soviets off each other while staying clear of unwanted commitments.[63] In many British colonies, this process brought Americans into a dominant role with lightning speed; they won government contracts soon after the British left and in some cases even earlier. The intellectual transfer of power was perhaps most dramatic in India, where the U.S. Technical Cooperation Administration (forerunner to the Agency for

International Development) and the Ford Foundation launched a massive community development program in the early 1950s, installing anthropologists, social workers, and other experts in villages across the country. It was a similar story even where the British retained formal political control. In Africa, Colonial Office administrators noticed uneasily in the late 1950s, American social scientists had surpassed their British counterparts in sheer numbers. By the end of the decade, an industrial psychologist from Michigan State University felt confident enough to deliver an epitaph for the imperial science of mind almost in passing. "As a burgeoning Africa becomes too big a problem for the metropole countries to handle," he announced, "there may be room for some Americans to assist Africans in developing Africa for Africans."[64]

Although American psychometrics had always loomed large in the British Empire, mental testers in the United States now pursued the imperial market more energetically than ever before. Officials at the Educational Testing Service (ETS) of Princeton, New Jersey—best known for administering the SAT—were reimagining their fill-in-the-bubble intelligence tests for global export and prioritized the training of "highly professional, expert measurement people" to administer them. With funding from the Carnegie Corporation and the Ford Foundation, they brought dozens of aspiring psychometricians from Asia, Africa, and the West Indies to the ETS campus at Princeton for six-week training sessions in test construction in the early 1960s. One ETS staffer, Morey Wantman, lived in Singapore for two years on another Carnegie-funded project; he served as a consultant to the Malayan Ministry of Education and guided a team of three trainees to design aptitude tests for the selection of students and civil servants. His trips to Africa and India were briefer but nonetheless useful in building demand for American psychometrics. As Wantman reported after a visit to East Africa in 1961, "the African leadership naturally shows a resentment toward the British" and "welcome the Americans, both because of the potential aid they can get and because we are not associated with colonialism."[65]

While this assessment may have overstated the enthusiasm for technical assistance from the United States, American resources did allow postcolonial leaders to pursue the modernizing promise of psychometrics while distancing themselves from its imperial origins. In 1960, the year of Nigerian independence, the new state commissioned the U.S. Agency for

International Development to design mental tests for school selection; six years later, the resulting assessments of verbal and quantitative aptitude had become part of the common entrance exam used everywhere in Anglophone West Africa.[66] The institution created to administer those tests, the West African Examinations Council (WAEC), received support from the Ford Foundation as well as the American government. Its African staffers studied mental measurement at the University of Pittsburgh and trained with ETS experts before assuming full control from the Americans in 1972.[67] Like British experts before them, American technical advisers sang from the hymn book of modernization, warning that only psychometric intervention could overcome "shortages of skilled manpower" and the threat of "depressed economies." But these arguments now came with a twist. Ignoring the proliferation of aptitude tests across the empire in the 1950s, the Americans and their African partners painted the British testing regime with the broadest of brushes, pointing to Oxbridge-style exams that favored English fluency as the ultimate symbol of imperial arrogance. With their fill-in-the-bubble choices and electronic scoring machines, American aptitude tests represented a dramatic departure from the musty Anglocentrism of the old system. Raw ability, not literary polish, would now receive its just reward.[68]

Of course, castigating the unfairness of the old system served a useful function: it strengthened the legitimacy of the new one. Once in power, nationalist movements that had long promised wider access to education expanded primary schools much more quickly than secondary schools, intensifying the selectivity of the system at the higher level.[69] The shortage of skilled jobs likewise remained pressing across the continent. As in the imperial era, aptitude testing helped deflect criticism from political leaders by allocating limited opportunities according to merit—or appearing to do so. Inheriting control of the Aptitude Testing Unit, then funded by the Ford Foundation, along with the portfolio of labor minister in 1962, Tom Mboya considered that "vast shortages of trained manpower" in East Africa required a psychometric response—"modern testing equipment and the means to design, prepare, interpret aptitude and achievement testing"—to maximize human resources. Following the same logic, WAEC expanded its purview from educational to vocational selection, surpassing the Aptitude Testing Unit to test more than ten thousand job seekers annually by the end of the 1960s. For everyone from watchmakers and electricians to airplane pilots and civil servants, standardized aptitude tests were now well established as the gateway to mobility in postcolonial Africa. Touted as a panacea for inefficiency, a corrective to imperial misrule, and a shortcut to modernization, aptitude testing still promised solutions to many problems.[70]

In some ways, then, an influx of American aid made it possible to write the imperial legacy out of the psychological experiments that began with the British and continued after they left. This was ironic not least because postcolonial leaders favored the same psychological language that British officials had once invoked to discredit decolonization. Even nationalists, that is, sometimes described nationalism as an emotionally powerful and potentially violent expression of resentment. For Nehru, the threat of internecine conflict in the new Indian state dictated a therapeutic response. To "achieve the psychological integration of our people," he advocated "a process similar to that of psychoanalysis," working through the shared history of India's diverse cultures without falling prey to "the overpowering and sometimes suffocating" weight of the past. Kenneth Kaunda, the first president of Zambia, favored the language of behaviorism rather than psychoanalysis: he warned in the 1960s that "political frustration" could result in "aggression, heightened suggestibility, and a reversion to non-constructive patterns of behavior" unless popular energies were channeled into the work of nation-building. Psychology played a central role in the pedagogical language of postcolonial rule as leaders stressed the need for new habits of thought and feeling to catch up with the West.[71]

Obscuring the British origins of postcolonial psychology also had ironies for the Americans who encouraged it. Eager to leverage their country's revolutionary heritage for Third World influence, U.S. officials in the Cold War era worked to craft an anticolonial image on the world stage even as they often supported British interests in practice. As one State Department planner argued, backing British imperialism too conspicuously could "limit our capacities for developing emotional adherence to our cause."[72] And yet, the aim of understanding, predicting, and ultimately changing inner life in other cultures united officials and experts on both sides of the Atlantic. From anticommunist propaganda to personality profiles of the Iranian shah to plans for the transformation of the Indian peasant, mind science shaped U.S. foreign policy in myriad ways.[73] Despite the abundance of expertise in America, these initiatives sometimes took cues from the British. Psychologists advising the U.S. government cited Morris Carstairs's study of the neurotic Brahmin personality as an explanation of the deep-seated resistance to change that supposedly plagued India.[74] State Department officials adopted some of the Tavistock techniques recommended by the World Federation for Mental Health, requiring diplomats bound for international conferences in the mid-1950s to first attend group therapy sessions so that they could examine their own "feelings, attitudes, and personal experiences," work through authoritarian impulses, and cultivate open-mindedness.[75]

If the democratic United States viewed the so-called Third World in a radically different way than imperial Britain, the contrast did not leave its mark on the field of psychology. Like the British researchers at the Institute of Race Relations, American experts at the Council on Foreign Relations in the mid-1950s were reading Mannoni and pondering how the emotional legacy of dependency posed obstacles to intervention. The postcolonial mind they imagined was essentially schizophrenic—sentimentally attached to the queen and a vague sense of Britain as "home" but also displaying an "almost pathological sensitivity" to assertions of Western dominance. In the mid-1960s, an American psychologist working in India was still citing Mannoni to explain the unstable combination of passivity and aggression he observed there. "Even today," Harvard researcher David Winter observed, "the Western scholar meets Indians who will say, 'Ah, you know, sahib, it was all better under the British.'" A Punjabi villager who suggested that economic progress depended on the Municipal Board and the Department of Agriculture exemplified what Winter saw as a crippling lack of individual initiative.[76] His boss, Harvard psychologist David McClelland, believed that only therapeutic intervention could create the psychological preconditions for economic growth. In a project funded by the Carnegie Corporation, the Ford Foundation, and the U.S. Agency for International Development, McClelland ran a seminar for Indian businessmen on the outskirts of Hyderabad that aimed to instill the "urge to improve" through role-playing, story-telling, and other creative exercises. Arguing that material progress in every society was determined by a single, measurable, motivational force—the need for achievement, or what he labeled "n Achievement"—McClelland inspired American researchers to quantify the inner capacity for modernization in cultures across Asia and Africa.[77]

Like their British counterparts at WHO, the World Federation for Mental Health, and elsewhere, Americans traced the pathologies of the postcolonial mind to dysfunctional families as well as the experience of colonization. Even after the hotly controversial reception of Englishman Geoffrey Gorer's "swaddling hypothesis," which traced Soviet authoritarianism to childhood experiences of discipline and indulgence, American experts kept turning to early life for explanations of political and economic behavior. A Council on Foreign Relations discussion group in the early 1950s worried that "patterns of family life and home-training" might be producing Asian and African leaders with authoritarian impulses: "anti-social attitudes," "class or national hatreds," "neurotic symptoms antithetical to effective leadership (excessive dependence, guilt-feelings, etc.)." For McClelland and other psychologists, too, parenting methods that encouraged self-reliance were critical to the formation of productive and democratic personalities. The handbook used by American aid workers in East Africa in the early 1960s even claimed that African children failed to develop an objective, mechanical outlook because they lacked exposure to toys and other "cultural objects." It was written by Gordon Wilson, an LSE-trained anthropologist and ex-imperial official in Kenya.[78]

The theories, methods, and language of imperial psychology endured because they furnished a rationale for continuing intervention in the decolonized world. Rendering inner life everywhere legible as well as malleable, mind science made difference less threatening. It contained the world's diversity within a framework of universalism; it softened the hard-edged abstractions of race and culture into a mass of individual subjects. As Indian social critic Ashis Nandy later put it, psychology served the ends of imperialism and modernization by striving to "remove the difference between the laboratory and life."[79] Psychology rarely, if ever, achieved the transformational effects that its most ardent champions hoped for— or that skeptics like Nandy feared. But thinkers and rulers were continually drawn to it anyway, seduced by the prospect of changing the world through the measurement of abilities and the management of emotions. The dream of making minds modern was a powerful one.

Conclusion

T HIS BOOK HAS TOLD the stories of the conduits, translators, and wanderers who made psychology an imperial project. Migrating across local, national, and regional spaces, they found their role navigating the places in between. Although psychology was not necessarily more portable than other human sciences, the rhetoric of universality that emerged from the laboratory encouraged its champions to believe it was. The struggle to reconcile universal claims with the stubborn realities of difference was a recurring theme of their experiments across the British Empire.

Imperial history becomes imperialist history when it uncritically accepts the stories contemporaries told about themselves and their actions. As this book has shown, however, the stories told by the practitioners of mind science in the empire—about the portability of their instruments, about their ability to redress social wrongs, about their power to suppress rebellions cleanly or develop economies from the nursery—rarely held up to the test of experience. Because the people involved in imperial psychology—belonging to many different professions and working in many different places—were so dispersed, an ambiguous or disappointing outcome in one case did not always prevent others from trying the same methods elsewhere. Then, too, experts who invented new tools or turned them to a novel purpose had a vested interest in declaring their success. It was difficult enough to confirm that psychometrics boosted a factory's output or that a propaganda pamphlet induced insurgents to surrender; it was virtually impossible to verify whether a theory of the unconscious explained what it was supposed to or whether a test measured what it claimed to. So if imperial psychology was too big—in terms of the ambitions proclaimed by its champions—to ever fully succeed, it was also too big—too diffuse, too important to careers, and too entangled with endless other variables—to definitively fail. Its appeal resisted refutation.

In some ways, then, the history of psychology and empire is a history of surprising continuity. But it is also a history of change over time. As the imperial state increasingly sponsored and acted on psychological knowledge, the anti-racist and anti-authoritarian possibilities of the field receded ever further into the background. It was not so much that human scientists tailored their views for the sake of winning patronage as that officials co-opted their expertise and absorbed their methods, fashioning ideologically diverse and sometimes radical currents of thought into bureaucratic tools and military weapons. The rigid hierarchies that Myers and Rivers challenged in the era of the First World War became a less meaningful target by the 1940s, as the paternalistic traditionalism of indirect rule gave way to the modernizing ethos of development. Objections to visual and inexpert assessments of mental ability likewise lost their force as intelligence testing gradually migrated from mission stations to military barracks, government schools, and factory floors. In the same way, the methods of researchers who analyzed the trauma of imperial subjects were later incorporated into the personality testing of imperial soldiers and ultimately adopted by counterinsurgency strategists and development planners. The impact of modernization theory and medicalized psychiatry—two areas where British and American influence were deeply entangled—played a part in this process of instrumentalization. But so did the fact that, for most of the twentieth century, ambitions to standardize and globalize depended on imperial networks. The institutional machinery that exported psychology around the world tamed idealism and suppressed subversion. The boundary between anticolonial protest and colonial knowledge, or radicalism and authority, was always unstable in the science of mind—an ideological malleability that may have undermined its effectiveness but also ensured its durability in the age of empire and beyond.

We are used to thinking about the power rather than the limits of expert knowledge and about harmony rather than conflict in the relationship between experts and the state. This book has questioned both assumptions. Psychology did not resolve the problems of ruling an empire so much as it dramatized them. Balancing difference with development, community with individuality, compulsion with autonomy, universality with particularity: these imperatives confronted researchers and rulers alike. Even when its theories and methods now seem quaint, psychology in the British Empire exposed tensions at the heart of every imperial project.

NOTES

Abbreviaions

ABCFM	American Board of Commissioners for Foreign Missions archive, Houghton Library, Harvard University
CC	Carnegie Corporation of New York archive, Columbia University Library
CHP	Center for the History of Psychology, University of Akron
CR	Colonial Research series, LSE archive
CSSRC	Colonial Social Science Research Council
CUL	Cambridge University Library
ETS	Educational Testing Service
FF	Ford Foundation archive, Rockefeller Archive Center
IEL	Institute of Education archive, University of London
IOR	India Office Records, British Library, London
IWM	Imperial War Museum, London
LOC	Library of Congress, Washington, DC
LSE	London School of Economics archive
MM	Margaret Mead papers, Library of Congress
NAG	National Archives of Ghana, Accra
NAI	National Archives of India, New Delhi
NAK	National Archives of Kenya, Nairobi
NAUK	National Archives of the United Kingdom, Kew
NAUS	National Archives and Records Administration of the United States, College Park, MD
NAZ	National Archives of Zambia, Lusaka
RAC	Rockefeller Archive Center, Sleepy Hollow, NY
RAI	Royal Anthropological Institute, London
RF	Rockefeller Foundation archive, Rockefeller Archive Center
RHO	Rhodes House Library, Oxford University
SLV	State Library of Victoria, Melbourne
UNNY	United Nations archive, New York
WFMH	World Federation for Mental Health

WHOG   World Health Organization archive, Geneva
  WL   Wellcome Library for the History of Medicine, London
 YUL   Yale University Library

Introduction

1. Nikolas Rose, *The Psychological Complex: Psychology, Politics and Society in England, 1869–1939* (London: Routledge, 1985); Nikolas Rose, *Governing the Soul: The Shaping of the Private Self* (London: Routledge, 1990); Ellen Herman, *The Romance of American Psychology: Political Culture in the Age of Experts* (Berkeley: University of California Press, 1995); John A. Mills, *Control: A History of Behavioral Psychology* (New York: New York University Press, 1998); Rebecca Lemov, *World as Laboratory: Experiments with Mice, Mazes, and Men* (New York: Hill and Wang, 2005); Stephen Jay Gould, *The Mismeasure of Man* (New York: W. W. Norton, 1981); John Carson, *The Measure of Merit: Talents, Intelligence, and Inequality in the French and American Republics, 1750–1940* (Princeton: Princeton University Press, 2007).

2. Graham Richards, *"Race," Racism and Psychology: Towards a Reflexive History* (London: Routledge, 1997); Chloe Campbell, *Race and Empire: Eugenics in Colonial Kenya* (Manchester: Manchester University Press, 2007); Saul Dubow, *Scientific Racism in Modern South Africa* (Cambridge: Cambridge University Press, 1995), ch. 6; Hussein Abdilahi Bulhan, "Psychological Research in Africa: Genesis and Function," *Race and Class* 23, no. 1 (1981): 25–41; Sunil Bhatia, "Orientalism in Euro-American and Indian Psychology: Historical Representations of 'Natives' in Colonial and Post-Colonial Contexts," *History of Psychology* 5, no. 4 (2002): 376–398; Christiane Hartnack, *Psychoanalysis in Colonial India* (New Delhi: Oxford University Press, 2001); Warwick Anderson, *The Cultivation of Whiteness: Science, Health, and Racial Destiny in Australia* (Carlton: Melbourne University Press, 2002), 206–209, 240–241. The related but distinct field of psychiatry, the branch of medicine concerned with the diagnosis and treatment of mental illness, has received even more attention. See Megan Vaughan, *Curing Their Ills: Colonial Power and African Illness* (Palo Alto: Stanford University Press, 1991), ch. 5; Jock McCulloch, *Colonial Psychiatry and "the African Mind"* (Cambridge: Cambridge University Press, 1995); Sloan Mahone and Megan Vaughan, eds., *Psychiatry and Empire* (New York: Palgrave Macmillan, 2007); Jonathan Sadowsky, *Imperial Bedlam: Institutions of Madness in Colonial Southwest Nigeria* (Berkeley: University of California Press, 1999); Lynette Jackson, *Surfacing Up: Psychiatry and Social Order in Colonial Zimbabwe, 1908–1968* (Ithaca: Cornell University Press, 2005); Shruti Kapila, "Masculinity and Madness: Princely Personhood and Colonial Sciences of the Mind in Western India, 1871–1940," *Past & Present* 187 (May 2005): 121–156; Sloan Mahone, "The Psychology of Rebellion: Colonial Medical Responses to Dissent in British East Africa," *Journal of African History* 47, no. 2 (2006): 241–258. On the French case, see Richard Keller, *Colonial Madness: Psychiatry in French North Africa* (Chicago: University of Chicago Press, 2007).

3. Helen Tilley, *Africa as a Living Laboratory: Empire, Development, and the Problem of Scientific Knowledge, 1870–1950* (Chicago: University of Chicago Press, 2011); Michal Shapira, *The War Inside: Psychoanalysis, Total War, and the Making of the Democratic Self in Britain* (Cambridge: Cambridge University Press, 2013); Peter Mandler, *Return from the Natives: How Margaret Mead Won the Second World War and Lost the Cold War* (New Haven: Yale University Press, 2013); Andrew Jewett, *Science, Democracy, and the American University: From the Civil War to the Cold War* (Cambridge: Cambridge University Press, 2014); John P. Jackson, Jr., *Social Scientists for Social Justice: Making the Case against Segregation* (New York: New York University Press, 2001). For a different critique of Foucauldian and Gramscian approaches, with an emphasis on popular psychology and democratic self-fashioning, see Matthew Thomson, *Psychological Subjects: Identity, Culture, and Health in Twentieth-Century Britain* (Oxford: Oxford University Press, 2006).

4. Edward Said, introduction to Rudyard Kipling, *Kim* (London: Penguin, 1989), 33.

5. Tilley, *Africa as a Living Laboratory*; Henrika Kuklick, *The Savage Within: The Social History of British Anthropology, 1885–1945* (Cambridge: Cambridge University Press, 1991), ch. 5; George W. Stocking, *After Tylor: British Social Anthropology, 1888–1951* (Madison: University of Wisconsin Press, 1995), ch. 8; Wendy James, "The Anthropologist as Reluctant Imperialist," in *Anthropology and the Colonial Encounter*, ed. Talal Asad (London: Ithaca Press, 1973); Joseph Morgan Hodge, *Triumph of the Expert: Agrarian Doctrines of Development and the Legacies of British Colonialism* (Athens: Ohio University Press, 2007), 226–230; William Beinart, Karen Brown, and Daniel Gilfoyle, "Experts and Expertise in Colonial Africa Reconsidered: Science and the Interpretation of Knowledge," *African Affairs* 108 (2009): 413–433; Sabine Clarke, "A Technocratic Imperial State? The Colonial Office and Scientific Research," *Twentieth-Century British History* 18, no. 4 (2007): 453–480, at 477–479; Richard H. Grove, *Green Imperialism: Colonial Expansion, Tropical Island Edens, and the Origins of Environmentalism, 1600–1860* (Cambridge: Cambridge University Press, 1995).

6. See especially Vaughan, *Curing Their Ills*, and David Arnold, *Colonizing the Body: State Medicine and Epidemic Disease in Nineteenth-Century India* (Berkeley: University of California Press, 1993).

7. Hodge, *Triumph of the Expert*; Frederick Cooper, *Decolonization and African Society: The Labor Question in French and British Africa* (Cambridge: Cambridge University Press, 1996); Frederick Cooper and Randall Packard, eds., *International Development and the Social Sciences: Essays on the History and Politics of Knowledge* (Berkeley: University of California Press, 1997); Karl Ittmann, *A Problem of Great Importance: Population, Race, and Power in the British Empire, 1918–1973* (Berkeley: University of California Press, 2013); John Darwin, "What Was the Late Colonial State?" *Itinerario* 23, nos. 3–4 (1999): 73–82.

8. Elazar Barkan, *The Retreat of Scientific Racism: Changing Concepts of Race in Britain and the United States between the World Wars* (Cambridge: Cambridge University Press, 1993); Nancy Stepan, *The Idea of Race in Science:*

Great Britain, 1800–1960 (Hamden, CT: Archon Books, 1982); Peter Mandler, *The English National Character: The History of an Idea from Edmund Burke to Tony Blair* (New Haven: Yale University Press, 2006), 157–159; Matthew Thomson, " 'Savage Civilisation': Race, Culture, and Mind in Britain, 1898–1939," in *Race, Science and Medicine, 1700–1960,* ed. Waltraud Ernst and Bernard Harris (London: Routledge, 1999), 240.

9. George Orwell, *The Road to Wigan Pier* (London: Penguin, 2001 [1937]), 147. See also Susan Pedersen, "Modernity and Trusteeship: Tensions of Empire in Britain between the Wars," in *Meanings of Modernity: Britain from the Late-Victorian Era to World War II,* ed. Martin Daunton and Bernhard Rieger (Oxford: Berg, 2001).

10. Edward Said, *Orientalism* (New York: Vintage, 1979), 72.

11. Saul Dubow, introduction to *The Rise and Fall of Modern Empires,* vol. 2, *Colonial Knowledges* (Farnham: Ashgate, 2013). On categories of difference in imperial rule, see Ronald Inden, *Imagining India* (Oxford: Blackwell, 1990); Bernard S. Cohn, *Colonialism and Its Forms of Knowledge: The British in India* (Princeton: Princeton University Press, 1996); Nicholas Dirks, *Castes of Mind: Colonialism and the Making of Modern India* (Princeton: Princeton University Press, 2001); Clare Anderson, *Legible Bodies: Race, Criminality, and Colonialism in South Asia* (New York: Berg, 2004); David Omissi, *The Sepoy and the Raj: The Indian Army, 1860–1940* (London: Macmillan, 1994), 10–35; Heather Streets, *Martial Races: The Military, Race, and Masculinity in British Imperial Culture, 1857–1914* (Manchester: Machester University Press, 2004): James Hevia, *English Lessons: The Pedagogy of Imperialism in Nineteenth-Century China* (Durham: Duke University Press, 2003), 174–183; James Hevia, *The Imperial Security State: British Colonial Knowledge and Empire-Building in Asia* (Cambridge: Cambridge University Press, 2012), 116–126; Vaughan, *Curing Their Ills,* 11; Archie Mafeje, "The Ideology of 'Tribalism,' " *Journal of Modern African Studies* 9 (1971): 253–261; Terence Ranger, "From Humanism to the Science of Man: Colonialism in Africa and the Understanding of Alien Societies," *Transactions of the Royal Historical Society* 26 (1976): 115–141; Terence Ranger, "Race and Tribe in Southern Africa: European Ideas and African Acceptance," in *Racism and Colonialism,* ed. Robert Ross (Leiden: Martinus Nijhoff, 1982); Leroy Vail, ed., *The Creation of Tribalism in Southern Africa* (London: James Currey, 1989); Mahmood Mamdani, *Citizen and Subject: Contemporary Africa and the Legacy of Late Colonialism* (Princeton: Princeton University Press, 1996).

12. Mathew Thomson, "The Psychological Body," in *Medicine in the Twentieth Century,* ed. Roger Cooter and John Pickstone (Amsterdam: Harwood, 2000), 292; Arjun Appadurai, "Putting Hierarchy in Its Place," *Cultural Anthropology* 3, no. 1 (1988): 36–49.

13. By contrast, the literature on colonial knowledge has emphasized the ease with which rulers could impose a sense of difference through classification—an approach that risks reifying those classifications, overstating the power of the colonizer, and portraying colonized society as a *tabula rasa.* For these criticisms, see Frederick Cooper, *Colonialism in Question: Theory, Knowledge, History* (Berkeley: University of California Press, 2005), 77–83; Mrinalini Sinha, "Empire, Colonies, and World History," in *A Companion to World History,* ed. Douglas Northrop (Malden, MA: Wiley-Blackwell, 2012), 262–63;

Terence Ranger, "The Invention of Tradition Revisited: The Case of Colonial Africa," in *Legitimacy and the State in Twentieth-Century Africa: Essays in Honor of A.H.M. Kirk-Greene* (London: Macmillan, 1993); Thomas Spear, "Neo-Traditionalism and the Limits of Invention in British Colonial Africa," *Journal of African History* 44 (2003): 3–27.

14. Thomson, " 'Savage Civilisation' "; George Stocking, *Victorian Anthropology* (New York: Free Press, 1987), ch. 6; Glenda Sluga, *The Nation, Psychology, and International Politics, 1870–1919* (New York: Routledge, 2006).

15. Among many possibilities, see Guy Ortolano, *The Two Cultures Controversy: Science, Literature and Cultural Politics in Postwar Britain* (Cambridge: Cambridge University Press, 2009); David Edgerton, *England and the Aeroplane: Militarism, Modernity, and Machines* (London: Penguin, 2013 [1991]), ch. 2; David Edgerton, *Warfare State: Britain 1920–1970* (Cambridge: Cambridge University Press, 2006); Cooper, *Decolonization and African Society*; Tilley, *Africa as a Living Laboratory;* Clarke, "Technocratic Imperial State?"; Hodge, *Triumph of the Expert;* Ittmann, *Problem of Great Importance*; Michael Worboys, "The Imperial Institute: The State and the Development of the Natural Resources of the Colonial Empire, 1887–1923," in *Imperialism and the Natural World,* ed. John M. MacKenzie (Manchester: Manchester University Press, 1990); Michael Worboys, "The Discovery of Colonial Malnutrition between the Wars," in *Imperial Medicine and Indigenous Societies,* ed. David Arnold (Manchester: Manchester University Press, 1988), 208–225. On expertise and development before the twentieth century, see especially Richard Drayton, *Nature's Government: Science, Imperial Britain, and the "Improvement" of the World* (New Haven: Yale University Press, 2000).

16. Duncan S. A. Bell, "Dissolving Distance: Empire, Space, and Technology in British Political Thought, 1770–1900," *Journal of Modern History* 77, no. 3 (2005): 523–562; Stephen Kern, *The Culture of Time and Space, 1880–1918* (Cambridge: Harvard University Press, 1983), ch. 8; Tony Ballantyne and Antoinette Burton, *Empires and the Reach of the Global, 1870–1945* (Cambridge: Harvard University Press, 2014), ch. 2; David Arnold, *Everyday Technology: Machines and the Making of India's Modernity* (Chicago: University of Chicago Press, 2013), 150–156; Edgerton, *England and the Aeroplane*; Katherine C. Epstein, "Imperial Airs: Leo Amery, Air Power and Empire, 1873–1945," *Journal of Imperial and Commonwealth History* 38, no. 4 (2010): 571–598; Chandra D. Bhimull, "Empire in the Air: Speed, Perception, and Airline Travel in the Atlantic World," Ph.D. thesis (University of Michigan, 2007); Priya Satia, "War, Wireless, and Empire: Marconi and the British Warfare State, 1896–1903," *Culture and Technology* 51, no. 4 (2010): 829–853.

17. Christophe Bonneuil, "Development as Experiment: Science and State Building in Late Colonial and Postcolonial Africa, 1930–1970," *Osiris* 15 (2000): 258–281. For standardization as a form of cultural imperialism, see Bruno Latour, *Science in Action: How to Follow Scientists and Engineers through Society* (Cambridge: MIT Press, 1987). On standardization and global connections more broadly, see Kern, *Culture of Time and Space,* 11–15; Nick Cullather, *The Hungry World: America's Cold War Battle against Poverty in Asia* (Cambridge: Harvard University Press, 2010), 18–19; C. A. Bayly, *The Birth of the Modern World, 1780–1914: Global Connections and Comparisons*

(Malden: Blackwell, 2004); David Livingstone, *Putting Science in Its Place: Geographies of Scientific Knowledge* (Chicago: University of Chicago Press, 2003), ch. 4; Theodore M. Porter, *Trust in Numbers: The Pursuit of Objectivity in Science and Public Life* (Princeton: Princeton University Press, 1995), 31–32; M. Norbert Wise, ed., *The Values of Precision* (Princeton: Princeton University Press, 2007), 229–230; Ian R. Bartky, *One Time Fits All: The Campaign for Global Uniformity* (Stanford: Stanford University Press, 2007); Mark Mazower, *Governing the World: The History of an Idea* (New York: Penguin, 2012), ch. 4.

18. Donna Mehos and Suzanne Moon, "The Uses of Portability: Circulating Experts in the Politics of Cold War and Decolonization," in *Entangled Geographies: Empire and Technopolitics in the Global Cold War,* ed. Gabrielle Hecht (Cambridge: MIT Press, 2011). For psychology and the laboratory, see especially Kurt Danziger, *Constructing the Subject: Historical Origins of Psychological Research* (Cambridge: Cambridge University Press, 1990), ch. 2, and Jimena Canales, *A Tenth of a Second: A History* (Chicago: University of Chicago Press, 2011). On psychology before the laboratory, see Fernando Vidal, *The Sciences of the Soul: The Early Modern Origins of Psychology,* trans. Saskia Brown (Chicago: University of Chicago Press, 2011).

19. David Hollinger, "Cultural Relativism," in *The Cambridge History of Science,* vol. 7, *The Modern Social Sciences,* ed. Theodore M. Porter and Dorothy Ross (Cambridge: Cambridge University Press, 2003); Robert Wald Sussman, *The Myth of Race: The Troubling Persistence of an Unscientific Idea* (Cambridge: Harvard University Press, 2014), ch. 5.

20. A classic statement of this view is, of course, James C. Scott, *Seeing Like a State: How Certain Schemes to Improve the Human Condition Have Failed* (New Haven: Yale University Press, 1998). For a critique, see Cooper, *Colonialism in Question,* 140–141.

21. Put another way, the shift from biological to cultural explanations was less clear-cut in the psychological sciences than the social sciences: see Thomson, " 'Savage Civilisation' "; Stuart Hall, "The Multi-Cultural Question," in *Un/Settled Multiculturalisms: Diasporas, Entanglements, Transruptions,* ed. Barnor Hesse (London: Zed Books, 2001); Chris Waters, " 'Dark Strangers' in Our Midst: Discourses of Race and Nation in Britain, 1947–1963," *Journal of British Studies* 36, no. 2 (1997): 207–238; Alana Lentin " 'Replacing 'Race,' Historicizing 'Culture' in Multiculturalism," *Patterns of Prejudice* 39, no. 4 (2005): 379–396.

22. Clifford Geertz, "Culture War," in *Available Light: Anthropological Reflections on Philosophical Topics* (Princeton: Princeton University Press, 2000).

23. Elizabeth Borgwardt, *A New Deal for the World: America's Vision for Human Rights* (Cambridge: Harvard University Press, 2005). For British development policy as a crusade against global poverty, see Harold Wilson, *The War on World Poverty: An Appeal to the Conscience of Mankind* (London: Victor Gollancz, 1953). On the statism of postwar development, see Stephen Constantine, *The Making of British Colonial Development Policy, 1914–1940* (London: Frank Cass, 1984), ch. 9; R. D. Pearce, *The Turning Point in Africa: British Colonial Policy 1938–48* (London: Frank Cass, 1982); J. M. Lee, *Colonial Development and Good Government: A Study of the Ideas Expressed*

by the British Official Classes in Planning Decolonization 1939–1964 (Oxford: Clarendon, 1967); J. M. Lee and Martin Petter, *The Colonial Office, War, and Development Policy* (London: M. T. Smith, 1982).

24. Scott, *Seeing Like a State.*

25. Cooper, *Decolonization and African Society,* 321; Emma Rothschild, "Psychological Modernity in Historical Perspective," in *Rethinking the Development Experience: Essays Provoked by the Work of Albert O. Hirschman* (Washington: Brookings Institution, 1994); Nils Gilman, *Mandarins of the Future: Modernization Theory in Cold War America* (Baltimore: Johns Hopkins University Press, 2003), 94–107, 167–174, 183, 187–188; David Ekbladh, *The Great American Mission: Modernization and the Construction of an American World Order* (Princeton: Princeton University Press, 2010), 4–5, 158, 161, 173, 184–185; Cullather, *Hungry World,* 77–94; Michael E. Latham, *Modernization as Ideology: American Social Science and "Nation Building" in the Kennedy Era* (Chapel Hill: University of North Carolina Press, 2000), 33–41; Michael Latham, *The Right Kind of Revolution: Modernization, Development, and U.S. Foreign Policy from the Cold War to the Present* (Ithaca: Cornell University Press, 2011), 46–48, 71, 96, 119.

26. 536 *Parl. Deb.,* H.C., 5th ser. (1954–1955), 1174. See also 465 *Parl. Deb.,* H.C., 5th ser. (1948–1949), 1591; 443 *Parl. Deb., H.C.,* 5th ser. (1947–1948), 2043–2107; 531 *Parl. Deb.,* H.C., 5th ser. (1953–1954), 1310.

27. For a similar argument about imperial sociology, see George Steinmetz, "A Child of the Empire: British Sociology and Colonialism, 1940s–1960s," *Journal of the History of the Behavioral Sciences* 49, no. 4 (2013): 353–378, at 357.

28. T. H. Pear, "Some Early Relations between English Ethnologists and Psychologists," *Journal of the Royal Anthropological Institute* 60, no. 2 (1960): 227–237; George W. Stocking, "Anthropology and the Science of the Irrational: Malinowski's Encounter with Freudian Psychoanalysis," in *Malinowski, Rivers, Benedict and Others: Essays on Culture and Personality,* ed. George W. Stocking (Madison: University of Wisconsin Press, 1986).

29. L. S. Hearnshaw, *A Short History of British Psychology, 1840–1940* (London: Methuen, 1964), 208.

30. Rose, *Psychological Complex;* Rose, *Governing the Soul;* Rhodri Hayward, *The Transformation of the Psyche in British Primary Care* (London: Bloomsbury, 2014); Jonathan Toms, *Mental Hygiene and Psychiatry in Modern Britain* (Basingstoke: Palgrave Macmillan, 2013).

31. Jordanna Bailkin, *The Afterlife of Empire* (Berkeley: University of California Press, 2012).

32. David Wade Chambers and Richard Gillespie, "Locality in the History of Science: Colonial Science, Technoscience, and Indigenous Knowledge," *Osiris* 15 (2000): 221–240; Warwick Anderson and Vincanne Adams, "Pramoedya's Chickens: Postcolonial Studies of Technoscience," in *The Handbook of Science and Technology Studies,* ed. Edward J. Hackett, et al. (Cambridge: MIT Press, 2007).

33. Bayly, *Birth of the Modern World,* 20–21, 320–322.

34. "AHR Conversation: On Transnational History," *American Historical Review* 111, no. 5 (2006): 1441–1464; Northrop, ed., *Companion to World History,* 321–388.

35. The literature is immense and growing, but see Alan Lester, *Imperial Networks: Creating Identities in Nineteenth-Century South Africa and Britain* (London: Routledge, 2001); David Lambert and Alan Lester, eds., *Colonial Lives across the British Empire: Imperial Careering in the Long Nineteenth Century* (Cambridge: Cambridge University Press, 2006); Gary B. Magee and Andrew S. Thompson, *Empire and Globalisation: Networks of People, Goods, and Capital in the British World, c. 1850–1914* (Cambridge: Cambridge University Press, 2010); Tamson Pietsch, *Empire of Scholars: Universities, Networks, and the British Academic World, 1850–1939* (Manchester: Manchester University Press, 2013); Zoe Laidlaw, *Colonial Connections, 1815–45: Patronage, the Information Revolution, and Colonial Government* (Manchester: Manchester University Press, 2010). On imperial networks of ideas, see Robert L. Tignor, "The 'Indianization' of the Egyptian Administration under British Rule," *American Historical Review* 68 (1963): 636–661; S. B. Cook, *Imperial Affinities: Nineteenth Century Analogies and Exchanges between India and Ireland* (New Delhi: Sage, 1993); Tony Ballantyne, *Orientalism and Race: Aryanism in the British Empire* (New York: Palgrave, 2002); Thomas R. Metcalf, *Imperial Connections: India in the Indian Ocean Arena, 1860–1920* (Berkeley: University of California Press, 2007); Durba Ghosh and Dane Kennedy, eds., *Decentering Empire: Britain, India, and the Transcolonial World* (New Delhi: Orient Longman, 2006); Brent M. Bennett and Joseph M. Hodge, eds., *Science and Empire: Knowledge and Networks of Science across the British Empire, 1800–1970* (New York: Palgrave Macmillan, 2011).

36. Pietsch, *Empire of Scholars*. On Britishness and empire, see also Carl Bridge and Kent Fedorowich, eds., *The British World: Diaspora, Culture, and Identity* (London: Frank Cass, 2003); Saul Dubow, "How British Was the British World? The Case of South Africa," *Journal of Imperial and Commonwealth History* 37, no. 1 (1999): 1–37; Anne Spry Rush, *Bonds of Empire: West Indians and Britishness from Victoria to Decolonization* (Oxford: Oxford University Press, 2011); A. G. Hopkins, "Rethinking Decolonization," *Past & Present* 200 (2008): 211–247.

37. E. S. Rosenberg, "Missions to the World: Philanthropy Abroad," in *Charity, Philanthropy, and Civility in American History,* ed. Lawrence J. Friedman and Mark D. MacGarvie (Cambridge: Cambridge University Press, 2003); Ian Tyrrell, *Reforming the World: The Creation of America's Moral Empire* (Princeton: Princeton University Press, 2010).

38. On overlapping networks of national, imperial, and international research, see also Tilley, *Africa as a Living Laboratory,* 7–10; Brett M. Bennett, "The Consolidation and Reconfiguration of British Networks of Science, 1800–1970," in *Science and Empire,* ed. Bennett and Hodge.

39. See especially John Darwin, *The Empire Project: The Rise and Fall of the British World-System, 1830–1970* (Cambridge: Cambridge University Press, 2011); John Darwin, *Unfinished Empire: The Global Expansion of Britain* (New York: Bloomsbury Press, 2013); Ged Martin, "Was There a British Empire?" *Historical Journal* 15, no. 3 (1972): 562–569.

40. C.A. Bayly, *Empire and Information: Intelligence Gathering and Social Communication in India, 1780–1870* (Cambridge: Cambridge University Press, 1996).

1. The Laboratory in the Field

1. Alfred C. Haddon diary, Haddon papers, envelope 1055, CUL.

2. A. C. Haddon, *Head-Hunters Black, White, and Brown* (London: Methuen, 1901), 23.

3. The group biography by Ben Shephard, *Head Hunters: The Search for a Modern Science of Mind* (London: Bodley Head, 2014), is an accessible introduction. See also Richard Slobodin, *W. H. R. Rivers* (New York: Columbia University Press, 1978); "Charles Samuel Myers," in *A History of Psychology in Autobiography,* vol. 3, ed. Carl Murchison (Worcester: Clark University Press, 1936); William McDougall, *An Introduction to Social Psychology* (London: Methuen, 1908); William McDougall, *Outline of Abnormal Psychology* (New York: Scribner, 1926), 188.

4. On the ideal of fieldwork as immersion, see especially George W. Stocking, Jr., "Maclay, Kubary, Malinowski: Archetypes from the Dreamtime of Anthropology," in *Colonial Situations: Essays on the Contextualization of Ethnographic Knowledge* (Madison: University of Wisconsin Press, 1991), at 9–10; George W. Stocking, Jr., "The Ethnographer's Magic: Fieldwork in British Anthropology from Tylor to Malinowski," in *Observers Observed: Essays on Ethnographic Fieldwork* (Madison: University of Wisconsin Press, 1983), 104–112; Susan Sontag, "The Anthropologist as Hero," in *Against Interpretation* (New York: Picador, 2001 [1961]).

5. On fieldwork with instruments as a process of inscribing meaning, see Bruno Latour, "Give Me a Laboratory and I Will Raise the World," in *Science Observed: Perspectives on the Social Study of Science,* ed. Karin Knorr-Cetina and Michael Mulkay (London: Sage, 1983); Matthew H. Edney, *Mapping an Empire: The Geographical Construction of British India, 1765–1843* (Chicago: University of Chicago Press, 1997); D. Graham Burnett, *Masters of All They Surveyed: Exploration, Geography, and a British El Dorado* (Chicago: University of Chicago Press, 2000)

6. The classic accounts of the colony as "laboratory of modernity" are Gwendolyn Wright, *The Politics of Design in French Colonial Urbanism* (Chicago: University of Chicago Press, 1991); Paul Rabinow, *French Modern: Norms and Forms of the Social Environment* (Chicago: University of Chicago Press, 1995); Ann Laura Stoler, *Race and the Education of Desire: Foucault's History of Sexuality and the Colonial Order of Things* (Durham: Duke University Press, 1995). Historians of British imperialism have since taken up the theme of imperial experiments in governance: see Philippa Levine, *Prostitution, Race, and Politics: Policing Venereal Disease in the British Empire* (New York: Routledge, 2003); Chandak Sengoopta, *Imprint of the Raj: How Fingerprinting Was Born in Colonial India* (London: Pan Books, 2004); Richard Philips, *Sex,*

Politics, and Empire: A Postcolonial Geography (Manchester: Manchester University Press, 2006), 136–62; James Vernon, *Hunger: A Modern History* (Cambridge: Harvard University Press, 2007), 104–117.

7. On the conceptualization of the trained observer's body as an instrument in the late nineteenth century, see Henrika Kuklick, "Personal Equations: Reflections on the History of Fieldwork, with Special Reference to Sociocultural Anthropology," *Isis* 102 (2011): 1–33; Simon Schaffer, "Astronomers Marking Time: Discipline and the Personal Equation," *Science in Context* 2, no. 1 (1988): 115–145; Simon Schaffer, *From Physics to Anthropology and Back Again* (Cambridge: Prickly Pear Press, 1994); Nélia Dias, *La mesure des sens: Les anthropologues et le corps humain au XIXe siècle* (Paris: Aubier, 2004), 184–188.

8. Daniel R. Headrick, *The Tools of Empire: Technology and European Imperialism in the Nineteenth Century* (New York: Oxford University Press, 1981). The representational and rhetorical uses of technology in the imperial context have received at least as much attention as the material uses: see Bell, "Dissolving Distance"; Michael Adas, *Machines as the Measure of Men: Science, Technology, and Ideologies of Western Dominance* (Ithaca: Cornell University Press, 1989); Timothy Mitchell, *Colonising Egypt* (Berkeley: University of California Press, 1991), 128–131.

9. Cf. Peter Galison, *Image and Logic: A Material Culture of Microphysics* (Chicago: University of Chicago Press, 1997), 2.

10. Sally Shuttleworth, *Charlotte Bronte and Victorian Psychology* (Cambridge: Cambridge University Press, 1996); Sharrona Pearl, *About Faces: Physiognomy in Nineteenth-Century Britain* (Cambridge: Harvard University Press, 2009); Lucy Hartley, *Physiognomy and the Meaning of Expression in Nineteenth Century Culture* (Cambridge: Cambridge University Press, 2001); Mary Cowling, *The Artist as Anthropologist: The Representation of Character and Type in Victorian Art* (Cambridge: Cambridge University Press, 2001).

11. Kuklick, "Personal Equations"; Martin Jay, *Downcast Eyes: The Denigration of Vision in Twentieth-Century French Thought* (Berkeley: University of California Press, 1993); Edney, *Mapping an Empire*, ch. 2; Dias, *La mesure des sens.*

12. Edney, *Mapping an Empire,* 83–84; David Gilmour, *The Ruling Caste: Imperial Lives in the Victorian Raj* (New York: Farrar, Straus and Giroux, 2008), 216; Anthony Kirk-Greene, *Symbol of Authority: The British District Officer in Africa* (London: I. B. Tauris, 2006), 125–126; Lynette Schumaker, "A Tent with a View: Colonial Officials, Anthropologists, and the Making of the Field in Northern Rhodesia, 1937–1960," *Osiris* 11 (1996): 237–258, at 241–242.

13. Richard Price, *Making Empire: Colonial Encounters and the Creation of Imperial Rule in Nineteenth-Century Africa* (Cambridge: Cambridge University Press, 2008), 199; Kuklick, *Savage Within,* 198–199.

14. Cf. Efram Sera-Shriar, *The Making of British Anthropology, 1813–1871* (London: Pickering & Chatto, 2013); Gould, *Mismeasure of Man*; Dias, *La mesure des sens.*

15. Sera-Shriar, *Making of British Anthropology;* Stocking, *Victorian Anthropology,* 93–94; Raymond E. Fancher, "Francis Galton's African

Ethnography and Its Role in the Development of His Psychology," *British Journal for the History of Science* 16, no. 1 (1983): 67–79.

16. Charles Darwin, *The Expression of the Emotions in Man and Animals* (New York: D. Appleton, 1873), 15–17.

17. Christine Bolt, *Victorian Attitudes to Race* (London: Routledge, 1971), 179–181; Kuklick, *Savage Within*, 197; C. A. Bayly, "Knowing the Country: Empire and Information in India," *Modern Asian Studies* 27 (1993): 3–23, at 3–4.

18. G. O. Trevelyan, *The Competition Wallah* (London: Macmillan, 1866), 345; Philip D. Curtin, *The Image of Africa: British Ideas and Action, 1780–1850* (Madison: University of Wisconsin Press, 1964); Joseph Turner Hutchinson and William Blanford Griffith, *Instructions to District Commissioners* (London: Stevens, 1899), 35.

19. John Lubbock, *The Origin of Civilisation and the Primitive Condition of Man* (New York: D. Appleton, 1889 [1870]), 7. On the decline of imperial liberalism, see Eric Stokes, *The English Utilitarians and India* (Oxford: Clarendon Press, 1959); V. G. Kiernan, *The Lords of Human Kind: European Attitudes Towards the Outside World in the Imperial Age* (London: Weidenfeld and Nicolson, 1969), 46–68; Thomas R. Metcalf, *Ideologies of the Raj* (Cambridge: Cambridge University Press, 1994); Catherine Hall, *Civilising Subjects: Metropole and Colony in the English Imagination, 1830–1867* (Chicago: University of Chicago Press, 2002); Karuna Mantena, *Alibis for Empire: Henry Maine and the Ends of Liberal Imperialism* (Princeton: Princeton University Press, 2010).

20. Rick Rylance, *Victorian Psychology and British Culture, 1850–1880* (Oxford: Oxford University Press, 2000), 57–61; Jan Goldstein, "Bringing the Psyche into Scientific Focus," in *Cambridge History of Science*, vol. 7, *Modern Social Sciences*, ed. Porter and Ross, 146–149; Hearnshaw, *Short History of British Psychology*, 1–2, 43; Robert M. Young, "Association of Ideas," in *Dictionary of the History of Ideas*, vol. 1, ed. Philip P. Wiener (New York: Scribner, 1973); John Stuart Mill, *Autobiography* (London: Penguin, 1989 [1873]), 114–115.

21. Robert M. Young, *Mind, Brain, and Adaptation in the Nineteenth Century: Cerebral Localization and Its Biological Context from Gall to Ferrier* (New York: Oxford University Press, 1990), ch. 5; Robert M. Young, *Darwin's Metaphor: Nature's Place in Victorian Culture* (Cambridge: Cambridge University Press, 1985), 74–76; Robert J. Richards, *Darwin and the Emergence of Evolutionary Theories of Mind and Behavior* (Chicago: University of Chicago Press, 1987), 396–398; Roger Smith, *Inhibition: History and Meaning in the Sciences of Mind and Brain* (Berkeley: University of California Press, 1992), 162–178.

22. Stocking, *Victorian Anthropology*, 216–228; Kuklick, *Savage Within*, 84–89; Kathleen Frederickson, "Liberalism and the Time of Instinct," *Victorian Studies* 49, no. 2 (2007): 302–312. Spencer's clearest statement of the psychological characteristics of "primitive man" is in *The Principles of Sociology*, vol. 1 (New York: D. Appleton, 1906 [1874–1875]), 54–93.

23. Edward B. Tylor, *Primitive Culture*, vol. 1 (London: John Murray, 1871), 10; Walter Bagehot, *Physics and Politics, or Thoughts on the Application of the*

Principles of "Natural Selection" and "Inheritance" to Primitive Society (New York: D. Appleton, 1873), 100. On the passage from homogeneity to heterogeneity as a theme in evolutionary thought, see also Daniel Pick, "Freud's 'Group Psychology' and the History of the Crowd," *History Workshop Journal* 40 (1995): 39–61, at 57–59.

24. Herbert Spencer, *Descriptive Sociology, or Groups of Sociological Facts,* 8 vols.(New York: D. Appleton, 1873–1881). See also Robert L. Carneiro and Robert G. Perrin, "Herbert Spencer's *Principles of Sociology:* A Centennial Retrospective and Appraisal," *Annals of Science* 59 (2002): 221–261, at 237–240. On the "spirit of encyclopaedism" in Victorian representations of the world, see Raymond Corbey, "Ethnographic Showcases, 1870–1930," in *The Decolonization of Imagination: Culture, Knowledge and Power,* ed. Jan Nederveen Pieterse and Bhikhu Parekh (London: Zed Books, 1995), 59, and Tony Ballantyne, "Empire, Knowledge and Culture: From Proto-Globalization to Modern Globalization," in *Globalization in World History,* ed. A. G. Hopkins (London: Pimlico, 2002), 123.

25. Omissi, *Sepoy and the Raj*; Streets, *Martial Races.*

26. Kipling, *Kim,* 207; Ian Ferguson Nicolson, *The Administration of Nigeria, 1900–1960: Men, Methods, and Myths* (Oxford: Clarendon, 1969), 107–108; Kathryn Tidrick, "The Masai and Their Masters: A Psychological Study of District Administration," *African Studies Review* 23, no. 1 (1980) 15–32; Bruce Berman, *Control & Crisis in Colonial Kenya: The Dialectic of Domination* (London: James Currey, 1990), 206; Brian Siegel, "The 'Wild' and 'Lazy' Lamba: Ethnic Stereotypes on the Central African Copperbelt," in *Creation of Tribalism,* ed. Vail; Syed Hussein Alatas, *The Myth of the Lazy Native: A Study of the Image of the Malays, Filipinos and Javanese from the 16th to the 20th Century and Its Function in the Ideology of Global Capitalism* (London: Frank Cass, 1977).

27. Nicholas Thomas, "The Force of Ethnology: Origins and Significance of the Melanesia/Polynesia Division," *Current Anthropology* 30, no. 1 (1989): 27–41.

28. Christopher Herbert, *Victorian Relativity: Radical Thought and Scientific Discovery* (Chicago: University of Chicago Press, 2010); Mira Matikkala, *Empire and Imperial Ambition: Liberty, Englishness, and Anti-Imperialism in Late Victorian Britain* (London: I. B. Tauris, 2011); David Weinstein, "Imagining Darwinism," in *Utilitarianism and Empire,* ed. Bart Schultz and Georgios Varouxakis (Lanham: Lexington Books, 2005).

29. "Myers," in *History of Psychology in Autobiography,* 217; Charles S. Myers, *Psychological Conceptions in Other Sciences* (Oxford: Clarendon Press, 1929), 5; Kuklick, "Personal Equations," 21n; James Urry, "From Zoology to Ethnology: A. C. Haddon's Conversion to Anthropology," in *Before Social Anthropology: Essays on the History of British Anthropology* (Abingdon: Routledge, 1993).

30. Shephard, *Head Hunters,* 45–47, 54–60.

31. Anita Herle and Sandra Rouse, introduction to *Cambridge and the Torres Strait: Centenary Essays on the 1898 Anthropological Expedition*

(Cambridge: Cambridge University Press, 1998), 12–13; Shephard, *Head Hunters*, 66–69; Kuklick, *Savage Within*, 195–198.

32. Haddon, *Head-Hunters*, x–xii, 111–113, 377, 405; Kuklick, *Savage Within*, 44–49.

33. In a vast literature, see especially Said, *Orientalism*, 240–242; Homi K. Bhabha, "Of Mimicry and Man: The Ambivalence of Colonial Discourse," in *The Location of Culture* (London: Routledge, 1994); Etienne Balibar, "Racism as Universalism," in *Masses, Classes, Ideas: Studies on Politics and Philosophy Before and After Marx*, trans. James Swenson (New York: Routledge, 1994); Immanuel Wallerstein, *European Universalism: The Rhetoric of Power* (New York: New Press, 2006); Uday Singh Mehta, *Liberalism and Empire: A Study in Nineteenth-Century British Liberal Thought* (Chicago: University of Chicago Press, 1999); Jennifer Pitts, *A Turn to Empire: The Rise of Imperial Liberalism in Britain and France* (Princeton: Princeton University Press, 2006); Theodore Koditschek, *Liberalism, Imperialism, and the Historical Imagination: Nineteenth-Century Visions of a Greater Britain* (Cambridge: Cambridge University Press, 2011); Warwick Anderson, "The Third World Body," in *Medicine in the Twentieth Century*, ed. Cooter and Pickstone.

34. Mandler, *English National Character*, chs. 3–4.

35. Ballantyne, *Orientalism and Race*.

36. David Cannadine, *Ornamentalism: How the British Saw Their Empire* (Oxford: Oxford University Press, 2001).

37. Jeffrey Cox, *Imperial Fault Lines: Christianity and Colonial Power in India, 1818–1940* (Palo Alto: Stanford University Press, 2002), 95–96, 222; Jean Comaroff and John Comaroff, *Of Reason and Revolution: Christianity, Colonialism, and Consciousness in South Africa*, vol. 1 (Chicago: University of Chicago Press, 1991), 108.

38. G. R. Searle, *A New England? Peace and War, 1886–1914* (New York: Oxford University Press, 2004), 31–36; Jose Harris, *Private Lives, Public Spirit: Britain 1870–1914* (London: Penguin, 1993), 236–237.

39. Klaus-Peter Köpping, *Adolf Bastian and the Psychic Unity of Mankind: The Foundations of Anthropology in Nineteenth-Century Germany* (Piscataway: Transaction, 2005); Kuklick, *Savage Within*, 80–82; Stocking, *After Tylor*, 5, 10, 136–137, 145–146.

40. R. B. Joyce, "John Douglas (1828–1904)," in *Australian Dictionary of Biography*, vol. 4 (Melbourne: Melbourne University Press, 1972); J. Douglas, "Islands of Torres Strait," *Queenslander* (Brisbane), 27 January 1900; Charles Hose and William McDougall, *The Pagan Tribes of Borneo*, vol. 2 (London: Macmillan, 1912), 222. Although credited as co-author, McDougall took pains in the preface to state that the ideas in the book were Hose's own.

41. Haddon, *Head-Hunters*, 2.

42. Patrick Brantlinger, *Dark Vanishings: Discourse on the Extinction of Primitive Races, 1800–1930* (Ithaca: Cornell University Press, 2003); Russell McGregor, *Imagined Destinies: Aboriginal Australians and the Doomed Race Theory* (Melbourne: Melbourne University Press, 1997).

43. Diary entry for 27 September 1899, Myers papers, Add. MS 8073, CUL.

44. Ibid.

45. Steve Mullins, *Torres Strait: A History of Colonial Occupation and Culture Contact 1864–1897* (Rockhampton: Central Queensland University Press, 1994), 81–82, 137–138; John Singe, *The Torres Strait: People and History* (St. Lucia: University of Queensland Press, 1989), 58–59, 60–63; Jeremy Beckett, *Torres Strait Islanders: Custom and Colonialism* (Cambridge: Cambridge University Press, 1987), 41–42.

46. W. H. R. Rivers, introduction to *Reports of the Cambridge Anthropological Expedition to Torres Strait,* ed. A. C. Haddon, vol. 2, *Physiology and Psychology* (Cambridge: Cambridge University Press, 1901), 1–3; A. C. Haddon diary, entry for 6 May 1898, Haddon papers, envelope 1055, CUL.

47. Haddon diary, entry for 6 May 1898, Haddon papers, envelope 1055, CUL; Kuklick, *Savage Within,* 142n; Graham Richards, "Getting a Result: The Expedition's Psychological Research," in *Cambridge and the Torres Strait,* ed. Herle and Rouse, 142–144.

48. Rivers, introduction to *Reports,* vol. 2, 4–5; C. S. Myers, diary entries for 4 June and 7 June 1898, Myers papers, Add. MS 8073, CUL.

49. See also Rivers, introduction to *Reports,* vol. 2, 1–2.

50. Lorraine Daston and Peter Galison, *Objectivity* (New York: Zone Books, 2007), ch. 4; Christopher D. Green, "Scientific Objectivity and E. B. Titchener's Experimental Psychology," *Isis* 101, no. 4 (2010): 697–721; Otinel E. Dror, "Seeing the Blush: Feeling Emotions," in *Histories of Scientific Observation,* ed. Lorraine Daston and Elizabeth Lunbeck (Chicago: University of Chicago Press, 2011).

51. Priya Satia, *Spies in Arabia: The Great War and the Covert Foundations of Britain's Empire in the Middle East* (New York: Oxford University Press, 2008); Patrick Brantlinger, *Rule of Darkness: British Literature and Imperialism, 1830–1914* (Ithaca: Cornell University Press, 1988), ch. 8; Danziger, *Constructing the Subject,* 147; Shephard, *Head Hunters,* 134. McDougall did maintain an interest in psychical research, but this was yet another sign of his distance from the rest of the Cambridge group: see Shephard, *Head Hunters,* 129–131, 231–232. On the wide influence of spiritualism in this period, see Alex Owen, *The Place of Enchantment: British Occultism and the Culture of the Modern* (Chicago: University of Chicago Press, 2004), and Janet Oppenheim, *The Other World: Spiritualism and Psychical Research in England, 1850–1914* (Cambridge: Cambridge University Press, 1985).

52. W. E. Gladstone, *Studies on Homer and the Homeric Age* (Oxford: Oxford University Press, 1858).

53. Danziger, *Constructing the Subject,* ch. 2; Henning Schmidgen, "Physics, Ballistics, and Psychology: The Chronoscope in/as Context," *History of Psychology* 8, no. 1 (2005): 46–78. On the significance of instruments in psychology, see also Michael M. Sokal, et al., "Laboratory Instruments in the History of Psychology," *Journal of the History of the Behavioral Sciences* 12 (1976): 59–64; Thomas Sturm and Mitchell G. Ash, "Roles of Instruments in Psychological Research," *History of Psychology* 8, no. 1 (2005): 3–34.

54. Arthur L. Blumenthal, "A Reappraisal of Wilhelm Wundt," *American Psychologist* 30 (1975): 1081–88; Canales, *Tenth of a Second,* 29–30, 45–48. On psychology before the laboratory, see Fernando Vidal, *The Sciences of the Soul: The Early Modern Origins of Psychology,* trans. Saskia Brown (Chicago: University of Chicago Press, 2011).

55. Dias, *La mesure des sens.*

56. Rivers, "Visual Acuity," in *Reports,* vol. 2, 12–13.

57. See, e.g., Spencer, "The Comparative Psychology of Man," *Popular Science Monthly* 8 (1876): 257–269. On the Spencer hypothesis, see also Richards, "Getting a Result"; Richards, *"Race," Racism and Psychology,* ch. 3.

58. Rivers, "Visual Acuity," in *Reports,* vol. 2, 42–45; Myers, "Reaction-Times," in *Reports,* vol. 2, 221–222. See also Kuklick, *Savage Within,* 148.

59. Cf. Arjun Appadurai, "Number in the Colonial Imagination," in *Orientalism and the Postcolonial Predicament: Perspectives on South Asia,* ed. Carol A. Breckenridge and Peter van der Veer (Philadelphia: University of Pennsylvania Press, 1993).

60. Myers, "Auditory Acuity," in *Reports,* vol. 2, 145.

61. C. S. Myers to John Bruce, 15 October 1907, Haddon papers, envelope 1002, CUL; Shephard, *Head Hunters,* 68; Beckett, "Haddon Attends a Funeral," 27; A. C. Haddon, "Incidents in the Life of a Torres Strait Islander," *Lippincott's Monthly Magazine* 45 (1890): 567–572, at 567.

62. Simon Schaffer, "Self Evidence," *Critical Inquiry* 18, no. 2 (1992): 327–362.

63. Schaffer, *From Physics to Anthropology,* 23; Myers, "Reaction-Times," in *Reports,* vol. 2, 206.

64. Myers, "Reaction-Times," in *Reports,* vol. 2, 205–207, 220; Rivers, "Visual Acuity," in *Reports,* vol. 2, 20; Haddon, *Head-Hunters,* 27; Canales, *Tenth of a Second,* 47–48.

65. Rivers, introduction to *Reports,* vol. 2, 3; Rivers notebook, Haddon papers, envelope 12080, CUL.

66. For the dependence of imperial ventures on local intermediaries, see also Dane Kennedy, *The Last Blank Spaces: Exploring Africa and Australia* (Cambridge: Harvard University Press, 2013), ch. 6; Simon Schaffer, et al., eds., *The Brokered World: Go-Betweens and Global Intelligence, 1770–1820* (Sagamore Beach: Watson, 2009); Benjamin N. Lawrance, Emily Lynn Osborn, and Richard L. Roberts, eds., *Intermediaries, Interpreters, and Clerks: African Employees in the Making of Colonial Africa* (Madison: University of Wisconsin Press, 2006); Lyn Schumaker, *Africanizing Anthropology: Fieldwork, Networks, and the Making of Cultural Knowledge in Central Africa* (Durham: Duke University Press, 2001).

67. Shephard, *Head Hunters,* 126–29; Richards, *"Race," Racism and Psychology,* 197–199; Thomson, " 'Savage Civilisation,' " 243–246.

68. Myers, "Reaction-Times," in *Reports,* vol. 2, 221–223, at 223; Kuklick, *Savage Within,* 154–157.

69. Myers, "Reaction-Times," in *Reports,* vol. 2, 220–221; Kuklick, *Savage Within,* 176–177.

70. Rivers, introduction to *Reports,* vol. 2, 4; C. S. Myers, diary entries for 4 June and 17 June 1898, Myers papers, Add. MS 8073, CUL.

71. On the standardization of individuality, see Michel Foucault, *The Birth of the Clinic: An Archaeology of Medical Perception,* trans. A. M. Sheridan Smith (New York: Vintage, 1994), ch. 6, and Warwick Anderson, *Colonial Pathologies: American Tropical Medicine, Race, and Hygiene in the Philippines* (Durham: Duke University Press, 2006), 161–162, 168.

72. C. S. Myers, diary entry for 17 June 1898, Myers papers, Add. MS 8073, CUL.

73. Stefan Collini, "The Idea of 'Character' in Victorian Political Thought," *Transactions of the Royal Historical Society,* 35 (1985): 29–50.

74. C. S. Myers, diary entry for 17 June 1898, Myers papers, Add. MS 8073, CUL.

75. Haddon, *Head-Hunters,* 27; "Psychology and Behaviour," in *Reports of the Cambridge Anthropological Expedition,* ed. A. C. Haddon, vol. 1, *General Ethnography* (Cambridge: Cambridge University Press, 1901), 286.

76. "Psychology and Behaviour," in *Reports,* vol. 1, 287; Jeremy Beckett, "Haddon Attends a Funeral: Fieldwork in Torres Strait, 1888, 1898," in *Cambridge and the Torres Strait,* ed. Herle and Rouse.

77. Franz Boas, *The Mind of Primitive Man* (New York: Macmillan, 1911), 117–118. On the relativizing influence of Boas's experiments with psycho-physics, see George W. Stocking, Jr., "From Physics to Ethnology," in *Race, Culture, and Evolution: Essays in the History of Anthropology* (New York: Free Press, 1968).

78. These are references to Haddon and Seligman, respectively: see Richards, *"Race," Racism and Psychology,* 49, and Barkan, *Retreat of Scientific Racism,* 30.

79. Stocking, *After Tylor,* 124–125; Barkan, *Retreat of Scientific Racism,* 65, 120.

80. Shephard, *Head Hunters,* 79–80, 121–124, 211–213. On the background of moral and ethical controversy, see especially Lorraine Daston, "British Responses to Psycho-Physiology, 1860–1900," *Isis* 69, no. 2 (1978): 192–208.

81. On Haddon and Rivers as social outsiders, see Edmund R. Leach, "Glimpses of the Unmentionable in the History of British Social Anthropology," *Annual Review of Anthropology* 13 (1984): 1–23; Ian Langham, *The Building of British Social Anthropology: W. H. R. Rivers and His Cambridge Disciplines in the Development of Kinship Studies, 1898–1931* (Dordrecht: D. Reidel, 1981), 52, 340n.

82. C. G. Seligman, "A Classification of the Natives of British New Guinea," *Journal of the Royal Anthropological Institute* 39 (1909): 314–333, at 317–323; C. G. Seligman, "Some Aspects of the Hamitic Problem in the Anglo-Egyptian Sudan," *Journal of the Royal Anthropological Institute* 43 (1913): 593–705, at 629–632.

83. Charles S. Myers, "The Future of Anthropometry," *Journal of the Anthropological Institute* 33 (1903): 36–40; C. S. Myers, "The Pitfalls of 'Mental Tests," *British Medical Journal* 2613 (1911): 195–197.

84. Samuel Hynes, *The Edwardian Turn of Mind* (Princeton: Princeton University Press, 1968), 138.

85. A. C. Haddon, "President's Address: Anthropology, Its Position and Needs," *Journal of the Anthropological Institute* 33 (1903): 11–23, at 13; C. G. Seligman, "A Golden Harvest," *Observer,* 26 July 1931, 7; Paul B. Rich, *Race and Empire in British Politics* (Cambridge: Cambridge University Press, 1986), 108.

86. Susan D. Pennybacker, "The Universal Races Congress, London Political Culture, and Imperial Dissent, 1900–1939," *Radical History Review,* 92 (2005): 103–117; Paul Rich, "The Baptism of a New Era: The 1911 Universal Races Congress and the Liberal Ideology of Race," in *Prospero's Return? Historical Essays on Race, Culture, and British Society* (London: Hansib, 1994); Paul Gilroy, *The Black Atlantic: Modernity and Double Consciousness* (Cambridge: Harvard University Press, 1993), 144, 214; Robert John Holton, "Cosmopolitanism or Cosmopolitans? The Universal Races Congress of 1911," *Global Networks: A Journal of Transnational Affairs* 2 (2002): 153–170; Marilyn Lake and Henry Reynolds, *Drawing the Global Color Line: White Men's Countries and the Global Challenge of Racial Equality* (Cambridge: Cambridge University Press, 2008), 251–261.

87. "The World in Conclave," *Mercury* (Hobart, Tasmania), 31 August 1912.

88. Charles S. Myers, "On the Permanence of Racial Mental Differences," in *Papers on Inter-Racial Problems Communicated to the First Universal Races Congress Held at the University of London* (London: P. S. King, 1911).

89. Lucien Lévy-Bruhl, *Les fonctions mentales dans les sociétés inférieures* (Paris: Félix Alcan, 1910), 7.

90. Lévy-Bruhl, *Les fonctions mentales,* 77; S.A. Mousalimas, "The Concept of Participation in Lévy-Bruhl's 'Primitive Mentality,'" *Journal of the Anthropological Society of Oxford* 21, no. 1 (1990): 33–46; Christina Chimisso, "The Mind and the Faculties: The Controversy over 'Primitive Mentality' and the Struggle for Disciplinary Space at the Inter-War Sorbonne," *History of the Human Sciences* 13, no. 3 (2000): 47–68.

91. Myers, "On the Permanence of Racial Mental Differences," 75–78; W. H. R. Rivers, "The Primitive Conception of Death," in *Psychology and Ethnology* (London: Kegan Paul, 1926), 53; W. H. R. Rivers, "Intellectual Concentration in Primitive Man," in *Psychology and Ethnology,* 46; [Seligman], "Psychology of Savages," n.d., Haddon papers, envelope 5378, CUL; C. G. Seligman, "The Unconscious in Relation to Anthropology," *British Journal of Psychology* 18, no. 3 (1928): 373–387, at 373; William McDougall, *The Group Mind: A Sketch of the Principles of Collective Psychology* (London: G. P. Putnam, 1920), 104–106.

92. Bronislaw Malinowski, "Baloma: The Spirits of the Dead in the Trobriand Islands," *Journal of the Royal Anthropological Institute* 46 (1916): 353–430, at 417–418; Malinowski, syllabus for course "Psychology of Culture," n.d., Malinowski papers, file 20/12, LSE; J. H. Driberg, *The Savage as He Really Is* (London: Routledge, 1929), 2; J. H. Driberg, *At Home with the Savage* (London: Routledge, 1932); F. C. Bartlett, *Psychology and Primitive Culture* (Cambridge: Cambridge University Press, 1923), 284–285; F. C.

Bartlett, "The Psychology of the Lower Races," in *Proceedings and Papers of the VIIIth International Congress of Psychology* (Groningen: P. Noordhoff, 1927), 200.

93. Clement C. J. Webb, *Group Theories of Religion and the Individual* (London: Allen & Unwin, 1916), especially ch. 6; [James Frazer], "Primitive Mentality," *Times Literary Supplement* (13 September 1923), 594; John Murphy, *Primitive Man: His Essential Quest* (London: Oxford University Press, 1927), 8–9, 89–90; Julian Huxley, *Africa View* (London: Chatto & Windus, 1931), 29; J. M. Evans, *Social and Psychological Aspects of Primitive Education* (London: Golden Vista, 1932), 35; Vernon Brelsford, *Primitive Philosophy* (London: John Bale, 1935), 14–15; W. B. Mumford and C. E. Smith, "Racial Comparisons and Intelligence Testing," *Journal of the Royal African Society* 37 (1938): 46–57, at 57; Arthur Mayhew, *Education in the Colonial Empire* (London: Longmans, 1938), 9. See also Kuklick, *Savage Within*, 119–120.

94. Robert Ackerman, *J. G. Frazer: His Life and Work* (Cambridge: Cambridge University Press, 1987), 225–229; Stocking, *After Tylor*, 163–172. On "British anthropology's long affair with Durkheimianism," as Stefan Collini had put it, see Collini, "Sociology and Idealism in Britain, 1880–1920," *European Journal of Sociology* 19, no. 1 (1978): 3–50, at 35; George W. Stocking, Jr., "Radcliffe-Brown and British Social Anthropology," in *Functionalism Historicized: Essays in British Social Anthropology*, ed. George W. Stocking, Jr. (Madison: University of Wisconsin Press, 1984); Joan W. Vincent, "Functionalism Revisited: An Unsettled Science," *Reviews in Anthropology* 13, no. 4 (1986): 331–339.

95. Roy Clive Abraham, *The Tiv People* (Lagos: Government Printer, 1933), 57–59; Brelsford, *Primitive Philosophy*, 22–23; Vaughan, *Curing Their Ills*, 11–12, 100–128.

96. Unsigned review of *Group Theories of Religion and the Individual*, *International Review of Missions* 5 (1916): 665–666; Edwin W. Smith, "A Study of 'Primitive Mentality,'" *International Review of Missions* 12 (1923): 133–135; Joseph Oldham, *Christianity and the Race Problem* (New York: George H. Doran, 1924), 80–83; Edwin W. Smith, *The Golden Stool: Some Aspects of the Conflict of Cultures in Modern Africa* (London: Holborn, 1926), 84–85; E. W. Smith, "Primitive Psychology," *International Review of Missions* 15 (1926): 760–763; A. B., review of *How Natives Think*, *The Southern Cross*, repr. in *Native Affairs Department Annual* 4 (1926): 126–128; A. S. Woodburne, "The Contribution of Psychology to Anthropology," *Indian Journal of Psychology* 5, nos. 1–2 (1930): 1–17, at 4–5; James W. C. Dougall, "Characteristics of African Thought," *Africa* 5, no. 3 (1932): 249–265; Edwin W. Smith, *Knowing the African* (London: Lutterworth Press, 1945), 38–39.

97. Joseph Oldham, *Christianity and the Race Problem* (New York: George H. Doran, 1924), 80–83. See also Tilley, *Africa as a Living Laboratory*, 232–233.

98. R. F. Alfred Hoernlé, "Prolegomena to the Study of the Black Man's Mind," *Journal of Philosophical Studies* 2, no. 5 (1927): 52–61, at 61; R. F. A. Hoernlé, "The Concept of the 'Primitive,'" *Bantu Studies* 2, no. 4 (1926): 327–332, at 332; J. D. Rheinallt Jones, "The Need of a Scientific Basis for South African Native Policy," *South African Journal of Science* 23 (1926): 79–91;

Edgar H. Brookes, *The Colour Problems of South Africa* (Lovedale, South Africa: Lovedale Press, 1934), 142; Peter Nielsen, *The Black Man's Place in South Africa* (Johannesburg: Juta, 1922), 51. See also the critics cited in Diana Jeater, *Law, Language, and Science: The Invention of the "Native Mind" in Southern Rhodesia, 1890–1930* (Portsmouth: Heinemann, 2007), 222–224.

99. J. W. Bews, *Human Ecology* (London: Oxford University Press, 1935), 116. On Bews, see also Peder Anker, *Imperial Ecology: Environmental Order in the British Empire, 1895–1945* (Cambridge: Harvard University Press, 2001).

100. Slobodin, *W. H. R. Rivers*, 80; "Myers," in *History of Psychology in Autobiography*, ed. Murchison, 228.

101. G. Elliot Smith, preface to W. H. R. Rivers, *Psychology and Politics and Other Essays* (New York: Harcourt, Brace, 1923), v; Rivers, "Education and Mental Hygiene," in *Psychology and Politics*, 105; W. H. R. Rivers, "The Government of Subject Peoples," in *Science and the Nation*, ed. A. C. Seward (Cambridge: Cambridge University Press, 1917); W. H. R. Rivers, "The Psychological Factor," in *Essays on the Depopulation of Melanesia*, ed. Rivers (Cambridge: Cambridge University Press, 1922).

102. W. H. R. Rivers, "The Concept of the Morbid in Sociology," in *Psychology and Politics;* John Forrester, "The 'English Freud': W. H. R. Rivers, Dreaming, and the Making of the Early Twentieth-Century Human Sciences," in *History and Psyche: Culture, Psychoanalysis, and the Past*, ed. Sally Alexander and Barbara Taylor (New York: Palgrave Macmillan, 2012).

103. Mandler, *English National Character*, 156; Jaap van Ginneken, *Mass Movements in Darwinist, Freudian and Marxist Perspective: Trotter, Freud and Reich on War, Revolution and Reaction, 1900–1933* (Apeldoorn: Het Spinhuis, 2007), ch. 4; Martin J. Wiener, *Between Two Worlds: The Political Thought of Graham Wallas* (Oxford: Clarendon Press, 1971), ch. 2; Gal Gerson, "Liberalism, Welfare and the Crowd in J. A. Hobson," *History of European Ideas* 30 (2004): 197–215; Reba N. Soffer, *Ethics and Society in England: The Revolution in the Social Sciences, 1870–1914* (Berkeley: University of California Press, 1978).

104. Ben Pimlott, ed., *The Political Diary of Hugh Dalton* (London: Jonathan Cape, 1986), 24; Rivers, "Concept of the Morbid," 78–80.

105. Kingsley Martin, "The Webbs in Retirement," in *The Webbs and Their Work*, ed. Margaret Cole (London: Frederick Muller, 1949), 285–286; Madeline Glasier, "London University Labour Party," *Clare Market Review* 2, no. 3 (1922): 24; R. H. Tawney, et al., letter to editor, *Manchester Guardian*, 25 March 1922; "Our London Correspondence," *Manchester Guardian*, 7 April 1922, 6.

106. J. A. Hobson, *The Psychology of Jingoism* (London: Grant Richards, 1901); Gregory Claeys, *Imperial Sceptics: British Critics of Empire, 1850–1920* (Cambridge: Cambridge University Press, 2010); Graham Wallas, *Human Nature in Politics* (London: Archibald Constable, 1908); Wiener, *Between Two Worlds*, 106.

107. W. H. R. Rivers, "An Address on Socialism and Human Nature," in *Psychology and Politics*.

108. Slobodin, *W. H. R. Rivers*, 81; H. G. Wells, open letter to London University electors, [October 1922], in *The Correspondence of H. G. Wells*, vol. 3, *1919–1934*, ed. Patrick Parrinder (London: Pickering & Chatto, 1998), 116–117; H. G. Wells, *The World, Its Debts, and the Rich Men: Report of a Meeting at Millbank School* (London: H. Finer, 1922), 10–11.

109. Brelsford, *Primitive Philosophy*, 12; Dougall, "Characteristics of African Thought," 255; McDougall, *Group Mind*, 104–105; Tylor, *Primitive Culture*, 70–159; Murphy, *Primitive Man*, 22; Bartlett, *Psychology and Primitive Culture*, 119–120; Malinowski seminar notes, 7 May 1936, Malinowski papers, file 6/12, LSE.

110. C. S. Myers to C. G. Seligman, n.d., MS 262/3/2/22, RAI.

2. A Dream Dictionary for the World

1. C. G. Seligman, "What Do You Dream About?" *The Listener,* 8 April 1931, 580–581. The major published sources for Seligman's life are the obituaries written by his colleagues: see Meyer Fortes, "Charles Gabriel Seligman, 1873–1940," *Man* 41 (1941): 1–6, and C. S. Myers, "Charles Gabriel Seligman, 1873–1940," *Obituary Notices of Fellows of the Royal Society* 3, no. 10 (1941): 627–646.

2. Maureen Perkins, "The Meaning of Dream Books," *History Workshop Journal* 48 (1999): 103–113; John Forrester, "Freud in Cambridge," *Critical Quarterly* 46, no. 2 (2004): 1–26; John Forrester, "1919: Psychology and Psychoanalysis, London and Cambridge," *Psychoanalysis and History* 10, no. 1 (2008): 37–94; R. D. Hinshelwood, "Psychoanalysis in Britain: Points of Cultural Access," *International Journal of Psycho-Analysis* 76 (1995): 135–151; Dean Rapp, "The Early Discovery of Freud by the British General Educated Public, 1912–1919," *Social History of Medicine* 3, no. 2 (1990): 217–243; Graham Richards, "Britain on the Couch: The Popularization of Psychoanalysis in Britain, 1918–1940," *Science in Context* 13 (2000): 183–230.

3. The literature is vast but the key works include Martin Stone, "Shell-Shock and the Psychologists," in *The Anatomy of Madness: Essays in the History of Psychiatry,* vol. 1, ed. W. F. Bynum, Roy Porter, and Michael Shepherd (London: Tavistock, 1985); Ben Shephard, *A War of Nerves: Soldiers and Psychiatrists, 1914–1994* (London: Pimlico, 2002); Peter Leese, *Shell Shock: Traumatic Neurosis and British Soldiers of the First World War* (New York: Palgrave Macmillan, 2002); Peter Barham, *Forgotten Lunatics of the Great War* (New Haven: Yale University Press, 2004).

4. Stocking, "Anthropology and the Science of the Irrational," 43.

5. Michael P. Steinberg, introduction to Aby M. Warburg, *Images from the Region of the Pueblo Indians of North America*, trans. Michael P. Steinberg (Ithaca: Cornell University Press, 1995), 61; Marianna Torgovnick, *Gone Primitive: Savage Intellects, Modern Lives* (Chicago: University of Chicago Press, 1991), ch. 10; Marianna Torgovnick, *Primitive Passions: Men, Women, and the Quest for Ecstasy* (New York: Alfred A. Knopf, 1997), 29–36; Blake W. Burleson, *Jung in Africa* (New York: Continuum, 2005).

6. On the critical and radical possibilities of psychoanalysis in the colonies, see Ranjana Khanna, *Dark Continents: Psychoanalysis and Colonialism* (Durham: Duke University Press, 2003); Shruti Kapila, "The 'Godless' Freud and His Indian Friends: An Indian Agenda for Psychoanalysis," in *Psychiatry and Empire,* ed. Mahone and Vaughan; Kapila, "Masculinity and Madness"; Rubén Gallo, *Freud's Mexico: Into the Wilds of Psychoanalysis* (Cambridge: MIT Press, 2010), ch. 7.

7. The key texts of the postwar moment are Frantz Fanon, *Black Skin, White Masks,* trans. Richard Philcox (New York: Grove Press, 2008 [1952]); Frantz Fanon, *The Wretched of the Earth,* trans. Constance Farrington (New York: Grove Press, 2004 [1961]); Octave Mannoni, *Prospero and Caliban: The Psychology of Colonization,* trans. Pamela Powesland (Ann Arbor: University of Michigan Press, 1990 [1950]); Albert Memmi, *The Colonizer and the Colonized,* trans. Howard Greenfeld (London: Earthscan, 2003 [1957]). On Fanon's prominent place in postcolonial theory, see Bhabha, *Location of Culture,* ch. 2; Homi K. Bhabha, "Remembering Fanon: Self, Psyche, and the Colonial Condition," in *Colonial Discourse and Post-Colonial Theory: A Reader,* ed. Patrick Williams and Laura Chrisman (New York: Columbia University Press, 1994). On Fanon, Mannoni, and Memmi as progenitors of the idea that "colonialism is itself psychopathological," see Megan Vaughan, "Madness and Colonialism, Colonialism as Madness: Re-Reading Fanon," *Paideuma* 39 (1993): 45–55, at 47. Despite this shared perspective, the three did not comprise a unified movement; they drew in varying degrees on Freud, Adler, and Lacan, and Fanon famously attacked Mannoni's Adlerian theory of a "dependency complex." For Fanon's indebtedness to existentialism and phenomenology as well as psychoanalysis, see David Macey, "The Recall of the Real: Frantz Fanon and Psychoanalysis," *Constellations* 6, no. 1 (1999): 97–107. On the problem of the unconscious in Memmi's work, see Suzanne Gearhart, "Colonialism, Psychoanalysis, and Cultural Criticism: The Problem of Interiorization in the Work of Albert Memmi," in *"Culture" and the Problem of the Disciplines,* ed. John Carlos Rowe (New York: Columbia University Press, 1998).

8. On tensions between liberation and regulation in psychoanalysis, see Warwick Anderson, Deborah Jenson, and Richard C. Keller, eds., *Unconscious Dominions: Psychoanalysis, Colonial Trauma, and Global Sovereignties* (Durham: Duke University Press, 2011), and Eli Zaretsky, *Secrets of the Soul: A Social and Cultural History of Psychoanalysis* (New York: Knopf, 2004).

9. Historians have usually identified the wartime mobilization and welfare statism of the 1940s as the key moment for the emergence of psychoanalytic politics in Britain: see Shapira, *War Inside*; Zaretsky, *Secrets of the Soul,* ch. 10; Rose, *Governing the Soul,* 157; Elisabeth Young-Bruehl, "Psychoanalysis and Social Democracy: A Tale of Two Developments," *Contemporary Psychoanalysis* 47, no. 2 (2011): 179–203.

10. On the ambiguity of this language in the American context, see Daryl Michael Scott, *Contempt and Pity: Social Policy and the Image of the Damaged Black Psyche, 1880–1996* (Chapel Hill: University of North Carolina Press, 1997).

11. Fortes, "Charles Gabriel Seligman," 1; T. H. Huxley, "On the Methods and Results of Ethnology," in *Man's Place in Nature and Other Essays* (London: Macmillan, 1910).

12. C. G. Seligman, "Eczema Papillomatosum among Papuans," *Transactions of the Pathological Society of London* 52 (1901): 145–149; C. G. Seligman, "A Note on Albinism, with Especial Reference to Its Racial Characteristics among Melanesians and Polynesians," *Lancet* 2 (1902): 803–805; C. G. Seligman, "On the Occurrence of New Growths among the People of New Guinea," *Scientific Report on the Investigations of the Imperial Cancer Fund* 3 (1908): 26–40; Seligman treatment notes, Seligman papers 10/1, LSE.

13. C. G. Seligman, *Races of Africa* (London: Oxford University Press, 1966), 2–3, 5; Barkan, *Retreat of Scientific Racism,* 29–31, at 31; Kuklick, *Savage Within,* 268. Racial classification formed an important part of Seligman's other major works as well: see his *The Melanesians of British New Guinea* (Cambridge: Cambridge University Press, 1910), 1–4, and with Brenda Z. Seligman, *The Veddas* (Cambridge: Cambridge University Press, 1911), 15–18, and *Pagan Tribes of the Nilotic Sudan* (London: Routledge, 1932), 11–13, 20, 114. For an example of his physiognomic observations while traveling, see the diary entry for 9 February 1922, Seligman papers 1/4/1, LSE.

14. Edith R. Sanders, "The Hamitic Hypothesis: Its Origin and Function in Time Perspective," *Journal of African History* 10, no. 4 (1969): 521–532; Seligman, *Races of Africa,* 100.

15. Hearnshaw, *Short History,* 126–131; Daston, "British Responses to Psycho-Physiology"; Thomas Dixon, *From Passions to Emotions: The Creation of a Secular Psychological Category* (Cambridge: Cambridge University Press, 2006), 213–216.

16. Soffer, *Ethics and Society in England,* 128–134, 157; Charles S. Myers, "Instinct and Intelligence," *British Journal of Psychology* 3 (1910): 209–218.

17. Deborah Cohen, *Family Secrets: Shame and Privacy in Modern Britain* (New York: Oxford University Press, 2013), 168–169; Peter Mandler, "Democratizing Psychoanalysis in Postwar Britain and America," paper presented at conference on History and Psychoanalysis in the Postwar Period, Columbia University, April 4, 2014.

18. Rapp, "Early Discovery of Freud"; Richards, "Britain on the Couch"; Thomson, *Psychological Subjects,* ch. 3.

19. Hinshelwood, "Psychoanalysis in Britain"; Jan Ellen Goldstein, "The Woolfs' Response to Freud: Water-Spiders, Singing Canaries, and the Golden Apple," *Psychoanalytic Quarterly* 43, no. 3 (1974): 438–476; J. H. Willis, Jr., *Leonard and Virginia Woolf as Publishers: The Hogarth Press, 1917–41* (Charlottesville: University of Virginia Press, 1992), 301–307; Shephard, *War of Nerves,* 161–163.

20. Hayward, *Transformation of the Psyche,* 3–4. For the dreams, mostly undated, see MS 262/5/1/9, /10, /15, /19, and /20, RAI.

21. Hayward, *Transformation of the Psyche,* 45–46; Ben Shephard, " 'The Early Treatment of Mental Disorders': R. G. Rows and Maghull, 1914–1918," in *150 Years of British Psychiatry,* vol. 2, *The Aftermath,* ed. H. L. Freeman and G. E. Berrios (London: Athlone, 1996), 443–444; Edgar Jones, "Shell Shock at

Maghull and the Maudsley: Models of Psychological Medicine in the UK," *Journal of the History of Medicine & Allied Sciences* 65, no. 3 (2010): 368–395.

22. Esther Fischer-Homberger, *Die traumatische Neurose: Vom somatischen zum sozialen Leiden* (Bern: Hans Huber, 1975); Wolfgang Schivelbusch, *The Railway Journey: The Industrialization of Time and Space in the 19th Century* (Berkeley: University of California Press, 1977), ch. 9; Michael Trimble, *Post-Traumatic Neurosis: From Railway Spine to Whiplash* (New York: Wiley, 1981); George Frederick Drinka, *The Birth of Neurosis: Myth, Malady, and the Victorians* (New York: Simon and Schuster, 1984), ch. 5; Ralph Harrington, "The 'Railway Spine' Diagnosis and Victorian Responses to PTSD," *Journal of Psychosomatic Research* 40, no. 1 (1996): 11–14; Mark S. Micale and Paul Lerner, eds., *Traumatic Pasts: History, Psychiatry, and Trauma in the Modern Age, 1870–1930* (Cambridge: Cambridge University Press, 2001).

23. Pear, "Some Early Relations between English Ethnologists and Psychologists," 232; Grafton Elliott Smith, preface to W. H. R. Rivers, *Conflict and Dream* (London: Kegan Paul, 1923), vii–ix.

24. Case no. 4, 31 July 1918; case no. 51931, n.d.; unnumbered case, 21 May 1918, Seligman papers 10/1, LSE.

25. Case no. 21861, 27 March 1918, Seligman papers 10/1, LSE.

26. Parna Sengupta, "An Object Lesson in Colonial Pedagogy," *Comparative Studies in Society and History* 45, no. 1 (2003): 96–121.

27. Lévy-Bruhl, *Les fonctions mentales*, 7; [Meyer Fortes?], "The anthropologist's contribution to psychology, with special reference to psycho-analysis," n.d., MS 262/1/3/23, RAI.

28. Kuklick, *Savage Within*, 169; Shephard, *War of Nerves*, 81–82.

29. Sonu Shamdasani, *Jung and the Making of Modern Psychology: The Dream of a Science* (Cambridge: Cambridge University Press, 2003), 45–47; "Classification of Reaction Associations," Seligman papers 10/2, LSE; Seligman notebooks, Seligman papers 10/3, LSE.

30. *Notes and Queries on Anthropology*, 5th ed. (London: Royal Anthropological Institute, 1929), 167; Seligman to Malinowski, 2 December 1918; Malinowski to Seligman, 21 January 1919; Seligman to Malinowski, 6 January 1923, Bronislaw Malinowski papers, series II, box 7, folio 566, YUL.

31. Seligman to Malinowski, 6 January 1923, Malinowski papers, YUL; Melville J. Herskovits, "Charles Gabriel Seligman," *American Anthropologist* 43 (1941): 437–439, at 437; Rivers, "Freud's Psychology of the Unconscious," *Lancet* 189 (1917): 912–914. Seligman, *Pagan Tribes*, makes a few discreet references to customs regarding adultery; cf. Malinowski, *The Sexual Life of Savages in North Western Melanesia* (London: Routledge, 1929).

32. Freud to Seligman, 24 August 1922, MS 262/5/1/19, RAI.

33. Sigmund Freud, *The Interpretation of Dreams*, trans. A. A. Brill (New York: Modern Library, 1994), 240–241; untitled dream narrative, n.d., MS 262/5/1/20, RAI.

34. Adam Kuper, *The Invention of Primitive Society: Transformations of an Illusion* (London: Routledge, 1988), 76–122.

35. Seligman, *Melanesians*, 10–12, 439–452; idem, *Races of Africa*, 2; idem, *Pagan Tribes*, 142–43. By the time of *Totem and Taboo* (1913), anthropologists

tended to think of totemism as an ideal type rather than an observable phenomenon. See Kuper, *Invention of Primitive Society*, 103–107; Henrika Kuklick, " 'Humanity in the Chrysalis Stage': Indigenous Australians in the Anthropological Imagination, 1899–1926," *British Journal of the History of Science* 39, no. 4 (2006): 535–568.

36. Lecture notes, n.d., Seligman papers 7/1, LSE, emphasis added. See also C. G. Seligman, "The Unconscious in Relation to Anthropology," *British Journal of Psychology* 18, no. 3 (1928): 373–387, at 376–377.

37. Shamdasani, *Jung and the Making of Modern Psychology*, 233; Rivers, *Conflict and Dream*, 177–180, at 180; Seligman to Alfred Thornton, 15 August 1923, MS 262/5/4/2, RAI.

38. Stocking, "Anthropology and the Science of the Irrational"; Bronislaw Malinowski, *Sex and Repression in Savage Society* (London: Routledge, 1927), 92–97, at 92.

39. Hartnack, *Psychoanalysis in Colonial India;* Kapila, " 'Godless' Freud and His Indian Friends," in *Psychiatry and Empire,* ed. Mahone and Vaughan.

40. Waltraud Ernst, *Mad Tales from the Raj: The European Insane in British India, 1800–1858* (London: Routledge, 1991); Dane Kennedy, *Islands of White: Settler Society and Culture in Kenya and Southern Rhodesia, 1890–1939* (Durham: Duke University Press, 1987), ch. 6. See also the review essay by Richard Keller, "Madness and Colonization: Psychiatry in the British and French Empires, 1800–1962," *Journal of Social History* 35, no. 2 (2001): 295–326, and for the American case, Warwick Anderson, "The White Man's Psychic Burden," in *Colonial Pathologies: American Tropical Medicine, Race, and Hygiene in the Philippines* (Durham: Duke University Press, 2006).

41. Eran J. Rolnik, *Freud in Zion: Psychoanalysis and the Making of Modern Jewish Identity,* trans. Haim Watzman (London: Karnac Books, 2012), 111; Mariano Ben Plotkin, *Freud in the Pampas: The Emergence and Development of a Psychoanalytic Culture in Argentina* (Stanford: Stanford University Press, 2001), 6, 118–121.

42. On the influence of this myth in imperial psychiatry, see Roland Littlewood and Maurice Lipsedge, *Aliens and Alienists: Ethnic Minorities and Psychiatry* (London: Routledge, 1997), 61–63; Megan Vaughan, "Suicide in Late Colonial Africa: The Evidence of Inquests from Nyasaland," *American Historical Review* 115, no. 2 (2010): 385–404, at 387–388; Leland V. Bell, *Mental and Social Disorder in Sub-Saharan Africa: The Case of Sierra Leone, 1787–1990* (New York: Greenwood, 1991), 1–3.

43. Brenda Seligman diary, 13 February 1922, Seligman papers 1/4/6, LSE; Northcote W. Thomas, *Thought Transference* (London: Alexander Moring, 1905); N. W. Thomas, *Crystal Gazing* (London: Alexander Moring, 1905); Kuklick, *Savage Within,* 199–201; Noel Machin, *Government Anthropologist: A Life of R. S. Rattray* (Canterbury: Centre for Social Anthropology and Computing, 1998), http://lucy.ukc.ac.uk/Machin; Theodore H. von Laue, "Anthropology and Power: R. S. Rattray among the Ashanti," *African Affairs* 75, no. 298 (1976): 33–54; Thomas Theodore Steiger Hayley memoir, Mss Eur F180/3, IOR; Andrew West, "Writing the Nagas: A British Officers' Ethnographic Tradition," *History and Anthropology* 8, no. 1 (1994): 55–88.

44. Northcote W. Thomas, *Anthropological Report on Sierra Leone,* vol. 1, *Law and Custom of the Timne and Other Tribes* (London: Harrison, 1916), 87; C. G. Seligman, "Anthropological Perspective and Psychological Theory," *Journal of the Royal Anthropological Institute of Great Britain and Ireland* 62 (1932): 193–228, at 216n; J. H. Hutton, *The Sema Nagas* (London: Macmillan, 1921), 247–248; J. H. Hutton, *The Angami Nagas* (London: Macmillan, 1921), 246–247; T. C. Hodson, *The Naga Tribes of Manipur* (London: Macmillan, 1911), 129–132.

45. C. G. Seligman, "Note on Dreams," *Man* 23 (1923): 186–188; C. G. Seligman to J. P. Mills, 10 January 1924, MS 262/6/3/3, RAI.

46. Geza Roheim, "Psycho-Analysis of Primitive Cultural Types," *International Journal of Psycho-Analysis* 13 (1932): 1–221, at 15; C. B. Guthrie to Seligman, 15 March 1922, MS 262/15/3/22; J. H. Hutton to Seligman, 6 December 1923, MS 262/6/3/19, RAI.

47. M. C. Blair to C. G. Seligman, 20 April 1926, MS 262/6/8/23; M. C. Blair to Seligman, 20 June 1926, MS 262/6/8/24, RAI.

48. M. C. Blair to Seligman, 20 June 1926, MS 262/6/8/24, RAI; J. H. Hutton to Seligman, 6 December 1923, MS 262/6/3/19, RAI; Malinowski, *Sex and Repression,* 92–93; [Meyer Fortes?] to Seligman, 1 November 1932, MS 262/3/2/21, RAI.

49. Geza Roheim to Seligman, 22 August 1932, MS 262/3/1/5; Hortense Powdermaker to Seligman, 14 November 1932, MS 262/3/1/8; Elizabeth J. Brown to Seligman, MS 262/3/1/9; Isaac Schapera to Seligman, 19 September 1932, MS 262/3/1/11, RAI.

50. Seligman, typescript notes, n.d., MS 262/1/3/25, RAI; J. P. Mills to Seligman, 7 November 1923, MS 262/6/3/6, RAI; Seligman, typescript notes, n.d., MS 262/6/3/7, RAI.

51. J. P. Mills to Seligman, 7 November 1923, MS 262/6/3/6, RAI; Seligman, typescript notes, n.d., MS 262/6/3/7, RAI.

52. Robert Keable, "A People of Dreams," *Hibbert Journal* 19 (1921): 522–531, at 527.

53. T. T. S. Hayley, *The Anatomy of Lango Religion and Groups* (Cambridge: Cambridge University Press, 1947), 170.

54. Hayley, "Some Evidence of Dreams Collected among the Lango of Uganda," n.d., MS 262/6/6/14.1, RAI. Oruro recorded his dreams in Lango, then turned the notebooks over to Hayley, who translated them into English.

55. Hayley, *Anatomy of Lango Religion,* 202; D. Anthony Low and R. Cranford Pratt, *Buganda and British Overrule, 1900–1955* (London: Oxford University Press, 1960), 176–177.

56. Hayley, "Some Evidence of Dreams," MS 262/6/6/14.1, RAI.

57. Seligman to T. T. S. Hayley, 7 September 1938, MS 262 6/6/15, RAI.

58. [A. C. Cardinall?], "Note on Dreams, Jukun Tribe, Nigeria," 19 May 1928, MS 262/6/5/13, RAI; J. H. Hutton to Seligman, 6 December 1923, MS 262/6/3/19, RAI; Cardinall, "Note on Dreams among the Dagomba and Moshi," *Man* 27 (1927): 87–88, also in MS 262/6/6/4, RAI; Seligman, "Anthropology and Psychology," 35–36.

59. *The Norwood Gypsy, or Universal Dream-Book* (London: J. Bailey, n.d.), MS 262/5/1/26, RAI.

60. Seligman, "Anthropology and Psychology," 42–45; Seligman, "Unconscious in Relation to Anthropology," 378–381.

61. C. G. Seligman, "Dreams," *Journal of the American Society for Psychical Research* 21 (1927): 355–357; Seligman, "Anthropology and Psychology," 41.

62. Roheim to Seligman, 13 June 1923, MS 262/6/1/3/2; Roheim to Seligman, 3 November 1923, MS 262/6/1/3/3, RAI.

63. Helen Atkinson to Seligman, n.d., MS 262/8/163; D. O'Brien to Seligman, 14 February 1924, MS 262/6/9/11, RAI.

64. Owen, *Place of Enchantment*; Jenny Hazelgrove, *Spiritualism and British Society between the Wars* (Manchester: Manchester University Press, 2000).

65. George S. Tanner to Seligman, 27 March 1931, MS 262/8/185; George C. Wheeler to Seligman, 24 March 1931, MS 262/8/94; B. A. Senior to Seligman, MS 262/8/186.3, RAI.

66. Seligman to Phyllis Love, 28 March 1931, MS 262/8/33.1, RAI; G. M. Hawkins to Seligman, MS 262/8/123; Edward Majoribanks to Seligman, MS 262/8/53; Mary C. Marshall to Seligman, 6 April 1931, MS 262/8/209, RAI; Seligman to Mrs. Adams, n.d., MS 262/6/2, RAI.

67. Seligman, "Anthropological Perspective," 217–219; Seligman, "What Do You Dream About?"

68. C. G. Seligman, letters to the editor, *Times,* 10 March 1925, 22 January 1925, and 22 April 1932; Barkan, *Retreat of Scientific Racism,* 286–287; Seligman, "Anthropology and Psychology," 24; C. G. Seligman, "Psychology and Racial Differences," in *Psychology and Modern Problems,* ed. J. A. Hadfield (London: University of London Press, 1935); Campbell, *Race and Empire,* 83; "The Empire and the Dying Races," *Sunday Times* (Perth), 21 August 1924, 9.

69. Francis Daniel Hislop, "Doctor Jung I Presume," *Corona* 12 (1960): 236–238.

70. Burleson, *Jung in Africa,* 142–143; C. G. Jung, *Memories, Dreams, Reflections,* ed. Aniela Jaffé (London: Fontana Press, 1995), 283.

71. Graham Greene, *Journey without Maps* (London: Penguin, 2006 [1936]), 16–17; Norman Sherry, *The Life of Graham Greene,* vol. 1, *1904–1939* (London: Jonathan Cape, 1989), 94–97; Laurens van der Post, *The Lost World of the Kalahari* (New York: William Morrow, 1958). On van der Post and Jung, see also Laurens van der Post, *The Dark Eye in Africa* (New York: William Morrow, 1955), and J. D. F. Jones, *Storyteller: The Many Lives of Laurens van der Post* (London: John Murray, 2001), 320–330.

72. Jung, *Memories, Dreams, Reflections,* 302–303; "What Dreams Reveal," *East African Standard,* 19 November 1925, 5. On Jung and primitivism, see also Burleson, *Jung in Africa,* 73, 121, and Torgovnick, *Primitive Passions,* 29–36.

73. Jung, *Memories, Dreams, Reflections,* 283, 293; Claire Douglas, ed., *Visions: Notes of the Seminar Given in 1930–1934 by C. G. Jung* (Princeton: Princeton University Press, 1997), vol. 1, 43, and vol. 2, 1023.

74. Jung, *Memories, Dreams, Reflections*, 282. For a sense of the spectacle, see Daniel Mark Stephen, " 'The White Man's Grave': British West Africa and the British Empire Exhibition of 1925–1925," *Journal of British Studies* 48 (2009): 102–128.

75. Bronislaw Malinowski, "Baloma: The Spirits of the Dead in the Trobriand Islands," *Journal of the Royal Anthropological Institute* 46 (1916): 353–430; Jung to Seligman, 20 January 1920, MS 262/5/1/27, RAI; C. G. Seligman, "Anthropology and Psychology: A Study of Some Points of Contact," *Journal of the Royal Anthropological Institute* 54 (1924): 13–46; Jung to Seligman, 3 September 1924, Seligman papers 8/10, LSE.

76. For "salvage colonialism," see George Steinmetz, *The Devil's Handwriting: Precoloniality and the German Colonial State in Qingdao, Samoa, and Southwest Africa* (Chicago: University of Chicago Press, 2007), 318–341.

77. C. J. Jung, *Modern Man in Search of a Soul,* trans. W. S. Dell and Cary F. Baynes (New York: Harcourt, s.d. [1933]), 213–214; cf. Torgovnick, *Gone Primitive,* 11.

78. Thomson, *Psychological Subjects,* 79–94; Zaretsky, *Secrets of the Soul;* Richard Overy, *The Morbid Age: Britain between the Wars* (London: Allen Lane, 2009), ch. 4; Luisa Passerini, *Europe in Love, Love in Europe: Imagination and Politics in Britain between the Wars* (London: I. B. Tauris, 1999), 81–100.

79. Martin Jay, *The Dialectical Imagination: A History of the Frankfurt School and the Institute for Social Research, 1923–1950* (Berkeley: University of California Press, 1996), ch. 3; Christopher Lasch, "The Freudian Left and Cultural Revolution," *New Left Review,* no. 129 (1981): 23–34; George Makari, *Revolution in Mind: The Creation of Psychoanalysis* (New York: Harper Perennial, 2009), 396–404; Elizabeth Ann Danto, *Freud's Free Clinics: Psychoanalysis & Social Justice, 1918–1938* (New York: Columbia University Press, 2007).

80. On the eclecticism of ideas about the unconscious in Britain, see especially Hayward, *Transformation of the Psyche,* ch. 2.

81. Raymond Williams, "The Bloomsbury Fraction," in *The Raymond Williams Reader,* ed. John Higgins (Oxford: Blackwell, 2001); Erik Linstrum, "The Making of a Translator: James Strachey and the Origins of British Psychoanalysis," *Journal of British Studies* 53, no. 3 (2014): 685–704.

82. Lytton Strachey, *Eminent Victorians* (New York: Penguin, 1986 [1918]), 190; Edward Glover, *War, Sadism, and Pacifism* (London: Allen & Unwin, 1946 [1935]), 43; Edward Glover, *The Dangers of Being Human* (London: Allen & Unwin, 1936), 35; [Edward Glover], "The Cost of Becoming Civilised," *The Listener,* 9 October 1935, 599–600, in MS 262/5/2/1, RAI; M. D. Eder, "Politics," in *Social Aspects of Psycho-Analysis,* ed. Ernest Jones (London: Williams & Norgate, 1924), 157; Thomson, *Psychological Subjects,* 85–94. On Eder's politics, see also Matthew Thomson, " 'The Solution to His Own Enigma': Connecting the Life of Montague David Eder (1865–1936), Socialist, Psychoanalyst, Zionist, and Modern Saint," *Medical History* 55 (2011): 61–84.

83. Bernard Houghton, *The Mind of the Indian Government* (Madras: Ganesh, 1922), 1–2; Bernard Houghton, *The Psychology of Empire* (Madras:

Ganesan, 1921), 10–12, 14–15; Bernard Houghton, *The Menace from the West* (Madras: Ganesan, 1922); Bernard Houghton, *Agitate!* (Madras: Ganesan, 1922), 6–7. Houghton's remarkable career has received almost no attention, but see the brief discussion in Suhash Chakravarty, *V. K. Krishna Menon and the India League, 1925–47,* vol. 1 (New Delhi: Har-Anand, 1997), 169–171.

84. See the correspondence in L/PJ/12/43, IOR.

85. J. S. Hoyland, *Letters from India* (Hoshangabad: s.n., 1918), 2; J. S. Hoyland, *An Investigation Regarding the Psychology of Indian Adolescence* (Jubbulpore: Christian Mission Press, 1921). For Hoyland's source, see Earl Barnes, ed., *Studies in Education, 1896–1902* (Philadelphia, 1902). On Hoyland's experiment in India, see also below, ch. 3.

86. Hoyland, *Letters from India,* 8; Hoyland, *Psychology of Indian Adolescence,* 18; J. S. Hoyland, *That Inferiority Feeling* (London: Allen & Unwin, 1937), 20–21; J. S. Hoyland, *Gandhi: In Defence* (London: Headley Bros, 1943), 35.

87. See, e.g., Adas, *Machines as the Measure of Men,* ch. 6.

88. Hoyland, *That Inferiority Feeling,* 13, 35, 45, 241–242. See also J. S. Hoyland, "The Basis of Social Experimentation," in *Experiments in Social Reconstruction,* ed. J. S. Hoyland (London: Allenson, 1937); J. S. Hoyland, *Digging with the Unemployed* (London: Student Christian Movement Press, 1934); J. S. Hoyland, *Digging for a New England* (London: Jonathan Cape, 1936); J. S. Hoyland, *The World in Union* (London: Peace Book Co., 1940); J. S. Hoyland, *Federate or Perish* (London: Federal Union, 1944). On the entanglement of ideas about motherhood, suburbanization, and psychopathology in this period, see also Rhodri Hayward, "Desperate Housewives and Model Amoebae: The Invention of Suburban Neurosis in Inter-War Britain," in *Health and the Modern Home,* ed. Mark Jackson (London: Routledge, 2007).

89. Bronislaw Malinowski, *Argonauts of the Western Pacific: An Account of Native Enterprise and Adventure in the Archipelagos of Melanesian New Guinea* (London: Routledge, 1922), 465–466; George Henry Lane Fox Pitt-Rivers, *The Clash of Cultures and the Contact of Races* (London: Routledge, 1927), 148–154, at 154; Stephen H. Roberts, *Population Problems of the Pacific* (London: Routledge, 1927), 139, 142–143. For the parallels between Rivers's analysis and missionary criticism of Belgian colonialism, see Nancy Rose Hunt, "Rewriting the Soul in a Flemish Congo," *Past & Present* 198 (2008): 185–215.

90. See especially Ruth Leys, *Trauma: A Genealogy* (Chicago: University of Chicago Press, 2000), 19–21.

91. Roheim, "Psycho-Analysis of Primitive Cultural Types," 154–156, 158, 164. On Roheim's expedition, see also Paul A. Robinson, *The Freudian Left: Wilhelm Reich, Geza Roheim, Herbert Marcuse* (Ithaca: Cornell University Press, 1990), 75–146; Joy Damousi, *Freud in the Antipodes: A Cultural History of Psychoanalysis in Australia* (Sydney: University of New South Wales Press, 2005), 93–96.

92. Fortes field notebook "33 8/36"; Fortes desk notebook "vol. I," 1936; Fortes desk notebook "vol. IV," February 1935; Fortes desk notebook "Voyage Home," 1935; Fortes to Malinowski, 12 July 1934, Fortes papers 1/45, CUL; M. Fortes, "Culture Contact as a Dynamic Process: An Investigation in the

Northern Territories of the Gold Coast," *Africa* 9, no. 1 (1936): 24–55, at 27–28.

93. Kapila, "Masculinity and Madness," 150–153.

94. Hartnack, *Psychoanalysis in Colonial India,* 51–55, 67–74; Mahone, "Psychology of Rebellion."

95. Sylvia Leith-Ross to Seligman, 5 January 1919; Leith-Ross to Seligman, 15 January 1920, C. G. Seligman papers, MS Add. 9396, box 1, CUL; Sylvia Leith-Ross, *Stepping-Stones: Memoirs of Colonial Nigeria, 1907–1960,* ed. Michael Crowder (London: Peter Owen, 1983), 17, 93.

96. Sylvia Leith-Ross, *African Women: A Study of the Ibo of Nigeria* (London: Routledge, 1965 [1939]), 175–176, 182–183.

97. Sylvia Leith-Ross, "Report on a Visit to the Nguru Area, Owerri Division, from the 7th May to the 1st June, and from the 13th June to the 29th June, 1935," Sylvia Leith-Ross papers, Mss. Afr. s. 1520, box 1, RHO.

98. William E. Hunt to Leith-Ross, 29 July 1935; Leith-Ross, "Report on a Visit to the Nguru Area"; Sylvia Leith-Ross, "The Small Coins: Nigeria, 1907–1969," 1972, Leith-Ross papers, box 1, RHO.

99. Margaret Field to Audrey Richards, 10 February 1959, Audrey Richards papers, file 16/22, LSE; Margaret Field grant application, 26 July 1955, Colonial Research papers 8/21, LSE; M. J. Field, *Religion and Medicine of the Ga People* (New York: Oxford University Press, 1937), 136n.

100. Margaret Field, *Search for Security: An Ethno-Psychiatric Study of Rural Ghana* (London: Faber and Faber, 1960); Vaughan, "Suicide in Late Colonial Africa," 388n; Field to Richards, 10 February 1959, Richards papers, file 16/22, LSE.

101. Vaughan, *Curing Their Ills.*

102. Field grant application, LSE; Mark Freshfield [Margaret Field], *The Stormy Dawn* (London: Faber and Faber, 1947), 29–30, 175–176

103. Field grant application, Colonial Research papers 8/21, LSE; [Field], *Stormy Dawn,* 59.

104. Nicholas Owen, *The British Left and India: Metropolitan Anti-Imperialism, 1885–1947* (Oxford: Oxford University Press, 2007); Susan Pedersen, *The Guardians: The League of Nations and the Crisis of Empire* (New York: Oxford University Press, 2015); Anthony Anghie, *Imperialism, Sovereignty, and the Making of International Law* (Cambridge: Cambridge University Press, 2007).

105. On Sachs, see the introductions by Saul Dubow and Jacqueline Rose in Wulf Sachs, *Black Hamlet* (Baltimore: Johns Hopkins University Press, 1996 [1937]), and Khanna, *Dark Continents,* 236–268.

106. Sachs, *Black Hamlet,* 71–72, 237–240; Wulf Sachs, "The Insane Native: An Introduction to a Psychological Study," *South African Journal of Science* 30 (1933): 706–713; Wulf Sachs, *Black Anger* (Boston: Little, Brown, 1947), 105.

107. Sachs, *Black Anger,* 95–96. On the political context of race in interwar South Africa, see Saul Dubow, *Racial Segregation and the Origins of Apartheid in South Africa, 1919–36* (London: Macmillan, 1989).

108. [John Rickman], "Wulf Sachs, 1893–1949," *International Journal of Psycho-Analysis* 31 (1950): 388–390; Wulf Sachs, "Racism: A Study in

Psychology," *The Democrat,* 4 November 1943, 5; Wulf Sachs, "Racism: The Solution," *The Democrat,* 20 January 1944, 15–16; Khanna, *Dark Continents,* 236.

109. Sachs, *Black Anger,* 147–148, 232, 304.

110. Sachs, *Black Hamlet,* 234–235; Sachs, *Black Anger,* 51–52.

111. Cathy Urwin and Elaine Sharland, "From Bodies to Minds in Childcare Literature: Advice to Parents in Interwar Britain," in *In the Name of the Child: Health and Welfare, 1880–1940,* ed. Roger Cooter (London: Routledge, 1992); Christina Hardyment, *Dream Babies: Childcare Advice from John Locke to Gina Ford* (London: Frances Lincoln, 2007), 167–179; John Newson and Elizabeth Newson, "Cultural Aspects of Childrearing in the English-Speaking World," in *The Integration of a Child into a Social World,* ed. Martin P. M. Richards (Cambridge: Cambridge University Press, 1974), 59–63. On the Edwardian origins of infant welfare, see Anna Davin, "Imperialism and Motherhood," *History Workshop Journal* 5 (1978): 9–65; Jane Lewis, *The Politics of Motherhood: Child and Maternal Welfare in England, 1900–1939* (London: Croom Helm, 1980); Deborah Dwork, *War Is Good for Babies and Other Young Children: A History of the Infant and Child Welfare Movement in England, 1898–1918* (London: Tavistock Publications, 1987). For the rise of theories about the social context of personality formation between the wars, see Rhodri Hayward, "The Invention of the Psychosocial: An Introduction," *History of the Human Sciences* 25, no. 5 (2012): 3–12, and Rhodri Hayward, "Enduring Emotions: James L. Halliday and the Invention of the Psychosocial," *Isis* 100 (2009): 827–838.

112. Zaretsky, *Secrets of the Soul,* 203–204, 213; Lasch, "Freudian Left," 24.

113. Mathew Thomson, *Lost Freedom: The Landscape of the Child and the British Post-War Settlement* (Oxford: Oxford University Press, 2013), 81–82; M. A. Payne, *Oliver Untwisted* (London: Edward Arnold, 1929), 51.

114. Vaughan, *Curing Their Ills,* 67–70, 117; Jennifer Beinart, "Darkly through a Lens: Changing Perceptions of the African Child in Sickness and Health, 1900–45," in *In the Name of the Child,* ed. Cooter, 233–234; Lenore Manderson, *Sickness and the State: Health and Illness in Colonial Malaya, 1870–1940* (Cambridge: Cambridge University Press, 1996), ch. 7.

115. J. F. Ritchie, *The African as Suckling and as Adult* (Manchester: Rhodes-Livingstone Institute, 1968 [1943]), 46, 61; cf. McCulloch, *Colonial Psychiatry,* 98.

116. J. F. Ritchie to W. V. Brelsford, 20 February 1944; Ritchie to Brelsford, 6 June 1944, William Vernon Brelsford papers, YUL.

117. Brelsford to Ritchie, 20 September 1943; Ritchie to Brelsford, 17 December 1943, Brelsford papers, YUL.

118. Ritchie, *African as Suckling,* 5.

119. Ritchie to Brelsford, 31 August 1944; Brelsford to Ritchie, 15 May 1944, Brelsford papers, YUL.

120. Barotse National School annual reports, 1940 and 1941, ED 1/2/15, NAZ.

121. Susan Pedersen, "The Maternalist Moment in British Colonial Policy: The Controversy over 'Child Slavery' in Hong Kong, 1917–1941," *Past & Present* 171 (2001): 161–202; Susan Pedersen, "National Bodies, Unspeakable

Acts: The Sexual Politics of Colonial Policy-making," *Journal of Modern History* 63, no. 4 (1991): 647–680. Indigenous nationalists could advance their own aims by participating in movements to protect children against "traditional" practices: see Mrinalini Sinha, *Specters of Mother India: The Global Restructuring of an Empire* (Durham: Duke University Press, 2006), ch. 4.

122. Cicely D. Williams, "Child Health in the Gold Coast," *Lancet* 231 (1938): 97–102.

123. C. Cox to Seligman, 21 Jan. 1938, MS 262/3/6/12; D. R. Macdonald to Seligman, 9 Oct. 1938, MS 262/3/6/25; Seligman to R. A. C. Oliver, 15 Feb. 1935, MS 262/4/3/11; Cyril Burt to Seligman, 24 Nov. 1934, MS 262/4/3/16; "Mental Differences in Races," n.d., MS 262/4/3/15, RAI.

3. Meritocracy or Master Race?

1. *Year Book of the United Theological College of South India and Ceylon at Bangalore* (Mysore: Wesleyan University Press, 1920), 14; *Year Book of the United Theological College of South India and Ceylon at Bangalore* (Mysore: Wesleyan University Press, 1915), 12; D. S. Herrick, "The Measurement of Intelligence and Its Value for Missionary Work," *Madras Christian College Magazine,* July 1923, and D. S. Herrick to William E. Strong, 7 February 1923, 16.1.9, vol. 28, ABCFM.

2. Herrick to Strong, 7 February 1923, ABCFM; American Madura Mission meeting minutes, January 1923, 16.1.9, vol. 26, ABCFM.

3. J. A. Richey, ed., *Provisional Series of Mental Intelligence Tests for Indian Scholars* (Calcutta: Bureau of Education, 1924), I; Elizabeth Buettner, *Empire Families: Britons and Late Imperial India* (Oxford: Oxford University Press, 2005).

4. D. S. Herrick biographical file, 77.1, box 33, ABCFM; D. S. Herrick to W. E. Strong, 5 June 1918, in *Papers of the American Board of Commissioners for Foreign Missions* (Woodbridge: Research Publications, 1982), reel 493; Frederick T. Simpson, "Psycho-Therapy," *Hartford Seminary Record* 18 (1908): 165–178; Samuel Edward Capen to George F. Dawson, 4 January 1919, box 31, folder 457, Hartford Seminary archive.

5. Carson, *Measure of Merit,* ch. 6; Leila Zenderland, *Measuring Minds: Henry Herbert Goddard and the Origins of American Intelligence Testing* (Cambridge: Cambridge University Press, 1998), 292; Herrick, "Measurement of Intelligence," 16.1.9, vol. 28, ABCFM.

6. Adas, *Machines as the Measure of Men,* 205–207; Ekbladh, *Great American Mission,* 26–27, 31, 107–108; Patrick Harries and David Maxwell, eds., *The Spiritual in the Secular: Missionaries and Knowledge about Africa* (Grand Rapids: Eerdmans, 2012); Norman Etherington, "Education and Medicine," in *Missions and Empire,* ed. Norman Etherington (Oxford: Oxford University Press, 2005), 275–284; Ronald Hyam, "The View from Below: The African Response to Missionaries," in *Understanding the British Empire* (Cambridge: Cambridge University Press, 2010), 190–191; Sujit Sivasundaram, *Nature and the Godly Empire: Science and Evangelical Mission in the Pacific, 1795–1850* (Cambridge: Cambridge University Press, 2005).

7. On racial identity in the Anglophone settler world, see especially Lake and Reynolds, *Drawing the Global Color Line;* Caroline Elkins and Susan Pedersen, eds., *Settler Colonialism in the Twentieth Century: Projects, Practices, Legacies* (New York: Routledge, 2005); Robert A. Huttenback, *Racism and Empire: White Settlers and Colored Immigrants in the British Self-Governing Colonies, 1830–1910* (Ithaca: Cornell University Press, 1976).

8. On nativism and American psychometrics, see Gould, *Mismeasure of Man,* 194–201, 218–221, 226–229, 252–262; Carson, *Measure of Merit,* 191–192; Daniel J. Kevles, *In the Name of Eugenics: Genetics and the Uses of Human Heredity* (New York: Knopf, 1985), 82–83; Alexandra Stern, *Eugenic Nation: Faults and Frontiers of Modern Breeding in Modern America* (Berkeley: University of California Press, 2005), 18–19, 93–94; Paul Davis Chapman, *Schools as Sorters: Lewis M. Terman, Applied Psychology, and the Intelligence Testing Movement, 1890–1930* (New York: New York University Press, 1988), 118–123. For a persuasively revisionist claim that one American mental tester, Henry Goddard, did not subscribe to the nativist and eugenicist views often attributed to him, see Zenderland, *Measuring Minds,* ch. 8. Ironically, Anglo-Saxonism generated far more enthusiasm among Americans looking toward Britain than among the British themselves: see Reginald Horsman, *Race and Manifest Destiny: The Origins of American Racial Anglo-Saxonism* (Cambridge: Harvard University Press, 1981); J.R. Hall, "Mid-Nineteenth-Century American Anglo-Saxonism: The Question of Language," in *Anglo-Saxonism and the Construction of Social Identity,* ed. Allen J. Frantzen and John D. Niles (Gainesville: University of Florida Press, 1997); Paul A. Kramer, "Empires, Exceptions, and Anglo-Saxons: Race and Rule between the British and United States Empires, 1880–1910," *Journal of American History* 88, no. 4 (2002): 1315–1353; Alex Zwerdling, *Improvised Europeans: American Literary Expatriates and the Siege of London* (New York: Basic Books, 1999).

9. Kevles, *In the Name of Eugenics,* 83–84; Jonathan Toms, *Mental Hygiene and Psychiatry in Modern Britain* (Basingstoke: Palgrave Macmillan, 2013), 37–38; Adrian Wooldridge, *Measuring the Mind: Education and Psychology in England, c. 1860–c.1990* (Cambridge: Cambridge University Press, 1994); Gillian Sutherland, *Ability, Merit, and Measurement: Mental Testing and English Education, 1880–1940* (Oxford: Clarendon Press, 1984). In the British context, eugenicist catchphrases such as "race quality" and "race suicide" referred to socioeconomic differences in fertility rather than the superiority of Anglo-Saxon stock: see Richard A. Soloway, *Demography and Degeneration: Eugenics and the Declining Birthrate in Twentieth-Century Britain* (Chapel Hill: University of North Carolina Press, 1995).

10. Cf. Nicholas Lemann, *The Big Test: The Secret History of the American Meritocracy* (New York: Farrar, Straus and Giroux, 2000), ch. 10. Compared to their American counterparts, Lemann argues, the British were more committed to a narrowly defined concept of intelligence and less enraptured with a vague idea of character as a means of sorting populations. But this account, focused on Cyril Burt and Michael Young's satirical *The Rise of the Meritocracy* (1958), exaggerates the dominance of psychometrics—and even the idea of meritocracy itself—in British school selection. See Ross McKibbin, *Classes and Cultures:*

England, 1918–1951 (Oxford: Oxford University Press, 2000), 229–231; Thomson, *Psychological Subjects,* 110–113; Peter Mandler, "The Crisis of the Meritocracy: Education and Democracy in Postwar Britain," paper presented at North American Conference on British Studies, Minneapolis, 7 November 2014.

11. Michael Young, *The Rise of the Meritocracy, 1870–2033: An Essay on Education and Equality* (London: Thames and Hudson, 1958).

12. Andrew Harold Walsh, "For Our City's Welfare: Building a Protestant Establishment in Hartford," Ph.D. thesis (Harvard University, 1995), 239–246; William Douglas Mackenzie, *South Africa: Its History, Heroes and Wars* (Chicago: Co-Operative Publishing Co., 1899), 270; Brian Stanley, *The World Missionary Conference, Edinburgh 1910* (Grand Rapids: Eerdmans, 2009), 316–317; World Missionary Conference, *Report of Commission V: The Training of Teachers* (Edinburgh: Oliphant, Anderson, and Ferrier, 1910), 161–162; Hartford Seminary, *Annual Register for the Seventy-Second Year, 1905–1906* (Hartford: Hartford Seminary Press, 1906), 26–32; Olav G. Myklebust, *The Study of Missions in Theological Education,* vol. 2 (Oslo: Egede Instituttet, 1957), 93.

13. "Happenings in the Seminary," *Hartford Seminary Record* 22 (1912): 226–252, at 247; *Who Was Who among North American Authors, 1921–1939,* vol. 2 (Detroit: Gale Research, 1976), 820.

14. Woodrow Wilson, "The Present Task of the Ministry," *Hartford Seminary Record* 19 (1909): 226–233; Samuel B. Capen, "The Seminary and the World," *Hartford Seminary Record* 19 (1909): 288–294, at 289–290; "Seventy-Seventh Anniversary," *Hartford Seminary Record* 21 (1911): 186–207, at 206; Edward Warren Capen, *Sociological Progress in Mission Lands* (New York: Fleming H. Revell, 1914), 35–39. On Mackenzie's enthusiasm for the League of Nations, see Mackenzie to Wilson, 22 October 1920, in Arthur S. Link, ed., *The Papers of Woodrow Wilson,* vol. 66 (Princeton: Princeton University Press, 1992), 259–291, and W. Douglas Mackenzie, *The Kingdom of God and the League of Nations* (Hartford: Hartford Seminary Press, 1919).

15. David Scudder Herrick, application form for missionary work in India, 12 February 1918, Home Department (Public), July 1918, part B, 146–157, NAI. On the limitations of Wilson's idealism, see Erez Manela, *The Wilsonian Moment: Self-Determination and the International Origins of Anticolonial Nationalism* (Oxford: Oxford University Press, 2007), ch. 1.

16. Sanford Gifford, *The Emmanuel Movement: The Origins of Group Treatment and the Assault on Lay Psychotherapy* (Boston: Francis Countway Library of Medicine, 1997); Robert C. Fuller, *Americans and the Unconscious* (New York: Oxford University Press, 1986), 102–104; Nathan G. Hale, *Freud and the Americans: The Beginnings of Psychoanalysis in the United States, 1876–1919* (New York: Oxford University Press, 1971), 248–249.

17. Mackenzie, "Colleges and Character," *Hartford Daily Times,* n.d., box 281, folder 3902, Hartford Seminary archive; Hartford Seminary, *Annual Register, 1905–1906,* 32.

18. Sutherland, *Ability, Merit, and Measurement,* 283; Wooldridge, *Measuring the Mind,* 47–48.

19. Earl Leslie King, *A Course in Diagnosis for Religious Educators* (Madras: Methodist Publishing House, 1928).

20. Herrick, "Measurement of Intelligence," ABCFM; David Herrick, "A Comparison of Brahman and Panchama Children in South India with Each Other and with American Children by Means of the Goddard Form Board," *Journal of Applied Psychology* 5, no. 3 (1921): 253–260.

21. Hoyland, *Investigation Regarding the Psychology of Indian Adolescence.*

22. E. L. King, *Ten Studies in Leadership* (Madras: Methodist Publishing House, 1921), 13; King, *Course in Diagnosis;* Frank N. Freeman, *Mental Tests: Their History, Principles & Applications* (Boston: Houghton Mifflin, 1939), 215–219; Herrick, "Measurement of Intelligence," ABCFM; Henry Herbert Goddard, *The Kallikak Family: A Study in the Heredity of Feeble-Mindedness* (New York: Macmillan, 1912); Zenderland, *Measuring Minds,* ch. 5.

23. Herrick, "Comparison of Brahman and Panchama Children"; Herrick, "Measurement of Intelligence," ABCFM; Hoyland, *Psychology of Indian Adolescence,* 176; Emil Wolfgang Menzel, "A Tentative Standardization of the Goodenough Intelligence Test for Central Provinces (India)," M.A. thesis (Washington University, 1934), 5, 60–71. See also Emil Menzel, "The Goodenough Intelligence Test in India," *Journal of Applied Psychology* 19, no. 5 (1935): 615–624.

24. Sinha, *Specters of Mother India,* 131–136.

25. Eugene P. Heideman, *From Mission to Church: The Reformed Church in America Mission to India* (Grand Rapids: Eerdmans, 2001), 493–497; Aparna Basu, *The Growth of Education and Political Development in India, 1898–1920* (Delhi: Oxford University Press, 1974), 105; J. H. Warnshuis, "The Arcot Mission Experiment in Tests," *Christian Education* 4 (1924): 1–25, at 1.

26. M. Olcott, "An Experiment with Intelligence Tests and their Evaluation," *Indian Journal of Psychology* 4, no. 1 (January 1929): 22–30, at 22–24; Warnshuis, "Arcot Mission Experiment," 2.

27. Zenderland, *Measuring Minds,* 291.

28. Warnshuis, "Arcot Mission Experiment," 3–5.

29. Dirks, *Castes of Mind,* 131–132, 141, 146–147; Duncan B. Forrester, *Caste and Christianity: Attitudes and Policies on Caste of Anglo-Saxon Protestant Missions in India* (London: Curzon, 1980); G. A. Oddie, *Social Protest in India: British Protestant Missionaries and Social Reforms, 1850–1900* (New Delhi: Manohar, 1979), ch. 2.

30. Bellenoit, *Missionary Education,* 117; Forrester, *Caste and Christianity,* 31; Herrick to Bell, 28 February 1910, *Papers of the American Board of Commissioners,* reel 493; John S. Hoyland, *They Saw Gandhi* (New York: Fellowship Publications, 1947), 58–62; Mason Olcott, *Village Schools in India: An Investigation with Suggestions* (Calcutta: Association Press, 1926), 59; J. H. Warnshuis, "Caste Levelling Movement in India," *Mission Field* 30, no. 10 (1918): 419; A. S. Woodburne, *Psychological Tests of Mental Abilities* (Madras: Government Press, 1924), 208.

31. J. A. Richey, "Mental Intelligence Tests for Indian Schools" (draft), Education Dept., Nov. 1931 Deposit, No. 48, NAI; Richey, ed., *Provisional*

Series, i; C. Herbert Rice, *A Hindustani Binet-Performance Point Scale* (Princeton: Princeton University Press, 1929), ix.

32. Hartog, *Examinations and Their Relation to Culture and Efficiency,* 1–2.

33. Minutes of the second meeting of the Central Advisory Board of Education, June 1921, Philip Hartog papers, MSS Eur E221/60, IOR.

34. Mabel Hartog, *P. J. Hartog: A Memoir* (London: Constable, 1949), 52; G. R. Searle, *The Quest for National Efficiency: A Study in British Politics and Political Thought, 1899–1914* (London: Ashfield, 1990 [1971]).

35. Wooldridge, *Measuring the Mind,* 203–205; P. J. Hartog, *Examinations and Their Relation to Culture and Efficiency* (London: Constable, 1918).

36. Central Advisory Board of Education minutes, June 1921, Hartog papers, IOR; Indian Statutory Commission, *Interim Report of the Indian Statutory Commission: Review of Growth of Education in British India* (London: H.M.S.O., 1929), 106, 144.

37. John Roach, *Public Examinations in England, 1850–1900* (Cambridge: Cambridge University Press, 1971); Roy MacLeod, ed., *Days of Judgment: Science, Examinations and the Organization of Knowledge in Late Victorian England* (Driffield: Nafferton Books, 1982); Robert John Montgomery, *Examinations: An Account of Their Evolution as Administrative Devices in England* (Pittsburgh: University of Pittsburgh Press, 1967); Stephen Wiseman, ed., *Examinations and English Education* (Manchester: Manchester University Press, 1961).

38. R. J. Moore, "The Abolition of Patronage in the Indian Civil Service and the Closure of Haileybury College," *Historical Journal* 7, no. 2 (1964): 246–257; Roach, *Public Examinations in England,* 23–27; C. J. Dewey, "The Education of a Ruling Caste: The Indian Civil Service in the Era of Competitive Examination," *English Historical Review* 88, no. 347 (1973): 262–282, at 272; Gilmour, *Ruling Caste,* 63–68.

39. A. J. Stockwell, "Examinations and Empire: The Cambridge Certificate in the Colonies, 1857–1957," in *Making Imperial Mentalities: Socialisation and British Imperialism,* ed. J. A. Mangan (Manchester: Manchester University Press, 1990); Sandra Raban, ed., *Examining the World: A History of the University of Cambridge Local Examinations Syndicate* (Cambridge: Cambridge University Press, 2008); J. M. Compton, "Indians and the Indian Civil Service, 1853–1879: A Study in National Agitation and Imperial Embarrassment," *Journal of the Royal Asiatic Society,* nos. 3–4 (1967): 99–113, esp. at 111–113; David C. Potter, "Manpower Shortage and the End of Colonialism: The Case of the Indian Civil Service," *Modern Asian Studies* 7, no. 1 (1973): 47–73, at 64–65.

40. Philip Hartog, *Some Aspects of Indian Education Past and Present* (London: Oxford University Press, 1939), 41.

41. Woolridge, *Measuring the Mind,* 93.

42. Rice, *Hindustani Binet Scale,* 1; Satyajivan Pal, *Tests of the Stanford Revision of the Binet-Simon Intelligence Scale, Adapted for Use with Bengali Boys and Translated into the Bengali Language* (London: Oxford University Press, 1925); [Corrie Gordon], "Report of the Binet-Simon Tests (Stanford

Revision) as Applied to the Children of the Model School, Teachers' College, Saidapet," Education Dept., November 1931 Deposit, No. 47, NAI.

43. Rice, *Hindustani Binet Scale,* 36–37, 99; Richey, ed., *Provisional Series,* 5–6, 9–10; [Gordon], "Report of the Binet-Simon Tests," Education Dept., NAI.

44. Ibid., 14; Lewis Terman, *The Measurement of Intelligence: An Explanation of and a Complete Guide for the Use of the Stanford Revision* (Boston: Houghton Mifflin, 1916), 166. On culture-bound images in the U.S. Army tests, see Gould, *Mismeasure of Man,* 200.

45. Woodburne, *Psychological Tests;* Rice, *Hindustani Binet Scale;* Partha Mitther, *Art and Nationalism in Colonial India, 1850–1922: Occidental Orientations* (Cambridge: Cambridge University Press, 1995), ch. 4.

46. Terman, *Measurement of Intelligence,* 215–216, 268–270; [Gordon], "Report of the Binet-Simon Tests," Education Dept., NAI; Rice, *Hindustani Binet Scale,* 150–156.

47. Wooldridge, *Measuring the Mind,* 94–95; Terman, *Measurement of Intelligence,* 115–118, at 115.

48. [Gordon], "Report of the Binet-Simon Tests," Education Dept., NAI; Woodburne, *Psychological Tests,* 211.

49. Woodburne, *Psychological Tests,* 4; Menzel, "Standardization of the Goodenough Intelligence Test," 2–3; Central Advisory Board of Education minutes, June 1921, Hartog papers, IOR; Richey, ed., *Provisional Series;* Corrie Gordon, ed., *Revised Series of Mental Intelligence Tests for Indian Scholars* (Calcutta: Government of India Central Publication Branch, 1930).

50. *Report on Public Instruction in the Bombay Presidency* (Bombay: Government Central Press, 1927), 51; "Mental Tests of Students," *Times of India,* 17 March 1933, 3.

51. For the example of Government College, Lahore, in the late 1920s, see Prakash Tandon, *Punjabi Century, 1857–1947* (Berkeley: University of California Press, 1968), 194.

52. G. Bose, "Progress of Psychology in India during the Past Twenty-five Years," in *The Progress of Science in India during the Past Twenty-five Years,* ed. B Prashad (Calcutta: Indian Science Congress Association, 1938), 336–339. For the research, see Haripada Maity, "A Report on the Application of the Stanford Adult Tests to a Group of College Students," *Indian Journal of Psychology* 1, no. 4 (1926): 214–222; A. K. Datta, "Intelligence Tests in Bengal," *Proceedings of the Indian Science Congress* 22 (1935): 443–444; B. Gupta, "Application of Binet, Simon, and Piaget Reasoning Tests," *Proceedings of the Indian Science Congress* 22 (1935): 445–446; G. C. Chatterjee, "Intelligence Tests for College Freshmen," *Indian Journal of Psychology* 2, no. 2 (1927): 74–79; B. Gupta, "Intelligence Tests for College Freshmen," *Proceedings of the Indian Science Congress* 14 (1927): 325–326; J. M. Sen, "The Measurement of the Intelligence of School Children by Group-Tests," *Proceedings of the Indian Science Congress* 12 (1925): 287; M. J. Mukherjea, "Intelligence Tests," *Proceedings of the Indian Science Congress* 15 (1928): 343.

53. Jalal Uddin to James Campbell Manry, 3 December 1928, James Campbell Manry papers, box 5, folder 1, Emory University Library, Atlanta; Emil W. Menzel, *Educational Adventures in India, 1924–1941* (Waverly: s.n., 1980), 76–77.

54. For the critique of Indian psychology as imitative, see Durganand Sinha, *Psychology in a Third World Country: The Indian Experience* (New Delhi: Sage, 1986); Ashis Nandy, "Non-Paradigmatic Crisis in Indian Psychology: Reflections on a Recipient Culture Science," *Indian Journal of Psychology* 49, no. 1 (1974): 1–20. For a revisionist view, see Aria S. K. Laskin, "The Politics of Psychology and the Psychology of Difference in the Age of India's Decolonisation," M.Phil. thesis (Cambridge University, 2009).

55. Gyan Prakash, *Another Reason: Science and the Imagination of Modern India* (Princeton: Princeton University Press, 1999); Benjamin Zachariah, *Developing India: An Intellectual and Social History, c. 1930–50* (New Delhi: Oxford University Press, 2005); Arnold, *Everyday Technology,* ch. 4; David Arnold, "Nehruvian Science and Postcolonial India," *Isis* 104 (2013): 360–370.

56. H. A. Yeole, *On Intelligence Testing* (Satara: Satara City Press, 1926), 13–15.

57. Robert Henderson Croll, *Wide Horizons: Wanderings in Central Australia* (Sydney: Angus & Robertson, 1937), 1, 14–15; Stanley D. Porteus, *A Psychologist of Sorts: The Autobiography and Publications of the Inventor of the Porteus Maze Tests* (Palo Alto: Pacific Books, 1969), 118.

58. S. D. Porteus, letter to *Times Literary Supplement,* 16 June 1932, 447. On extinction discourse, see especially McGregor, *Imagined Destinies*; Andrew Markus, *Governing Savages* (Sydney: Allen & Unwin, 1990); Brantlinger, *Dark Vanishings.* On the setting of the expedition as a "death space," see Warwick Anderson, "Hermannsburg, 1929: Turning Aboriginal 'Primitives' into Modern Psychological Subjects," *Journal of the History of the Behavioral Sciences* 50, no. 2 (2014): 127–147.

59. Porteus, *Psychologist of Sorts,* 1–2, 12–14. Porteus has usually figured in national rather than imperial histories: see Anderson, *Cultivation of Whiteness,* 207–208, 240–241; Geoffrey Gray, *A Cautious Silence: The Politics of Australian Anthropology* (Canberra: Aboriginal Studies Press, 2007), 97–102; Geoffrey Gray, "Looking for Neanderthal Man, Finding a Captive White Woman: The Story of a Documentary Film," *Health and History* 8, no. 2 (2006): 69–90; Alison M. Turtle, "Péron, Porteus, and the Pacific Islands Regiment: The Beginnings of Cross-Cultural Psychology in Australia," *Journal of the History of the Behavioral Sciences* 27 (1997): 7–20.

60. For his long memory of British slights, see S. D. Porteus, *Porteus Maze Test: Fifty Years' Application* (Palo Alto: Pacific Books, 1965), 10–11; Porteus, *Psychologist of Sorts,* 47–49. For the origin of "colonial science," and the diffusionist, metropole-to-periphery model associated with it, see George Basalla, "The Spread of Western Science," *Science* 156 (1967): 611–622. Even critiques of Basalla have reaffirmed the idea of a struggle for independence from British influence in Australia: see Ian Inkster, "Scientific Enterprise and the Colonial

'Model': Observations on Australian Experience in Historical Context," *Social Studies of Science* 15 (1985): 677–704; Roy MacLeod, "On Visiting the 'Moving Metropolis': Reflections on the Architecture of Imperial Science," in *Scientific Colonialism: A Cross-Cultural Comparison,* ed. Nathan Reingold and Marc Rothenberg (Washington: Smithsonian Institution Press, 1987); Jan Todd, *Colonial Technology: Science and the Transfer of Innovation to Australia* (Cambridge: Cambridge University Press, 1995). More recent work has suggested discarding the concept of "colonial science" altogether, stressing the importance of exchanges in both directions and the existence of intellectual networks that do not map neatly onto an imperial framework. See Harrison, "Science in the British Empire," and Tilley, *Africa as a Living Laboratory,* 10–11.

61. Porteus, *Psychologist of Sorts,* 34–43; Porteus, *Fifty Years',* 1–7.

62. Porteus, *Fifty Years,* 13; Cyril Burt, *Mental and Scholastic Tests* (London: P. S. King, 1922), 242–244; Cyril Burt, *Handbook of Tests for Use in Schools* (London: P. S. King, 1923), 94–96; Katherine Treat, "The Significance of Test Results in Predicting Efficiency in Garment Machine Operating," *Psychological Clinic* 19 (1930): 218–230; G. Mennens, "Étude expérimentale de différentes aptitudes psychiques chez les prisonniers," *Journal de psychologie* 28 (1931): 283–302; A. Zeckel and J. J. V. D. Kolk, "Eine vergleichende Intelligenz-Untersuchung einer Gruppe erblich taubstummer und hörender Kinder mittels der Porteus-Intelligenz-Probe," *Psychiatrische en Neurologische Bladen* 43 (1939): 141–150; J. C. Tsao, "A Note on Porteus Maze Test," *Chinese Journal of Psychology* 1 (1937): 252–264.

63. Porteus, *Fifty Years,* 249; Rice, *Hindustani Binet Scale,* 1; I. D. MacCrone, "Preliminary Results from the Porteus Maze Tests Applied to Native Children," *South African Journal of Science* 25 (1928): 481–484; R. A. C. Oliver, "Report on the Construction of a Battery of Individual Tests of Intelligence for Adult Natives in East Africa," 14 July 1931, series III. A, box 196, folio 6, CC.

64. Porteus, *Fifty Years,* 6–7, 246–254; Porteus, *Psychologist of Sorts,* 38, 43–44; Porteus, *The Maze Test and Mental Differences* (Vineland: Smith Printing and Publishing House, 1933), 176–188; S. D. Porteus, "Human Studies in Hawaii," [1931], series 214, box 1, folder 6, RF.

65. S. D. Porteus, "Mental Tests with Delinquents and Australian Aboriginal Children," *Psychological Review* 24, no. 1 (1917): 32–42; S. D. Porteus, *Primitive Intelligence and Environment* (New York: Macmillan, 1937), 252, 255, 289. On Kidd's theory and its influence, see Dubow, *Scientific Racism in Modern South Africa,* 199–203; Gaurav Desai, *Subject to Colonialism: African Self-Fashioning and the Colonial Library* (Durham: Duke University Press, 2001), 28–32.

66. S. D. Porteus, "Race and Social Differences in Performance Tests," *Genetic Psychology Monographs* 8, no. 2 (1930): 93–208, at 101; Porteus, *Maze Test and Mental Differences,* 101–102.

67. Terman and the other Army testers, however, showed far more enthusiasm for restricting immigration than Goddard did: see Gould, *Mismeasure of Man,* 254–262, and Zenderland, *Measuring Minds,* 264–266, 281–294.

258

68. S. D. Porteus, "Psychological Service in Hawaii: The Work of the University Clinic," *University of Hawaii Bulletin* 18, no. 5 (1939): 3–17, at 3; Oswald F. Black, *Race Psychology in Hawaii with Special Reference to Clinical Methods* (Pretoria: Carnegie Corporation, 1936); Michael Haas, *Institutional Racism: The Case of Hawai'i* (Westport: Praeger, 1992), 55–57.

69. A. N. Dean, "A Proposed Station for Racial Research," 13 April 1926; S. D. Porteus, "Research Programme on Racial Differences," 21 October 1927, series 214, box 1, folder 3, RF.

70. George W. Stocking, "Philanthropoids and Vanishing Cultures: Rockefeller Funding and the End of the Museum Era in Anglo-American Anthropology," in *The Ethnographer's Magic and Other Essays in the History of Anthropology* (Madison: University of Wisconsin Press, 1992); Henrika Kuklick, " 'Humanity in the Chrysalis Stage': Indigenous Australians in the Anthropological Imagination, 1899–1926," *British Journal of the History of Science* 39, no. 4 (2006): 535–568, at 542; Gray, *Cautious Silence*, 6–13; Charles B. Davenport to Edwin Embree, 3 March 1924, series 410, box 3, folder 23, RF.

71. Porteus, "Human Studies in Hawaii," [1931], series 214, box 1, folder 6, at 35, RF; Porteus, "General Survey of Racial Investigations," 7 October 1930, series 214, box 1, folder 5, RF.

72. Stanley D. Porteus, *The Psychology of a Primitive People: A Study of a Primitive People* (London: Edward Arnold, 1931), 316–407; Paul Withington, "By Truck across Australia," *Atlantic Monthly* 147, no. 1 (1931): 88–97; H. A. Heinrich to Porteus, 12 June 1932, Robert Henderson Croll papers, MS 8910, box 1207, file 3(b), SLV.

73. Field record card, series 214, box 1, folder 5, RF; Porteus, *Psychology of a Primitive People*, 95, 301–307, 336, 399–401; S. D. Porteus, *Primitive Intelligence and Environment* (New York: Macmillan, 1937), 215–221.

74. Patricia M. Greenfield, "You Can't Take It with You: Why Ability Assessments Don't Cross Cultures," *American Psychologist* 52, no. 10 (1997): 1115–1124.

75. Porteus, *Psychology of a Primitive People*, 308, 361.

76. Ibid., 378, 420.

77. A. P. Elkin, "The Social Life and Intelligence of the Australian Aborigine," *Oceania* 3, no. 2 (1932): 101–113, at 109; Porteus, *Psychology of a Primitive People*, 360–361.

78. McGregor, *Imagined Destinies*, ch. 5; Elkin, "Social Life and Intelligence," 113; Porteus, *Psychology of a Primitive People*, 379, 387–388; "Australian Aborigines," *The Barrier Miner* (Broken Hill, NSW), 2 September 1929, 3.

79. [R. H. Croll], "The Extinction of the Aboriginal," n.d., Croll papers, MS 8964, box 1220, folder 1, at 14, SLV; [idem], "Hopeless! Our Half-Caste Problem," 26 October 1929, Croll papers, MS 8964, box 1223, folder 3(a), at 1, SLV; Porteus, *Psychology of a Primitive People*, 131.

80. For notable examples from Australia, see Rudolphe Samuel Schenk, *The Educability of the Native* (Perth: Service Printing, 1936); A. P. Elkin, "Native Education, with Special Reference to the Australian Aborigine," *Oceania* 7, no. 4 (1937): 459–500; Peter Biskup, *Not Slaves, Not Citizens: The Aboriginal Problem in Western Australia, 1898–1954* (St. Lucia: University of Queensland Press, 1973), 192. For Africa, see Julian Huxley, "African Education," *Atlantic*

Monthly 146 (1930): 256–262, at 256; H. S. Scott, "A Note on the Educable Capacity of the African," *East African Medical Journal* 9, no. 5 (1932): 99–110; F. L. Fick, *The Educability of the South African Native* (Pretoria: South African Council for Educational and Social Research, 1939).

81. Dubow, *Scientific Racism,* 213–218; Paul Rich, "Race, Science, and the Legitimization of White Supremacy in South Africa, 1902–1940," *International Journal of African Historical Studies* 23, no. 4 (1990): 665–686.

82. On Australia, see R. J. A. Berry and S. D. Porteus, *Intelligence and Social Valuation: A Practical Method for the Diagnosis of Mental Deficiency* (Vineland: Training School, 1920), 25–36; H. K. Fry and R. H. Pulleine, "The Mentality of the Australian Aborigine," *Australian Journal of Experimental Biology and Medical Science* 8 (1931): 153–167; Anderson, *Cultivation of Whiteness,* 215–219; Mary Cawte, "Craniometry and Eugenics in Australia: R. J. A. Berry and the Quest for Social Efficiency," *Historical Studies* 22, no. 86 (1986): 35–53. On Africa, see Sloan Mahone, "East African Psychiatry and the Practical Problems of Empire," in *Psychiatry and Empire,* ed. Mahone and Vaughan; McCulloch, *Colonial Psychiatry and "the African Mind,"* 47–49; Campbell, *Race and Empire,* 82–94; Tilley, *Africa as a Living Laboratory,* 235–243.

83. Charles T. Loram to J. D. Rheinallt Jones, 28 November 1933, South African Institute of Race Relations records, AD843B, 93.4.8, University of the Witwatersrand, Johannesburg; C. T. Loram, *The Education of the South African Native* (London: Longmans, 1917), 206–207.

84. Stocking, "Philanthropoids and Vanishing Cultures," 188; Frederick Paul Keppel, "The Southern Dominions of the British Empire," in *Philanthropy and Learning with Other Papers* (New York: Columbia University Press, 1936), 154; Porteus, "South African Project, 1934," with Porteus to Edgar Brookes, 17 November 1933, South African Institute of Race Relations records, AD843B, 93.4.8, University of the Witwatersrand; Porteus, *Primitive Intelligence and Environment,* 1–3.

85. Porteus, "Psychological Studies of Native in South Africa: Progress Report, May–Sept. 1934," n.d., III.A, box 295, folio 16, CC.

86. Porteus, "Progress Report, May–Sept. 1934," series III.A, box 295, folio 16, CC; Porteus, *Primitive Intelligence and Environment,* 5–6, 213.

87. Lois Dwight Cole to John Russell, 13 July 1937, series III.A, box 295, folio 16, CC; Porteus to Croll, 16 November 1937, Croll papers, MS 8964, box 1207, file 3(b), 1, SLV; R. F. Alfred Hoernlé, "Intelligence & Environment: Are There Racial Differences?" *Johannesburg Star,* 7 December 1937; Gray, "Looking for Neanderthal Man," 86.

88. "Culture and Savages: New Light on the Aborigine," *Melbourne Argus,* 5 January 1932; "The Aboriginal of Australia: More Intelligent than Supposed," *Adelaide Advertiser,* 2 January 1932, 14; "Care of Aborigines: Work in This State Commended," *West Australian,* 11 May 1934, 20; "A Primitive People," *Melbourne Age,* 2 January 1932; "Study of Aborigines," *Melbourne Age,* 27 November 1937; "The Aboriginal Race: Two Arresting Questions," *Western Mail,* 23 February 1939, 45.

89. J. W. Bews, *Human Ecology* (London: Oxford University Press, 1935); [Clement Martyn Doke], review of *Primitive Intelligence and Environment,*

Bantu Studies 12 (1938): 64–65; [Christian Louis Leipoldt], review of *Primitive Intelligence and Environment, South African Medical Journal* 11 (1937): 890.

90. Barkan, *Retreat of Scientific Racism;* Wilhelm E. Mühlmann, *Rassen und Völkerkunde: Lebensprobleme der Rassen, Gesellschaften, und Völker* (Braunschweig: Friedrich Vieweg, 1936), 414–419. The copy of Mühlmann's book held by Harvard University Library bears the stamp of the Nazi Party archive in Munich. Mühlmann expressed some doubt about the Australian research on methodological grounds but praised Porteus for questioning whether the aborigines were "intelligent enough to adapt themselves to the advancing European civilization."

91. Ruth Benedict, review of *Primitive Intelligence and Environment, New York Herald Tribune Weekly Book Review,* 10 October 1937; Otto Klineberg, review of *Psychology of a Primitive People, American Anthropologist,* n.s., 35, no. 3 (1933): 524–527; Otto Klineberg, review of *Primitive Intelligence and Environment, Annals of the American Academy of Political and Social Science* 197 (1938): 281–282; [Joseph Peterson], review of *Temperament and Race, American Journal of Psychology* 40, no. 4 (1928): 640–641; Anne Anastasi, *American Journal of Psychology* 51, no. 1 (1938): 192–194.

92. Porteus to Sydnor Walker, 17 June 1938, series 214, box 1, folder 9, RF; F. P. Keppel to E. L. Thorndike, 13 January 1939, Porteus to Charles Dollard, 19 Nov. 1938, and Porteus to Keppel, 26 February 1936, series III.A, box 295, folio 16, CC.

93. [Bartlett], review of *Primitive Intelligence and Environment, Nature* 142 (1938): 774; Meyer Fortes, review of *Psychology of a Primitive People, Man* 32 (1932): 98–100; Meyer Fortes, review of *Primitive Intelligence and Environment, Man* 40 (1940): 144; R. R. Marett, review of *Psychology of a Primitive People, Philosophy* 7, no. 27 (1932): 349–350; R. R. Marett, "The Bushman and the Examiner: Civilized Tests," *Times Literary Supplement,* 1 January 1938, 6; S. F. Nadel, "The Application of Intelligence Tests in the Anthropological Field," in *The Study of Society: Methods and Problems,* ed. F. C. Bartlett, et al. (New York: Macmillan, 1939), 185–186; J. H. Driberg, "Pacific Psychology," *Spectator* 148 (1932): 418–419; Arthur Wilberforce Jose, "The Australian Aborigine," *Times Literary Supplement,* 24 December 1931, 1036; review of *Psychology of a Primitive People, British Medical Journal,* no. 3726 (1932): 1038; review of *Primitive Intelligence and Environment, British Journal of Psychology* 29 (1938): 80–81; Fortes to Philip Vernon, 12 May 1937, Fortes papers 2/1937, CUL.

94. Beatrice Blackwood, *A Study of Mental Testing in Relation to Anthropology* (Baltimore: Williams & Wilkins, 1927), 45; Vernon to Meyer Fortes, 8 June 1937, Fortes papers, 2/1937, CUL; Burt to Seligman, 24 November 1934, MS 262/4/3/16, RAI. Blackwood was quoting Wilson Wallis, an American anthropologist who studied under R. R. Marett as a Rhodes Scholar at Oxford.

95. Mumford and Smith, "Racial Comparisons and Intelligence Testing," 57; Nadel, "Intelligence Tests in the Anthropological Field," 196–197; F. C.

Bartlett, "Psychological Methods and Anthropological Problems," *Africa* 10, no. 4 (1937): 401–420, at 412–414; R. A. C. Oliver, *General Intelligence Test for Africans: Manual of Directions* (Nairobi: Government Printer, 1932), 10–12.

96. Nadel, "Intelligence Tests in the Anthropological Field," 185; Bartlett, "Psychological Methods," 411–412.

97. Bartlett, lecture on "Contact of Cultures," n.d., Frederic Bartlett papers, MS Add. 8076, file B12, CUL. On the proposals for aptitude testing, see below, ch. 4.

98. On the tension between officials and settlers, see especially Huttenback, *Racism and Empire;* Ronald Hyam, "Bureaucracy and Trusteeship in the Colonial Empire," in *Oxford History of the British Empire,* vol. 4, ed. Judith M. Brown and Wm. Roger Louis (Oxford: Oxford University Press, 1999).

99. Mayhew, *Education in the Colonial Empire,* 4, 9. On Mayhew, see also Clive Whitehead, *Colonial Educators: The British Indian and Colonial Education Service, 1858–1983* (London: I. B. Tauris, 2003), ch. 8.

100. Board of Education, *Report of the Consultative Committee on Psychological Tests of Educable Capacity and Their Possible Use in the Public System of Education* (London: H.M.S.O., 1924). See also Wooldridge, *Measuring the Mind,* 221–224.

101. "Note on Psychological Tests of Educable Capacity and on the Possibility of Their Use in the Colonies," 1929, CO 323/1036/20, NAUK, my emphasis. Mayhew was quoting University of London education expert Sir Percy Nunn on "alleged" differences.

102. Bartlett, lecture on "Contact of Cultures," n.d., Bartlett papers, file B12, CUL; Congrès international des sciences anthropologiques et ethnologiques, *Compte-rendu de la première Session* (London: Royal Anthropological Institute, 1934), 211–212; "Anthropologists in Congress," *Journal of the Royal African Society* 33, no. 133 (1934): 398–403, at 401; Tilley, *Africa as a Living Laboratory,* 256–257.

103. J. W. C. Dougall, "The Provision of Basic Material for Elementary Education in Native Schools in Kenya Colony," [1927?], and F. P. Keppel to Godfrey Thomson, 2 December 1927, series III.A, box 196, folio 6, CC; extract from minutes of the Advisory Committee on Education in the Colonies, 17 October 1929, International Missionary Council archives, box 223, School of Oriental and African Studies, London. On Oliver, see also Campbell, *Race and Empire,* 148–156; Tilley, *Africa as a Living Laboratory,* 245–250; Richard Pearson, John D. Turner, and Gerry M. Forrest, eds., *The Psychologist as Educator: The Writings of R. A. C. Oliver* (Manchester: University of Manchester, 1989).

104. Oliver, "Report on the Construction of a Battery of Individual Tests of Intelligence for Adult Natives in East Africa," 14 July 1931, series III.A, box 196, folio 6, CC; Richard A. C. Oliver, "Mental Tests in the Study of the African," *Africa* 7, no. 1 (1934): 40–46, at 44.

105. Oliver, *General Intelligence Test for Africans,* 10–11; Oliver, "Mental Tests," 45–46.

106. R. A. C. Oliver to F. P. Keppel, 4 June 1931, Dougall to Keppel, 13 August 1932, and Oliver to Keppel, 1 November 1932, series III.A, box 196, folio 6, CC; Tilley, *Africa as a Living Laboratory,* 250–258.

107. William Malcolm Hailey, *An African Survey: A Study of Problems Arising in Africa South of the Sahara* (Oxford: Oxford University Press, 1938), 37–40.

108. R. A. C. Oliver to J. M. Russell, 15 January 1936; Russell to Oliver, 18 September 1936, series III.A, box 196, folio 6, CC; H. S. Scott, preface to Oliver, *General Intelligence Test,* 3.

109. Oliver, "Final Report to the Carnegie Corporation on Educational Research in East Africa," 7 February 1933; Oliver to Keppel, 10 February 1938; Menzel to Oliver, 18 January 1938, series III.A, box 196, folio 6, CC; Menzel, *Suggestions for the Use of New-Type Tests,* 154.

110. Hartog, *Some Aspects of Indian Education,* 144.

111. Dougall to Keppel, 25 November 1932; Oliver to Keppel, 1 November 1932, series III.A, box 196, folio 6, CC.

4. Square Pegs and Round Holes

1. F. H. Vinden memoir, Vinden papers, Documents.5565, at 102–105, IWM.

2. Cooper, *Decolonization and African Society;* Cooper, "Modernizing Bureaucrats, Backward Africans, and the Development Concept." See also Heath Pearson, "*Homo Economicus* Goes Native: The Rise and Fall of Primitive Economics," *History of Political Economy* 32, no. 4 (2000): 933–989.

3. Arjun Appadurai, *Modernity at Large: Cultural Dimensions of Globalization* (Minneapolis: University of Minnesota Press, 1996); Benedict Anderson, *Imagined Communities: Reflections on the Origin and Spread of Nationalism* (London: Verso, 2006), ch. 10; Keletso E. Atkins, " 'Kafir Time': Preindustrial Temporal Concepts and Labour Discipline in Nineteenth-Century Colonial Natal," *Journal of African History* 29, no. 2 (1988): 229–244; Vanessa Ogle, "Whose Time Is It? The Pluralization of Time and the Global Condition, 1870s–1940s," *American Historical Review* 118, no. 5 (2013): 1376–1402.

4. "British Scientists in India," *Times of India,* 18 December 1937; C. S. Myers to J. G. Laithwaite, 17 June 1937, Home (Political), file 136/37, NAI.

5. Minutes of the Executive Committee, 22 March 1938, National Institute of Industrial Psychology papers 2/2, LSE; John Anderson to Lord Linlithgow, 18 July 1937; Linlithgow to Anderson, 14 July 1937, Home (Political), file 136/37, NAI.

6. Matthew Hale, *Human Science and Social Order: Hugo Münsterberg and the Origins of Applied Psychology* (Philadelphia: Temple University Press, 1980); Richard Gillespie, *Manufacturing Knowledge: A History of the Hawthorne Experiments* (Cambridge: Cambridge University Press, 1991), 133–136. On Taylorism, see the classic accounts by Charles S. Maier, "Society as Factory," in *In Search of Stability: Explorations in Historical Political Economy* (Cambridge: Cambridge University Press, 1987), and Anson

Rabinbach, *The Human Motor: Energy, Fatigue, and the Origins of Modernity* (New York: Basic Books, 1990).

7. Wendy Hollway, "Efficiency and Welfare: Industrial Psychology at Rowntree's Cocoa Works," *Theory & Psychology* 3, no. 3 (1993): 303–322; Thomson, *Psychological Subjects,* 145–147; Daniel Ussishkin, "Morale: Social Citizenship and Democracy in Modern Britain," Ph.D. thesis (University of California, Berkeley, 2007), ch. 4; Charles S. Myers, *Industrial Psychology in Great Britain* (London: Jonathan Cape, 1926), 28–30.

8. Royal Commission on Labour in India, *Report of the Royal Commission on Labour in India* (London: H.M.S.O., 1931), vol. 3, part 2, 94; vol. 1, part 1, 265, 285; vol. 1, part 2, 121; vol. 2, part 1, 64; vol. 2, part 2, 84, 130; vol. 3, part 2, 158–159, 163, 179.

9. Satyashraya Gopal Panandikar, *Industrial Labour in India* (Bombay: Longmans, 1933), 215–216. See also Rajani Kanta Das, *Factory Labor in India* (Berlin: W. de Gruyter, 1923), 125–129; Margaret Read, *From Field to Factory: An Introductory Study of the Indian Peasant Turned Factory Hand* (London: Student Christian Movement, 1927), 25; A. A. Purcell and J. Hallsworth, *Report on Labour Conditions in India* (London: Trades Union Congress, 1928), 6–12; Ahmad Mukhtar, *Factory Labour in India* (Madras: Methodist Publishing, 1930), chs. 6–8; H. R. Soni, *Indian Industry and Its Problems,* vol. 1, *Factors in Industrial Development* (London: Longmans, 1932), 296–324.

10. David Munro to Thomas Stanton, 4 May 1932, CO 822/47/5, NAUK; "Memorandum of Sir David Munro," n.d., BY/26/7, Kenya National Archives, Nairobi (KNA).

11. G. St. J. Orde Browne, *The African Labourer* (London: Oxford University Press, 1933), 9; [Arthur Landsborough Thomson] to L. Haden Guest, 16 January 1936, FD 1/3143/56, NAUK; David Munro to F. C. Bartlett, 18 December 1933, FD 1/3143/56, NAUK; David Munro to H. L. Gordon, 21 February 1933, FD 1/3143/56, NAUK; David Munro to A. T. Stanton, 21 February 1933, FD 1/3143/56, NAUK; David Munro to H. L. Gordon, 4 May 1932, FD 1/3143/56, NAUK.

12. Angus Calder, *The People's War: Britain 1939–45* (London: Jonathan Cape, 1986 [1969]), 457–477; William Harrington and Peter Young, *The 1945 Revolution* (London: Davis-Poynter, 1978), ch. 7; Edgerton, *Warfare State;* David Edgerton, *Britain's War Machine: Weapons, Resources, and Experts in the Second World War* (London: Allen Lane, 2011); Ortolano, *Two Cultures Controversy.*

13. Shephard, *War of Nerves;* Jeremy A. Crang, *The British Army and the People's War 1939–1945* (Manchester: Manchester University Press, 2000); Robert Ahrenfeldt, *Psychiatry in the British Army in the Second World War* (London: Routledge, 1958); Philip E. Vernon and John B. Parry, *Personnel Selection in the British Forces* (London: University of London Press, 1949).

14. J. C. Raven, "Report of the Work Carried Out During the Year 1941–42," 3 February 1942, FD 1/5499, National NAUK; Bernard Ungerson, "Personnel Selection," 1953, WO 277/19, NAUK, 19; Vernon and Parry, *Personnel Selection,* 43–46; Crang, *British Army and the People's War,* 13–15.

15. Tom Harrison, *Bion, Rickman, Foulkes, and the Northfield Experiments: Advancing on a Different Front* (London: Jessica Kingsley Publishers, 2000); Crang, *British Army and the People's War*, ch. 2; Ahrenfeldt, *Psychiatry in the British Army*, 38; Vernon and Parry, *Personnel Selection*, 55–56, 61.

16. F. H. Vinden, "The Introduction of War Office Selection Boards in the British Army: A Personal Recollection," in *War and Society: A Yearbook of Military History*, vol. 2, ed. Brian Bond and Ian Roy (London: Croom Helm: 1977); Shephard, *War of Nerves*, 192–195; Crang, *British Army and the People's War*, 31–33; Ahrenfeldt, *Psychiatry in the British Army*, 60–63; Vernon and Parry, *Personnel Selection in the British Forces*, ch. 4.

17. J. R. Rees, *The Shaping of Psychiatry by War* (London: Chapman and Hall, 1945), 63. Other British intellectuals in this period also translated traditional ideas of military character into modern psychological language: see Frederic Bartlett, *Psychology and the Soldier* (Cambridge: Cambridge University Press, 1927); Norman Copeland, *Psychology and the Soldier: The Art of Leadership* (London: Allen & Unwin, 1944); Lord Moran, *The Anatomy of Courage* (London: Constable, 1945). On the Victorian origins of morale, see Ussishkin, "Morale," chs. 2–3.

18. [Wilfred Bion], "Technical Memorandum No. 1: 'Leaderless Group Test,'" 30 November 1942, GC/135/B.1/2, Napsbury Mental Hospital collection, WL; "W.O.S.B. Standing Orders," Appendix A, "M.T.O.'s Report Form on Candidate for O.C.T.U.," Jock Sutherland papers, box 20, Tavistock Institute Library, London; Edward Leslie Wenger, interview by David M. Blake, 10–11 September 1990, IOR; Simeon W. Gillman, "Officer Selection in the Army," *British Journal of Psychiatry* 93 (1947): 101–111.

19. "Note by Director of Exams on Visit to No. 10 War Office Selection Board," 17 October 1944, L/SG/7/267, IOR; N. V. Brindley to Aileen Brindley, 24 January 1943, N. V. Brindley papers, Documents.11784, IWM; Bion, "'Leaderless Group Test,'" WL; Donald Portway, *The Quest of Leadership: With Special Reference to the Circumstances of India* (Bombay: Thacker, 1945), 26.

20. Rees, *Shaping of Psychiatry by War*, 70; Vinden, "Introduction of War Office Selection Boards," 126; Wooldridge, *Measuring the Mind*, 213–219.

21. Rees quoted in Crang, *British Army and the People's War*, 35; Wooldridge, *Measuring the Mind*, 208–212, 216; Walter Greenhalgh, interview with Conrad Wood, 12 August 1992, catalogue no. 11187, IWM.

22. Vinden memoir, at 1, IWM. Vinden does not mention his father's occupation, but F. W. Vinden of Exeter appears in the records of trade association meetings. See "British Pharmaceutical Conference," *Year-Book of Pharmacy* (London: Churchill, 1904), 396; "Pharmaceutical Association Meetings," *Pharmaceutical Journal*, 25 January 1908, 92.

23. Donald Portway, *Militant Don* (London: Robert Hale, 1964); Donald Portway, *Memoirs of an Academic Old Contemptible* (London: Leo Cooper, 1971), 27; Michael Longford, *The Path That Led to Africa* (Leominster: Gracewing, 2003), 133; F. H. Vinden, "A Race Apart," *The Listener*, 13 November 1947, 852–861.

24. Omissi, *Sepoy and the Raj,* ch. 5; Sri Nandan Prasad, *Expansion of the Armed Forces and Defence Organisation, 1939–45* ([Delhi]: Combined Inter-Services Historical Section of India and Pakistan, 1956), ch. 11; Pradeep P. Barua, *Gentlemen of the Raj: The Indian Officer Corps, 1817–1949* (Westport: Praeger, 2003), 78–82.

25. Crang, *British Army and the People's War,* 35–37; Ahrenfeldt, *Psychiatry in the British Army,* 63–65; Shephard, *War of Nerves,* 195; House of Commons, *Reports from the Select Committee on Estimates* (London: H.M.S.O., 1946), 429; Richard A. Chapman, *Leadership in the British Civil Service: A Study of Sir Percival Waterfield and the Creation of the Civil Service Selection Board* (London: Croom Helm, 1984), 100.

26. Crang, *British Army and the People's War,* 27, 35; Greenhalgh interview, IWM.

27. Vinden memoir, IWM.

28. Vinden memoir, at 106–109, IWM; F. W. Perry, *The Commonwealth Armies: Manpower and Organisation in the Two World Wars* (Manchester: Manchester University Press, 1988), 102–119; Prasad, *Expansion of the Armed Forces,* chs. 5–6.

29. Shephard, *War of Nerves,* chs. 14–15; Mark Harrison, *Medicine and Victory: British Military Medicine in the Second World War* (Oxford: Oxford University Press, 2004), 120–126, 170–178, 221–223; Nafsika Thalassis, "Treating and Preventing Trauma: British Military Psychiatry during the Second World War," Ph.D. thesis (University of Salford, 2004), ch. 5.

30. R. F. Tredgold, "The West in the East," letter to *Lancet,* 4 August 1945, 154. See also R. F. Tredgold, et al., "Serious Psychiatric Disability among British Officers in India," *Lancet,* 24 August 1946, 257–261, at 260.

31. A. P. Wavell, "The Training of the Army for War," *Journal of the Royal United Services Institute* 78 (1933): 254–273, at 258, 271; Vinden memoir, at 107, IWM.

32. Vinden memoir, at 109–112, IWM; Portway, *Quest of Leadership,* iii.

33. Perry, *Commonwealth Armies,* 110; Prasad, *Expansion of the Armed Forces,* 182–183.

34. Charles Alexander Wilson, interview by Conrad Wood, 16 February 1977, catalogue no. 894, IWM.

35. Stanley Menezes, interview by BBC, October 2003, catalogue no. 25448, IWM; S. K. Sinha, *A Soldier Recalls* (New Delhi: Lancer, 1992), 66–67; Portway, *Quest of Character,* 116, 141.

36. G. M. Ray diary, entry for 2 July 1946, MSS EUR F256/9, IOR.

37. Vinden memoir, IWM; W. T. B. Grounds letter, 1 April 1944, W. T. B. Grounds papers, Documents.735, IWM.

38. "New Way of Selecting Indian Army Officers," *Indian Information* 12, no. 111 (1943): 268; "Tests of Intelligence, Fitness and Personality," *Madras Mail,* 22 April 1946; Portway, *Quest of Leadership,* 117.

39. N. V. Brindley to Aileen Brindley, 24 January 1943, IWM; John Arnold Victor Routledge, interview by Conrad Wood, 17 January 1996, catalogue no. 16417, IWM; Grounds letter, 1 April 1944, IWM; George Macdonald Fraser, "Monsoon Selection Board," in *The General Danced at Dawn* (London: Barrie

& Jenkins, 1970); Richard O'Connor, farewell speech, 1946, Richard O'Connor papers 6/1/27, Lidell Hart Centre for Military Archives, King's College, London; Wenger interview, IOR.

40. Mohammad Ayub Khan, *Friends Not Masters: A Political Autobiography* (New York: Oxford University Press, 1967), 14–15; Gurbachan Singh, "The Indian Army Officer," *Spectator* 177 (1946): 110–111; "Government's Scientific System: Tests for Personality and Intelligence of Candidates," *Times of India,* 28 January 1947, 5.

41. Rees, "Report to the Director General of Army Medical Services on Tour to Malta, Paiforce, India," December 1944–March 1945, GC/135/B.1/2, Napsbury Mental Hospital collection, WL; Portway, *Quest of Leadership,* 101.

42. Vinden memoir, at 115, IWM; D. T. Watterson, "Selection of Personnel for the Public Service," *Indian Journal of Psychology* 22 (1947): 100–112; David C. Potter, "Manpower Shortage and the End of Colonialism: The Case of the Indian Civil Service," *Modern Asian Studies* 7, no. 1 (1973): 47–73, at 54–62; R. M. J. Harris, "Visit to FPSC Selection Board," 13–17 December 1944, L/SG/7/267, IOR.

43. Ray, diary entry for 6 January 1946, IOR; K. G. Rama Rao, "Memorandum on 'Officer Selection Procedure' in India during World War II," *Indian Journal of Psychology* 23 (1948): 103–138.

44. Wenger interview, IOR.

45. Rao, "Memorandum on 'Officer Selection Procedure' "; Wenger interview, IOR.

46. Rao, "Memorandum on 'Officer Selection Procedure,' " 112–113, 118; T. N. Kaul, *Reminiscences, Discreet and Indiscreet* (New Delhi: Lancers, 1982), 106–108.

47. Ray, diary entries for 1, 2, 8, and 23 January and 22 February 1946, IOR.

48. Ray, diary entry for 26 March 1946, IOR; Wenger interview, IOR; A. H. Williams, "Prophylactic Selection of Indian Troops," *Journal of the Royal Army Medical Corps* 87 (July 1946): 1–9.

49. Wenger interview, IOR; Ray, diary entry for 24 January 1946, IOR; Kaul, *Reminiscences.*

50. Ray, diary entries for 7 February, 13 April, and 3 March 1946, IOR.

51. Wenger interview, IOR; Rao, "Memorandum on 'Officer Selection Procedure,' " 104, 128.

52. Rees, "Report by Consulting Psychiatrist to the Army on a Visit to the Overseas Forces in Gibraltar, North Africa and Middle East," 25 May–29 June 1943, and Rees, "Tour to Malta, Paiforce, India," GC/135/B.1/2, Napsbury Mental Hospital collection, WL.

53. "Government's Scientific System"; "Army Officers' Selection," *Times of India,* 25 April 1947, 3; "A Selection Bureau for India," *British Medical Journal,* 21 September 1946, 431.

54. Jonathan Fennell, *Combat and Morale in the North African Campaign: The Eighth Army and the Path to El Alamein* (Cambridge: Cambridge University Press, 2010), ch. 3; Gillman, "Methods of Officer Selection"; G. W. B. James, "Psychiatry in the Middle East Force, 1940–1943," in *History of the Second World War: Medicine and Pathology,* ed. V. Zachary Cope

(London: H.M.S.O., 1952), 372–373; F. A. E. Crew, "The Army Psychiatric Service: Middle East Force, 1940–1943," in *The Army Medical Services,* vol. 2 (London: H.M.S.O., 1957), 483–485.

55. R. E. Tunbridge, "Psychiatric Experiences of a General Physician in Malta, 1941–43," *Lancet,* 10 November 1945, 587–590; Ungerson, "Personnel Selection," NAUK.

56. R. F. Barbour, "Quarterly Report for 1 October to 31 December 1943" and "Quarterly 1 January to 31 March 1944," WO 222/1299, NAUK; Crew, "Army Psychiatric Service, 484–485; Gillman, "Officer Selection in the Army," 108; Tunbridge, "Psychiatric Experiences," 588.

57. Peter Quentin Logan, interview by John D. Charmley, catalogue no. 3864, IWM; "Selection of African Personnel: Results of the Discussion on Selection in East Africa," n.d., CO 927/77/3, NAUK; Timothy H. Parsons, *The African Rank-and-File: Social Implications of Colonial Military Service in the King's African Rifles, 1902–1964* (Portsmouth: Heinemann, 1999), 81–86; David Killingray, *Fighting for Britain: African Soldiers in the Second World War* (Woodbridge: James Currey, 2010), 42–43.

58. Evelyn Baring to Eric Machtig, 16 March 1945, DO 35/1184, NAUK.

59. "Statement of Problems Encountered in the Recruitment and Training of Africans in the West African Command," 21 April 1945, CO 927/77/3, NAUK; "Proficiency in Spoken English—AORs," 9 February 1945, CSO 18/1/329, NAG.

60. Killingray, *Fighting for Britain,* 85–88; Parsons, *African Rank-and-File,* 109.

61. Parsons, *African Rank-and-File,* 86–89; C. H. Stoneley, "Memories of the King's African Rifles," *Journal of the Royal Signals Institution* 14, no. 6 (1980): 253–267, at 258.

62. "Statement of Problems," NAUK.

63. A. Macdonald, "Interim Report on the Selection of African Personnel," 2 April 1945; A. Macdonald, "Selection of African Personnel: Summary of the Final Report on the Work of the Selection of Personnel Technical and Research Unit, Middle Eastern Forces," n.d., CO 927/77/3, NAUK.

64. Macdonald, "Summary of Final Report"; "War Office (DSP) Covering Note to Macdonald's Final Report," 29 January 1946; C. W. F. Footman to A. D. Buchanan Smith, 28 February 1946, CO 927/77/3, NAUK.

65. S. R. Ashton and S. E. Stockwell, eds., *Imperial Policy and Colonial Practice, 1925–1945, Part II: Economic Policy, Social Policies, and Colonial Research* (London: H.M.S.O., 1996), 355–361.

66. F. C. Bartlett, *Remembering: A Study in Experimental and Social Psychology* (Cambridge: Cambridge University Press, 1932), 249; Alison Winter, *Memory: Fragments of a Modern History* (Chicago: University of Chicago Press, 2012), ch. 9; D. E. Broadbent, "Frederic Charles Bartlett, 1886–1969," *Biographical Memoirs of Fellows of the Royal Society* 16 (November 1970): 1–13.

67. Bartlett, "Psychological Problems in the Government of Native Races," n.d., Frederic Bartlett papers, file B42, CUL.

68. Ibid.; F. C. Bartlett, "Anthropology in Reconstruction," *Journal of the Royal Anthropological Institute* 73, nos. 1–2 (1943): 9–16, at 12.

69. Bartlett, lecture on social psychology, 1930, Bartlett papers, file B3, CUL; Bartlett, "Psychological Problems," CUL.

70. Bartlett, "Anthropology in Reconstruction," 11. On the emergence of "attitude" as a measurable concept in psychology, see Kurt Danziger, *Naming the Mind: How Psychology Found Its Language* (London: Sage, 1997), ch. 8.

71. F. C. Bartlett, "Psychological Methods for the Study of 'Hard' and 'Soft' Features of Culture," *Africa* 16, no. 3 (1946): 145–155, at 153–154; "Report of the Colonial Psychology Research Group to Colonial Research Council," 1944, CR 8/2, LSE.

72. David Mills, "Anthropology at the End of Empire: The Rise and Fall of the Colonial Social Science Research Council, 1944–62," in *Empires, Nations, and Natives: Anthropology and State-Making,* ed. Benoît de l'Estoile, Federico Neiburg, and Lygia Sigaud (Durham: Duke University Press, 2005); Kuklick, *Savage Within,* 190–192; Stocking, *After Tylor,* 416, 420–421.

73. "Godfrey Thomson," in *A History of Psychology in Autobiography,* ed. Edwin G. Boring, et al., vol. 4 (Worcester: Clark University Press, 1952); Wooldridge, *Measuring the Mind,* 213–216; Sutherland, *Ability, Merit, and Measurement,* 192–193.

74. "Godfrey Thomson," 292; Godfrey Thomson, foreword to C. M. Bhatia, *Performance Tests of Intelligence under Indian Conditions* (London: Oxford University Press, 1955); Godfrey Thomson to P. A. Wilson, 5 December 1946, CO 927/77/3, NAUK; CSSRC minutes, 9 January 1945, CR 8/6, LSE; "Statement on Research Needs," 1945, CR 8/10, LSE.

75. Parsons, *African Rank-and-File,* 94; A. Taylor, "The Development of Personnel Selection in the Institute of Education, University College of Ghana," in *Educational and Occupational Selection in West Africa,* ed. A. Taylor (London: Oxford University Press, 1962),7; David Akpode Ejoor, *Reminiscences* (Lagos: Malthouse, 1989), 9.

76. L. J. Holman, "An Assessment of the Value of the Selection Tests Used for Malayans," 22 April 1959, WO 291/2465, NAUK; I. G. Ord, *Mental Tests for Pre-Literates: Resulting Mainly from New Guinea Studies* (Brisbane: Jacaranda Press, 1970); R. M. Waite and H. Lewis, "Selection of Gurkha Boys for the Gurkha Boys' Company," 1958, WO 291/1715, NAUK.

77. Dubow, *Scientific Racism in South Africa,* 236–242; Johann Louw, "South Africa," in David B. Baker, ed., *The Oxford Handbook of the History of Psychology: Global Perspectives* (Oxford: Oxford University Press, 2012), 502–506; Stuart Coupe, "Testing for Aptitude and Motivation in South African Industry: The Work of the National Institute for Personnel Research, 1946–1973," *Business History Review* 70, no. 1 (1996): 43–68.

78. Louw, "South Africa," 505; notes of telephone conference between Edith Mercer and Clifford Frisby, 11 March 1957; Frisby to Audrey Richards, 12 March 1957; Frisby memorandum, 9 May 1960, National Institute of Industrial Psychology papers 10/22, LSE.

79. Shell-BP Petroleum Development Co. of Nigeria contract, 23 January 1959, John C. Raven papers 1/2/5, WL; A. Taylor, "The Development of Personnel Selection in the Institute of Education, University College of Ghana," in *Educational and Occupational Selection in West Africa,* ed. A. Taylor

(London: Oxford University Press, 1962), 8–9; "Man O' War Bay in the News," *West African Review* 31 (1960): 16–18; James H. B. Vant to T. J. F. Gavaghan, 29 October 1960, RZ/9/20, NAK; V. L. Allen, "Management and Labor in Africa," *Listener,* 15 August 1963, 225.

80. "Ombe Trade Centre: Aptitude Testing," *Times Educational Supplement,* 6 February 1959, 205; Mildred Adams, "When Tribesmen Shift from Jungle to Jobs," *Think* 27, no. 2 (1961): 29–32; Gambia, *Report of the Education Department for the Triennium 1961–63* (Bathurst: Government Printer, 1964), 3; James H. B. Vant, "Artisan Training in Kenya: Selection and Classification," *Journal of Cross-Cultural Psychology* 10, no. 3 (1979): 294–323, at 318.

81. Bulhan, "Psychological Research in Africa," 28; B. Nzimande, "Industrial Psychology and the Study of Black Workers in South Africa: A Review and Critique," *Psychology in Society* 2 (1984): 54–91, at 57; Johan Louw, " 'This Is Thy Work': A Contextual History of Applied Psychology and Labor in South Africa," Ph.D. thesis (University of Amsterdam, 1986), 202–203.

82. S. Biesheuvel, *African Intelligence* (Johannesburg: South African Institute of Race Relations, 1943); S. Biesheuvel, "Objectives and Methods of African Psychological Research," *Journal of Social Psychology* 47 (1958): 161–168, at 161–162; S. Biesheuvel, "The Occupational Abilities of Africans," *Optima* 2 (1952): 18–22, at 18.

83. Y. Glass, *Industrial Man in Southern Africa* (Johannesburg: National Institute for Personnel Research, [1961]), 14; Coupe, "Testing for Aptitude and Motivation"; Louw, "South Africa."

84. T. G. Askwith, "Rehabilitation," 6 January 1954, CO 822/794, NAUK; W. R. L. Addison to J. H. Butter, 24 January 1959, ACW/36/6, NAK; James H. B. Vant, "Artisan Training in Kenya: Selection and Classification," *Journal of Cross-Cultural Psychology* 10, no. 3 (1979): 294–323; Caroline Elkins, *Imperial Reckoning: The Untold Story of Britain's Gulag in Kenya* (New York: Henry Holt, 2005), 111–120, 148–149, 327–328.

85. "Aptitude Testing Unit," n.d., ACW/36/6, NAK; "Selection of Administrative and Executive Trainees," n.d., RZ/9/20, NAK; J. J. Adie to Treasury Secretary, 22 February 1963, RZ/9/20, NAK; A. O. H. Roberts, "Report to Kenya Labour Department," 4 September 1962, reel 776, FF.

86. Program Actions 59–318a and 59–318b, 24 June 1959 and 3 May 1963; Request for Grant Action, 9 June 1959, reel 776, FF.

87. "Aptitude Testing Unit," n.d., ACW/36/6, NAK; "Selection of Administrative and Executive Trainees," n.d., RZ/9/20, NAK; "Report to the Ford Foundation on the Activities of the Aptitude Testing Unit," August 1960, reel 776, FF; Vant, "Artisan Training"; J. H. Vant, "The Selection of Convicted Prisoners for Occupational Training: A Preliminary Report," August 1955, NAK Library.

88. "Aptitude Testing Unit," n.d., and G. M. Wilson to R. A. Lake, 12 February 1962, RZ/9/20, NAK.

89. C. H. Northcott to P. A. Wilson, 31 January 1947, CO 927/81/4, NAUK; C. H. Northcott, *African Labour Efficiency Survey* (London: H.M.S.O., 1949), 16–17, 26–27, 34.

90. Reginald Robins to Northcott, n.d., CR 8/100, LSE; Robins to Northcott, 9 December 1947, CR 8/98, LSE; Northcott, *African Labour Efficiency Survey,* 16, 69; Arnold Plant to Northcott, 4 March 1948, CR 8/100, LSE.

91. 464 *Parl. Deb.*, H.C., 5th ser. (1948–1949), 1004–1005, 1401–1402.

92. 465 *Parl. Deb.*, H.C., 5th ser. (1948–1949), 1642; "Labour in Africa," *The Economist,* 30 April 1949, 786.

93. "Extracts of the Minutes of the Principal Finance and Establishment Officers' Meeting," 17 August 1962, RZ/9/20, NAK.

94. P. W. Watson to General Mines Manager, 29 October 1958, and acting general mines manager to secretary, 23 November 1960, Ashanti Goldfields papers, London Metropolitan Archive.

95. Raymond Grainger, "Forget Africanization or Europeanization . . . and Choose the Best Man for the Job!" *West African Review,* August 1947, 9–13.

96. Philip Foster, *Education and Social Change in Ghana* (London: Routledge, 1965), 148–153, 169–171; Lewis Brownstein, "Mass Education in a Developing Society: The Case of the Kenya Preliminary Examination Candidate," Ph.D. thesis (Johns Hopkins University, 1969), 61–66; John Anderson, *The Struggle for the School: The Interaction of Missionary, Colonial Government and Nationalist Enterprise in the Development of Formal Education in Kenya* (London: Longman, 1970), 76–79; David R. Morrison, *Education and Politics in Africa: The Tanzanian Case* (Montreal: McGill-Queen's University Press, 1976), 46–47; T. E. Dorman, *African Experience: An Education Officer in Northern Rhodesia (Zambia)* (London: Radcliffe Press, 1993), 35–36; Jack C. E. Greig, "Education in Northern Rhodesia and Nyasaland: The Pre-Independence Period" (Oxford Development Records Project, 1985), 16–17; Daniel R. Headrick, *The Tentacles of Progress: Technology Transfer in the Age of Imperialism, 1850–1940* (New York: Oxford University Press, 1988), 312–315, 345.

97. Geoffrey Tooth, "Draft Proposals for Psychological Research," January 1950; Geoffrey Tooth to P. A. Wilson, 16 July 1948; Geoffrey Tooth, "Report of Discussions with Nigerian Government on Selection Tests," n.d., CO 927/172/3, NAUK; W. E. H. Stanner, "Reports on Proposal to Establish an Institute of Social Research at Makerere and on Soc Science Research in Uganda and Tanganyika," n.d., CR 8/25, LSE.

98. Cooper, *Decolonization and African Society;* Killingray, *Fighting for Britain,* ch. 6; Joanna Lewis, *Empire State-Building: War and Welfare in Kenya, 1925–52* (Oxford: James Currey, 2000), 198–204; Frank Furedi, "The Demobilized African Soldier and the Blow to White Prestige," in David Killingray and David E. Omissi, eds., *Guardians of Empire: The Armed Forces of the Colonial Powers, c. 1700–1964* (Manchester: Manchester University Press, 1999).

99. T. Barton to Tooth, 4 February 1950, CO 927/172/3, and Tooth, "Report of Discussions with Nigerian Government," CO 927/172/3, NAUK; Tooth to P. A. Wilson, 12 December 1947, CR 8/14, LSE.

100. Quoted in P. A. Wilson, "Psychological Research in West Africa," 6 May 1947, CO 927/76/2, NAUK.

101. Tooth to Wilson, 12 December 1947, LSE; Tooth, "Report to the CSSRC on the Use of Unadapted Tests of Intelligence, Attainment, and Aptitude for the Selection of Candidates for Secondary and Technical Education in Nigeria and the Gold Coast," March 1953, CR 8/51, LSE; Tooth, "A Survey of Juvenile Delinquency in the Gold Coast," December 1946, CR 8/27, LSE.

102. Tooth to Wilson, 12 December 1947, LSE.

103. E. D. Roberts, "Intelligence Tests," 11 July 1953, E. D. Roberts papers, Mss. Afr s. 1755, box 5, file 25b, RHO.

104. Douglas Milne and P. K. Stevenson, "Selection for African Secondary Schools in Northern Rhodesia," Oversea Education 31, no. 2 (1959): 61–69; R. H. Stone, "Common Entrance in Eastern Nigeria," Oversea Education 29, no. 1 (1957): 10–24; "Southern Highlands Province Secondary Selection Exam," 1957, Philip H. C. Clarke papers, Mss. Afr s. 1755, box 42, file 119c, RHO; F. H. H. Hall, "Annual Report of the Educational Psychologist (Salisbury Region)," 19 December 1959, ED 1/2/106, NAZ.

105. Stone, "Common Entrance in Eastern Nigeria"; "Southern Highlands Province Secondary Selection Exam," Clarke papers, RHO; R. R. Campbell and A. G. Smith, The Campbell Picture Test Handbook (London: Longmans, 1955), 3.

106. J. D. Clarke, "Performance Tests of Intelligence for Africa: Part I," Oversea Education 20 (1948): 777–787.

107. S. H. Irvine, "A Psychological Study of Selection Problems at the End of Primary Schooling in Southern Rhodesia," Ph.D. thesis (University of London, 1964), 341.

108. Gold Coast, Accelerated Development Plan for Education, 1951 (Accra: Government Printing Department, 1951), 3. See also Kenya, African Education in Kenya (Nairobi: Government Printer, 1949).

109. Hall, "Annual Report," 1959, NAZ.

110. A. K. Wareham, "Methods of Selection for the Government Secondary Grammar Schools in Eastern Nigeria," in A. Taylor, ed., Education and Occupational Selection in West Africa (London: Oxford University Press, 1962), 66; S. S. A. Akeju, "Large-Scale Assessment of Educational Aptitude in Nigeria," in S. H. Irvine and John W. Berry, eds., Human Assessment and Cultural Factors (New York: Plenum Press, 1983), 36; Betty Stein George, Education in Ghana (Washington: Government Printing Office, 1976), 133; H. C. A. Somerset, "Who Goes to Secondary School? Relevance, Reliability and Equity in Secondary School Selection," in David Court and Dhara P. Ghai, eds., Education, Society, and Development: New Perspectives from Kenya (Nairobi: Oxford University Press, 1974).

111. Wooldridge, Measuring the Mind, ch. 12.

112. See below, ch. 6.

113. Taylor, "Development of Personnel Selection"; Jonathan Silvey, "Testing Ability Tests: Issues in the Measurement of Ability among African Schoolboys," in Makerere Institute of Social Research, Conference Papers, January 1963; R. S. MacArthur, et al., Northern Rhodesia Abilities Survey (Lusaka: Rhodes-Livingstone Institute, 1964).

114. Taylor, "Development of Personnel Selection"; Philip E. Vernon, "Administration of Group Intelligence Tests to East African Pupils," British Journal of Educational Psychology 37 (1967): 282–291.

115. I. Addae-Mensah, J. S. Djangmah, and C. O. Agbenyega, Family Background and Educational Opportunities in Ghana ([Legon]: Ghana Universities Press, 1973); H. C. A. Somerset, "Aptitude Tests, Socio-Economic Background,

and Secondary School Selection: The Possibilities and Limits of Change,"
discussion paper (Institute of Development Studies, University of Nairobi,
March 1977).

116. "Summary for an Application for a Colonial Research Fellowship by
B. J. Bedell," n.d., CR 8/2, LSE; "Application of A. Deans Peggs," CR 8/7, LSE;
B. J. Bedell, progress report for January 1948–March 1949, CR 8/24, LSE; B. J.
Bedell to Godfrey Thomson, 8 February 1949, CO 927/77/2, NAUK.

117. A. Deans Peggs, "Note on a 'New' Non-Verbal Intelligence Test Item,"
British Journal of Psychology 42, nos. 1–2 (1951): 177–179; P. E. Vernon,
*Selection for Secondary Education in Jamaica: A Report to the Minister of
Education* (Kingston: Government Printer, 1961), 13; D. R. Manley, "Mental
Ability in Jamaica," *Social and Economic Studies* (1963): 51–71, at 52.

118. Vernon, *Selection for Secondary Education in Jamaica*, 2, 47–48.

5. The Truth about Hearts and Minds

1. P. B. Humphrey, "A Study of the Reasons for Entering the Jungle within a
Group of Surrendered Chinese Communist Terrorists in Malaya, Part VII: A
Study of the Differences between Opinions Held by SEP and by Workers Who
Had a Similar Opportunity to Become Terrorists but Who Did Not in Fact Do
So," 25 March 1955, WO 276/532, NAUK.

2. Ibid.

3. Robert Thompson, *Defeating Communist Insurgency: Experiences from
Malaya and Vietnam* (London: Chatto & Windus, 1966); Richard L.
Clutterbuck, *The Long Long War: Counterinsurgency in Malaya and Vietnam*
(New York: Praeger, 1966); Julian Paget, *Counter-Insurgency Operations:
Techniques of Guerilla Warfare* (New York: Walker, 1967), chs. 6–7; Andrew
R. Molnar, et al., *Undergrounds in Insurgent, Revolutionary, and Resistance
Warfare* (Washington: Special Operations Research Office, 1963), 170–173,
259–262; Richard Stubbs, *Hearts and Minds in Guerilla Warfare: The Malayan
Emergency, 1948–1960* (Oxford: Oxford University Press, 1989); Thomas R.
Mockaitis, *British Counterinsurgency, 1919–60* (London: Macmillan, 1990);
Department of the Army, *The U.S. Army/Marine Corps Counterinsurgency
Field Manual* (Chicago: University of Chicago Press, 2007).

4. A. F. Derry, "Emergency in Malaya: The Psychological Dimension" (mim-
eograph, 1982), Joint Services Command and Staff College Library, Defence
Academy of the U.K., Shrivenham; Stubbs, *Hearts and Minds*, 180–184; John
Cloake, *Templer, Tiger of Malaya: The Life of Field Marshal Sir Gerald
Templer* (London: Harap, 1985), 234–239; Kumar Ramakrishna, *Emergency
Propaganda: The Winning of Malayan Hearts and Minds, 1948–1958*
(Richmond: Curzon, 2002), ch. 5; Noel Barber, *The War of the Running Dogs:
How Malaya Defeated the Communist Guerillas, 1948–60* (London: Collins,
1971), ch. 10; Sir Hugh Greene, *The Third Floor Front: A View of Broadcasting
in the Sixties* (London: Bodley Head, 1969), 33–37.

5. General Rob Lockhart, quoted in "Winning the Shooting War in Malaya,"
Observer, 4 January 1953, 1.

6. Paul Dixon, " 'Hearts and Minds'? British Counter-Insurgency from Malaya to Iraq," *Journal of Strategic Studies* 32, no. 3 (2009): 353–381, at 377. See also John Newsinger, *British Counter-Insurgency: From Palestine to Northern Ireland* (New York: Palgrave Macmillan, 2002); David French, *The British Way in Counter-Insurgency, 1945–1967* (Oxford: Oxford University Press, 2011); Hew Strachan, "British Counter-Insurgency from Malaya to Iraq," *Journal of the Royal United Services Institute* 152 (2007): 8–11.

7. See, e.g., K. R. Brazier-Creagh, "Malaya," *Journal of the Royal United Service Institution* 99 (May 1954): 175–190, at 180; "Noll," "The Emergency in Malaya," *Army Quarterly* (1954): 46–65, at 62; David Dimbleby, "Britain's Forgotten War," *New Statesman,* 18 December 1964, 959–960, at 959; Edgar O'Ballance, *Malaya: The Communist Insurgent War, 1948–1960* (London: Faber, 1966), 168.

8. Keller, *Colonial Madness,* 152–159; Marnia Lazreg, *Torture and the Twilight of Empire: From Algiers to Baghdad* (Princeton: Princeton University Press, 2008), ch. 3; Paul and Marie-Catherine Villatoux, *La République et son armée face au "péril subversif": guerre et action psychologiques, 1945–1960* (Paris: Les Indes savantes, 2005); Paul Villatoux, "L'institutionnalisation de l'arme psychologique pendant la guerre d'Algérie au miroir de la guerre froide," *Guerres mondiales et conflits contemporains,* 208 (2002): 35–44; Marie-Catherine Villatoux, "Traitement psychologique, endoctrinement, contre-endoctrinement en guerre d'Algérie: le cas des camps de detention," *Guerres mondiales et conflits contemporains,* 208 (2002): 45–54; Philippe Raggi, "Services speciaux et action psychologique en Indochine," *Revue historique des Armées,* 194 (1994): 44–53. For an important argument on the entwinement of coercion and "hearts and minds" in British counterinsurgency, see Karl Hack, "Everyone Lived in Fear: Malaya and the British Way of Counter-Insurgency," *Small Wars & Insurgencies* 23, nos. 4–5 (2012): 671–699.

9. Bailkin, *Afterlife of Empire,* 8.

10. Herman, *Romance of American Psychology,* chs. 5–6; Ron Theodore Robin, *The Making of the Cold War Enemy : Culture and Politics in the Military Intellectual-Complex* (Princeton: Princeton University Press, 2001); Mandler, *Return from the Natives*; Christopher Simpson, *Science of Coercion: Communication Research and Psychological Warfare, 1945–1960* (New York: Oxford University Press, 1994); David C. Engerman, *Know Your Enemy*: Culture and Politics in the Military Intellectual-Complex (Princeton: Princeton University Press, 2001): *The Rise and Fall of America's Soviet Experts* (New York: Oxford University Press, 2009); Christopher Simpson, ed., *Universities and Empire: Money and Politics in the Social Sciences during the Cold War* (New York: New Press, 1998); Mark Solovey, *Shaky Foundations: The Politics–Patronage–Social Science Nexus in Cold War America* (New Brunswick: Rutgers University Press, 2013); Mark Solovey and Hamilton Cravens, eds., *Cold War Social Science: Knowledge Production, Liberal Democracy, and Human Nature* (New York: Palgrave Macmillan, 2012); Joy Rohde, *Armed with Expertise: The Militarization of American Social Research during the Cold War* (Ithaca: Cornell University Press, 2013).

11. Joel Isaac, "The Human Sciences in Cold War America," *Historical Journal* 50, no. 3 (2007): 725–746.

12. Robin, *Making of the Cold War Enemy.*

13. Edgerton, *Warfare State,* 166–172, 181–189.

14. H. N. Brain to C. F. A. Warner, 16 March 1949, FO 110/220, NAUK; Harold Evans to A. F. J. Reddaway, 10 October 1955; M. A. C. Cruickshank to A. F. J. Reddaway, 8 October 1955, FCO 141/3727, NAUK; Hugh Foot to E. Melville, 21 April 1959, CO 1027/180, NAUK.

15. Bailkin, *Afterlife of Empire,* 7; David Mills, *Difficult Folk? A Political History of Social Anthropology* (New York: Berghahn, 2008), 89; Steinmetz, "Child of the Empire," 8–9. Of the 19 chairs in psychology at British universities in 1960, 11 were established after 1945: see B. M. Foss, ed., *Psychology in Great Britain: Supplement to the Bulletin of the British Psychological Society* (London: s.n., 1970), 9–13.

16. Edith Mercer, "A Woman Psychologist at War," *The Psychologist* 4, no. 9 (1991): 413–415; T. N. Harper, *The End of Empire and the Making of Malaya* (Cambridge: Cambridge University Press, 1999), 60; Charles Preston Rawson, "An Investigation into the Phenomena of Aggressiveness," Ph.D. thesis (London School of Economics, 1934); *British Imperial Calendar and Civil Service Calendar* (London: H.M.S.O., 1956), col. 751.

17. Pietsch, *Empire of Scholars,* 377; Steinmetz, "Child of the Empire," 2–4; Mills, *Difficult Folk?* 80–84. On the Rhodes-Livingstone Institute, see Lyn Schumaker, *Africanizing Anthropology: Fieldwork, Networks, and the Making of Cultural Knowledge in Central Africa* (Durham: Duke University Press, 2001). The researchers were Max Marwick at Rhodes-Livingstone and Mary Ainsworth, Leonard Ainsworth, Leonard Doob, and A. J. Laird in East Africa.

18. Mandler, *Return from the Natives;* Dunlap and Associates, "Analysis of Strategic Crop Weapons Systems (U)," 1962, available online at www.dtic.mil/dtic/tr/fulltext/u2/334517.pdf.

19. Lee J. Cronbach, "Psychology in British Universities," 11 June 1956, and Norman Pelner, "The Clinical Psychiatry Section of Maudsley Hospital, London," 18 May 1961, Office of Naval Research folder, Saul B. Sells papers, CHP. On the postwar vogue for human sciences research in the U.S. Navy, see Mandler, *Return from the Natives,* 178–179, 192–193.

20. Special Operations Research Office, *U.S. Army Area Handbook for the United Arab Republic (Egypt)* (Washington: Government Printing Office, 1964); T. W. Adams, *U.S. Army Area Handbook for Cyprus* (Washington: Government Printing Office, 1964); Norman C. Walpole, *U.S. Army Area Handbook for India* (Washington: Government Printing Office, 1964).

21. Lee, *Colonial Development and Good Government,* 23–24.

22. "Fostering Research within NATO on Military Applications of Mass Communication," [1955], FO 1110/720, NAUK. On Anglo-American cooperation in Cold War propaganda, see Andrew Defty, *Britain, America, and Anti-Communist Propaganda, 1945–53: The Information Research Department* (London: Routledge, 2008); John Jenks, *British Propaganda and News Media in the Cold War* (Edinburgh: Edinburgh University Press, 2006), 98–104; J. R. Vaughan, *The Failure of American and British Propaganda in the Arab Middle East, 1945–57: Unconquerable Minds* (New York: Palgrave Macmillan, 2005);

Hugh Wilford, "The Information Research Department: Britain's Secret Cold War Weapon Revealed," *Review of International Studies* 24 (1998): 353–369.

23. Ortolano, *Two Cultures Controversy*, 208–209; Frederick Cooper, "Development, Modernization, and the Social Sciences in the Age of Decolonization: The Examples of British and French Africa," *Revue d'histoire des sciences humaines* (2004): 9–38.

24. Alfred J. Marrow, *The Practical Theorist: The Life and Work of Kurt Lewin* (New York: Basic Books, 1969), 164–172, 222–224; Jean E. Neumann, "Kurt Lewin at the Tavistock Institute," *Educational Action Research* 13, no. 1 (2005): 119–136; Nuno Torres, "The Psycho-Social Field Dynamics: Kurt Lewin and Bion," in *Bion's Sources: The Making of His Paradigms,* ed. Nuno Torres and R. D. Hinshelwood (Hove: Routledge, 2013).

25. Young-Bruehl, "Psychoanalysis and Social Democracy"; Mathew Thomson, "Before Anti-Psychiatry: 'Mental Health' in Wartime Britain," in *Cultures of Psychiatry and Mental Health Care in Postwar Britain and the Netherlands,* ed. Marijke Gijswijt-Hofstra and Roy Porter (Amsterdam: Rodopi, 1998); Daniel Pick, *In Pursuit of the Nazi Mind: Hitler, Hess, and the Analysts* (Oxford: Oxford University Press, 2012); Herman, *Romance of American Psychology,* 34–36; David F. Smith, "Juvenile Delinquency in the British Zone of Germany, 1945–51," *German History* 12 (1994): 39–63.

26. Marrow, *Practical Theorist,* 191–221; Leland P. Bradford, *The National Training Laboratories: Its History, 1947–1970* (Bethel: Bradford, 1974). For more critical interpretations, see William Graebner, "Confronting the Democratic Paradox: The Ambivalent Vision of Kurt Lewin," *Journal of Social Issues* 43, no. 3 (1987): 141–146; Elisabeth Lasch-Quinn, *Race Experts: How Racial Etiquette, Sensitivity Training, and New Age Therapy Hijacked the Civil Rights Revolution* (Lanham: Rowan & Littlefield, 2002).

27. Steve Joshua Heims, *The Cybernetics Group* (Cambridge: MIT Press, 1991), 216–218.

28. Daniel Immerwahr, *Thinking Small: The United States and the Lure of Community Development* (Cambridge: Harvard University Press, 2015); Matthew S. Hull, "Communities of Place, Not Kind: American Technologies of Neighborhood in Postcolonial Delhi," *Comparative Studies in Society and History* 53, no. 4 (2011): 757–790; Matthew Hull, "Democratic Technologies of Speech: From WWII America to Postcolonial Delhi," *Linguistic Anthropology* 20, no. 2 (2010): 257–282; Cullather, *Hungry World,* 78–94; Latham, *Right Kind of Revolution,* 71–72.

29. Colonial Office, *Mass Education in African Society* (London: H.M.S.O., [1943]); Rosaleen Smyth, "The Roots of Community Development in Colonial Office Policy and Practice in Africa," *Social Policy & Administration* 38, no. 4 (2004): 418–436; Colonial Office Summer Conference on African Administration, *The Encouragement of Initiative in African Society* (s.n., 1948), 14–15.

30. Lewis, *Empire State-Building*; Lee, *Colonial Development and Good Government,* 166–167; "Text of a Talk Given by the Community Development Officer to the Members of the Eastern Regional Conference," 9 August 1950, Alec Dickson papers, Nigeria 1/4, RHO.

31. A. I. K. Quainoo, "Formal and Informal Education in the Gold Coast Village," in *Perspectives in Mass Education & Community Development,* ed. L. J. Lewis (London: Thomas Nelson, 1955).

32. Report of Study Group on Special Problems of Rural Conservatism in Kenya, Conference on Education for Nationhood, April 1958, BZ/5/3, NAK; D. E. Faulkner, *A Pilot Scheme in Community Development* (s.n., 1950), Dickson papers, Nigeria 2/7, RHO; "The District Welfare Officer," n.d., DC/MKS/8/10, NAK; Alec Dickson, notes on G. B. Masefield, "Psychology of Agriculture Extension Work," n.d., Dickson papers, Mass Education 1/1, RHO.

33. Community Development Reading Lists, June 1951, IE/COL/C/1/3; Mass Education Reading List, n.d., IE/COL/C/1/2, IEL. On the postwar reform of colonial training, see A. H. M. Kirk-Greene, *On Crown Service: A History of HM Colonial and Overseas Civil Services, 1837–1997* (London: I. B. Tauris, 1999), 46–49; Robert Heussler, *Yesterday's Rulers: The Making of the British Colonial Service* (London: Oxford University Press, 1963), ch. 7.

34. Madge Gill, "Notes on the Discussion Group Work in the Community Development Course, 1950–1953," September 1953, IE/COL/C/1/3, IEL.

35. Great Britain, *Catalogue of the Colonial Office Library, London* (Boston: G. K. Hall, 1964), 5: 339, 8: 662–663. On the internal divisions that make "culture and personality school" something of a misnomer, see Robert A. LeVine, "Culture and Personality Studies, 1918–1960: Myth and History," *Journal of Personality* 69, no. 6 (2001): 803–818.

36. Hearnshaw, *Short History of British Psychology,* 210–213; Walter Laqueur, "Interpretations of Terrorism: Fact, Fiction, and Political Science," *Journal of Contemporary History* 12, no. 1 (1977): 1–42, at 4–5. Frederic Bartlett at Cambridge was one skeptic of the frustration-aggression hypothesis: see Raj Narain to Gardner Murphy, 17 June 1950, Gardner and Lois Murphy papers, M1804, folder 3, CHP.

37. Colonial Office, *Encouragement of Initiative in African Society,* 72; Batten, *Communities and Their Development,* 220–223; *Measures for the Economic Development of Under-Developed Countries: Report by a Group of Experts Appointed by the Secretary-General of the United Nations* (New York: United Nations, 1951), 15.

38. Community Development Reading Lists, June 1951, IE/COL/C/1/3; Mass Education Reading List, n.d., IE/COL/C/1/2, IEL. On the postwar convergence of the psychological and the social, see Thomson, *Psychological Subjects,* 231–241; Chris Waters, "The Homosexual as a Social Being in Britain, 1945–1968," *Journal of British Studies* 51, no. 3 (2012): 685–710; Harrison, *Bion, Rickman, Foulkes, and the Northfield Experiments.*

39. "Report of Group IV: Incentives to Progress in African Society," in Colonial Office, *Encouragement of Initiative,* 6; M. McMullen, "The Psychology of Disengagement," *Corona* 10 (1958): 448–450.

40. T. R. Batten, *The Non-Directive Approach in Group and Community Work* (Oxford: Oxford University Press, 1967), 29; T. R. Batten, "The Human Factor in Programmes of Social Change," n.d., Batten papers, box 253, Avec Archive, Oxford Brookes University.

41. T. R. Batten, *Communities and Their Development: An Introductory Study with Special Reference to the Tropics* (London: Oxford University Press, 1957), 30, 225–227.

42. Sluga, *The Nation, Psychology, and International Politics.*

43. Mark Mazower, *No Enchanted Palace: The End of Empire and the Ideological Origins of the United Nations* (Princeton: Princeton University Press, 2009), ch. 2; Ian Hall, *Dilemmas of Decline: British Intellectuals and World Politics, 1945–1975* (Berkeley: University of California Press, 2012), 132–138, at 137. On the Frankfurt School and psychoanalysis, see Jay, *Dialectical Imagination,* 226–227, 234–252.

44. Nicholas Owen, "Four Straws in the Wind: Metropolitan Anti-Imperialism, January–February 1960," in *The Wind of Change: Harold Macmillan and British Decolonization,* ed. L. J. Butler and Sarah Stockwell (Basingstoke: Palgrave Macmillan, 2013); Ortolano, *Two Cultures Controversy,* 205–211; John Strachey, quoted in "In Place of Empire," 18 January 1960, reel T124, BBC Written Archives, Reading; Bertrand Russell, "Pros and Cons of Nationalism," in *Fact and Fiction* (London: Allen & Unwin, 1961), 118; Rita Hinden, "Socialism and the Colonial World," in *New Fabian Colonial Essays,* ed. A. Creech Jones (London: Hogarth Press, 1959), 15.

45. Robert H. Thouless, "'ASPRIT': International Tensions and Social Psychology," *Bulletin of the British Psychological Society,* no. 36 (1958): 21–24, at 21; W. F. Gutteridge, "The Nature of Nationalism in British West Africa," *Western Political Quarterly* 11, no. 3 (1958): 574–582, at 579; Alix Strachey, "Psychological Problems of Nationhood," *Year Book of World Affairs* 14 (1960): 260–285, at 268, 272.

46. Bailkin, *Afterlife of Empire,* 119–125; Brian Crozier, *The Rebels: A Study of Post-War Insurrections* (Boston: Beacon Press, 1960), 13–14.

47. Leonard H. Ainsworth and Mary D. Ainsworth, "Acculturation in East Africa (I): Political Awareness and Attitudes toward Authority," *Journal of Social Psychology* 57 (1962): 391–399; Ainsworth and Ainsworth, "Acculturation in East Africa (II): Frustration and Aggression," *Journal of Social Psychology* 57 (1962): 401–407; Mary Ainsworth to Audrey Richards, 12 March 1962, Audrey Richards papers, file 16/2, LSE; Leonard W. Doob, *Becoming More Civilized: A Psychological Exploration* (New Haven: Yale University Press, 1960), 79.

48. T. S. Simey to Millais Culpin, 9 July 1945, T. S. Simey papers, file D396/8/1, Sydney Jones Library, University of Liverpool; Simey, *Welfare & Planning,* 93–101, at 98; T. S. Simey, *Welfare & Planning in the West Indies* (Oxford: Clarendon Press, 1946), 99–100; T. S. Simey, "Colonial Discontents: The Psychology of Nationalism," *Manchester Guardian,* 2 February 1948, 1.

49. C. V. D. Hadley, "Transfer Experiments with Guinea-Pigs," *British Journal of Psychology* 18, no. 2 (1927): 189–224; C. V. D. Hadley, "Personality Patterns, Social Class, and Aggression in the West Indies," *Human Relations* 2 (1949): 349–362, at 358.

50. Lewis Davidson, "Outline of a Psychological Study of Jamaican Society," n.d., CR 8/7, LSE. On Clarke, see Christine Barrow, "Edith Clarke: Jamaican Social Reformer and Anthropologist," *Caribbean Quarterly* 44 (1998): 15–34.

51. CSSRC minutes, 5 September 1944, CR 8/1, LSE; Audrey Richards to Raymond Firth, 3 November 1949, Firth papers, file 7/3/1, LSE; Margaret Mead to Madeline Kerr, 9 June 1944, MM, box C11, folder 9, LOC.

52. Edith Clarke to Madeline Kerr, 9 January 1950, Firth papers 7/3/1, LSE.

53. Madeline Kerr, *Personality and Conflict in Jamaica* (Liverpool: Liverpool University Press, 1952).

54. Jules Henry, et al., "Symposium: Projective Testing in Ethnography," *American Anthropologist* 57, no. 2 (1955): 245–270; Cyril J. Adcock and James E. Ritchie, "Intercultural Use of the Rorschach," *American Anthropologist* 60, no. 5 (1958): 881–892.

55. Kerr, *Personality and Conflict*, 83, 176–188.

56. Madeline Kerr, *The People of Ship Street* (London: Routledge, 1958). Kerr was commenting on a heated debate between former Kenya governor Philip Mitchell and anthropologist Max Gluckman in the pages of the *Manchester Guardian:* see Gluckman, "The Mau Mau Rituals: Tribal Religion and Witchcraft," *Manchester Guardian,* 19 March 1954; Mitchell, "The Mau Mau Rituals: 'Fancy and Fact,' " *Manchester Guardian,* 10 May 1954.

57. Madeline Kerr, "Some Psychological Factors in the Jamaican Culture Pattern," 16 February 1948, Clarke papers, file 77, LSE; Kerr, *Personality and Conflict.*

58. Gustav Jahoda, *White Man: A Study of the Attitudes of Africans to Europeans in Ghana before Independence* (London: Oxford University Press, 1961), 118, 129; Marie Jahoda, *Race Relations and Mental Health* (Paris: UNESCO, 1960); Henri Tajfel, *Human Groups and Social Categories: Studies in Social Psychology* (Cambridge: Cambridge University Press, 1981), 140. Marie Jahoda (no relation to Gustav) lost her job with a government broadcasting service during the war by predicting on the air that India would soon gain its independence. See Marie Jahoda, "Rekonstruktionen," in *Ich habe die Welt nicht verändert: Lebenserrinerungen einer Pioneirin der Sozialforschung* (Weinheim: Beltz, 2002), 74.

59. R. E. Robinson, minute, 7 October 1948, CO 927/172, NAUK; Sally Chilver, "The Secretaryship of the Colonial Social Science Research Council: A Reminiscence," *Anthropological Forum* 4, no. 2 (1977): 239–248, at 244.

60. P. A. P. Robertson, "Zanzibar—Crossroads of East Africa," *Journal of the Royal Society* 112 (1964): 605–615, at 608; John Glubb, "A Further Review of the Middle East," *Journal of the Royal United Services Institution* 103 (1958): 324–335, at 328; Philip Mitchell, circular letter, 1949, CO 537/6569, NAUK; Margery Perham, "Psychology of Mau Mau," n.d., Margery Perham papers 347/5, RHO.

61. Margery Perham, "The Mood of African Nationalism," 7 August 1960, Perham papers 240/3, RHO; Perham, "The Psychology of African Nationalism," *Optima* 10 (1960): 27–36, at 36; Alan Burns, *Colour Prejudice: With Particular Reference to the Relationship between Whites and Negroes* (London: Allen & Unwin, 1948), 140–141; W. R. Crocker, *Self-Government for the Colonies* (London: Allen & Unwin, 1949), 91.

62. On the pedagogical impulse in British imperialism, see Mehta, *Liberalism and Empire*, and Hevia, *English Lessons.*

63. W. E. F. Ward, "Education for Citizenship," 18 July 1946, CO 859/89/8, NAUK, reproduced in Ronald Hyam, ed., *The Labour Government and the End of Empire, 1945–1951,* part IV, *Race Relations and the Commonwealth* (London: H.M.S.O., 1992), 52–53; Robert H. Thouless, *Straight and Crooked Thinking* (New York: Simon & Schuster, 1932); Colonial Office, *Education for Citizenship in Africa* (London: H.M.S.O., 1948), 17–19; "Education for Citizenship in Africa: Reply from Sir Philip Mitchell," 19 May 1949, CO 859/171/1, NAUK.

64. A. G. Dickson, "Batten on Community Development," *Community Development Bulletin* 9, no. 2 (1958); A. G. Dickson, "Mass Education in the Gold Coast & Togoland," n.d., Dickson papers, Gold Coast 6/14, RHO.

65. Arthur Creech Jones to Batten, 20 November 1944, Batten papers, box 259, AA; Colonial Office, *Education for Citizenship,* 36–40; Institute of Education, *Bakht er Ruda: Twenty Years Old* (Khartoum: Publications Bureau, 1954); V. L. Griffiths, *Character Aims: Some Suggestions on Standards for a Rising Nation* (London: Longmans, 1949); V. L. Griffiths, *An Experiment in Education* (London: Longmans, 1953), 114.

66. V. L. Griffiths, *Character: Its Psychology* (London: Longmans, 1953); Barbara H. Rosenwein, "Worrying about Emotions in History," *American Historical Review* 107 (2002): 821–845.

67. Griffiths, *Character Aims,* 16–17, 21, 26.

68. Jean M. Sargent to Christopher Cox, 29 October 1948, 668/11/49; Cox to H. M. Grace, 8 November 1948, 668/11/52–53; Christopher Cox to Griffiths, 13 January 1949, 668/11/60–61, Sudan Archive, University of Durham.

69. Griffiths, *Character: Its Psychology,* 83.

70. "First Report of the Committee on Character Training," *Northern Rhodesia African Education Journal* 2, no. 1 (1951), in Dickson papers, Mass Education 2/4, RHO; Director of Education to principals of primary training colleges, 12 September 1960, Mss Afr. s. 1755 (154), RHO; E. D. Roberts, "Teaching for International Understanding," n.d., E. D. Roberts papers, Mss Afr s. 1755, box 5, file 25b, RHO; W. H. Ingrams, minute, 13 April 1951, CO 875/58/2, NAUK.

71. *Man O' War Bay Training Centre* (London: Edgar G. Dunstan, [1958]); Alec Dickson, *A Chance to Serve,* ed. Mora Dickson (London: Dennis Dobson, 1976), ch. 4; Mora Dickson, *New Nigerians* (London: Dennis Dobson, 1960). On Outward Bound, see Mark Freeman, "From 'Character Training' to 'Personal Growth': The Early History of Outward Bound, 1941–1965," *History of Education* 40, no. 1 (2011): 21–43; Mark Freeman, "Muscular Quakerism? The Society of Friends and Youth Organisations in Britain, c. 1900–1950," *English Historical Review* 125 (2010): 642–669. On the Dicksons, see also Bailkin, *Afterlife of Empire,* ch. 2.

72. *Man O' War Bay Training Centre,* 34; "Man O' War Bay Students List, 1951–54," Dickson papers, Man O' War Bay 7/20, RHO; Hyacinth Nuaji Agbani diary, entry for 3 April 1952, Dickson papers, Man O' War Bay 3/7,

RHO; Alec G. Dickson, "Man O' War Bay," *Geographical Magazine* 26 (1954): 557–561; exam paper, n.d., Perham papers 244/4, RHO.

73. David Martin Jones and M. L. R. Smith, "Myth and the Small War Tradition: Reassessing the Discourse of British Counter-Insurgency," *Small Wars & Insurgencies* 24, no. 3 (2013): 436–464.

74. Campbell Stuart, *Secrets of Crewe House: The Story of a Famous Campaign* (London: Hodder and Stoughton, 1920); Philip M. Taylor, *The Projection of Britain: British Overseas Publicity and Propaganda, 1919–1939* (Cambridge: Cambridge University Press, 1981); Charles Roetter, *The Art of Psychological Warfare, 1914–1945* (New York: Stein and Day, 1974); Charles Greig Cruickshank, *The Fourth Arm: Psychological Warfare, 1938–1945* (London: Davis-Poynter, 1977).

75. Ian McLaine, *Ministry of Morale: Home Front Morale and the Ministry of Information in World War II* (London: Allen & Unwin, 1979).

76. Susan L. Carruthers, *Winning Hearts and Minds: British Governments, the Media, and Colonial Counter-Insurgency, 1944–1960* (London: Leicester University Press, 1995).

77. N. C. Willmott, "Is 'Morale Warfare' (Psychological Warfare) an Air Force Interest and/or Duty?" 1956, AIR 20/9599, NAUK; "Staff Officers' Guide to Psychological Warfare" (second draft), [1959], CO 1027/179, NAUK.

78. Thompson, *Defeating Communist Insurgency*, 38–39; Kenneth W. Yarnold, "Fear: A Field Survey in Palestine," [1949], W. S. Cole papers, Documents.15656, 7/34/4, IWM.

79. Carruthers, *Winning Hearts and Minds*, 31, 92, 138, 221.

80. John Macpherson to Frederick Hoyer Millar, 30 October 1957, FO 1110/985, NAUK; "Colonial Information Policy and Problems," November 1952, CO 1027/27, NAUK.

81. "Suggested Heads and Sub-Heads for Brigadier Baker on Propaganda, Information, and Publicity" (draft), [1958?]; A. F. J. Reddaway to Leslie Glass, 28 November 1955; Psychological Warfare Staff, "Mau Mau Emergency in Kenya, Part I: Some Psychological Aspects of the Emergency in Retrospect," [1956], FCO 141/3727, NAUK.

82. Carruthers, *Winning Hearts and Minds*, 92.

83. F. H. Lakin, "Psychological Warfare Research in Malaya, 1952–55," in *Report of the Annual Army Human Factors Research and Development Conference* (Washington: Office of the Chief of Research and Development, 1965); Thomas J. Maguire, "Interrogation and 'Psychological Intelligence': The Construction of Propaganda during the Malayan Emergency, 1948–1958," in *Interrogation in War and Conflict: A Comparative and Interdisciplinary Analysis*, ed. Christopher Andrew and Simona Tobia (New York: Routledge, 2014).

84. P. B. Humphrey, "Study of Reasons for Entering the Jungle (V): Mental Ability and Educational Factors in Terrorist Recruitment and Surrender," 7 May 1954, WO 291/1780, NAUK.

85. Lakin, "A Study of the Communist Terrorist Group," WO 211/1765, NAUK; "Turning a New Leaf," n.d., FO 1110/534, NAUK.

86. Humphrey, "A Preliminary Study of Entry Behaviour among Chinese Communist Terrorists in Malaya," n.d., WO 291/1764, NAUK; Lucian Pye, *Guerrilla Communism in Malaya: Its Social and Political Meaning* (Princeton: Princeton University Press, 1956), 144–146; Cheng Leng Lim, *The Story of a Psy-Warrior: Tan Sri Dr. C. C. Too* (Selangor Darul Ehsan: Lim Cheng Leng, 2000), app. 2. A copy of one such pamphlet is in FO 1110/534, NAUK.

87. Lakin and Humphrey, "A Study of Reasons for Entering the Jungle among Chinese Communist Terrorists in Malaya (IV): Some Social Factors," 29 March 1954, WO 291/1779, NAUK; Psychological Warfare Directive No. 1, 12 November 1952, FO 1110/534, NAUK.

88. Ramakrishna, *Emergency Propaganda*, 116, 147, 188.

89. Margaret Read to E. M. Chilver, CO 927/164/8, NAUK.

90. Peggy Thornton, "Progress Report No. 1," 30 December 1953, CR 8/30, LSE; Peggy K. Thornton, "Visual Perception among the Peoples of Malaya," D.Phil. thesis (University of Reading, 1956), 54, 148.

91. F. H. Lakin, "Psychological Warfare Research: Its Role in Cold War," March 1956, WO 291/1509, NAUK.

92. Deputy Governor [of Cyprus] minute, 31 May 1958, FCO 141/3727, NAUK; "Some Past Recommendations on Psychological Operations Support," 9 June 1969, DEFE 11/884, NAUK; H. A. H. Cortazzi minute, 24 Oct 1957, FO 1110/986, NAUK; A. D. C. Peterson, "Inadequate Information Services," *East Africa and Rhodesia* 35 (1959): 1411.

93. George Davy to P. Storrs, 14 August 1957, FCO 141/3727, NAUK; Peter Watson, *War on the Mind: The Military Uses and Abuses of Psychology* (London: Hutchinson, 1978), 382.

94. H. A. H. Cortazzi minute, 24 October 1957, FO 1110/986, NAUK; "Some Past Recommendations on Psychological Operations Support," 9 June 1969, DEFE 11/884, NAUK; A. D. C. Peterson, "Inadequate Information Services," *East Africa and Rhodesia* 35 (1959): 1411; "Psychological Warfare Requirements in Limited War and Police Actions," 20 December 1957, FO 1110/986, NAUK; H. A. A. Bray, "Psychological Operations Lecture Notes," 28 November 1962, DEFE 25/85, NAUK; "Establishment—Psychological Operations Units," [1961], DEFE 28/2, NAUK; D. E. Ryan, "Future of the Army Information Team, East Africa Command," 3 October 1963, DEFE 28/171, NAUK; H. N. H. Wild, "Psychological Operations in the Far East," 19 April 1963, DEFE 11/236, NAUK.

95. F. H. Lakin to J. C. Penton, 15 December 1957, WO 342/2, NAUK.

96. Staff Officers' PW Course 1958, 9–27 June, FO 1110/1102, NAUK; "Extract of Draft Time-Table for Psychological Warfare Staff Course, Joint Concealment Centre, 1957," FO 1110/981, NAUK; Alec Seath Kirkbride, *A Crackle of Thorns: Experiences in the Middle East* (London: John Murray, 1956); Mandler, *Return from the Natives*, 34–40; "Staff Officers' Guide," NAUK.

97. C. Y. Carstairs minute, 25 October 1957, CO 1027/178, NAUK; Psychological Warfare Staff, "Some Psychological Aspects of the Emergency," Part I, NAUK.

98. Lakin to Penton, 15 December 1957, NAUK; W. M. T. Magan, "Grivas: A Personality Sketch," 11 March 1959, FCO 141/4488, NAUK; "Suggested Heads and Sub-Heads for Brigadier Baker," NAUK.

99. Clutterbuck, *Long Long War,* 106; Barber, *War of the Running Dogs,* ch. 10.

100. Psychological Warfare Staff, "Some Psychological Aspects of the Emergency," and Psychological Warfare Staff, "Mau Mau Emergency in Kenya, Part II: Present Organization of Propaganda and Psychological Warfare in East Africa," [1956], FCO 141/3727, NAUK, emphasis added.

101. "Surrender Propaganda," [1955], and Ian Henderson, "Propaganda Schemes: Scheme for Consideration by the Surrender Propaganda Committee," [1955], WO 276/532, NAUK; E. B. David minute, 17 August 1953, CO 822/701, NAUK; Bray, "Psychological Operations Lecture Notes," NAUK.

102. Bray, "Psychological Operations Lecture Notes," and Psychological Warfare Staff, "Some Psychological Aspects of the Emergency," NAUK.

103. Kathleen Gough, review of *The Psychology of Mau Mau, Man* 54 (1954): 143–144; A. T. Culwick, letter to editor, *Manchester Guardian,* 3 June 1954, 6; Max Gluckman, "The Mau Mau Rituals: Tribal Religion and Witchcraft," *Manchester Guardian,* 19 March 1954, 8; Philip Mitchell, "The Mau Mau Rituals: 'Fancy and Fact,'" *Manchester Guardian,* 10 May 1954, 6; Madeline Kerr, "The Study of Personality Deprivation through Projection Tests," *Social and Economic Studies* 4, no. 1 (1954): 83–94, at 83.

104. Alfred W. McCoy, *A Question of Torture: CIA Interrogation from the Cold War to the War on Terror* (New York: Metropolitan Books, 2006); Dominic Streatfeild, *Brainwash: The Secret History of Mind Control* (New York: St. Martin's, 2007); Ian Cobain, *A Secret History of Torture* (Berkeley: Counterpoint, 2012). For a persuasively skeptical view of claims that scientific research drives torture practices, see Darius Rejali, *Torture and Democracy* (Princeton: Princeton University Press, 2009), 28, 375–377, 420–425.

105. *Opinion of George Cooper, Q.C., Regarding Canadian Government Funding of the Allan Memorial Institute in the 1950s and 1960s* (Ottawa: Minister of Supply and Services, 1986), appendix 12; Parker Committee on Interrogation Procedures minutes, 22 December 1971, RV 1/2, NAUK; Cyril Cunningham, *No Mercy, No Leniency: Communist Mistreatment of British Prisoners of War in Korea* (London: Leo Cooper, 2000), 140–141; Army Psychiatric Advisory Committee minutes, 21 April 1960, 30 June 1961, and 9 December 1965, WO 32/13462, NAUK.

106. Howard Lakin, memorandum, 3 June 1959, WO 342/2, NAUK; F. H. Lakin, "Exercise White Knight," 11 July 1959, WO 342/2, NAUK.

107. On the brainwashing scare in America, see Robin, *Making of the Cold War Enemy,* ch. 8; Susan Carruthers, *Cold War Captives: Imprisonment, Escape, and Brainwashing* (Berkeley: University of California Press, 2009), ch. 5; John Marks, *The Search for the "Manchurian Candidate": The CIA and Mind Control* (New York: Times Books, 1979).

108. Alwyn Crow to Henry Tizard, 2 August 1950, DEFE 9/37, NAUK.

109. E. D. Adrian to Tizard, n.d., and Himsworth to Tizard, 4 December 1950, NAUK.

110. Solandt to Tizard, 2 May 1951, DEFE 9/21, NAUK; Medical Intelligence Working Party and Consultant Panel on Psychiatry minutes, 15 March 1956, DEFE 7/1809, NAUK; Streatfeild, *Brainwash,* 69–73.

111. Medical Intelligence Working Party and Consultant Panel on Psychiatry minutes, 19 February 1957, DEFE 7/1809, NAUK; R. M. Bremner, "Interrogation in Internal Security Situations since 1945," 21 November 1971, DEFE 23/109, NAUK.

112. Bremner, "Interrogation in Internal Security," NAUK; F. H. Lakin to J. C. Penton, 23 January 1958, WO 342/2, NAUK. For the controversy over resistance-to-interrogation training at home, see Keith Thompson, "Brainwash Shocks: War Office Admits Grilling Tests on Elite Troops," *Daily Mail,* 9 March 1960, and subsequent official discussions in PREM 11/2900, NAUK.

113. J. Constant, "The Psychology of Interrogation," 21 February 1957, WO 342/2, NAUK; John Sankey, interview by Conrad Wood, 1988, catalogue no. 10300, IWM; Chief Inspector Luther to Secretary of State for the Colonies, 21 November 1958, CO 926/888, NAUK; Laurence Oldmeadow Crosland, interview by Conrad Wood, 23 June 1988, catalogue no. 10232, IWM.

114. Bremner, "Interrogation in Internal Security," NAUK; J. S. Parry to J. C. Penton, 17 January 1957, J. R. Kemp to "the Select Committee on Brain-Washing," 19 February 1957, J. C. Penton to M. W. Hodges, 27 March 1957, and Director of Military Intelligence to Penton, 10 April 1957, WO 342/2, NAUK.

115. Bremner, "Interrogation in Internal Security," NAUK; "Interrogation: Note of a Meeting Held at the Home Office," 21 October 1971, DEFE 24/968, NAUK; "A Note on 'Deep Interrogation,'" n.d., WO 296/67, NAUK; "KUBARK," 83–85.

116. T. Shallice, "The Ulster Depth Interrogation Techniques and Their Relation to Sensory Deprivation Research," *Cognition* 1, no. 4 (1972): 385–405; John McGuffin, *The Guineapigs* (Harmondsworth: Penguin, 1974); Peter Deeley, *Beyond Breaking Point* (London: Barker, 1971).

117. V. W. Whitman, "Meeting with Mr. Healey," 24 November 1971, and "Background Note," n.d., DEFE 23/109, NAUK.

118. Rejali, *Torture and Democracy,* 300–301, 331; John Sankey, interview with Conrad Wood, 1988, catalogue no. 10300, IWM; Costas Montis, *Closed Doors: An Answer to* Bitter Lemons *by Lawrence Durrell,* trans. David Roessel and Soterios G. Stavrou (Minneapolis: Nostos, 2004), 44; Cobain, *A Secret History of Torture,* 94; Elkins, *Imperial Reckoning,* 155, 158; French, *British Way,* 161n.

119. Jessica Wolfendale, "The Myth of 'Torture Lite,'" *Ethics & International Affairs* 23, no. 1 (2009): 49–61; French, *British Way,* 160–162; Geoffrey Strickland to Peter Emery, 4 April 1960, WO 32/17501, NAUK; Calder Walton, *Empire of Secrets: British Intelligence, the Cold War, and the Twilight of Empire* (London: Overlook, 2013), 192–193.

120. Rejali, *Torture and Democracy;* Elkins, *Imperial Reckoning;* Charlie Standley, "The British Army, Violence, Interrogation, and Shortcomings in Intelligence Gathering during the Cyprus Emergency, 1955–59," in *Interrogation*

in War and Conflict, ed. Andrew and Tobia. On the popular culture of brain-washing, see David Seed, *Brainwashing: The Fictions of Mind Control: A Study of Novels and Films since World War II* (Kent: Kent State University Press, 2004); Alan Burton, "Mind Bending, Mental Seduction, and Menticide: Brainwashing in British Spy Dramas of the 1960s," *Journal of British Cinema and Television* 10, no. 1 (2013): 27–48.

121. Minute by Director of Welfare Services, 17 May 1957, and "Pyroi Detention Camp: Report on the First Six Months' Work," [January 1958], FCO 141/3641, NAUK. For the idea of the "total institution," see Erving Goffman, *Asylums: Essays on the Social Situation of Mental Patients and Other Inmates* (Chicago: Aldine, 1961).

122. Elkins, *Imperial Reckoning;* Katherine Bruce-Lockhart, " 'Unsound' Minds and Broken Bodies: The Detention of 'Hard Core' Mau Mau Women at Kimiti and Gitamayu Detention Camps, 1954–1960," *Journal of East African Studies* 8, no. 4 (2014): 1–20; Derek R. Peterson, *Ethnic Patriotism and the East African Revival: A History of Dissent, c. 1935–1972* (Cambridge: Cambridge University Press, 2013), 236.

123. S. H. la Fontaine, "Establishment Athi River Internment Camp," 8 September 1953, FCO 141/5666, NAUK; Eric Griffith-Jones, " 'Dilution' Detention Camps: Use of Force in Enforcing Discipline," [1957], CO 822/1251, NAUK. Designated as the camp for "deeply indoctrinated Mau Mau," Athi River had a unique status in the detention system because of the authority granted to missionaries and the intensity of "reeducation" efforts—although this did not diminish the use of physical violence. See Elkins, *Imperial Reckoning,* 198–201.

124. Griffith-Jones, " 'Dilution' Detention Camps," NAUK.

6. Psychology beyond Empire

1. Thomson, "Before Anti-Psychiatry; Eugene B. Brody, *The Search for Mental Health: A History and Memoir of WFMH, 1948–1997* (Baltimore: Williams & Wilkins, 1998); Heims, *Cybernetics Group,* 172–176; Jonathan Paul Toms, "From Mental Hygiene to Civil Rights: MIND and the Problematic of Personhood, c. 1900 to 1980," Ph.D. thesis (University College London, 2005). On the limited internationalism of the interwar movement, see Mathew Thomson, "Mental Hygiene in Britain in the First Half of the Twentieth Century: The Limits of International Influence," in *International Relations in Psychiatry: Britain, Germany, and the United States to World War II,* ed. Volker Roelcke, Paul J. Weindling, and Louise Westwood (Rochester: University of Rochester Press, 2013); Mathew Thomson, "Mental Hygiene as an International Movement," in *International Health Organisations and Movements, 1918–1939,* ed. Paul Weindling (Cambridge: Cambridge University Press, 1995); Hans Pols, "Managing the Mind: The Culture of American Mental Hygiene, 1910–1950," Ph.D. thesis (University of Pennsylvania, 1997).

2. *Mental Health and World Citizenship* (London: World Federation for Mental Health, 1948), 16. On this theme in British psychoanalysis after the war, see especially Shapira, *War Inside*.

3. John R. Rees, *Reflections: A Personal History and an Account of the Growth of the World Federation for Mental Health* (New York: United States Committee of the World Federation for Mental Health, 1966), 72.

4. "Minutes of the Organizational Meeting to Found the World Federation of Mental Health," 18 August 1948, MM, box F50, folder 11, LOC; J. C. Flugel, ed., *International Congress on Mental Health, London, 1948* (London: H. K. Lewis, [1948]); J. R. Rees, "Report on Discussion with Representatives of McGill University with Regard to Their Co-Operation with WFMH," 1956, MM, box F53, folder 2, LOC.

5. On the imperial legacy in international organizations, see especially Ittmann, *Problem of Great Importance;* Mazower, *No Enchanted Palace;* Glenda Sluga, "UNESCO and the (One) World of Julian Huxley," *Journal of World History* 21, no. 3 (2010): 393–418; Joseph M. Hodge, "British Colonial Expertise, Post-Colonial Careering, and the Early History of International Development," *Journal of Modern European History* 8 (2010): 24–46; Matthew Connelly, *Fatal Misconception: The Struggle to Control World Population* (Cambridge: Harvard University Press, 2008); Chloé Maurel, *Histoire de l'UNESCO: Les trentes premières années, 1945–1974* (Paris: Harmattan, 2010).

6. For critiques of the apolitical rhetoric of "development," see also Cooper and Packard, eds., *International Development and the Social Sciences;* Gilbert Rist, *The History of Development: From Western Origins to Global Faith* (London: Zed Books, 2001); Arturo Escobar, *Encountering Development: The Making and Unmaking of the Third World* (Princeton: Princeton University Press, 1994); James Ferguson, *The Anti-Politics Machine: "Development," Depoliticization, and Bureaucratic Power in Lesotho* (Cambridge: Cambridge University Press, 1990); Akhil Gupta, *Postcolonial Developments: Agriculture in the Making of Modern India* (Durham: Duke University Press, 2000); Frédérique Apffel Marglin and Stephen A. Marglin, eds., *Dominating Knowledge: Development, Culture, and Resistance* (Oxford: Clarendon Press, 1990).

7. Bailkin, *Afterlife of Empire*, 9.

8. Anthony Kirk-Greene, "Decolonization: The Ultimate Diaspora," *Journal of Contemporary History* 36, no. 1 (2001): 133–151; Hodge, "British Colonial Expertise"; Connelly, *Fatal Misconception*, 311.

9. Maurel, *Histoire de l'UNESCO,* 102, 121–122; Farley, *Brock Chisholm,* 73, 78.

10. Julian Huxley, *UNESCO: Its Purpose and Its Philosophy* (Washington: Public Affairs Press, 1947), 45; Sluga, "Julian Huxley," 404; John Farley, *Brock Chisholm, the World Health Organization, and the Cold War* (Vancouver: University of British Columbia Press, 2008), 40–42.

11. Maurel, *Histoire de l'UNESCO,* 221–226; Heims, *Cybernetics Group,* 171; Teresa Tomás Rangil, "Citizen, Academic, Expert, or International Worker? Juggling with Identities at UNESCO's Social Science Department, 1946–1955," *Science in Context* 26, no. 1 (2013): 61–91, at 74–76.

12. "Statement of Tensions Affecting International Understanding," 8 July 1948, file 327.5, part I, UNESCO archive, Paris; Hadley Cantril, ed., *Tensions That Cause Wars* (Urbana: University of Illinois Press, 1950), 19; Mandler, *Return from the Natives,* 271.

13. T. Adeoye Lambo, mimeograph, "Rapid Development Can Threaten Mental Health," 7 April 1959. On Lambo, see also Sadowsky, *Imperial Bedlam,* 42–47; Matthew M. Heaton, *Black Skin, White Coats: Nigerian Psychiatrists, Decolonization, and the Globalization of Psychiatry* (Athens: University of Ohio Press, 2013).

14. P. N. Kirpal, "Committee of the Indian National Commission for Co-Ordination of the Study of Tensions," 16 December 1950, Gardner and Lois Murphy papers, M1804, folder 1, CHP; K. P. Chattopadhyay to Arvid Broderson, 31 July 1947, file 327.5, part II, UNESCO archive; B. Pattabhi Sitaramayya, "Group Prejudices," in *Group Prejudices in India,* ed. Nanavati and Vakil; B. S. Guha, *Studies in Social Tensions Among the Refugees from Eastern Pakistan* (Calcutta: Government of India Press, 1959), viii.

15. Randall M. Packard, "Post-Colonial Medicine," in *Medicine in the Twentieth Century,* ed. Roger Cooter and John Pickstone (Amsterdam: Harwood, 2000); Erez Manela, "A Pox on Your Narrative: Writing Disease Control into Cold War History," *Diplomatic History* 34, no. 2 (2010): 299–323.

16. "WHO Mental Health Programme Beginning 1950," 19 January 1949, 606-1-13, WHOG.

17. Cf. Sunil S. Amrith, *Decolonizing International Health: India and Southeast Asia, 1930–65* (New York: Palgrave, 2006); Farley, *Brock Chisholm;* Ernesto Venturini and Stefania Atti, "Per una politica di salute mentale: il ruolo svolto dall'Organizzione Mondiale della Sanità in Africa," *Africa* (Rome) 39, no. 3 (1984): 375–390.

18. "Mental Health Programme Beginning 1950," WHOG.

19. "Discussion after Dr. Soddy's Lecture," 15 December 1958, MM, box F66, folder 1, LOC.

20. Mandler, *Return from the Natives,* 267; David Cohen, "Psychiatric Imperialism," in *Forgotten Millions* (London: Paladin, 1988); Thomson, "Before Anti-Psychiatry."

21. "Presentation of Reports of the Working Groups," 5 September 1950, MM, box F52, folder 2, LOC; "Notes on Discussions of Group VII—Mental Health Aspects of International Relations," 23 August 1949, file S-0FF1-55-5, UNNY.

22. Tara Zahra, *The Lost Children: Reconstructing Europe's Families after World War II* (Cambridge: Harvard University Press, 2011), ch. 3; John Welshman, "Evacuation and Social Policy during the Second World War: Myth and Reality," *Twentieth Century British History* 9 (1998): 28–53.

23. Shapira, *War Inside,* 203–214; Ben Mayhew, 'Between Love and Aggression: The Politics of John Bowlby,' *History of the Human Sciences* 19, no. 4 (2006): 19–35; Frank C. P. van der Horst, *John Bowlby from Psychoanalysis to Ethology: Unraveling the Roots of Attachment Theory* (Chichester: Wiley-Blackwell, 2011). For the classic criticism that Bowlby encouraged a conservative view of the family, by implying that mothers who

pursued careers outside it risked damaging their children for life, see Juliet Mitchell, *Psychoanalysis and Feminism* (New York: Pantheon, 1974). For more sympathetic interpretations which attempt to distinguish the nuances of Bowlby's own thought from "Bowlbyism," see Thomson, *Lost Freedom,* ch. 3; Denise Riley, *War in the Nursery: Theories of the Child and Mother* (London: Virago, 1983); Jeremy Holmes, *John Bowlby and Attachment Theory* (London: Routledge, 1993), 41–50.

24. John Bowlby, *Attachment and Loss,* vol. 1, *Attachment* (London: Hogarth Press, 1969).

25. Inge Bretherton, "The Origins of Attachment Theory: John Bowlby and Mary Ainsworth," *Developmental Psychology* 28 (1992): 759–775; Mary Ainsworth, *Infancy in Uganda: Infant Care and the Growth of Love* (Baltimore: Johns Hopkins University Press, 1967); Bowlby, *Attachment,* 199–201; Mary Ainsworth to Audrey Richards, 4 October 1962, Mary Ainsworth papers, box M3167, folder 1, CHP.

26. G. R. Hargreaves, "A Web Woven of Many Threads," in *Mental Health and the World Community,* ed. Fraser Brockington (London: World Federation for Mental Health, 1954); Bretherton, "Origins of Attachment Theory," 6.

27. Marcelle Geber and R. F. A. Dean, "Gesell Tests on African Children," *Pediatrics* 20 (1957): 1055–1065.

28. Sally Craddock, *Retired Except on Demand: The Life of Dr. Cicely Williams* (Oxford: Green College, 1983); Cicely Williams, "Child Health and Child Welfare," United Nations Social Welfare Seminar for the Arab States in the Middle East, August–September 1949, PP/CDW/D.7; Cicely Williams, "The Pre-School Child in Africa," June 1955, PP/CDW/E.2/1; Cicely Williams, "Report of Maternal and Child Health Adviser to South East Asia," November 1949–August 1951, PP/CDW/D.4, WL.

29. "Consultants Furnished to Governments at Their Request," n.d., PP/CDW/D.3, WL; "Training Course of Indian Nurses in Rural Social Life," n.d., PP/CDW/D.10, WL; Williams, "Report of Maternal and Child Health Adviser"; Expert Committee on Maternal and Child Health, "Report on First Session," 21 February 1949, PP/CDW/D.3, WL.

30. "Mental Health Programme Beginning 1950," WHOG; Eduardo Duniec and Mical Raz, "Vitamins for the Soul: John Bowlby's Thesis of Maternal Deprivation, Biomedical Metaphors, and the Deficiency Model of Disease," *History of Psychiatry* 22 (2011): 93–107.

31. McCulloch, *Colonial Psychiatry,* 50–76; Elkins, *Imperial Reckoning,* 106–107; David Anderson, *Histories of the Hanged: The Dirty War in Kenya and the End of Empire* (New York: W.W. Norton, 2005), 283–284.

32. J. C. Carothers, *The African Mind in Health and Disease: A Study in Ethnopsychiatry* (Geneva: World Health Organization, 1953).

33. Jules Henry, "A Report on 'The African Mind in Health and Disease' by JC Carothers," [January 1956]; "Extracts from Reviews of Carother's [*sic*] African Mind in Health and Disease," [February 1956], file M4/445/13, WHOG; cf. McCulloch, *Colonial Psychiatry,* 62.

34. Carothers, *African Mind,* 97–106.

35. J. C. Carothers, *The Psychology of Mau Mau* (Nairobi: Government Printer, 1954), 24–25; Colin Carothers to Margaret Mead, 1 March 1955, MM, box C31, folder 7, LOC.

36. Margaret Mead, review of *African Mind in Health and Disease*, *Psychiatry* 17, no. 3 (1954): 303–306; "Comments on Jules Henry's Report to the American Orthopsychiatric Association on the WHO Monograph 'The African Mind in Health and Disease,'" February 1956, file M4/445/13, WHOG.

37. G. R. Hargreaves to Melville Herskovits, 8 March 1954, MM, box F78, folder 5; Hargreaves to Antonio J. de Liz Ferreira, 16 May 1955, MM, box C31, folder 7, LOC.

38. Scientific Committee minutes, 11–15 September 1956, MM, box F55, folder 1, LOC, 9; "Identity: Working Paper for Discussion," September 1956, MM, box F55, folder 1, LOC, 10; Kenneth Soddy, ed., *Identity/Mental Health and Value Systems* (London: Tavistock Publications, 1961), 65–66, 110–111, 171, 176–177, 204.

39. Kenneth Soddy, "The Concept of Mental Health," [1958], MM, box F66, folder 3, LOC; Soddy, ed., *Identity/Mental Health*, 201.

40. Committee on Anthropology and Sociology minutes, Colonial Social Science Research Council, 9 August 1949, CR 8/106, LSE; minute by E. M. Chilver, 19 September 1949, CO 927/172, NAUK; G. Morris Carstairs, *The Twice-Born: A Study of a Community of High-Caste Hindus* (London: Hogarth Press, 1957), 318–325; Lenora Foerstel, "Margaret Mead from a Cultural-Historical Perspective," in *Confronting Margaret Mead: Scholarship, Empire, and the South Pacific* (Philadelphia: Temple University Press, 1994), ed. Lenora Foerstel and Angela Gilliam, 62.

41. Carstairs, *Twice-Born*, 146, 158.

42. "Quarterly Report on Action Taken by WFMH, Relative to the Agreement between WHO and the Federation," August 1951, CC 4-4/78 (1), WHOG; Charles Hogan to Gustavo Martinez Cabañas, 12 January 1956, S-0FF1–55–6, UNNY; *Social Implications of Technical Assistance* (London: World Federation for Mental Health, 1955); *Mental Health Aspects of Urbanization* (London: World Federation for Mental Health, 1957); *Africa: Social Change and Mental Health* (London: World Federation for Mental Health, 1959).

43. *Mental Health Aspects of Urbanization*, 20, 23.

44. J. R. Rees to Charles Hogan, 5 January 1956, S-0FF1–55–7, UNNY; *Technical Assistance for Economic Development* (Lake Success: United Nations, 1949), 15, 273.

45. Ernest Grigg and T. Nasr to Julia Henderson, 8 August 1955, S-0FF1–55–7, UNNY; Hans W. Singer, interview with Richard Jolly, 2 January 2000, in *The Complete Oral History Transcripts from* UN Voices (New York: United Nations Intellectual History Project, 2007), CD-ROM; *Measures for the Economic Development of Under-Developed Countries*, 14.

46. Minutes of the U.S. Regional Inter-Professional Advisory Committee, 8 December 1949, MM, box F51, folder 5, LOC; "Presentation of Reports of the Working Groups," 5 September 1950, MM, box F52, folder 2, LOC.

47. Margaret Mead, ed., *Cultural Patterns and Technical Change: A Manual Prepared by the World Federation for Mental Health* (Paris: UNESCO, 1953),

286–292; Social Welfare Adviser, "Report for the Period 1942–44" (draft), n.d., T. S. Simey papers, folder D396/9, Sydney Jones Library, University of Liverpool; cf. Mandler, *Return from the Natives*, 266–273. Mead and her American collaborator, Lawrence Frank, pointed to "the British suggestion for a study of individuals and authority" as a starting point for their work: see Lawrence Frank and Margaret Mead, "The Advisory Inter-Professional Committee," [1949], MM, box F51, folder 4, LOC.

48. A. T. N. Wilson, "The Interview in Cross-Cultural Selection," [1959], reel 546, grant file 58–350, FF.

49. H. V. Hodson, *Twentieth-Century Empire* (London: Faber and Faber, 1948), 177; Paul B. Rich, "End of Empire and the Rise of 'Race Relations,'" in *Race and Empire in British Politics;* Chris Mullard, *Race, Power, and Resistance* (London: Routledge, 1985), 13–18; Bailkin, *Afterlife of Empire*, 50–53; Philip Mason, *An Essay on Racial Tension* (London: Royal Institute of International Affairs, 1954), viii; [Philip Mason], "Application to the Ford Foundation," [1960], reel 2544, grant file 60–447, FF.

50. Philip Mason, foreword to Octave Mannoni, *Prospero and Caliban: The Psychology of Colonization,* trans. Pamela Powesland (London: Methuen, 1956); Philip Mason, "Race as an Obstacle to Progress," 17 December 1963, reel 2544, grant file 60–447, FF; Guy Hunter, *The New Societies of Tropical Africa: A Selective Study* (London: Oxford University Press, 1962), 19–21, 304–306; Hugh Tinker, "A Proposal for . . . Race Relations Study," [1969], reel 2544, grant file 60–447, FF. On Anglophone readings of Mannoni, see also Erik Linstrum, "Specters of Dependency: Psychoanalysis in the Age of Decolonization," in *Psychoanalysis in the Age of Totalitarianism,* ed. Daniel Pick and Matt Ffytche (London: Routledge, 2016).

51. Margaret Read notebook, 1959, Read papers, MR/E/31, IEL; Read notebooks, 1964, Read papers, MR/E/38–39, IEL; Margaret Read, *Children of Their Fathers: Growing Up among the Ngoni of Nyasaland* (London: Methuen, 1959); Philip Mason, *The Birth of a Dilemma: The Conquest and Settlement of Rhodesia* (London: Oxford University Press, 1958), 84–85.

52. Kathleen W. Jones, *Taming the Troublesome Child: American Families, Child Guidance, and the Limits of Psychiatric Authority* (Cambridge: Harvard University Press, 2002); Jacques Donzelot, *The Policing of Families,* trans. Robert Hurley (New York: Pantheon, 1979).

53. Farley, *Brock Chisholm*, 78; Javed Siddiqi, *World Health and World Politics: The World Health Organization and the UN System* (Columbia: University of South Carolina Press, 1995), 218.

54. Brody, *Search for Mental Health;* Rich, "End of Empire and the Rise of 'Race Relations'"; Mullard, *Race, Power, and Resistance.*

55. Gustav Jahoda, interview with author, 9 October 2009; Andrew Cohen, "Africa in Transition," in *Africa: Progress through Cooperation,* ed. John Karefa-Smart (New York: Dodd, Mead, 1966); Margery Perham, "Political Tensions in Development," in *Restless Nations: A Study of World Tensions and Development* (New York: Dodd, Mead, 1962); T. J. Mboya, "Tensions in Development," in *Restless Nations;* Arthur Gaitskell, "The Oxford Conference Discussions," *Journal of the Council on World Tensions* (1962): 2–12, at 2;

Jawaharlal Nehru, "UNESCO and the Future of Humanity," in *Selected Works of Jawaharlal Nehru,* ed. S. Gopal, 2nd ser., vol. 16, part 1 (New Delhi: Jawaharlal Nehru Memorial Fund, 1984), 134.

56. L. F. Urwick, "Management for India," [1956], file 17/1/1; Urwick, lecture at University of Bombay, 2 March [1956], file 25/3/12; Urwick, lecture at University of Bombay, 3 March [1956], file 25/3/13, Lyndall Urwick papers, Henley Business School Library, Henley-on-Thames.

57. Shyam Swaroop Jalota, *Scientific Personnel Selection Procedure: A Study* (Banaras: Hind Art Press, 1950); E. V. Parkman to John C. Raven, 27 August 1947, John C. Raven papers, file 1/2/6, WL.

58. P. C. Mahalanobis, "The Approach of Operational Research to Planning in India," *Sankhya* 16 (1955). For Mahalanobis's earlier research on mental testing, see P. C. Mahalanobis, "Studies in Group Tests of Intelligence," *Proceedings of the Indian Science Congress* 18 (1931): 437; P. C. Mahalanobis, "A Comparison of Different Statistical Measures of Intelligence Based on a Group Test in Bengali," *Proceedings of the Indian Science Congress* 20 (1933): 439.

59. W. Leslie Barnette, "Survey of Research with Psychological Tests in India," *Psychological Bulletin* 52, no. 2 (1955): 105–121; Suhrichandra Sinha, *Fifty Years of Science in India: Progress of Psychology* (Calcutta: Indian Science Congress Association, 1963), 10–12; George Chacko, "E.T.S. for India," part II, 15 February 1956, box 48, folder 514, Educational Testing Service archive, Princeton, NJ.

60. Christiane Hartnack, "Vishnu on Freud's Desk: Psychoanalysis in Colonial India," *Social Research* 57, no. 4 (1990): 921–949, at 929; Hartnack, *Psychoanalysis in Colonial India;* Kapila, "The 'Godless' Freud and His Indian Friends"; Ashis Nandy, *The Savage Freud and Other Essays on Possible or Retrievable Selves* (Princeton: Princeton University Press, 1995); G. Bose, "Report on the Working of the Applied Section"; Maya Deb, *Researches on Industrial Psychology, Department of Psychology, Calcutta University, 1916–1976* (Calcutta: Job & Art Printers, 1977).

61. Mana Sarabhai Brearley, interview by author, 26 November 2010, London; A. K. Rice, *Productivity and Social Organization: The Ahmedabad Experiment* (London: Tavistock Publications, 1958), 121–123; Prakash, *Another Reason,* 231–232.

62. "A Note on Management Training," n.d., 4–5, and Fritz Roethlisberger to Mr. and Mrs. Rolf Lynton, 1 October 1959, carton 1, folder 4, Fritz Roethlisberger papers, Baker Library, Harvard Business School, Cambridge, MA; F. J. Roethlisberger, *Understanding: A Prerequisite of Leadership* (Cambridge: Harvard University Press, 1938); F. J. Roethlisberger, *Management and Morale* (Cambridge: Harvard University Press, 1941); Ahmedabad Textile Industry Research Association, *Administrative Practices: Cases and Concepts* (July 1960), Tavistock Institute Library, London, 60, 67. Roethlisberger was followed to Ahmedabad a few years later by Erik Erikson, who wrote much of his famous study of Gandhi while staying at the Sarabhai family compound. See Lawrence J. Friedman, *Identity's Architect: A Biography of Erik H. Erikson* (New York: Scribner, 1999), 326–329.

63. UNESCO, *Report of the Director General on the Activities of the Organisation* (Paris: UNESCO, 1956), 186, 188; A. Taylor and G. D. Bradshaw, "Secondary School Selection: The Development of an Intelligence Test for Use in Nigeria," *West African Journal of Education* 9 (1965): 6–12, at 6. On the Cold War and technical assistance, see especially Latham, *Right Kind of Revolution*, ch. 3.

64. Cullather, *Hungry World,* 77–91; Dennis Merrill, *Bread and the Ballot: The United States and India's Economic Development, 1947–1963* (Chapel Hill: University of North Carolina Press, 1990); Lee, *Colonial Development and Good Government,* 23–24; Frederic R. Wickert, "Industrial Psychology in Africa," *American Psychologist* 15 (1960): 163–170, at 165.

65. M. J. Wantman to Henry Chauncey, memorandum, 30 March 1961, and Wantman to Chauncey, memorandum, 28 April 1961, Henry Chauncey papers, folder 362, ETS archive; M. J. Wantman, "Report on the Malayan Project Sponsored by the Educational Testing Service," in *Educational and Occupational Selection in West Africa,* ed. Taylor.

66. American Institutes for Research (AIR), "Test Development and Research Office, West African Examinations Council," 1968, http://pdf.usaid.gov/pdf _docs/PNAAM298.pdf, 30; AIR, "The Lagos Conference on Testing in the Developing Countries," 1967, http://pdf.usaid.gov/pdf_docs/pnaad246.pdf.

67. Francis Agbodeka, *The West African Examinations Council, 1952–2002: Half a Century of Commitment to Excellence and Regional Co-Operation* (Accra: Woeli, 2002), 127–132, 170–172; Mary Dillard, "Testing Freedom: A History of the West African Examinations Council" Ph.D. thesis (University of California, Los Angeles, 2001), 166, 175–184.

68. Paul A. Schwarz, *Aptitude Tests for Use in the Developing Nations* ([Pittsburgh]: American Institute for Research, [1961]), 1, 5–6; American Institutes for Research, "Lagos Conference on Testing," 12. On the Anglophone bias of colonial examinations, see also Ngũgĩ wa Thiong'o, *Decolonising the Mind: The Politics of Language in African Literature* (Nairobi: East African Educational Publishers, 1986), 12.

69. Foster, *Education and Social Change in Ghana,* 182–199; Anderson, *Struggle for the School,* 149–154; Morrison, *Education and Politics in Africa,* 121–122, 128–132, 195–210.

70. Tom Mboya, *The Challenge of Nationhood: A Collection of Speeches and Writings* (London: Heinemann, 1972), 204–205; American Institutes for Research, "Test Development and Research Office," 25–26, 60; Paul A. Schwarz and Robert E. Krug, *Aptitude Testing in Developing Countries: A Handbook of Principles and Techniques* (New York: Praeger, 1972).

71. Jawaharlal Nehru, *Letters to Chief Ministers,* vol. 3, *1952–1954* (Delhi: Jawaharlal Nehru Memorial Fund, 1988), 377, 387; Jawaharlal Nehru, *The Discovery of India* (Delhi: Oxford University Press, 1994 [1946]), 36; Kenneth D. Kaunda, *A Humanist in Africa: Letters to Colin M. Morris* (London: Longmans, 1967), 48–57. On postcolonial politics as pedagogy, see Dipesh Chakrabarty, "The Legacies of Bandung: Decolonization and the Politics of Culture," in *Making a World after Empire: Bandung and Its Political*

Afterlives, ed. Christopher J. Lee (Athens: Ohio University Press, 2010). On Nehru and psychoanalysis, see also Benjamin Zachariah, *Nehru* (London: Routledge, 2004), 143–147.

72. Kenneth Osgood, *Total Cold War: Eisenhower's Secret Propaganda Battle at Home and Abroad* (Lawrence: University of Kansas Press, 2006), 123–133; Allan Evans memorandum, 27 December 1950, RG 59, entry P310, box 13, folder 10.071, NAUS.

73. Scott Lucas, "Campaigns of Truth: The Psychological Strategy Board and American Ideology, 1951–53," *International History Review* 18, no. 2 (1996): 279–302; Andrew Warne, "Psychoanalyzing Iran: Kennedy's Iran Task Force and the Modernization of Orientalism, 1961–63," *International History Review* 35, no. 2 (2013): 396–422; Cullather, *Hungry World,* 78–85.

74. Hadley Cantril, *Some Observations of a Psychologist in India: An Informal Discussion* (Princeton: Institute for International Social Research, 1958); David G. Winter, "Some Notes on Indian Political Culture," 19 January 1965, David McClelland papers, HUGFP 145, box 18, folder 1, Harvard University Archives.

75. Mottram Torre, "Application of Group Therapy Insights and Techniques to Governmental Problems," 12 August 1954, MM, box F53, folder 6, LOC. On the pursuit of non-authoritarian personalities in the American human sciences, see also Jamie Cohen-Cole, *The Open Mind: Cold War Politics and the Sciences of Human Nature* (Chicago: University of Chicago Press, 2014).

76. Discussion Group on Economic Development in Africa minutes, 8 March 1956, series 3, box 159, folder 4; Edwin J. Cohn to William Diebold, 27 August 1957, series 3, box 164, folder 5; Discussion Group on Colonialism minutes, 24 January 1956, series 3, box 158, folder 5, 5–7; Discussion Group on the Colonial Problem minutes, 13 November 1956, series 3, box 161, folder 1, Council on Foreign Relations archive, Mudd Manuscript Library, Princeton University.

77. David C. McClelland, *The Achieving Society* (Princeton: Van Nostrand, 1961); David C. McClelland and David G. Winter, *Motivating Economic Achievement* (New York: Free Press, 1969); Robert A. LeVine, *Dreams and Deeds: Achievement Motivation in Nigeria* (Chicago: University of Chicago Press, 1966); Corhann Okorodudu, "Achievement Training and Achievement Motivation among the Kpelle in Liberia: A Study of Household Structure Antecedents," Ed.D. thesis (Harvard University, 1966); John M. Ostheimer, "The Achievement Motive among the Chaga of Tanzania," Ph.D. thesis (Yale University, 1967); Thomas M. Fraser, *Reports on Achievement Motivation* (Amherst: University of Massachusetts, 1968). On McClelland, see also Gilman, *Mandarins of the Future,* 97–100.

78. Mandler, *Return from the Natives,* ch. 6; Council on Foreign Relations, "Study Group on Problems of Strengthening Democratic Leadership Abroad," [1950?], RG 59, entry P310, box 12, folder 9.0491, NAUS; McClelland, *Achieving Society,* 340–362; David C. McClelland, A. Rindlisbacher, and Richard DeCharms, "Religious and Other Sources of Parental Attitudes toward Independence Training," in *Studies in Motivation,* ed. David C. McClelland (New York: Appleton-Century-Crofts, 1955); John Wesley Mayhew Whiting, et

al., *Field Guide for a Study of Socialization in Five Societies* (New York: Social Science Research Council, 1954); Gordon M. Wilson, *Understanding Social Change* (Nairobi: Marco Surveys, 1962).

79. Ashis Nandy, "Towards an Alternative Politics of Psychology," in *Bonfire of Creeds: The Essential Ashis Nandy* (New Delhi: Oxford University Press, 2004), 326.

ACKNOWLEDGMENTS

Every book takes a village, and this one is no exception. Funding from the Center for European Studies, the Weatherhead Center for International Affairs, the Committee on African Studies, and the History Department at Harvard University made long periods of research possible. I am especially grateful to the Institute of Historical Research; its director, Miles Taylor; and the Andrew W. Mellon Foundation for a productive year in British archives. A fellowship with the Belfer Center for Science and International Affairs in the Kennedy School of Government at Harvard and the Society of Fellows at the University of Michigan afforded me invaluable time to write after my return. The Dean of the College and Graduate School of Arts and Sciences and the Vice President for Research at the University of Virginia have generously supported the final passage from manuscript to publication.

Many librarians and archivists around the world helped me to navigate their collections in the course of my research. Special thanks are due to Richard Ambani at the National Archives of Kenya in Nairobi; Jaya Ravindran at the National Archives of India in New Delhi; Lucy McCann at Rhodes House Library in Oxford; and Sarah Walpole at the Royal Anthropological Institute in London. Thanks also to Danae Karydaki for her assistance with research in London. A number of conferences and seminars provided valuable opportunities to present work in progress over the past few years. I owe an especially large debt to the Decolonization Seminar of the National History Center, led by the inimitable Roger Louis and expertly administered by Marian Barber, for a month of research and fellowship at the Library of Congress.

Many scholars have responded to questions, offered advice, and encouraged my research. I am deeply grateful to all of them and especially those who took the time to offer thoughtful comments on parts of the manuscript: David Edgerton, Dane Kennedy, the late Riki Kuklick, and Philippa Levine. Two anonymous readers for Harvard University Press also provided unusually thoughtful and constructive feedback. I was fortunate to have Daniel Pick serve as a mentor during my year at the Institute of Historical Research and thank him for his support in the years since. Deborah Cohen has surpassed the call of duty as a mentor and offered an inspiring example as a scholar. I thank Peter Mandler, too, for his generosity, wisdom, and enthusiasm from the early days of this project.

At the University of Michigan, Don Lopez and Linda Turner made the Society of Fellows a happy home for two years of work on this book. I am grateful to all of my fellow fellows, junior and senior, for many inspired conversations. A cadre of faculty and graduate students associated with Michigan's History Department and the Program in Science, Technology, and Society offered useful comments on the manuscript and a lively interdisciplinary environment. Thanks to John Carson, Geoff Eley, Joy Rohde, Perrin Selcer, and Minnie Sinha for welcoming me to Ann Arbor and offering a fresh perspective on my work. This book took its final shape in the Department of History at the University of Virginia. I thank Paul Halliday, Will Hitchcock, Erin Lambert, Sarah Milov, Robert Stolz, and Josh White, among many others, for their warm welcome and collegial support. Kent Merritt, Kathleen Miller, and Ella Wood have overseen a seamless transition, and I am grateful to each of them as well.

I could not ask for a more thoughtful or professional editor than Andrew Kinney and am grateful to him and his colleagues at Harvard University Press for shepherding the book into print. *Ruling Minds* began in the History Department at Harvard, where Ann Blair, Erez Manela, and Judith Surkis all deepened my passion for history and made me a better scholar. David Armitage helped to draw me into imperial history from my very first semester as a graduate student. Carrie Elkins, too, was present at the beginning; her scholarship and her mentorship have challenged me to reflect on what it means to write about empire. I was fortunate to begin my studies under the tutelage of David Blackbourn, who taught me how to think like a historian and encouraged me to follow my curiosity wherever it led me. My debts to Maya Jasanoff, *il miglior fabbro,* are many. I will always be grateful for her example as a researcher, writer, and scholar and for her generosity as a mentor. Friends at Harvard and beyond—including Ahmad Al-Jallad, Hannah Callaway, Elizabeth Hinton, Philip Johnston, Mira Siegelberg, Matt Spooner, Julie Stephens, and Mason Williams—set a high bar as fellow scholars but also made things fun.

This book would not have been written without the love and support of my parents. It is dedicated to Sheela, my partner in everything, who made it possible and made it worthwhile.

INDEX